Rifted
Clouds

Rifted Clouds

by

Bella Cooke

**White Tree Publishing Edition
combining all three parts**

This edited edition ©White Tree Publishing 2018

Paperback ISBN: 978-1-912529-09-4

Available as an eBook mid 2018
e-Book ISBN: 978-1-912529-08-7

Published by
White Tree Publishing
Bristol
UNITED KINGDOM

wtpbristol@gmail.com

Full list of books on our website

www.whitetreepublishing.com

**WHITE
TREE
PUBLISHING**

Original Dedication

Memories of my Father's love, written in prayer and pain,
are dedicated to my dear children and grandchildren as a
memento of the love that never ceased to cherish them.

Bella Cooke 1821–1908

Yours in Jesus
Bella Cooke

Publisher's Notes

The three *Rifted Clouds* books by Bella Cooke are long in total, and our original intention was to produce a considerably abridged combined edition. However, in the first two volumes we could find nothing that could be removed without losing much of value, although long sentences and paragraphs have been broken into shorter lengths, in line with modern publishing practice.

The third part, *Rifted Clouds, The Life Story of Bella Cooke Concluded*, was published by Bella Cooke's daughter, Mary Pullman, after her mother's death in 1909. It contains new writing by Bella Cooke, but it was padded by similar memories from friends of events already told in the two earlier books, with many newspaper tributes and memorial addresses, in order to make a full length book. Much of this has been abridged, as clearly Part 3 will not now be read in isolation. The chapter numbers in Part 3 do not match those of the original publication.

Many entries in the original books were out of date order. After the publication of the first volume of *Rifted Clouds*, earlier material was discovered, and put into the second volume. Similarly with the third part. We have done out best to put everything in chronological order in this combined edition.

For readers who would like to read the original lengthy Introductions to each of the three volumes in full, and the addresses at Bella Cooke's funeral and memorial services, they are at the end of the book, with the page numbers in the Contents.

Bella Cooke's Bible knowledge was amazing, and although writing on her back while bed bound, she was able to quote (perhaps from memory) many Scripture promises.

Only rarely does she give their references. As these will be useful to many readers today, we have inserted nearly 400 Bible references throughout the book in square brackets [like this]. Standard brackets (like this) are in the original books. Bella Cooke's spelling of Saviour has been retained. All her other American spellings are as in the original.

Introductory Notes Part 1
Abridged

Full Introductory Notes for all three parts are at the end of the book. See Contents.

Henry Dickinson
Brooklyn, N. Y.
The Christian reader who follows this providential story to its close will find new proofs that the God and Father of our Lord Jesus Christ is a living and unchangeable God.

S. A. Lankford Palmer
316 E. 15th St.
New York
The life of Bella Cooke is truly a life of faith, and believing that her testimony, as it is found in her journals and letters will strengthen the heart of many fearful ones in Zion, we ask for her offering a prayerful acceptance.

The volume is published at the request of many friends. A few letters written by old friends were solicited and inserted by the Editor in the belief that they will add to the interest and usefulness of the book. It is a touching tale of singular providences, of patient endurance and overcoming faith.

Contents

Part 3
Rifted Clouds
The Life Story of Bella Cooke Concluded

Chapter 1

Early Years

I remember the days of old; I meditate on all Thy works; I muse on the work of Thy hands (Psalm 143:5).

The living, the living, he shall praise Thee, as I do this day; the father to the children shall make known Thy truth (Isaiah 38:19).

I was born July 13th 1821, in Hull, England. Of my parents I would speak with reverence. They were devoted followers of the meek and lowly Jesus. My father, John Beeton, was born August 1772, in Norfolk, England. My mother, Elizabeth Smawfield, was born December 2nd 1776, in Epworth, the birthplace of the Wesleys.

My grandfather was in the shoe business, and the Wesley family traded with him. My grandmother Smawfield was a devoted follower of Christ, and died when my mother was about twenty-one years of age. I have often heard my mother speak of the deathbed scene.

She being the eldest daughter felt the responsibility for the younger children rest heavily upon her, and when friends were praying at the bedside of her mother, "Not our will, but Thine be done," she would not say it, but felt in her heart to say, "A little of my will, Lord. Oh, spare my mother."

When her mother saw her weeping, she said, "My daughter, weep not; as I am only stepping out of my Father's kitchen into His parlor." Thus, as the daughter of a King, she passed on to her Father's house on high.

Two years later a regiment of the British army was stationed in her town, and a young soldier, tall and of imposing figure, made my mother's acquaintance. Soon after, he proposed marriage, and although he was not a member of society – that is a professor of religion and a Methodist – yet because she loved him they were married. This was against the rules of the society, and in due form, after prayer on the part of the Church, she was expelled from her membership.

When informed of this, my mother answered, "Thank God they cannot read me out of Heaven."

They were very happy in their married life, yet many were the hardships which they endured while in the army. During a short term of peace, when their first child was about three years old, father bought his discharge from the service.

They went to Hull and settled there. My dear mother again joined the Wesleyan Society, and my father, seeing her consistent walk, gave his heart to God, and until death they walked with Him. They had nine children, of whom I was the youngest and the household pet.

In the spring of 1827 my parents moved to Sheffield, where my two sisters and I went to the Red Hill Sunday school, and later to the Ebenezer Chapel, a Methodist church where we all attended service.

I was about nine years old, and had been for some time greatly troubled about my sins. I do not remember the time, when I heard of the death of anyone, that the question did not arise in my mind – were they ready to die?

At two different times, when about eight or nine years old, I had told an untruth, and the anguish of mind it caused me was terrible. Once, when mother had gone to Hull and I longed to have her home, I told sister Bessie that we were to go to the coach office to meet mother. She asked if father said so. I answered yes.

We went, I thinking that we should meet her, but of course she was not there for us. When father came home, my sister said, "We went to the office, but mother was not there."

Father asked, "Why did you go?"

Sister replied, "Bella said you wished us to do so."

Dear old man, he talked with me, and of course punished me severely, yet that was but little to what I felt in my mind. I hardly dared to go to sleep lest I should be lost. Thus things went on till I was about ten years old.

Father had a prayer meeting at our house every Sunday evening after chapel service. One evening, when they were about to close, my sister Hannah, who was home on a visit, became anxious about her soul. At nine o'clock the meeting was closed.

A few remained to pray with her, and I was sent to bed; but I crept down and sat on the stairs, and, oh, how I wished I could go in and be prayed for, but dared not do so. I waited until I heard "Hallelujah, a soul is saved," and my dear mother singing, "Praise God from whom all blessings flow," after which I ran upstairs to bed.

My sister Hannah was very fashionable, and wore her hair in long curls. In the morning I thought, now I will see if my sister is converted. The curl papers were lying on the dressing table, so I took them downstairs, and said, "Sister, here are your curl papers."

She said, "No, my dear, they are the devil's curl papers. I do not want them now. I do not intend to serve him anymore."

Then I was satisfied that she was converted. That dear sister lived a most earnest and devoted Christian life, and was for many years an acceptable class leader. She died in

1852 in New York, after years of great suffering.

About that time I heard that they were having a service at Norfolk Street Chapel every morning at five o'clock. I got father to let me go with a Mr. and Mrs. Wright — he was a local preacher.

I went with them for some weeks, and felt I was saved and that my sins were forgiven. But being of a diffident nature, I did not like to tell anyone, although I often tried to do so. By this I lost my peace of mind, and then it seemed that I was worse than ever I had been before, and might as well give up trying to be good.

I was sorely tempted, and yielded to many wrong things. When I would hear dear father pray at family worship, pleading for his children that they all might be the saved of the Lord, I would often turn and look at that old gray head bowed in earnest supplication and would weep, I felt so bad, and think, "Shall I ever be saved? Can I ever be forgiven, or shall I be lost?"

I had heard the passage discussed by friends at my mother's, "For if we sin willfully after that we have received the knowledge of the truth, there remaineth no more sacrifice for sins." [Hebrews 10:26.]

The opinion of some was that it was doubtful if any could be saved who had thus done, repeating the words, "Ephraim is joined to idols, let him alone." [Hosea 4:17.] How careful older Christians should be in conversing before children of these things!

Shortly after this, I had several serious attacks of illness. [We read in Part 3 that Bella had been dropped as a small child, and suffered a serious spine injury. This, among other afflictions, would lead to over fifty years in bed.]

Oh, what sorrow I would feel, yet dared not tell mother or sisters for fear they would question me, and tell me there was no mercy for me because I had been so naughty after having promised to serve the Lord. These lines were often in my thoughts,

> "What after death for me remains,
> Celestial joys or hellish pains
> To all eternity?"

Thus I was until the spring of 1834, when I heard a sermon from, "The Spirit and the bride say, Come; and let him that heareth say, Come, and let him that is athirst come, and whosoever will, let him take the water of life freely." [Revelation 22:17.]

The latter clause was dwelt upon, and I saw some light but little comfort. When our Sunday school anniversary sermons were preached, I was one of a number chosen to sing on a platform in chapel, but it gave me no pleasure, I was so unhappy. One of the hymns was,

> "Daughter of Zion, awake from thy sadness,
> Awake, for thy foes shall oppress thee no more."

These words fastened in my mind, and I thought, "My sins are my foes, and if they are pardoned they will oppress me no more." Then, about nine o'clock in the Ebenezer Chapel, after the sermon I was enabled to cast my burden at the feet of Jesus, and felt He did forgive me all my sins.

That was fifty years ago, and thus far the Lord hath led me on. I did not hesitate to tell my dear mother, my best friend, and this was a great help to me. I joined Mr. Benjamin Wood's class, became a teacher shortly after, and did what I could for Jesus.

My sisters were married, one in January, and the other in February 1835, and thus I was left at home alone with my dear parents.

I became acquainted with, and was much in the company of a lovely family, Mr. and Mrs. Goodwin, members of the Society of Friends. I loved them and their children very much, and watched their Christian life. A younger sister of Mrs. G. was often there, Miss Grace Davy, now Mrs. Henry Dickinson, of Brooklyn, with whom I began at that time a lifelong friendship. I was present at her marriage, and felt that I would like to join their Society, for their plainness suited me.

I could never think it right for me to wear a bow of ribbon or a breastpin or ring, though I had nothing to say about others doing so. I went to Mr. Brown, my class leader, and told him how I felt about the Friends.

He said, "Sister Bella, I do not hear a call for you to leave the Methodists, but I tell you what we will do. We will meet at seven o'clock each morning for ten minutes in special prayer for three months. Speak to your parents, and if at that time you still feel drawn to leave us for the Friends I will get you your transfer."

I did so, and although we met every week in class we never spoke of it again until the end of the three months. I kept the contract to the letter, and when I told my parents, they said, "Follow your leader's advice, and if at that time you still wish to go, you shall have our consent."

At the end of the three months I went to him and told him I should remain a Methodist. Yet I always loved the Friends, and had great respect for anyone who belonged to their Society.

When about six years old in Hull, the Sunday school belonging to the Wesleyan Chapel was so far away from our home that I attended the Sunday school and morning service of the Church of England, as a favor of the officers of the said Sunday school. There I learned to love, though so young, their mode of worship.

I also attended a day school belonging to the Establishment and so learned their catechism, in addition to the Wesleyan catechism, for which I have many times been thankful. I often look back to the leadings of Providence as preparing me for the wonderful introduction to so many different denominations that I have met with during my confinement in my little home, thus divesting me of anything like sectarianism, and teaching me that all who love the Lord Jesus are one in and with Him.

When about sixteen, my health was very feeble, yet I often wanted to enter into things my parents felt I was not able to do. At that time, early morning prayer meetings were held in some of the chapels, and I had some years before been so much blessed at such meetings that I wanted to attend them.

Mother objected on account of my health. I heard that the meetings were very spiritual and I longed to go, and my zeal ran away with my obedience to my parents.

I went again; then my dear father took the key out of the door. Still once more I persisted in going, and this time I got out of the window. When I reached home they were at breakfast. I saw my father was displeased and I did not want any breakfast.

After some time father said, "Bella, what is the first commandment with promise?"

I repeated it. He talked very tenderly with me; how terribly I felt! I would have given anything if I could have undone what I had done. I had much rather he had given me a good whipping. He told me it was their loving care for me; that they did not want me to go because my health would not admit of it.

Chapter 2

The Young Disciple

Sweet bondage of love; I am willingly led
By the hand of the Master divine;
I fear not the dangers that round me are spread,
I heed not the gathering clouds overhead,
For His love and protection are mine.

When about seventeen years old I felt I must do more work for Him who had done so much for me. One afternoon I went to take tea with one of my classmates, and in the evening we went to the monthly tract meeting. Mr. Henry Longdon was president; he was also the superintendent of the Ebenezer Sunday school where I was a teacher.

He asked who would take the "Isle," a vicious district in Sheffield. As no one spoke, I said I would take it.

He said, "No, my child, you cannot take it."

I said, "Not in my own strength, but in the strength of my Master I thought I could."

He gave me the tracts for the district and I went home delighted, but I saw father was displeased. I was one quarter of an hour late home.

Mother said, "You had better go right upstairs. Father is not pleased."

So I did not feel that I could say one word about what I had done or was going to do.

I often took a walk in the afternoon, and so I took my Testament and tracts in my little bag on my arm and went to the "Isle," but failed to gain admittance to a single house. I prayed each day very earnestly that if the Lord was pleased with my efforts He would grant me success.

I went forth trembling, as the place was the worst place in Sheffield, like the New York Five Points in former years. In England we lend our tracts and exchange them each week.

The next week I gained access to one house. From another a dog was set at me (and I was terribly afraid of dogs), but this one did not seem to frighten me. One of the men called the dog off, saying in his strong Irish brogue, "What are you about there? Sure what harm is she doing?"

Next week I got into three houses, and had permission to read and offer a short prayer. In a few weeks I had access to all but two or three houses. Thus I had been getting along when one day I was met by a woman who said, "It is yourself. We were watching for you, honey."

I asked her what was the matter, and she took me to a room where was a young woman apparently dying, with her dead babe beside her.

She said, "It was yourself I wanted to see." I asked her what I could do for her. "I want to hear more of the dear Jesus ye were speaking to me about."

I read to her the Saviour's invitation, "Come unto me all ye that labor and are heavy laden and I will give you rest." [Matthew 11:28] Also about "the new heaven and the new earth," [Revelation 21] but I tried to tell her how it was only those who came to Jesus and believed in Him that could reach that happy place and find that rest.

I prayed with her and asked her if she did not want to see her priest. She said, "No, I only want to see you or one of your ministers." Then I was in a dilemma and needed my mother's advice.

I went home and asked mother to go upstairs with me, I had something to tell her. She did so, and first I asked her not to be displeased with me. I told her my story; she looked amazed. "To the 'Isle,' child?"

I said, "Yes, no one else would take it."

She said, "Well, dear, our preachers live so far away you had better go up to the vicarage and get the curate to go with you."

We lived near the parish church and vicarage. I went and saw the old vicar – a grand old man. He called the curate. "To the Isle?" he said, in surprise. "Yes, I will go with you, but it is only money they want."

I said, "No, indeed, it is not."

We found the poor woman delighted to see us. He talked and prayed with her; and there, in that miserable, dirty place, in the corner of a room with many people in it, on a pallet of straw a precious soul was redeemed, saved by grace divine.

She lived a few days. The curate, a true man of God, visited her every day and told me he never saw a brighter conversion. Is anything too hard for the Lord of hosts?

I continued my work in Sheffield until I became too feeble, and had to be sent to Hull to my native air, where I stayed with my brother's family six months. During that time I became acquainted with a young man who was preparing to go as a missionary to New Zealand.

I had always wanted to be a missionary, and I now thought that I would have an opportunity to do so, and was pleased with the idea that I might some day go to work for the Master. But my brother, who was a local preacher and class leader at the same chapel, thought I was both too young and too feeble to receive the attention of anyone. He also knew the young man better than I did, and requested me not to receive any more attention from him. He wrote to father and I was sent for to return home.

Soon after, I went to call on my first class leader, Mr. Benjamin Wood. I found that his wife had died, that he had

broken up his home, had become intemperate and was boarding. I felt very badly and could hardly believe it. They were holding extra meetings in Norfolk Street Chapel. I prayed much about Mr. Wood, and felt impressed to go and seek him out.

I went to where they told me he boarded. It was a long way from where we lived, but I went and waited for him to come from work to his tea. He was surprised to see me. I told him what I had heard. He said, yes, he was at first innocent of the charge, but afterward gave way to temptation, and then gave up going to Chapel altogether.

I told him I had come to take him to Chapel. He asked if I would walk with him through the streets. He wanted me to leave him and he would come some other night. I replied that I had come for him, and I did not wish to go without him.

We went to God's house together. He sat in the back seat and refused to go farther in. He promised to be there the next night, and not only kept his promise, but went forward as a penitent and was restored to the joys of salvation.

What a happy man he was! As long as I remained in Sheffield he kept in the good old way. "I will heal their backslidings, I will love them freely." [Hosea 14:4.]

My health was very poor for some time. I was taken with great pain in my knee, which seemed to baffle the skill of the physicians for a long time. Very severe treatment was used, but to no purpose, when it seemed to one of the physicians that it might proceed from the spine.

The day had been fixed to have the limb taken off, but my doctor said he could not bear the idea of this. He studied much about it. The spine was examined, and there was found the cause of all the trouble. Again, very severe treatment of issues and leeches and blisters was used, but in a few months I was able to walk again.

In about a year I was taken very ill with inflammation of the brain. I lay in spasms for a long time. My head was shaved, and again severe treatment was used; but in answer to the earnest pleadings of my parents, the Lord blessed the means and I was restored, quite against the expectations of the physicians.

When better, I was sent to my oldest sister in Derbyshire, but I became ill again. Her physician, Dr. Gregory, was a sincere Christian. The trouble was inflammation of the brain again. He bled me nine times in the arm in three weeks. The last time he thought I was dead, and he pleaded with God most powerfully to spare me to my parents. He said that I must have had a glimpse into the spirit world during this illness.

The curate of the church visited me often, as there was no Methodist minister within three miles of our village. I enjoyed his visits and teachings very much, and was cheered and helped by them.

It was at my sister's that I first met Mr. Cooke, where he was a frequent visitor. He was a devoted Christian man, a class leader in the church, also Sunday school superintendent, steward and chorister. He was in very comfortable circumstances, owned two lead mines and had shares in a third. Mr. Cooke was several years older than myself, but from the first day of my second visit at my sister's he began to pay attention to me.

He said to my sister, Mrs. Lees, "That young woman will be my wife. Don't you remember a dream I told you I had some time ago? Well, it is she I saw in my dream." He had not seen me at the time of the dream.

He dreamed that a young woman came to the village, that he asked her in marriage, but she would not consent to be married, except from her father's house and the parish church in Sheffield; and, said he, "This is she, but do not tell her my dream." Nor did I hear of it until after we were married.

My father heard that someone was keeping company with me, and came to see the young man and inquire into the matter. He found Mr. Cooke all he could ask, and gave the consent which was asked the first opportunity after my father came.

Mr. Cooke said to me, "I have one request to make?" I asked what it was. "Are you willing that our house should be the preachers' home when they come to preach?"

I answered that it would be a pleasure to have it so. He said when his father was living, his house was their home, but since his father's death they had been greatly put about for a steady stopping place. So as soon as we could, we furnished a little upper room and called it the "prophet's chamber."

They preached for us every other Sabbath and every Wednesday, and stayed all night When they had tarried a while, they left a blessing behind. Especially did I feel it so after our financial losses fell upon us, but never did I permit them to see our straits and difficulties.

We were very nicely settled. I went to work in the Sabbath school, distributed tracts, collected missionary money. Also from the local church subscribers, from a penny to one shilling per week.

Thus time sped on until our first baby came, when my life was despaired of. For two weeks the babe was taken away to be cared for by others. But the Lord in mercy spared my life and raised me up again. Our next babe, Mary Elizabeth, seemed to bring sorrows with her.

Up to that time our married life had been bright and prosperous, for our only trial was the parting with sisters and their families who left England for the United States. I seemed to be left alone.

But when our dear child Mary was a few days old, misfortunes, as they are called, began to fall upon us. By dishonesty and robbery my husband lost much of his property. We were greatly depressed, but even in this affliction may I not trace the hand of Providence, for had things gone on prosperously we would never have come to this country [the United States], nor is it likely that I would have been so peculiarly led to live in Him a life of faith, and learn by experience the riches of His loving kindness.

During this summer, the celebrated Rev. Robert Newton came to preach our Sunday school anniversary sermons. We always tried to have some noted preachers for the occasion, at which times the children appeared in white on the platform and sang the hymns.

Mr. Newton made his home at our house. Mary was in the cradle; I took her up and kissed her, and earnestly prayed that she might be spared to be a useful woman in the Lord's vineyard.

In August 1845, another little one was given to us: Agnes Ann, a lovely babe, who seemed to be more of heaven than of earth. In 1840 my sister Lees came to visit us from New York, but only stayed two days.

The next month I was going to buy some fruit from a dealer at the door. I ran upstairs for a basket and the little one crept to the door. Just then a wagon load of hay on the street come in contact with the fruiterer's cart and turned it over upon my darling. We picked her up for dead after the horse and wagon were raised.

Oh, the anguish it caused me! All thought her dead, but she partially recovered and was with us until April 1846, when God took her.

Chapter 3

The Shadows of the Sea

> I am bringing my child to the heavenly land,
> I am leading her day by day,
> And am asking her now, whilst I hold her hand,
> To come home by a rugged way.
>
> By a way that she never herself would choose,
> For its beauties she doth not see;
> And she knows not yet what her soul would lose
> If she trod not this path with me.

In January 1847, my dear husband, on account of repeated losses in business which reduced us greatly, decided to go to New York. Accordingly, after many severe trials and heartrendings in bidding adieu to parents and friends, we embarked on board the ship *Cambridge*, Captain Peabody, at Liverpool, on the 4th of April 1847.

After lying in the Mersey six days, we bade a final farewell to our native land, where we had been taught to bow the knee in prayer, and lisp Our Father, and the sweet name of Jesus.

Every stranger knows it is not a small trial to set out for a strange land. Mine had been a favored lot, as I was blessed with parents who walked with God, and I felt assured that it was a final farewell. But in this trying hour the Lord stood by me, and although living far below my privileges in Christ, He did not cast me off, but was still whispering in my heart, "Come closer, this is the way, walk thou in it." [Isaiah 30:21.] But my rebellious heart would say, "Nay, Lord, but in this way."

Oh, the wonderful long-suffering of an offended God. He cast me not off in my lukewarmness, but in answer to the prayer of Him who ever liveth to intercede for me, He cut me not down as a cumberer of the ground, but pruned the unfruitful branch that it might bring forth more fruit. [See Luke 13:7.]

> "Tears of joy my eyes o'erflow,
> That I have any hope of Heaven;
> Much of love I ought to know
> For I've had much forgiven."

In the ship, the Lord raised up friends for us. The captain and his wife were very kind; also the other officers of the ship. There were 350 Romanists in the steerage, and among them was our lot cast; but the goodness of the Lord gave us favor in the sight of the captain. The fare of the first-class stateroom was more than we felt able to pay, as there were five of us. But how to live in that place we knew not. For two nights I could not undress, and in our trouble we cried to the Lord, and unworthy as I was, He answered.

On the third day, Captain Peabody called for me and asked how I was getting along. I told him I did not know how we could live there for five or six weeks, that we had no idea of being put in such a place and company, but if I could not have my circumstances to my mind, I would try to bring my mind to my circumstances.

He replied, "That is a very good way, but I never intended you to be down there. You would never live to get to New York."

Nor do I think we could. For to say nothing of the dirt, it was a constant uproar of fiddling and dancing, cursing and swearing, and sometimes fighting. The captain called two of his men and bade them take up our baggage and put it in the house on the deck, and then took me by the hand and led me into the cabin, saying, "Here, Mrs. Cooke, is your place."

I replied, "We cannot not pay the difference in the fare."

He answered, "You have nothing more to pay. I have an interest in the vessel, and it is my wish for you to be here."

Then he went and sent my dear husband and children to me. We could not sufficiently express our gratitude to him. All this from a stranger. We could scarcely believe it. Mr. Cooke observed, "If this is the way Americans treat strangers (for the officers of the ship were Americans) we have not much to fear."

That night was the first time since being on board that we could have our little ones around us and read undisturbed the word of God. And oh, how earnestly did my dear husband plead with the Lord to guide us safely to our destined port, and thank Him for His loving kindness.

Our companions were very kind, and so were the captain and his lady in their notice of our children, and their pleasure in hearing them sing.

On the 14th of the month our dear little Agnes was taken with ship dysentery. The captain did all he could to save her, also the first mate; but the Great Captain ordered it otherwise. He saw fit to take her from the voyage of life and land her where no rude blast should trouble her more.

She lingered on in great suffering until the 22nd, and at two a.m. the precious Saviour called her to Himself, and sheltered the tender lamb in His bosom. But oh, how my heart rebelled, and would not be submissive; would not give her up. I could not say, "Thy will be done."

I entreated the Lord, in agony of soul, to spare her. How could I give her beautiful body to the deep? She was my idol. My dear husband entreated me to give her up, but no, I could not. Yet the Lord took her. Mr. Taylor the first mate was with us, and when all was over he desired me to lie down, but I replied that as long as I could keep her, I would not leave her for a moment.

At five o'clock the captain came and found me clinging to that loved form. He, with his wife and Mr. Taylor, wept – the strong men wept. It was a solemn time.

Though so rebellious, this passage was given with great force to my mind, "The sea shall give up its dead." [Revelation 20:13.] The Holy Spirit strove with me, showing me how wrong it was for me to feel and act in this way. As I was the only professor of religion among the women, I should have set an example of resignation and patience. But how could I, when I did not feel it?

The captain called Mr. Cooke aside and asked if he knew the mode of burial at sea. He answered that he did, after which the captain said, "I will encase that little body and put ballast to it myself, and also give you back her passage money. You have lost enough by losing her."

He returned and told me, and we were completely overcome with the goodness of God in putting it into the heart of the captain to treat us with such unexpected kindness. But, oh, my hard heart, I could not take comfort in any of these things. I only looked at the dark side, thinking how hardly I was dealt with by Providence – away from parents and friends in my affliction, upon the trackless deep, and my idol about to be consigned to a watery grave.

I was almost wild with grief. How many times since then have I been lost in wonder at the long suffering of my heavenly Father, that He did not strip me of all my children or husband, and leave me to the hardness of my heart.

Yet amid all this I would occasionally plead for perfect resignation, and feel as if I was about to enter that "rest" promised the children of God; but soon again I would find myself in the waste howling wilderness of unbelief.

"In darkness willingly I strayed;
I sought Thee, yet from Thee I roved,
And wide my wandering thoughts were spread;
Thy creatures more than Thee I loved;
And now if more at length I see,
'Tis through Thy light and comes from Thee."

Yes, blessed Lord, it was because Thy mercies fail not that I was not consumed. After I had with my own hands washed and dressed my precious babe, at ten in the morning it was taken out to the side of the ship for burial.

The boatswain piped, "All hands to bury the dead." The ship was hove to, and the officers and many passengers gathered around the gangway with uncovered heads. The good captain read the burial service, but three times during the reading he turned aside and wept, and then,

"The heavy-shotted hammock shroud
Dropped in its vast and wandering grave."

My heart sank down beneath the waters with my darling, but a voice still whispered, "The sea shall give up its dead."

In the afternoon we perceived that Mary was sick, and for twelve days we watched her, expecting her to follow Agnes, for three of our fellow passengers passed away in the meantime. But the Lord spared our child.

Before we reached quarantine, the captain came to me and said, "When your trunks have been examined you will have to pass the doctor, and for your children's sake look as cheerful as possible, lest you have to go to the hospital. Although you have no fever, you look dreadfully bad."

While waiting on deck for my turn to pass to the boat, a poor woman stood near me with her babe in her arms closely covered. I asked if it was sick. She looked around, and then said, "Ain't you the lady that lost the beautiful child?"

I said, "Yes."

"Och, then," she said, "it isn't yourself would betray the likes o' me if I were after telling you it's dead my child is, after losing one of your own and having it buried in the great sea. Sure, then, I'd jump in after it, for I could not myself bear the like of it."

No, it was not I that could betray the poor creature. She got to the city with the dead baby, and I trust met with friends who could sympathize with her.

While watching to see if there was anyone looking for us, a fine young man came on board and asked for his father and mother. The names were looked over, and they were among those we had left behind in the deep. He was shown their baggage, but took no notice of it, and his cries were beyond anything I have ever heard.

While thinking of his distress, a hand was laid upon my shoulder. It was my brother-in-law, John Evans. The first word was, "Where is the baby?"

My brother-in-law, George Lees, was with him, and took us to his home. My sister, holding out her arms, exclaimed, "Where is the baby?"

The wound was probed again. I said, "Agnes is no more."

"Well, dear, let us thank God that you and Joseph are spared."

I was thankful it was so, but could not praise the Lord for all that was past, or trust Him for the future. I had settled down into a sort of melancholy, and my thoughts were, "It is very easy for them to talk; they have not lost a child."

Oh, the long-suffering of the Lord to me!

Sabbath, the 16th of May 1847, was our first day of rest in the New World, and in the evening Mr. John Pullman and Miss Wilson came to see the strangers. They received us very kindly, and Brother Pullman said, "Well, friends, would you like to go to church?"

I said we would, and he took us to Rose Hill Church. They were singing these words as we entered,

> "He in the days of feeble flesh
> Poured out strong cries and tears,
> And in His measure feels afresh
> What every member bears."

Chapter 4

The Rugged Way

The Lord preserveth the strangers (Psalm 146:9).

> Oh, it is hard to work for God,
> To rise and take His part
> Upon this battlefield of earth
> And not sometimes lose heart.

On Monday, Rev. Mr. Perry called upon us and advised us to join the church. We had our certificate of membership, but by some means it was mislaid; but we showed our last quarter's tickets and Mr. Cooke's class I took, with which he was perfectly satisfied. Besides, his acquaintance with my sister assured him that there was no deception on our part.

On Tuesday evening I joined class, and my husband did the same on Thursday evening. Oh, how thankful I am that my feet were ever led to that little church, and that He gave me a place in the hearts of His people. For they have indeed cared for us with a fatherly care, and watched over us in all our affliction. It is my earnest prayer that the Lord, even our God, will stand by them one and all and give them an abundant entrance into the heavenly kingdom.

The next question was, "Where shall my husband find employment?" For our means were limited. My sister Evans took Mary E. with her to Meriden, Ct., for the summer. My sister Longdon took Hannah with her to Wethersfield for some months. For all this I was very thankful, yet it was a trial to me and the children, as they had never been separated from me before.

Mr. Cooke traversed the city daily in search of work, but in vain. In July 1847, Brother Pullman called to say he thought he had met with just the right thing for us. He had been talking with Peter Cooper about Mr. Cooke, and he was to go to Andover to take charge of the mines belonging to Mr. Cooper, and with great joy he left me, thinking how well we would get along.

But "the Lord's ways are not our ways, nor His thoughts as our thoughts." [Isaiah 55:8.] Husband was to come or send for us in four weeks, but when he arrived there, the agent had engaged another man, but he desired Mr. Cooke to stay two or three weeks and give them some ideas of the English methods of mining, for which he was liberally paid. He returned home with our hopes crushed, not knowing what to do.

I was ready to say, "All these things are against me." [Genesis 42:36.]

One day, while sitting and looking out of the window on the East River, I was musing upon that which was often in my thoughts: the death of my babe; also upon my honored father's removal, which we heard of three weeks after we landed, and the last words he uttered as he leaned upon his son's breast, "My son, live to God."

He, the aged pilgrim, and the little child, had met where parting is not known, when these sweet words were given to me with great power,

> "Give to the winds thy fears,
> Hope and be undismayed,
> God hears thy sighs and counts thy tears,
> God shall lift up thy head.
> Through waves and clouds and storms
> He gently clears the way;
> Wait thou His time, so shall this night
> Soon end in joyous day."

My thoughts followed the hymn to its close. I sang it over twice, and besought the Lord earnestly with groans and tears to give me that sweet peace which I had read of in the lives of Mrs. Hester Ann Rogers, Carvosso, Bramwell, and others, which I had in a measure possessed some years before, but had let slip from me, so that for the last two years I had been very unhappy.

I could not get away from self, and hide in the Redeemer, but thought I must become better before I dare trust for that state of grace. As I sang and prayed, I felt lightened a little of my load, but did not dare to reckon myself dead indeed to sin. It was the almost constant breathing of my heart,

> "When, gracious Lord, when shall it be
> That I shall find my all in Thee?"

Oh, how dark things looked. There was no light upon what we should do through the coming winter. I would not dare to say I could not trust the Lord, yet I did not trust Him. I was full of doubts and fears.

In September 1847, I became unable to do anything as I had done for my sister, and she kindly gave us a room in her house for ourselves. How could I keep house in one room? Well, I must try; no other way was left. Husband had no work except a day now and then, and the children soon to come home from the country, the little money we had was going very fast.

Sometimes I was almost beside myself, but would not let anyone know if I could help it, and hid it all in my own heart. I have since often wondered that I kept my reason, thinking of my coming sickness, our dismal prospects, my husband and my children. It was almost more than feeble nature could sustain.

But the loving kindness of my Heavenly Father and the intercession of my High Priest prevailed. "Spare her yet a little longer," was mercy's cry. Truly it may be said of me, if I hold my peace the very stones might cry out against me. No, blessed Jesus,

> "I will Thy boundless love proclaim
> With every fleeting breath."

About this time I became acquainted with the late Miss Martha Cooper and Mrs. Ryer, of precious memory, also Miss Kate Busteed and others who had known my sister Lees. I often heard these dear women converse about the blessing of perfect love, but never dared to ask them anything about it. Strange to say, they never addressed anything to me on the subject, although I believed they all lived in its possession.

On the 1st of November 1847, we had another little one added to our family, Ann Evans. At this time I was brought very low, but in addition to the pain of the body was the agony of my soul, for I remembered that without holiness no one can see the Lord. I deeply felt that there was a nearness to God and rest in Him, to which I was still a stranger. My unfaithfulness and unbelief were a grievous burden to me.

Oh, I thought if only someone would speak to me on the subject, for I could not tell my feelings. But they could not see the troubled waters that were ready to overwhelm the poor, sinking soul, and supposed that all was peace within. Oh, that Christians would deal more plainly with each other, and draw out the timid ones to tell of their spiritual troubles, and the workings of the Spirit to those who might instruct and help them.

One day in January 1848, Sisters Busteed and Ryer called for my sister to go to the female prayer meeting in our church. I was not asked to go. I suppose they thought I could not take the child or leave it. This hurt me sorely, but as soon as they were gone I wrapped up the child and followed, hoping to hear something that would bring comfort to my soul.

What was my surprise when in the meeting a dear sister, who I thought lived in the enjoyment of the blessing of perfect love, rose and said that she did not think a mother could retain so high a grace. Here was a good hold for the enemy, who lost no time in telling me that if one in her station of life could not retain this grace, it was useless for me to seek it any longer with my three little ones, a poor feeble body, and so many other things to try me.

I might as well give it up, and try and live as nearly right as I could in my humble way; but for me to seek after purity of heart at present was of no use. And thus instead of casting my burden upon the Lord, I was making up my mind to trudge on with it as best I could.

My dear husband would often say, "What makes you so happy? Cannot you trust the Lord when He hath done so much for us? We shall never want. Something will turn up by and by."

He thought all my sorrow was on account of outward trials. We were very fond of singing, but I could not get up the ladder any higher than such hymns as,

> "Depth of mercy, can there be
> Mercy still reserved for me?"

> "My Saviour doth not yet appear,
> He hides the brightness of His face."

Sometimes I would get on as far as,

"God is love, I know, I feel
Jesus weeps and loves me still."

When in church or anywhere else the people sang hymns of praise and triumph, I would stop. I dared not sing what I did not feel, as I considered it would be mocking God, for I did not serve with filial love, but with a servile fear, and I would not knowingly displease Him. And still I was displeasing Him all the time by not making a full surrender of *all I was* and *had to Him.*

The Comforter continued to stay near me, and I wonder He did not say, "Ephraim is joined to idols; let him alone." [Hosea 4:17.] But no, the prayer had gone forth, "Father, I will that these whom Thou hast given Me be where I am, that they may behold My glory." [John 17:24.]

Although so unworthy and so unfaithful, I had never lost the evidence that I was one of His little ones, and often did I hear the gentle voice, "Come unto me that ye may have life; yea, come that ye may have it more abundantly." [John 10:10.]

One afternoon in the following March it seemed as if I had almost become desperate, and giving the babe to Mr. Cooke, I said, "I must go to the prayer meeting. Would you not like to take care of baby?"

He answered "Yes."

I went. There was quite an assembly, and Mrs. Sarah Lankford led the meeting. I had seen her before, but not to speak with her. She gave out the beautiful hymn,

"Jesus, Thy blood and righteousness
My beauty are, my glorious dress."

I could not sing, only wept. Sister Lankford remarked that, "The new sister who appears very much depressed, we should like to hear from."

I tried to speak, but utterance was choked. Sister L. spoke of my feeling so badly. A sister replied that any of them would feel badly if they were in a strange land, with little children, and husband without work.

Then Mrs. Lankford came forward, and laying her hand upon my shoulder said, "Darling, cannot you trust the Lord?"

I replied that I was trying to trust Him, but it seemed of no use. She then asked me what Mr. Cooke could do.

I told her he was willing to do anything to earn an honest living for his family.

She replied, "He may come down to Dr Palmer's tomorrow morning, and I think Mr. Lankford, will engage him," and looking at Mary, asked if that was one of my little ones, with so much affection that it won my heart and the child's heart also.

With what joy did I go home, and as soon as I entered the door, said, "Pa, there is hope of work."

It was so unexpected that he said, "Not for me?"

I said, "Yes, for you."

The tears started into his eyes while he asked me about it. Oh, how anxiously did he wait for the morning, which at last came, and he went to meet Mr. L., who thought Mr. C. was not strong enough for his work.

He said, "If you will only try me, I will endeavor to please you."

But Mrs. Lankford said, "I want you to engage him, for I want his wife and children with us up at Caldwells."

Mr. L. replied that he could try, but it was evident he had not been used to such hard work as was needed. It was agreed that he should go up the following Tuesday and try for a month, and then take up his family if he succeeded. He came home like a new man.

As he entered the door he clapped his hands, saying, "I am going. The gentleman has engaged me."

Oh, what rejoicings were in that little home! My sister said, "I am so glad the Lord has opened your way to go there. You will be well cared for."

This dear sister had always had a mother's care over me. Surely here was the hand of the Lord directing my steps to the prayer meeting, and also the steps of Sister Lankford, for she but seldom attended that meeting; and for this I will praise the Lord through all eternity.

The coming week he left us, earnestly praying that the Lord would open his way before him and give him favor in the sight of his people.

After two weeks sister L. came down and told me to get ready, for they could not part with Mr. Cooke, and he would be down for us in two weeks. My joy was almost unbounded; what to say I knew not. Mr. L. was trying to have a little cottage prepared for us, and if he could not succeed, would let us have two rooms and make us comfortable. How happy I was! Constant work, our own bread, and a home!

The following Monday my husband came, but Mary was sick with scarlet fever. My things were all packed, and he could not be away from his work another day; but my way was opened, for sister wished to keep Mary and take care of her.

April 9th 1848, we reached Caldwells, a beautiful place on the Hudson, above Haverstraw.

Happy time, happy change. Mrs. L. came down to the boat to meet us and gave us a hearty welcome. We went with her to dinner, after which Mrs. Lankford said, "I have to go to the city for a few days. The cottage is not ready for you yet. You had better remain here until my return."

After she left, I told Mr. Lankford I preferred to go to the cottage. He said it was not ready. Still I wished to go, and did so. I said I could clean it and we could sleep on the floor. I longed to be in our own home. Besides, I feared the children would be troublesome.

With what joy did we close the door of our cottage, for it was the first time we had had a house to ourselves since we broke up our home in Derbyshire.

Often did I think of Mother Cooke's words, "Bella, you will never have another home like this." And my brother, as we were parting at the railway station, said, "Bella, this is a wild goose chase; you have broken up a lovely home. Will you ever have another like it?"

Chapter 5

The Victory of Faith

> What hast thou done in all these years,
> Since Christ in love dispelled thy fears,
> And in their place gave peace of mind,
> And access to His throne to find?
> Tell me, my soul!
>
> Oh, glorious liberty! Freedom indeed,
> Deliverance, full and complete;
> Since He gives me so freely
> The grace that I need,
> I willingly follow where'er He doth lead,
> And I'll ever keep low at His feet.

I felt thankful to have a home once more. Yet even here, with everything done that was reasonably possible for our comfort, I was not happy. The thought came that we were having more than we earned, and thereby we were more dependent than it suited me. Oh, my poor unsubdued spirit, what a training thou hadst to go through before finding thy resting place.

A few days after, Mrs. Lankford returned from the city. I was glad to see her. But when a little more than a week had passed, and she asked me how I liked my new home, she was disappointed in not finding me as happy as she had hoped.

Mrs. Lankford said she would like me to spend a little time every afternoon with her for reading, conversation and prayer. I was very thankful for the privilege.

On the second day, she said, "How do you get along? Do

you think you will like it up here with us?"

I said I liked the place very well, but could not stay, for my husband was not earning all we received; neither he nor I was satisfied on that point. She smiled and said she did not think that I especially had anything to do with that. Mr. Lankford was perfectly satisfied with Mr. Cooke, but she added, "I think I know what is the matter. You need a little more religion. Do you not think so?"

I said "No."

She then said, "Well, what do you need?"

I said "I need much more, but I cannot stay here. The swells from the steamboats almost drown my heart every time they pass up the river, and I bury my little one over again. And besides, I cannot be dependent."

Mrs. Lankford said, "You will get used to the swells, and that high, proud English spirit will have to come down. Do you enjoy the blessing of perfect love?"

I answered that I did not, and there was no use for me to seek it, as I had heard a sister say she did not think a mother could keep it.

Mrs. Lankford replied, "My dear child, it is just what you want to keep you, instead of you keeping it. Do you not believe the Bible?"

I was astonished at the question, for had I not loved it from my childhood? But I had been so unfaithful.

Mrs. Lankford replied, "If we confess our sins, He is faithful and just to forgive us our sins, and to cleanse us from all unrighteousness, is He not? [1 John 1:9.] Do you not believe that His grace is free?"

"Oh yes."

"Then why not for you? Let us kneel right down and ask the Lord just now for that clean heart."

Taking the Bible, blessed book, she read a part of the 36th chapter of Ezekiel, beginning at the 25th verse. [Then will I sprinkle clean water upon you, and ye shall be clean: from all your filthiness, and from all your idols, will I cleanse you.]

She then earnestly entreated the Lord for Christ's sake to receive me and cleanse me from all sin, after which we arose and sang, "How do thy mercies close me round," repeating the last verse, "Me for Thine own Thou lov'st to take."

We again knelt. I tried to pray, and Mrs. Lankford said, "I want you to pray. It is you who are seeking this blessing. Remember, you are committing suicide to carry such a burden with that poor frail body. The Saviour asks you to cast it all at His feet. He will carry it for you. The faith shall bring the power. The Lord is waiting to be gracious *now*;" and then she led in prayer again. And there just *then*, at about four o'clock p.m., I rested.

The Lord stretched out His arm and I was saved, yes, saved with a full salvation. It seemed to me I was stripped and clothed, unclothed and clothed upon; filled with the love of God. Husband, children, and everything were taken away, given to the Lord, no longer mine. Everything seemed to be new and lovely.

Sister L. understood just how I felt, and said, "Let us sing,

> O love, thou bottomless abyss,
> My sins are swallowed up in thee."

Then we sang, "Praise God from whom all blessings flow."

And I was a new creature in Christ Jesus. Oh the sweet, calm, settled peace! It was beyond expression. I, who had for years been seeking this promised rest, at last had found it.

I have often been lost in wonder when thinking of that

day. As long ago as 1845 I had gone with two children to Sheffield to hear the Rev. James Caughey preach in Brunswick Chapel, a distance of twenty miles, hoping to find "where His flocks rested at noon," [Song of Solomon 1:7] for my soul longed to find rest. After preaching, Mr. C. gave out that all seeking the blessing of holiness might meet him in the vestry.

I attended the vestry meeting, but found no resting place, and returned to my village home more cast down than ever, having rode forty miles and walked eight. I was weary in body and anxious in mind, almost ready to despair. O cruel unbelief! How many hast thou kept in sorrowful darkness!

I thought again if I might see my old class leader he could perhaps throw some light upon my way. Here faith was again at fault. I could not take hold of the promises and claim them mine. No, they were for others – for all the world, but not for me.

In 1846 my sister came to visit me and brought *The Way of Holiness*. I read it with eagerness, and felt a little comforted, but could not reckon myself dead indeed unto sin, and thought if I could only see the author and converse with her. In this I was still looking to the creature instead of the great *I Am*.

When we came to America in May 1847, I determined to see Mrs. Palmer and find that which I had been seeking after; but no, circumstances did not permit it. But in April 1848, in an upper room with her dear sister's advice to cast all upon my Saviour, give up all, and believe that my Father did accept me, not for my sake, but for the sake of His Son whom He gave as a ransom for my sins, the just for the unjust – take Him and His word, that He would sprinkle clean water upon me – I was enabled by grace to plunge into that fountain which is open in the house of David, and to believe that I was accepted of the Beloved.

Truly that room was a Bethel to me, for there the Lord met me and spoke with me as it were face to face. And now I raise my Ebenezer, for "hitherto the Lord hath helped me." [1 Samuel 7:12.] Although I have many times erred through lack of judgment, or shunning the cross, yet I have ever been enabled to look up to Him with childlike confidence and say, "I am Thine, save me; and thus His smile has been the light of my life."

I returned to my home with my new treasure, and when my dear partner came in we rejoiced together in the Lord. Oh what a change! Every breath seemed to bring with it "Praise the Lord." There was no great outburst of feeling, but a calm, serene resting in the arms of my Beloved; a persuasion that I had given myself with all my powers over into His care, to do with me just as He pleased, only to make and keep me fully His.

The following Sabbath I was almost afraid to speak out boldly of what the Lord had done for me, when this passage came to my mind, "They that honor Me, I will honor, and he that is ashamed of Me, of him will I be ashamed before My Father and His holy angels." [Luke 9:26.] With this before me, I resolved by His grace to,

"Tell to all around
What a dear Saviour I have found."

Whenever opportunity offered, or I was called upon, I would tell the wonderful dealings of the Lord to me. Accordingly, I went to meeting, and in the strength of the Lord spoke freely in class meeting. And oh, the power that came down! It almost overcame me. I hardly knew whether I was in or out of the body. I then felt a strong desire for my dear husband to enter into this rest, and that my dear little ones should be saved.

Shortly after, the Lord gave me the assurance that my children should be saved; yet I dared not claim it for them during my life. I knew it would be done. I felt that Jehovah had promised them to me, but the time and the manner I knew nothing about; and thus I continued to keep them before the Lord, for they were His.

Thus passed the summer of 1848 very pleasantly, but the next winter I was the subject of very sore temptations. Sometimes it seemed as if Satan were let loose upon me for a season, and once or twice I yielded in a measure, but praise my Heavenly Father, He enabled me to go right to the blood of sprinkling and wait to be made whole.

During the winter we had no opportunity of worshiping God with the Methodists, as there was no preaching place in the vicinity. Mrs. L. was away in New York, the river was frozen, and there was no communication between the city and us; but we held church and Sabbath school in our own room.

My dear husband would read, and explain what he read in the Blessed Book. We would sing and pray together, and hear the children recite the Scripture which they had learned during the week. Although we were alone, our Sabbaths were a delight. We welcomed them as a day of rest and refreshing from the Lord.

We invited our neighbors to join us, but they were so busy on that holy day, drawing wood or mending their barns, that they thought they had no time to worship Him who gave them life and all its comforts.

In the spring of 1849 I had a sore trouble. A reproachful charge was made against me, of which I was perfectly innocent. This was a painful wound, but I felt that I had a sure resting place. And "though an host should encamp against me," [Psalm 27:3] one thing I would seek after, that I might dwell in His presence for ever, and be approved of Him.

Oh, with what joy I hailed Mrs. L. back in April, that I might again be profited by her counsel and prayer.

Chapter 6

Thy Maker Is Thy Husband

Thy Maker is thine Husband; the Lord of Hosts is His name
(Isaiah 55:5).

> "Give me the cup, my Master! See me clasp
> With willing hands this remedy from Thine.
> Forgive the mortal shudder, mortal gasp
> That proves me human, proves me not divine.
> Slowly each drop I'll taste, and one by one,
> For Thee I drink, Lord; let Thy will be done."

It seemed as if my cup of blessing was full. The summer came, and with it came many dear friends from the city with whom I was permitted to take sweet counsel, and we often met for social conversation and prayer.

In July 1849, Mr. and Mrs. Kellogg, and Mr. and Mrs. Hall were with us. The cholera was raging at a fearful rate in the city, and this was the theme of conversation. Mr. Hall said that he knew the Lord would preserve him and his family from it, for the Lord had said, "No evil shall befall thee, or plague come nigh thy dwelling." [Psalm 91:10.]

I replied that I could not say so, for if my husband or children should be taken with it, I could not look upon it as an evil. It would certainly be a great trial, but not an evil, and I believed the Lord would sustain me through it.

He said I was welcome to my views, and he would keep his.

On the evening of the 18th of August, after supper the children were in bed, we sat on the steps of our house watching the steamboats sailing up the river, and the beautiful moon shining brightly on the waters.

We sang many hymns, after which, when about to retire, Mr. Cooke said, "Well, dear, tomorrow would have been Mr. Loomis' day to preach, but he is gone, and we cannot tell who may be the next." (Mr. L. had died the previous week with the cholera.)

We had prayers and went to bed. About half-past two a.m. the babe awoke and wanted a drink. Mr. Cooke said, "Can you get her a drink, dear? I feel sick."

I did so, and gave him a drink also. In about an hour he was very sick, and I went against his wishes to Mrs. Lankford for some medicine. Mrs. Lankford said, "If Mr. Cooke is not better in an hour let me know, and I will go and see him."

He got no relief, and as I stood with his head leaning against me, he looked up very sweetly, and said, "My dear, I am going home today."

I said, "Oh, no, Papa, do not say so. You will be better soon, I hope."

He replied, "No, I am going home today."

I went for Mrs. Lankford. She, with Mr. L., came at once, about half-past four a.m. Mr. L. took a man and boat and went to Peekskill and brought a physician.

Mrs. L. said, "Brother Cooke, you are very sick."

He replied, "Yes, I am going home today."

Mrs. L. said, "I hope not, for the sake of those dear children and your dear wife," when he again repeated it.

When the doctor came, he gave us very little hope. Mr. L. took him back and brought another doctor. He gave us no more encouragement than the first. Everything was done for him that could be done, but of no avail.

All through that last fatal day, amid cramps and sore distress, he was laboring for Christ – warning sinners or urging believers to a closer walk with God; asking them what he could do now if he had to make his peace with God, often saying he was almost home.

When he heard the bell for Sabbath school, he said, "Tell them it is the last time I shall hear the Sabbath bell, but I shall be with Jesus, for I shall get home today."

Then he told us how he loved his duties as superintendent and teacher in his own land. In the afternoon Mrs. L. said, "Brother Cooke, you are almost home. Is Jesus precious?"

He answered, "Yes, yes, very precious."

"Is the prospect clear?"

"Oh, yes; clear and bright."

"Praise the Lord!"

To which he sweetly responded, "Yes, praise to Him."

Can anyone wonder at my strong love for that dear sister, who has been with me and stood by me in all my sorrow? At half-past four that morning she came with Mr. L. and cared for that poor suffering body all day, except the little time for food. Fear of infection seemed not to enter their minds. They saw he was hasting home, but strange to tell I could not see it. At six his speech left him, yet I could see no danger.

At six p.m. Mrs. L. urged me to go down and take a cup of tea she had prepared for me, but I did not wish to leave him. He heard the request and looked very earnestly at me. As I leaned over him, he said, "Go, dear."

I kissed him and left him for a moment. When I returned, his speech had left him. I never, never heard that gentle voice again. Oh, how I reproached myself for leaving him for that brief minute.

When about to put the children to bed I thought it strange that Mrs. L. should wish me to send them to her house. After seeing them to bed, I took my stand at the head of the dear sufferer, one arm under his head, the other holding one of his hands, and Mrs. L. holding the other and fanning him, Mr. L. standing at the foot.

The room and yard were full of people, when about seven o'clock Mr. Coles stood upon the doorstep and said to those without, "Come in and see how the Christian dies. We may well say, mark the perfect man, and behold the upright, for the end of that man is peace." [Psalm 37:37.]

I wondered at those words, for Mr. Coles was not one who professed to follow the meek and lowly Jesus, but he had to acknowledge the power of God to sustain in the trying hour of death.

There we stood, when at twenty minutes to eight, p.m., I heard Mrs. L. saying, "Happy soul, thy days are ended."

I looked at her and said, "Is it so?"

"Yes," she replied, "our brother is with the blessed;" but so calm, so much like falling asleep, I could scarcely believe it. Truly he slept in Jesus, blessed sleep. All I could think of was, "It is my Father, and He is too good to be unkind. *My Father! My Father!*"

Thus passed away a good and kind husband, an affectionate father and a devoted Christian; one whom the Master made ready as a shock of corn to be gathered into the garner of the Lord.

We remained silent for some time, when Mrs. L. said to me, "Come, dear, you must go with me. Mr. L. will care for the poor body. You can trust it with him, can you not?"

So after getting the things necessary for them, I went with Mrs. L. to her home where the little ones had been taken, with the baby in the cradle. She led me to her room, where my sleeping little ones were unconscious of the loss they had sustained.

We knelt, and Mrs. L. poured forth her soul in prayer and supplication to our dear Father in Heaven, that He would be the Father of the fatherless and the widow's God, and pleaded the promise and assurance in Isaiah, "Thy Maker is thy Husband and thy Redeemer, the Holy one of Israel, the Lord of Hosts is His name." [Isaiah 54:5.]

I had read those words many times, but never before did I see the force of them. It seemed as if I did take the Lord at His word and cleaved to Him as my husband. After some time we rose from our knees and Mrs. L. gave me a little room adjoining hers, the maid having been told to prepare it for me. I entered, but not to sleep. I went over the past day, trying to realize it, for it seemed as a dream.

My eyes rested on the pillows of the bed. Certain passages of Scripture were on the pillowcase, and I read, "I will never leave thee, nor forsake thee, but lo, I am with thee alway, even unto the end of the world" [Hebrews 13:5 and Matthew 28:20.] Also, "He that keepeth Israel shall neither slumber nor sleep." [Psalm 121:4.]

No one can tell the comfort I derived from those Scriptures. I seemed fixed to the chair as I read and re-read. Oh, how sweet were the blessed words! I knew it was not done intentionally by anyone, for the girl was not a Christian. At last I laid down, but not to sleep – I felt perfectly secure in the arms of Israel's God.

At early dawn my little ones awoke and asked why they were there, and was papa better. The baby could not be pacified. She wanted papa. All her cry was, "My papa."

It seemed as if my heart and brain would burst. I could not weep; tears refused to flow. Even before breakfast Mr. L. came to ask what commands I had and what I would like to have done. I had nothing to say, but would like, if possible, to have the remains laid in a Methodist burial ground.

He said it should be done, if possible. A spot was obtained in Peekskill, and he had already sent to New York to my friends, sisters and brother-in-law. The dear remains he had brought to his own house, where he had the services.

I have often wondered at this love in comparative strangers, that they should take pains and care for us in such a manner in a time when some might have fear of infection. I was perfectly astonished, and have often thought it might have appeared strange to them that I had so little to say in the way of thanks.

Mr. L. had all things ready, and went to Peekskill again for the Rev. Mr. Young to speak at the funeral, as the regular minister was absent. The house was full, and the minister spoke from these words, "Then shall the dust return to the earth as it was, and the spirit shall return to God who gave it," [Ecclesiastes 12:7] and sang the hymn,

"And must this body die?
This well-wrought frame decay?"

A procession of seven boats took us across the beautiful Hudson, and as we passed over I thought of another glorious river – a pure river of water of life, clear as crystal, proceeding out of the throne of God and of the Lamb, where there shall be no more curse, and there shall be no night there, and they shall reign for ever and ever. [Revelation 22:1.]

On the other side, a hearse and carriages were waiting to take us to my dear partner's final resting place. Amid all this my mind was kept sweetly stayed upon God. No distracting thoughts were permitted to distress or agitate my soul, but the 23rd Psalm was given me by the Comforter. This sustained and cheered my poor, crushed, yet trusting, heart, for I felt that it was the Lord, let Him do what seemeth Him good.

There were my little ones, the eldest just eight years old, the baby one year and eight months old. My health was feeble, and with nothing of worldly goods beforehand, yet I felt secure in the hands of my Heavenly Father, assured that He who had taken away my earthly prop would not leave me to suffer.

No, "The Lord is my Shepherd" was with me constantly. I had nothing to fear, but much to praise Him for, inasmuch as He had raised up for me such friends in a strange land.

After laying the precious relics in the silent tomb we returned to Mr. L's, where my three little fatherless ones met me at the door, and the baby crying for her papa. A silent solemnity pervaded the house. We were not permitted to return to our home that night.

In the evening Mr. L. said, "Well, I have had many men to work for me in my life, but I never had one like Mr. Cooke, nor do I ever expect to have another so truly conscientious and good."

This was a great comfort to me. Mrs. L. told me the next morning that they would fit up a room in their house until I should be over my approaching illness. I was very thankful for this new token of love, but my sister in New York wanted me with her.

"Well, then," she said, "leave me one of your little ones and I will keep her until then." She took Mary, and instead of a few months, provided for her eleven years, even until the child was fitted to teach.

> "Pause, my soul, adore and wonder.
> Ask, Oh, why such love to thee?"

It needed all that my husband had earned to pay the funeral expenses, and when I returned to the city to rest a little, Mrs. L. gave me twelve dollars. I also sold some things that I did not need. I told my sister I could help her through the winter, and my sister Longdon took Hannah, so I had but one child with me.

On the following 20th of March 1850, another child was given me, Josephine Lankford, a lovely child, but oh, who but those who have passed through such circumstances can tell the feelings of a mother to the child? My physician, a kind Christian gentleman, waited until it was dressed, when he brought it to me and said, "The Lord has given you a lovely babe. Nurse and care for it for Him."

I said, "Oh, Dr. Fitch, but her father!"

He replied, "Yes, my dear, God will be her Father," and before he would go down to eat some breakfast, he said, "Let us kneel and thank the Lord for sparing the life of our dear sister," and with great fervor he approached the throne of grace in my behalf and for my little ones.

After this, my life was despaired of, but I was raised up in answer to prayer.

Chapter 7

The Widow's God

For He shall deliver the needy when he crieth; the poor also, and him that hath no helper (Psalm 72:12).

Leave thy fatherless children, I will preserve them alive: and let thy widows trust in Me (Jeremiah 10:11)

In April, Mrs. Lankford came to ask me what were my wishes for the future. I said if I could, I should like a little home of my own, and would be very thankful. She said it should be so. Two little rooms were hired, where I removed on the 6th of May.

Few can tell what were my feelings when I for the first time locked the door of my habitation against the remains of the one I held most dear on earth. But I found it very sweet to take my little ones and kneel and claim a Father's care and blessing. Nor did we ask in vain. Dear Mrs. L brought me $15 to commence housekeeping with.

Being settled in my little home, I went to the coal yard and asked for a bushel of coal, wishing to have it sent home. The gentleman in the office said he would like to ask me a few questions, and hoped I would not think it was idle curiosity that prompted him.

He had seen me passing and re-passing for some months, had missed me for a while, and now saw me with a babe. Was I not a widow, and to what church did I belong? And what were my means, or had I a competency? For I had been very much on his mind.

I told him I was a widow and belonged to the Methodist

Church, and had the promise of the Father of the fatherless and the widow's God. He said he thought so. He belonged to the Forsyth Street Methodist Church, and would send the coal and would not take any pay; and when I wanted more, I must not hesitate to go and tell him.

Ten days rolled round. It was Saturday evening. I was somewhat perplexed. I needed coal, and did not like to go to the yard. It seemed like begging it. I did not like to go anywhere else: that would appear ungrateful. I sat down with my head on my hand and was asking my Heavenly Father to guide me, when a man called out, "Mrs. Cooke, here is some coal."

I knew that it was from the same gentleman; I never learned his name. For two or three weeks I got along very well, but then my strength began to fail, and the doctor said the child must be put to nurse and I must get to the country by short and easy stages, by which my life might be prolonged through the summer — or in a few weeks, to all human appearances, I would be done with all the cares of life.

Accordingly, my kind friends gathered around and got a nurse for the baby, and made me up a purse. Mrs. Stephenson and Mrs. Howe were ever ready to help me. They sent me to Miss Busteed's, at Tarrytown, until I was able to go to Mrs. Lankford's.

After about two months I was much better, and was able to take the baby and Hannah and go to my sister Evans, who had sent for me, and where I remained until September, when I returned to the city, much improved in health, and determined if possible to get work and take care of my little ones.

I solicited sewing from my friends and went to work, having my three children until December, when Mary came home. I worked nearly night and day to provide food necessary for myself and little ones.

Early in February 1851, I had a trial of my faith. I had some shirts to make, and when done I took them home on Thursday evening, expecting to get six dollars, having spent my last six cents going down in the stage. But what was my surprise when told that the lady had left the city and would not be home until Tuesday. My heart replied, "Though Thou slay me yet will I trust in Thee." [Job 13:15.]

It was a bitter cold night, and I hurried home and found my Hannah had tea ready. I had but part of a small loaf of bread, nothing to cook, and no milk for my baby. I gave the children their supper, took a cup of tea, and gave baby some sweetened water. I knew if I could get along until Saturday I should have a dollar.

We went to bed and slept soundly. In the morning we had very little, and dear Hannah wanted to go and get a loaf of bread so that I could have some. I said, "No, not this morning."

Mary said, "Mama, I am sure I could eat more;"

I replied, "You shall have all the bread you want for dinner."

Then Hannah spoke up and said, "But, mama, you say that we ought not to eat fresh bread, that it is extravagant."

Again I said, "You shall have all you want for dinner. Mama does not wish any now."

At family worship, when pleading the promises, there was such a holy calm with the full belief that deliverance was at hand that my little room seemed filled with the presence of God. I sat down to my work and sang, and never was happier.

About eleven o'clock, I thought I would go to my sister's and ask her to lend me twenty-five cents.

I went through the heavy storm, and found her sewing. I sat down a little while, but could not tell her what I wanted.

I rose to go when she went into the back room, singing, "Come Thou fount of every blessing."

I stood for a moment, speaking to my brother-in-law, when she called to me.

"Come here, Bella. Would you not like a loaf of home-made bread? I have been baking this morning."

She met me with a loaf. I took it, and went home and laid it on the table, and went to my little room to return thanks to my kind good Father who pitied me as a father pitieth his children. [Psalm 103:13.] I had my breakfast, or rather my dinner, and it tasted so good.

The children asked, "Mama, where did you get this new bread?"

I told them the Lord gave it to me, for I wished to impress on their minds His great care over us.

"Never have I seen the righteous forsaken, nor his seed begging bread." [Psalm 37:25.] And so the Lord sealed my mouth and worked in His own way and time.

In the evening I thought I would tell my sister; and with tears she said, "Why did you not tell me?"

I said, "I could not. The Lord seemed to seal my lips."

I went home, and H. met me, saying, "Oh, ma, do hurry."

I went in, and on the first chair was a large piece of corned beef, a cabbage, a loaf of bread, and some potatoes. I asked where they came from.

She said, "A man brought them, and he said the Lord sent them to mother."

I never knew from whence they came. So the good Lord provided for us in a wonderful manner. All that I could say was, "I thank Thee, my Father. When He hath tried me I shall come forth as gold." [Job 23:10.]

To no one had I said a word of my necessity, but my kind good Father, whose ear is ever open to His children when they cry, knew my wants.

Faint yet Pursuing

Straits and poor health continued until late in February 1851. One day while I was sitting sewing, Mrs. Thompson called. I had just sent Hannah to our coalhouse to pick up what she could. She asked me if I had plenty of coal, and how I had got along through the winter thus far. I merely said I had some coal.

Just then Hannah came in, and said, "There, ma, is every bit I can find."

I shook my head at her, but Mrs. Thompson asked, "What is it, Hannah?"

I begged her to excuse her, but she pressed the question, and Hannah said it was all the coal she could find.

Mrs. Thompson said, "I thought you said that you had coal."

I replied, Yes, I had, and before that was burnt I would either have coal or money.

She stood at the door to leave, when a knock led her to open it, and there stood a man with a whip in his hand and asked if Mrs. Bella Cooke lived there. "Here is a ton of coal for her."

I said, "It must be a mistake, I have not ordered any."

He said, "If that is your name, and you are a widow, it is for you."

Mrs. Thompson said that I was as bad as they were when praying for Peter's release from Herod's prison, when he stood at the gate and they would not believe it. [Acts 12.] "You said you would either have coal or money, and now it is just here."

My heart went up in praise to God for all His goodness to me. "He knoweth our frame and remembereth that we are dust." (Psalm 103:14.)

In March I was taken very sick, not able to sit up. Through the winter I had been working till twelve and one o'clock at night, and up again at five in the morning, for I knew that my children would want new clothes in the spring — four little ones at my feet, the oldest but nine years.

Then I was laid up for a month. Dear Mrs. Lankford went to work and clothed Hannah and Mary, and my sister Evans came and asked me if I would give her Annie. I said I could not give any of them away, but I would lend Annie to her a little while if she could coax her to go with her.

She did so, and when she had gone halfway home the little thing cried, and said, "There, now, take me back to my poor dear mama. I have been with you far enough; take me home." But she had to go on, and for months after when she heard the train whistle, she would say, "They are coming to take me to my mama."

I continued feeble, and the physicians said I must get to the country. Mrs. Lankford sent Mary to school. The rest of us went to my sister's in Meriden, then to Wethersfield till the last of July.

After our return, my dear baby was taken ill.

New York
August 18th 1851
My dear Sisters,
I just write to say that my dear baby still breathes. Dear lamb, we have been watching ever since Wednesday for every breath to be her last. She has had convulsions with very little intermission, after which she would lie in a state of stupor. She has lost the use of her left side.

I have been looking for letters from you. Mrs. Lankford came from camp meeting, as Dr. Palmer sent her word baby was so sick. And what a comfort she is to me. How kind they all are! May our dear Father in heaven reward, them for their kindness to the widow and the fatherless. Give my love to the children, and tell them dear little Josey is near home – will soon be with that dear Jesus who said, "Suffer little children to come unto me," and with her dear father who would have loved her so much if he had lived to see her.

This morning at three o'clock she raised her right hand as high as she could, and pointing upward said three times, "See there! There! There! Papa, papa!" The only thing she has said for eight days, except on Thursday, about midnight, raising the same hand and opening her eyes said, "See there! Papa, papa!"

Who can tell but that she saw into that land of spirits to which she is hastening? Pray for me.

Your stricken sister,
Bella Cooke

[Every letter from Bella, even to close family members, is "signed" Bella Cooke, or B. Cooke. These letters were borrowed from the recipients by Bella's son-in-law, Joseph Pullman, for this publication, and presumably out of respect for family members and others he has not always copied any informal Bella may have used, and probably not always copied the opening name by which the recipient is addressed.]

On the 19th of August Josephine went home to join her dear father and sister. He doeth all things well. Praise the Lord! Both the Drs. Palmer attended my darling babe and were very tender over her.

As I sat and watched that lovely form waste away, I felt that all was well, not one stroke too many.

The Sabbath before she died, sister Shipman was with me. When, laying her hand upon my shoulder, she said, "Don't forget, dear, that the Saviour said, 'What I do thou knowest not now, but thou shalt know hereafter.'" [John 13:7.]

It was a word of comfort, but I felt no repining, for I knew I was my Beloved's, and He was mine, and that He did all things well.

New York
August 24th 1851
My Dear Sisters,

I received your kind notes on my return from Peekskill, where we had been laying the remains of my precious babe. Truly, I found it a great trial, but blessed be the Lord, He sweetly enabled me to say, "It is well with me, it is well with my husband, it is well with the child."

Yes, it is well with them. They are, "Far from a world of grief and sin, with God eternally shut in," and by and bye, if faithful, I, too, will be permitted to enter those pearly gates where I shall never in the anguish of my soul cry out, "My child! My child!" But there every tear shall be forever wiped from our eyes, and we shall no more say, "I am sick."

On Tuesday, Mr. and Mrs. Lankford and Mrs. Shipman came up and made arrangements how to proceed. Mr. Lankford went to Peekskill and had the same ground opened for father and babe to lie together. Carriages to meet us at ten o'clock on Thursday morning, and on his return called and brought Mary with him.

The minister here, Mr. Perry, improved the occasion from the words, "Is it well with thee? Is it well with thy husband? Is it well with the child? And she answered, It is well." [2 Kings 4:26.]

Yes, praise the Lord, it is well. This service was on Wednesday afternoon, and the next morning Mr. and Mrs. Lankford and Mrs. Shipman went up with me to Peekskill with Miss Cannon and the children. Mrs. Shipman repeated over the grave these words,

> "Unveil thy bosom, faithful tomb,
> Take this new treasure to thy trust,
> And give these sacred relics room
> To slumber in thy silent dust."

Mr. Lankford paid for the grave opening, carriages and railroad fare, and told Mr. Lees to keep an account of anything else, and he would pay it. "Praise the Lord, O my soul, for He hath done great things for thee."

What a friend He hath given me in dear Mrs. Lankford, who stands by me in all my trouble.

Help me, dear sisters, to praise the Lord.

Your sister,

Bella Cooke

Chapter 8

Joy In the Will of God

Nevertheless, afterward it yieldeth the peaceable fruit of righteousness (Hebrews 12:11).

> What shall Thine "afterward" be, O Lord,
>   For this dark and suffering night?
> Father, what shall Thine "afterward" be?
>   Hast Thou a morning of joy for me
>   And a new and joyous light?

About a fortnight after this I was seized with spasms. My faithful little Hannah was my housekeeper, and she went for some friends who remained with me through the night, and who, with Doctors W. C. and M. W. Palmer, and my pastor, Rev. J. J. Matthias, thought I could not live, but the Master spared me a little longer.

I was soon up again and worked pretty hard, and suffered much in body, but my soul leaned upon God. He was my present help.

The following March 1852, the Lord saw fit to put me through another trial. He took from me my sister Lees, my last prop. She being so much older than myself, I leaned upon her, although my other sisters were equally kind. She calmly fell asleep in Jesus after having suffered with dropsy for six years.

After the death of my sister, my health sunk very much, and friends, at the doctor's advice, with great care carried me to my sisters at Meriden and Wethersfield. I was several weeks on a sickbed, but by the blessing of God on the labors of a kind physician, Dr. Brown, of Hartford, and the incessant care of my sisters, I was spared.

Doctor Brown left me one night at twelve o'clock, not expecting to see me alive when he returned in the morning. Two days before this I had a very bad turn. I do not know how it was. I was feeling badly, and asked my sister to raise me up. She did so, when to all appearances I died.

She alarmed the house. My brother-in-law ran to the next house for help. Mr. Boardman came and begged them to let me alone, as I was dead; but they continued their efforts to resuscitate me.

At last my brother-in-law poured my mouth and throat full of brandy, and that seemed to choke me and I rallied. I was in this state about twenty-three minutes, and strange to say, although I could hear everything that was said, I could not move a finger or toe, or any part of my body; and though I heard their cries and moans, I was not in the slightest degree affected by them.

But all that I ever did wrong seemed to come up in array before me, and beside them stood my Saviour, and it seemed as though I saw His wounds and heard Him say, "I suffered this for thee; thou art Mine."

I felt as if suspended between earth and heaven. Oh, the depth of unworthiness that I felt! It seemed as if it would sink me down, but my Saviour held me up. Nothing on earth – children, sisters or friends – gave me the least concern. Through all this the Lord spared me, and here I am a monument of His power to save. How many times have physicians given me up to die, and felt no more could be done to continue my life.

The last of September I returned home again and strove to labor for the bread which perisheth. Yet I thought I must do something for Him who had done so much for me. So I devoted one or two hours in the day to labor among the poor in Bellevue Hospital and on First Avenue, taking the streets from Twenty-Eighth to Thirty-Fourth, and from Third Avenue to the river.

I found many cases of distress which were helped and aided, and some professed to find the "pearl of great price." As we believe that prayer shall not return void, we may hope to find some precious souls at the right hand of God.

Miss Mary Cannon sometimes went with me to the Hospital, and dear Mary Stephenson, now Mrs. De Lamater, went with me to the houses.

You may say, "Where did you get the money, clothes and food you needed in your visits?" Well, I was widely known on Third Avenue, and many of the storekeepers would give me food when I presented my bad cases.

Mrs. A. G. Phelps and her daughter, Mrs. Stokes, lived in the old homestead then, and they would always help me with clothing and sometimes with money, as also did some of the brethren of our own church, for funerals. I was hardly ever refused by anyone, as I always laid the cases before the Lord before I went out, and asked of Him to appoint my way and direct me where to go.

Neither fevers nor smallpox detained me. It was the Master's work, and I believed if He wished me to go, He would protect me – and He did. Of course I took every precaution not to carry infection to others. "He that hath a bountiful eye shall be blessed." [Proverbs 22:9.]

In December 1852, I was very poorly and not able to work much. Again I was in need of coal, and did not know what to do but go to my Father, who seeth in secret, and tell Him all my wants. I did so, and earnestly poured out my soul to Him in prayer. And while I was yet asking, the answer came. The doorbell rang, and the person on the first floor called out,

"Mrs. Cooke, it is for you." And lo, a ton of coal!

I stood amazed, for although I was asking and felt I was heard, I hardly expected an answer so soon. But there it was. I could only praise and adore.

Mr. Warner, who lived downstairs, said, "What did you pay for coal?"

I answered, "Nothing. My Heavenly Father paid for it."

On the next evening Mr. J. D. Smith, who kept a fancy store on Fourth Avenue, called on me and asked, Had I a ton of coal come?

I told him "Yes," and that I was just then asking for some.

He said that was strange, as that morning he said to his wife, "Eliza, I don't think we give enough away. We are not prospering in business as we might. I think we ought to send Mrs. Cooke some coal."

She said, "Well, do so."

He went immediately to the coal yard and ordered the coal that came to me. He then went down town to sell sewing-silk, and that day cleared twenty-five dollars – more than he had sold for a long time. Thus did our Father in heaven show His approbation of the act by blessing the labor of his hands before he slept, restoring to him fourfold what he had given to His needy child. Yes, our heavenly Father knoweth that we have need of these things and we will praise Him, for He is worthy.

Oh, the Lord was very good to shield and give me favor with His children. So that I might not be chargeable to others, as I read, "Be not slothful in business," [Romans 12:11.] I went back to my work, and would sit up *one, two, three* hours at night to make up the time I had spent in going my rounds, and how sweet were the hours spent for my Saviour!

"He spoke, and my poor name He named,
Of Me thou hast not been ashamed."

But this little labor was not to last long. The poor body gave way, and after much struggling with pain and nervousness I was induced by Mrs. S. G. Smith and Mrs. Mason, in September 1855, to go to The Woman's Hospital. I felt I must consult Mrs. Lankford and Dr. Palmer.

Mrs. Lankford objected. The other two ladies wished her to visit the hospital and see Dr. Sims. They met at my house, and we all prayed over the matter. Then they went round, and the doctor told them that without help and treatment there, I could not live three months, as my spine, lungs and liver were much diseased.

He did not know if he could help me at all, but I should have the best of care, and should go in immediately. Dear Mrs. Lankford returned with the decision that I should go at once. Then she took Mary, and Mrs. Cooper took Hannah, and on the 17th my pastor and Miss Mary Stephenson took me to the hospital.

Was on the second floor where were nine beds, all occupied but one. All were respectable, intelligent women, but not one did I see bow the knee in prayer or read the word of God.

On Saturday my dear young friend, Miss Stephenson, came to see how I got along. I told her it seemed as if I would starve to death.

"Why," said she, "do they not give you enough to eat?"

"Oh, yes, but we have no spiritual food."

Then she said, "Would you like to see pa? I will tell him to come."

That evening a lady, Miss Ellis, came in. She took out her Bible, read and knelt in prayer. On Monday Mrs. Boden came to me, as I was the only one confined to the bed, and said, "You think we have not much regard for the Sabbath or God here, I suppose."

I told her how I had felt, and hoped by another Sabbath some Christian friends would visit us; and that I missed family prayer so much, and wished we could have this blessing; and that if she would pray I would read. But she said, "No, you must pray and I will read, for you are a Methodist and I am a Presbyterian."

So we determined to put it to vote with the ladies and have their decision. We found we had Baptists, Presbyterians and others, and I was a Methodist. So we called them all to my bed, and laid the matter before them, and they all said "Yes," and some lamented with tears that they had been so ashamed of Jesus, and had not honored Him by taking up their cross.

The next thing was to speak with the matron and managers. Dear Mrs. Doremus said she was so glad, and they were very sorry that in their anxiety for other things they had overlooked provision for the soul.

With much trembling we commenced daily worship, and on the Sabbath Mr. Stephenson, with his wife and daughter, were with us to sing and pray. Truly the Lord of Hosts was with us, and we felt that the God of Jacob was our refuge. Praise the Lord! He is the same, unchangeable, yesterday, today and forever. [Hebrews 13:8.]

Brother Stephenson and part of his family came every Sabbath while I was there. No weather deterred them or friends who came with them. Things went on pretty smoothly, and souls were stirred up and blessed through the prayers of the brethren. But Satan does not like to see his kingdom in danger. He aroused one who had the power to put a stop to our services, who told me that the doctor said I must quit praying.

I said, "I cannot."

Then she said the doctor said it was an injury for me to rise so early and to kneel. I usually rose about seven, and would sit up for breakfast and family worship. I said, "Very well, I will stay in bed till after breakfast, and then we can have prayers after the chambermaids are through and the doctor has been his rounds."

She was quite displeased, and spoke harshly. I answered, "I thought you loved me more than anyone in the hospital."

She said, "Well, I do."

Then I said, "Will you take from me the greatest comfort I have?"

At this she had nothing to say, but that I could pray as much as I liked and kill myself. I said that we would not only continue them in the morning, but we meant to commence in the evening, as it had been a great blessing to all of us. But if the managers disapproved, that would alter the case, and I was willing to sit in my chair and not kneel if the doctor did not allow me to do so.

We rejoiced when we were alone, as some of the patients were afraid I would yield the point, and yet they dared not say a word.

The next day, when the Doctor came to me, I asked him if it would hurt me to sing and pray. He said, "No, if it is done in moderation; but why do you ask me?"

"Well, Mrs. H. thought it did, and that we had better give up morning worship."

"Oh," said he, "don't give that up. I often come in at the back door and listen. It does me good, but I would rather you would not kneel."

Then there an attempt to hinder our Sabbath evening meetings, and I spoke to Mrs. Doremus and Mrs. Mason, and they stood by me and said they would not permit any interference with our worship. Mrs. Doremus came several evenings to be with us, and went through the house inviting others to come and join us, as they had been forbidden by Mrs. H.

I suffered much from this source, but the winter rolled away, and in the spring I was not able to walk out at all. I asked Dr. Sims if he thought I would ever be any better, and what his opinion was of my case. "I can bear to know it."

"Can you?"

"Oh, yes, tell me just what you think."

"Well, you will never be any better."

"Will I not be able to sit up a little at a time and sew awhile?"

"No, you will not."

For a moment I looked up to my Father, and then victory came. I had to exclaim, "Thanks be unto God, who giveth us the victory, through our Lord Jesus Christ." [1 Corinthians 15:57.]

The Doctor turned and wept, but my poor heart was kept in peace.

In the evening our kind friends came to sing and pray with us, and I told them what the Doctor had said. Brother Stephenson said, "Sister Cooke, if you have anything you would like me to attend to, with regard to your children or yourself, let me know, and it shall be done."

I could only thank him and say, "Another token of my Father's love. 'Leave thy fatherless children, I will preserve them alive, and let thy widows trust in Me.'" [Jeremiah 49:11.] Oh, how His promises have been verified!

A Few Memories of Former Labors

In 1854 I was sent for to see a lady who was ill and wanted some fine sewing done for her little girls. It was Mrs. Tieman, a sister of John Stephenson. The word was that

Mrs. T. was much pleased with my work. I did not see her, but her sister. The next day I was sent for by her maid.

I went trembling, for I said, "She is not pleased with the work, and if not, what shall I do?" To rip that fine work I could not, without spoiling the goods.

One of her sisters met me at the door. "Mrs. Cooke, Mrs. T. wants you in her room."

She was very ill. She requested her sister to leave the room, then she said, "Mrs. Cooke, do you think I am going to die?"

I said, "I do not know, dear. You are very feeble."

"Well," she said, "I don't want to die. The doctors say I must, and I *cannot* die. What, leave my husband and six little children! No, no, don't tell me that God is love, and have Him take me away from them."

I tried to calm and soothe her, but she was in great distress of mind. I asked to read to her, but she did not wish it. When leaving she said, "Come tomorrow;"

I went, no change. Still, "Come tomorrow." Thus I went for four days, and then she said if I wanted to, I could read a little. I did so, and committed her in prayer to her father's God, for he had gone to his reward, and her mother tremblingly told me if only Jane was ready, we could give her up.

I went home and I pleaded earnestly with the Lord, that He would arouse her, as she still would not believe she must die. But I got the answer, and felt prayer was heard. I told her mother and sisters that I knew she would leave a bright testimony when she should be called – that she had gone to be with Jesus.

On the next Sabbath, while we prayed together, she was seized with deep conviction of sin. I soothed her as much as I could. Her friends were distressed for her, one sister coming to my house to talk with me about her. I told them I had the answer and I knew she would be saved. I asked her to see Rev. Dr. Floy or Mrs. Lankford.

She said, "No, I only want you."

I continued my visits all the week, and on the following Sabbath she found peace to her hungry soul. Her joy was very great. She sat up in bed rejoicing in the God of her salvation. Her husband came in and tried to quiet her. But she turned to him, saying, "Would you have me hide my joy and praise? Let the doctors tell me now that I must die, and I shall say amen."

He stood there in amazement, and there also stood the aged mother, a mother in Israel, also her sister, weeping for joy. I asked, "Will you allow me to bring Mrs. Lankford up now, and Mr. Floy?"

"Yes, anybody."

She lived on for a few weeks. I went all I could, but, being feeble, could not be there as much as she wished, but left word, should it appear that she was about to pass away, to send for me. She had several of her dear children dedicated to God in baptism at her bedside.

On a Friday eve I was sent for and stayed nearly all night. Went early the next morning, and as I sat holding her hand her husband brought a cup of coffee to see if she would not take a drink with him. She looked up sweetly at him and said, "No, dear, nothing more till I drink the new wine in my Father's kingdom."

At noon she sweetly went to meet her risen Lord.

A Strange Case

In this year 1854, I was deceived by a poor family in a strange way. Having heard of a case of great distress in Thirty-First Street, I visited the house and found a sick man laid on the floor on straw, several children in rags, and an untidy mother. Moved by their distress I went to Mrs. A. G.

Phelps and Mrs. James Stokes and secured flannels, clothing, a new bed; from others I obtained food and money.

Miss Mary Stephenson visited the family with me, and we made them comfortable. After some days the wife came to say her husband was dead, that she had no money to bury him. I told her to get what she could, and I would do the rest. She got $5 but needed $30. At the time I was very feeble, but felt that I must bury the poor man, so I went forth and got $20, and took it to the woman.

I found the corpse stretched out with a cloth over the face and the woman weeping and lamenting. I tried to comfort her, and left. Having reached the street I turned back to talk of some plans for the children, but on opening the door what was my surprise to find the man sitting up, and his wife standing beside him as they counted the money.

I was startled, and said, "You have deceived me."

The woman was not at all abashed, and replied, "Sure, then, it's dying he is; and isn't the priest after giving him holy unction; an' it's dead he'll be soon."

I said a few words on the wickedness of doing so and left, well knowing he could not live long. He lived about two weeks, then died, and I saw him really dead. Those who visit the very poor must be prepared for anything. Most of the money was gone. I got her a coffin from the city, as I could not beg any more money.

I have had frequent applications for money to bury the dead, but never give anything until I find out if the story is true. This is a plan often pursued by the lower classes, as they think ladies will not go to see, but their sympathies will be wrought upon. But I have only been deceived once in this way.

"Labor and Sorrow"

At one time an old black woman came to me and said, "Mrs.

Cooke, there is a poor woman in great distress on First Avenue, near Thirtieth Street. Will you go and see her?"

I went, and found the poor woman had buried her husband two months earlier, and now she had three children sick, one of whom lay dying. I went out and got her some food and raiment for them. Her rooms were wretched, stripped of every comfort − no bed, no stove, a few old chairs, a bit of straw in a corner and an old lounge completed her store of household goods. The children were almost naked.

I tried to point her to the Saviour. In two days the babe died. I went out and begged money to bury it. We laid it away. In a week the other one died. I repeated my work, begged the money from friends and buried it. Then the third took sick. I sat with it night and day a large part of the time amid great dirt and filth, but the poor mother was so crushed she could do nothing. In a few days this one died also.

I did not know where to go for funds to bury this one, so I got in a streetcar to go down town to some of the business places of gentlemen I knew. While in the car it occurred to me to speak to an old gentleman who sat beside me. I asked him if he were a father. He said, Yes, he was a grandfather. I told him my story. Others listened, and the result was $5 from those good people.

Then I went to the office of the *Evening Post* to see Mr. Timothy A. Howe, to Liberty Street to see Mr. Pullman, also to Mr. James Stokes, and got what I needed to lay away the little one; and shoes were bought and other things for the mother and remaining girl of about ten years.

We had her removed to another and better apartment, got a bed and bedstead, a stove, some chairs and a table, some food in the pantry, coal in the cellar, and paid one month's rent. Work was also found for her; and thus set on her feet we left her feeling that she had begun a new life, trusting in God.

Another time I was called to a poor family where the poor man had fallen and broken his leg, and two children were sick with smallpox. Everybody avoided them. I went and did all I could. They were very poor. I went to Mrs. Stokes, who then lived in the Old Homestead, She gave me a little money, and said her cook should place some cooked food in a certain part of the garden where I could go each day and get it for them.

We buried one of the little sick ones, but it was very sweet to see the resignation of those poor stricken parents and their thankfulness that no more of their eight little ones were taken from them.

I always changed my clothing before and after I went, so as not to carry infection to my own dear little ones or others. By God's blessing, though often exposed to contagious diseases, I never contracted any of them or carried them to others.

I could give many similar cases, but these will suffice.

Madison Avenue Hospital
Wednesday, December 19th 1855

This day three months ago I came to this house, and have been partaker of unnumbered blessings. The Lord has been my support and strength. Three times I have been brought to the verge of the grave, yet the Lord hath spared me a little longer. Let me show by my life that I have given myself unreservedly to Thee – body, soul, and all my powers. Have been favored today with a visit from Sister Lankford and Dr. Bangs.

December 20th 1855
Mrs. Stephenson came to see me, and tells me that all my

furniture has been carefully stored away. How shall I thank my Heavenly Father for the kindness of Christian friends! Truly I find it a privation to give up my home, the place where together my little ones and I have spent so many happy hours, and may never meet in one home again on earth.

Yet, my soul, why shouldst thou for one moment dwell on these things, although thou knowest not why these things are so? Thy Heavenly Father hath told thee thou shalt know hereafter, and He hath also said, "I will never leave thee nor forsake thee." [Hebrews 13:5.] Enough that He hath given me a place in the hearts of so many Christian friends.

December 24th 1855
Have suffered much since last I wrote, but the everlasting arms are round about me. Was again able to lead in family worship. O my Father, grant that these precious seasons may be as bread cast upon the waters and found after many days. [Ecclesiastes 11:1.]

December 25th 1855
Considered the Saviour's birthday. A precious thought that He came down and took upon Him our nature, was tempted as we are, yet without sin, and even suffered in our stead. O my Father, help me to adorn the doctrine of Christ in all things. Feel very poorly, but the Lord is my Shepherd.

January 1st 1856
Full of pain, but it is the Lord. Let Him do as seemeth Him good. Another year has flown, and in a manner I am laid aside. Yet I am Thine; save me.

Wednesday was led to see it my duty to commence family worship in the evening, and have been much blessed in the attempt. There is some opposition, but I must go on, for the battle is the Lord's. It is not to the strong, but to those that endure to the end that shall be saved. Truly I feel that I am unworthy and incompetent to take the lead. I know my weakness on this point, but shall I, for fear of feeble man, "the Spirit's course in me restrain?" "He that honoreth Me I will honor." [1 Samuel 2:30.] Can I for one moment bear the thought of forsaking my Saviour?

"Ashamed of Jesus! That dear friend
On whom my hopes of Heaven depend?
No! When I blush be this my shame,
That I no more revere His name."

May 30th 1856
After a month of extreme weakness, early in May I was taken with inflammation in the stomach, and was watched over to die. Sister Lankford was sent for, and remained with me one or two days. Sister Mason also came, and they supposed I was dying. The doctor would come in through the night and look if I was still alive.

The sisters prayed with me, and at one of their visits I could not forbear although so weak. I had to say, "What have I to fear? He has promised to be with me to the end;" and then I repeated the lines,

"With Him I on Zion shall stand,
For Jesus hath spoken the word;
The breadth of Emmanuel's land
I survey by the light of my Lord."

My soul seemed just to bask in the presence of God, in the full light of His countenance. But not yet was I to sit down with Him in glory. This sickness was to bind Christian hearts to mine, to raise up friends to care for me and mine.

How wonderfully the Lord works to carry out His designs! Chain after chain is filled out, link by link made into one.

Here I was a confirmed invalid with no means, yet did my soul dwell in peace, for I felt the word of the Lord had gone forth. Heaven and earth should pass away, but not any of all things in His promises should fail in being fulfilled. The gold and the silver were His, and the cattle upon a thousand hills, and all hearts He held in His hands. [See Psalm 50:10.]

A letter to my eldest daughter
From The Woman's Hospital
Madison Avenue
June 9th 1856
My dear Hannah,
Through the mercy of an all-wise God, I am permitted once more to write to you, although I am very feeble, not able to be out of bed. I have had my bed made but once in nearly four weeks, but hope ere long to be able to sit up, and go and see you. Since I last wrote to you myself, I was given up to die.

The doctor and all others thought I could not live, but the Lord's ways are not as our ways, nor His thoughts as our thoughts. In His mercy He has spared me to you a little longer. Oh, my dear child, I want you to help me praise Him for His goodness and tender mercies toward us. Yet the doctor says it is not likely I will be long with you. I may rally through the summer, and I may not; but, my dear child, whichever way, all will be well.

I know you will feel it to be a very severe blow, but in every time of need, cast your care upon your Heavenly Father, and He who has proved Himself your Father so long, will not leave you. No, my dear, He will never forsake you. He is the God of thy fathers, and will not only be found of thee, but will bless and sustain thee. What should I have done in all my sickness and bereavement without the precious promises? They are indeed, "a sovereign balm for every wound, a cordial for every fear."

If I am spared, it must be a life of suffering, and no one but my Heavenly Father knoweth how much. Yet if it is his will I should live three score of years, and by so doing I could bring any glory to His name, I would gladly do it. Yet, the rest from pain and temptation to sin looks very sweet. I can truly say,

> "Give joy or grief, give ease or pain,
> Take life or friends away;
> But let me find them all again,
> In that eternal day."

My dear, I am glad to hear from you at all times. It does me good to hear of the welfare of my children, and you all were never dearer to me than now. It would have been a great comfort to have had you with me when I was so ill, but that could not be, and I am thankful you are with your uncle and aunt, and have so good a home.

I hope you strive to do all you can, and the best you can. In all things, my dear, ask your Heavenly Father to guide you, even in little things, just as you would ask an earthly parent, and He will do so.

My love to your dear little sister. Mary is well, and happy at school. She was to see me a week ago. She has a good home. Mrs. Smith sends love to you and other friends also. I hope you will never forget the kindness of friends to your poor mother and you all for these many years.

I wrote this letter yesterday, and received yours this morning, but I want to say to you, do not fret, dear child, for whatever you may have said or done before for want of thought, I most freely forgive, and love you most dearly. And if spared, I want you to be a companion and comfort to me, which I know you will strive to be, will you not?

Your affectionate and loving mother, Bella Cooke

Praise in the Fire

To Mrs. Evans
Madison Avenue
June 10th 1856
My Dear Precious Sister,
I received your very kind letter, and was so glad to hear from you; but, dear sister, I cannot bear to have you feel so badly about my being so feeble. Remember, dear, that He who sits as a refiner will not let the precious metal burn, but when His image is reflected He will say, "It is enough."

No matter how fiercely the fire may burn, He hath said, "*I will never leave thee nor forsake thee.*" [Hebrews 13:5.] He is ever saying unto me, "Fear thou not, for I am with thee; be not dismayed, for I am thy God. I will strengthen thee; yea, will uphold thee with the right hand of my righteousness." [Isaiah 41:10.] And surely this is enough, and how can we fear?

Dearest sister, if I should be called to rest a little before you, do not fear. There is indeed grace to help in every time of need. Oh yes, He is our God and Guide, even unto the end. Praise the Lord, we will trust Him where we cannot trace Him. I know my loss would be a great trial to you, but ere long we will meet never more to part.

Dear sister, the rest looks very sweet, but what must it be to be there! Let us ever stand on the watchtower, that whether He shall come at the early dawn or evening shade, all will be well. I am so tired. Believe me still,

Your affectionate sister, Bella Cooke

With many forebodings I had left my little home in the fall of last year for The Woman's Hospital, and now Dr. Sims orders me to the country as his last hope, that a change of air may do me good.

Never can I forget the great kindness received while here from the managers and patrons of the Hospital, as well as from my old friends who still called upon me. Among these friends, the wise and good Mrs. T. C. Doremus deserves special mention, both for her devotion to the institution and for her interest in all its inmates.

She is untiring in her efforts to promote our comfort, and her cheerful, "Good morning, ladies, what can I do for you today?" as morning after morning she visits us, is a cordial better than medicine, and can never be forgotten by any of us. In the early morning she visits Washington Market in order to secure provisions for the house, and from that hour till evening most of her time is devoted to our welfare.

Afflicted women will ever owe a large debt to Mrs. Doremus for the support she gave to our physician in establishing this hospital, for at the first he met with opposition and discouragement on all sides. But at last he made the acquaintance of this elect lady, and her great motherly heart at once enlisted her in his plans, while her social position and high character won new friends and brought success to the enterprise. Hundreds of poor suffering women who have been relieved or cured, bless God for such spirits as Mrs. Doremus and Doctor Marion Sims.

June 1856

The doctor said I must be taken to the country, as nothing was left for me but a change of air. And the next question was, "How could I be taken there?"

Brother Stephenson, with others, decided that a carriage

could be brought with a mattress, on which I was laid, and so carried to the cars. There everything was in readiness for all my wants and ease as much as possible.

Mrs. Lankford, Mrs. Mulholland, and Mr. De Lamater went with me to Meriden, where my sister Evans did all in her power to restore me to a measure of health. I stood the journey better than was expected, as the doctor had said he would not be surprised if I died before they got me there.

Ten days before I left the hospital, Mrs. Peck, one of the managers, was saying they were sorry I had to leave them.

I answered, "Had I known that I could never be better, I would not have stayed to be a burden."

She said, "You have not been a burden, dear Mrs. Cooke. We wished you here at the first meeting of the ladies after you came. The doctor told us he could do nothing for you. Your case was incurable, but we must keep you and not tell you that it was so, or you would not stay. But we were delighted to keep you and do all we could for you."

Here was kindness! Oh, what love. Nothing but loving kindness strews my path. I stayed with my sister Evans until August, then was taken to East Hartford to my sister Longdon, where I remained until the middle of September.

Chapter 9

Waiting and Serving

We sometimes wonder why our Lord doth place us
Within a sphere so narrow, so obscure,
That nothing we call work can find an entrance;
There's only room to suffer, to endure.
Well, God loves patience; souls that dwell in stillness,
Doing the little things or resting quite,
May just as perfectly fulfill their mission,
Be just as pleasing in the Father's sight.

July 3rd 1856
Have passed through a very trying ordeal today, but think I never felt the force of that promise as at this time, "My grace is sufficient for thee." [2 Corinthians 12:9.] Praise the Lord, it is sufficient; it can and does sustain. I will trust and not be afraid.

When about to retire, while suffering much pain, this was brought to my mind: "He giveth his beloved sleep." [Psalm 127:2.] I lay me down and slept, for the Lord sustained me. Yes, He gave me more sleep than I had had for some time in one night. Oh, how good, how kind, thus to condescend to one so unworthy. I would indeed say,

"Take my body, spirit, soul,
Only Thou possess me whole.
Simply to Thy cross I cling."

July 4th 1856
While left alone, had a most refreshing time from on high. The Lord God of Hosts is my refuge, whereunto I can run and take shelter. I was led to pondering on the longsuffering

of our God. The portion for today is, "Faint, yet pursuing." [Judges 8:4.]

Though so weak and feeble I need not fear, for He hath told me, and His word is firmer than the pillars of heaven, that "He will not break the bruised reed, nor quench the smoking flax." [Matthew 12:20.] No, He will never forsake them that trust in Him. I will not forget His benefits, but praise His holy name.

July 9th 1856

Have been very much blessed while reading in Revelation, "To him that is faithful shall be given a crown of life." [2:10.] Oh, that I may be of that number! Although it is with trembling, I cannot refuse to say, "He hath given me the bread and the white stone with a new name written thereon. For hath He not said I have called thee by a new name; thou art Mine." [Revelation 2:17.] Glory be to His Holy Name.

> "Jesus ever lives above,
> For me to intercede;
> His all redeeming love,
> His precious blood to plead."

Keep me close to Thy bleeding side, however various maybe the current of my life, that my "loins may be continually girt about," to be ready when Thou shalt call me. [Ephesians 6:14.]

Thursday, July 15th 1856

Oh, this weakness, this extreme prostration of body. Strengthen me, my Father, I beseech Thee, that I may endure Thy righteous will; not only patiently, but rejoicing in Thy salvation; that I may in all things, and at all times, give thanks, for truly Thy loving kindness is better than life.

"Courage, my soul, on God rely,
Deliverance soon will come,
A thousand ways has Providence
To bring believers home."

So I will not faint, but praise God.

To Mrs. H. V. Butler
Hanover, W. M.
August 1st 1856
Dear Mrs. Butler,
I cannot tell you how thankful I was to have a letter from you. I would have written before, but I was not able. Since you saw me I have been very feeble, sometimes scarcely able to lift my hand to my head, and am now suffering a great deal. I am glad you and the dear little ones are quite well, and have a comfortable home. It must be pleasant, so near the beautiful ocean.

I would like to sit with you on the rocks and talk over the dealings of our Father in His loving kindness and longsuffering to me, so weak and so unworthy a child. Will you not, dear friend, help me to praise Him? Truly "not more than others I deserve, yet God hath given me more."

I am very glad to hear you have such pleasant company. How sweet to converse with the children of God, with those who are traveling to the same city.

"And if our fellowship below,
In Jesus be so sweet,
What heights of rapture shall we know,
When round His throne we meet."

Yes, meet in those mansions which our Saviour hath gone to prepare for those that endure to the end, and to the finally faithful. Pray for your unworthy friend, that I may endure patiently all my Father's righteous will.

I have been very much blessed in reading the Revelation, especially part of the twenty-first chapter, where we are told that, "God shall wipe away all tears from our eyes." No more sorrow, crying, pain, or death. Oh, is it not worthwhile to suffer a few trials and privations, to be let into all this! I can truly say, no cross, no suffering I decline.

"Lo, I am with you," is my constant comfort. I am glad to hear you will be in New York in September, and hope, if spared, to meet you again. I do not know where my lot may be cast, but the Scriptures assure me, "The Lord will provide." [Philippians 4:19.]

Although my earthly path may appear mysterious, or even dark to some, I know that my Heavenly Father knows I have need of these earthly comforts, and He doeth all things well.

It is very pleasant here to see the green and beautiful grass, all so fresh and cheering. Yet I have not been able to walk out since I came, but if able, will go to East Hartford the thirteenth of this month, and be in New York early in September.

I often think of you, dear Mrs. B., and your kindness to me, a stranger, in a strange land. I pray our Father to bless you and yours, and give you all an abundant entrance into the Heavenly kingdom. Please excuse this, as I have to write as I lie on my back, and my brain is much confused.

With much love, believe me,

Your true, though unworthy friend,

B. Cooke

In the middle of September [1856] I was brought to this house [492 Second Avenue] by kind friends, Miss Lispenard and Mrs. Stephenson, who prepared all and placed my furniture therein. Oh, how thankful I was, once more to get into a little spot of my own, with one of my dear children with me. But how were rent and fuel to be met, besides food and clothes?

Faith was brought into exercise, and triumphed. Praise the Lord! None ever trusted in Him and was put to shame. Dear Mrs. Doremus and Mrs. Butler came, and were very kind. Mrs. Lankford was about to send Mary to Charlotteville to school, but her mother, Mrs. Worrall, said she thought I would rather have Mary at home.

She had been with her a year, and when Mrs. L. spoke to me about it, I replied that I would much rather have her at home, and let her go to the public school. I longed to have my children with me, and I thought the education at one of these schools more thorough. So she came home, and I began my housekeeping, by faith, in the Second Avenue.

Bella Cooke's room in 492 Second Avenue.
Original retouched photo

In October, I was taken to my bed. A friend sent for Dr. Barker, who said nothing more could be done for me. Then my ever-kind friend Dr. M. W. Palmer, came again to see me, and did, and does still, all in his power for my improvement.

"Thus far the Lord hath led me on,
Thus far His power prolongs my days,
And every evening shall make known,
Some fresh memorial of His grace."

492 Second Avenue

Divine Support

January 13th 1857

Dear Sister Mason and Miss Jacques were to see me. O my Father, why this boundless love to me, the least of Thy children? And so many other dear friends were with me. "Bless the Lord, my soul, and all that is within me bless His holy name." [Psalm 103:1.]

January 23rd 1857

Since I last wrote I have been as it were on the borders of the New Jerusalem, but my Father sent me back into the vineyard for a time, and may He enable me to let patience have her perfect work, that I may labor faithfully for Him — for in no position can a Christian be placed but he has a work to do. Every day Thou art showing me Thy goodness in raising up friends to care for this poor body. For all this I thank Thee, O my Father.

Sabbath, January 25th 1857

Feeling somewhat easier today, I praise the Lord for His goodness. The room appeared filled with the power of God while some brethren were with me in prayer and praise. He heard and answered. I'll praise Him while He lends me breath.

January 28th 1857

Was sorely tried and tempted today, but shall I therefore let Him go — basely to the tempter yield? No! No! In the strength of Jesus I will never give up my shield.

Sisters Lankford and Wendell were here, and we feasted at the throne of grace. My old and tried friend Mrs. Dickinson was with me, also Mrs. Worrall, who told me, anything I wanted, to let her know and she would get it for me.

January 30th 1857
Very feeble, but the Lord is very near, and I feel that glorious hope of perfect love. It bears me up on eagle's wings. Glory! Glory! How thin the veil between the golden city and me!

When He hath tried me I shall come forth as gold. He will come and say, "Child, come home," then I will clap my glad wings and soar away, thus be forever with the Lord.

February 11th 1857
The Lord was very near while Sisters Shipman, Worrall and Lankford were with me. They think my race is almost run. Well, the Lord is a stronghold, "beneath and round about me are the everlasting arms." [Deuteronomy 33:27.]

Such love, such care calls for songs of loudest praise. Very, very feeble. Hard work to guide my pen, but I must praise Him, for He doeth all things well.

While the sisters were at prayer, such a blessing came down that it seemed as if the windows of heaven were opened. Enlarge our faith's capacity and our souls forever fill.

February 14th 1857
Mrs. Butler was here to see if I had coal to keep me warm. Thou, precious Saviour, who had not where to lay Thy head, carest for me. Not a hair of my head shall fall to the ground without Thy notice.

While we are asking, Thou dost answer. In His own good time deliverance comes. "Leave thy fatherless children, I will preserve them alive." [Jeremiah 49:11.]

February 25th 1857
Am very feeble. Art Thou about to unloose the fluttering spirit, that it may rest in the mansions of glory? Thy will be done. All is well. Thou canst take care of my dear girls and

watch over them with a Father's care and, I doubt not, will bring them in Thine own good time to meet those gone before.

Father, bless and reward all those dear sisters for their labor of love to me. Oh, how many cups of cold water have they given to me, and Thou hast said, "Not one shall go unrewarded," [Matthew 25:40], and Thy word is true. Glory! Glory! Children of a king; heirs of God; joint heirs with Jesus Christ. [Romans 8:17.] We will praise Him.

March 2nd 1857
Have been feeling the heat of the furnace keenly the past few days, but the Refiner sat by and would not let the precious metal burn. No! No! But when His image is perfectly reflected, He will say, "It is enough; come up higher;" then to be in His presence and be like Him. Oh rapturous thought! Well might Thy saint exclaim, "Glory, glory dwelleth in Emmanuel's land."

March 11th 1857
Sister Lankford was here with a Brother Hall from Canada, and we were much blessed while talking of Jesus, for He was in our midst, and we were ready to say, "Let us build tabernacles." [Matthew 17:4.]

March 18th 1857
Brother Hall called again. He came to hear what great things the Lord had done for me. Be Thou to me a mouth and wisdom, that I may with the Spirit tell of Thy goodness, not only in word but in deed, that I may in all things adorn the doctrine of Christ my Saviour, that others may see that I have been with Jesus, and that I live and dwell in Him. To think He calls a worm His friend!

March 22nd 1857
Have felt today very much oppressed, but why I know not. Surely by and by He that will come shall come and will not tarry. Mould and fashion me as Thou wilt, only as I have borne the image of the earthly so I may bear the image of the heavenly. Make me all like Thee.

April 1st 1857
Have this day seen Brother Hull for the last time on earth, as he leaves for home. But I trust to meet him with all the redeemed in our Father's house, and worship around the throne without alloy. His blood avails for me.

April 17th 1857
My sister Evans, with my darling Annie, came to see me today to stay awhile. Truly the Lord is good, and grants us the desires of our hearts. Much as I would like to have my dear child with me at home, yet I know she is well cared for. Well might the Psalmist cry out, "Oh, that men would praise the Lord for His wonderful works to the children of men." [Psalm 107:31.]

April 20th 1857
Yesterday had more kind friends to see me and talk over the loving kindness of the Lord. Truly it is no vain thing to wait upon Him. What a mercy it is that we need not go to the temple or to Jerusalem to worship Him, but that He is in our hearts, if we only believe.

> "Lord, I believe Thy every word,
>   Thy every promise true;
> And, lo! I wait on Thee, my Lord
>   Till I my strength renew."

April 26th 1857
Have decided to remove on the 1st of May, if the Lord wills it. Cannot see *why*, only it seems I must. My Father knows best. He has some wise end in it, no doubt, for He doeth all things well. I have not sought it, and He says He will direct my steps. It has been much prayed over. I must believe He does appoint the way.

May 1st 1857
Brother Stephenson kindly sent the men to remove me and my goods to my new home, corner of Twenty-Eighth Street; but I was not able to be taken any farther than downstairs to Mrs. Marshall's room, where she has kindly invited me to stay until I have recovered from the fatigue.

Sabbath, May 3rd 1857
Had a visit from my leader and other brethren, and though very feeble in body I feel the force of those words, "When I am weak then I am strong." [2 Corinthians 12:10.]

Yes, praise the Lord, He does give strength to the weary sufferer. He is ever saying, "Fear not; I, the Lord thy God, will hold thy right hand." [Isaiah 41:13.] Oh, what love! It is immense and free, to think it ever found out me.

While they were singing,

"I shall behold His face,
I shall His power adore;
And tell the wonders of His grace
For ever, evermore,"

it seemed as if I were translated to His right hand. But again the Master bade me wait. Give me patience to suffer all Thy righteous will. I want a trumpet voice to tell of His goodness. Praise the Lord!

"If such a worm as I can spread
The common Saviour's name;
Let Him who raised Thee from the dead
Quicken my mortal frame."

Chapter 10

Answered Prayer; Happy Deaths

The Lord shall preserve thy going out and thy coming in from this time forth, and even for evermore (Psalm 121:8).

> "Thou, Lord, hast blest my going out,
> Oh, bless my coming in;
> Compass my weakness round about,
> And keep me safe from sin."

May 10th 1857
On the 4th I was brought here in a chair. It was a painful ordeal, and I suffered so that it seemed as if it would prove too much for the frail body, but I am in His hands. I earnestly pray that He will bless my coming in, and open my way.

My dear girls had everything nicely fixed, and Mrs. Stephenson sent a very nice and good carpet, as she thought mine was too much worn to put down again. Oh, how kind that dear family is and has been, and may the Lord reward them.

June 4th 1857
Surely goodness and mercy hath followed me all my days.

> "None is like Jeshurun's God,
> So great, so strong, so high;
> Lo! He spreads His wings around,
> He rides upon the sky.

> "Israel is His first-born Son,
> God, the Almighty God, is thine;
> See Him to thy help come down,
> The Excellence Divine."

June 28th 1857

Have just been on the verge of the Celestial City, yet all is well. Praise the Lord! I am hastening on to where sickness and sorrow, pain and death, are felt no more.

Many of my dear friends with whom I have taken sweet counsel, and who have aided me, are leaving for the country, among whom are Mrs. Camman and daughter. Mrs. Butler has been to say goodbye. Go with them each, my Father, and bless them.

Sister Mason has been here. She is a precious spirit. What a comfort she has been to me! Have had a feast of fat things. Truly the Lord was with us while partaking of the emblems of His dying love. Oh, for the time when we shall drink of the new wine of the kingdom.

My dear pastor, Rev. T. G. Osborne, Mrs. Lankford, Mrs. Butler, and Mrs. S. G. Smith – God, bless them all. Had a visit from my old pastor, Rev. G. Taylor and wife. Goodness and mercy crown my life.

> "From human eye 'tis better to conceal
> Much that I suffer, much I hourly feel;
> But, oh, the thought doth tranquilize and heal,
> All, all is known to Thee."

I am one of those of whom it is said, "Ye shall not need to fight in this battle; set yourselves, stand ye still, and see the salvation of the Lord with you." [2 Chronicles 20:17.]

> "They also serve who only stand and wait."

Oh, what a fullness in the oneness with Christ! What a joy, a rest and peace. And then, how much is laid up for them that fear Thee! There is laid up for *me* a crown of righteousness, reserved in Heaven for us – for me – to be enjoyed fully only in His presence where there is fullness of joy and pleasure for evermore.

The spiced wine shall be given, and the juice of the pomegranate, all pleasant fruits, and drinks from the river of His pleasures. Oh, what love is here for me! He gave Himself for me. He is my Beloved, and I am His, bought with His most precious blood, kept by His power, and fed by His hand. [From Song of Solomon.]

> "Oh, for this love, let rocks and hills
> Their lasting silence break."

Most of my friends are in the country. Faith is being tried, but my God has promised, "Your bread shall be given, and your water sure." [Isaiah 33:16.]

Jehovah Jireh, the same yesterday, today and forever. He will provide. In Him is my trust. Praise the Lord! All is "Yea, and Amen" in Christ Jesus to them that believe. [2 Corinthians 1:20.]

> "Who fed thee last, will feed thee still;
> Be calm and sink into His will."

Thou art my Husband, Brother, all in all, my present help in time of need, therefore will we not fear. [Psalm 46:1.] "One thing have I desired of the Lord, that will I seek after, that I may dwell in the house of the Lord forever." [Psalm 27:4.]

Last Sabbath I asked Brothers Stephenson, Pullman and Armstrong to join me each day in prayer for the convicting power of the Holy Ghost upon the heart of my neighbor, Mr. Enever, who is quite ill with consumption, but says he has no need of a change, and will not die at this time.

His wife is not willing that anyone should speak to him of his state, for he has wronged no one, and is as good as many who go to church. But I cannot rest. I feel the man will die, and he will be lost unless he is roused to see his fallen state and flee to Christ as his Saviour. Lord, give us strong, mighty faith that laughs at impossibilities, and cries, "It shall be done."

Clothe these, Thy servants, with great faith, that they may not be deterred by the crowd, but if need be, take him up and let him down through the tiles, and so bring him to Jesus, that he may be healed of his malady. "Seeing their faith, He healed him." [Luke 5:20.]

To Mrs. H. V. Butler
New York
July 21st 1857
My Dear Mrs. Butler,
When your very kind letter came to hand I was so overjoyed that my full heart cried out, "Oh, my Father, why is it that Thou art so mindful over me?" It was such a comfort, dear Mrs. Butler, to hear from you, for I have missed your visits so much; but I try to put this among "the all things."

And what a blessing to know and feel that our blessed Lord Jesus never leaves us, but in the dark and silent night, when tossed about with pain and sore distress of body, then He is saying, "Fear not, be not dismayed, I, the Lord, will help thee; yea, will uphold thee with the right hand of My righteousness." [Isaiah 41:10.] And when we know that the "Great I Am" hath said this, and that not one jot or tittle of His word shall fall to the ground till all be fulfilled, may we not say, "Praise the Lord?" [Matthew 5:18.]

We will trust and not be afraid. Oh, Glory! Glory! It seems, dear friend, as if the veil between us and the Father's face is very thin, and must soon be rent in twain to let this happy spirit quit this house of clay and grasp the Saviour in the skies. I find it as you say, "Any place with Jesus is very sweet," but it takes more to say with the poet,

> "I'll gladly linger on my three score years,
> Till my Deliverer comes,"

than to say, "Come, Lord Jesus, come quickly." Still, if by enduring even four score years, I could, by the grace of God, encourage one poor soul, or in any way glorify my Father, I would gladly stay.

I was glad to hear the children are well, and if it please our Father to strengthen your poor, feeble body, I would be very happy; but this we must ask in submission to His will.

I was sorry to hear the preaching was such as you could not enjoy. I know you cannot feel as easy as in your own Christian circle, and under the instructions of your own pastor; but does it not draw you nearer to the side of our precious Saviour?

When you were telling me about the way you were situated, it took me, in spirit, to the marriage supper of the Lamb, and to the City of our God, the New Jerusalem.

I know you wish to hear about this poor body. It has had much to contend with since I saw you, and is suffering a good deal now, but I could not let Mary write to you as long as I can hold a pen; so excuse all errors.

The weather has been very hot, indeed; but how much better off I am than many of the poor in Bellevue Hospital. In comparing myself with them, well may I say, "What am I, or my father's house, that Thou art so mindful of me?" [|See Psalm 8:4.]

I opened the note you left for me on the first of the month, and found two dollars. Oh, my dear friend, how can I thank you for unceasing love and Christian kindness? I never can, but God bless and reward you, and may all your dear family be gathered on high. There we will never be tired or sick. Praying that you may be filled with all the fullness of God,

Believe me to be,
Your affectionate sister in Christ,
Bella Cooke

August 19th 1857

The anniversary of the transplanting of my dear husband and child. Looking back over these years of widowhood I have to say the promises have been more than fulfilled. The Lord, the Lord mighty in battle, has stood by me all the way through. He has brought me by a way that I knew not. "He has led me through green pastures; He anoints my head with oil, and my cup runneth over." [Psalm 23.]

I praise Him that we see some little gleaming of light with regard to Mr. Enever. The fallow ground is breaking up. I have prevailed on them to see Sister Lankford and my pastor, and may the Lord soften his heart.

This morning my dear pastor, Brother Osborne, came in and asked "how faith stood?" Leaning his head on his hand, he said, "Oh, sister Cooke, pray, if faith is strong, pray. The doctors say my poor wife cannot live, and she does not find her evidence as clear as she would like."

I sent down for Sister Lankford to come up and see her and cheer her heart. It is no small trial to leave her little children and husband. Lord, grant that this painful dispensation may be blessed to him, and make him more than ever alive in Thy cause, and that the Church may be aroused to a closer walk with God — that holiness to the

Lord may be written on all their hearts, and may our aim be one, to bring sinners to Christ.

August 21st 1857

Sent for a few sisters to come in and join me in prayer for that dear sufferer, on the promise that where two or three unite as touching the kingdom, it shall be done. [Matthew 18:20.]

The Lord was very near, the little room was filled with His presence; the answer is given, it shall be done. A glorious testimony shall be left. Satan in his last attempt shall be foiled. The struggle is great, but the victory is greater. Oh, Thou glorious conqueror, the honor, the glory is Thine, and soon she will be with Thee in Thy kingdom.

Sabbath, August 23rd 1857

Dear Sister Osborne still lingers on the shores of time. If it be possible, ease her sufferings. Grant her an easy passage unto eternal life. Praise the Lord, her sky is clear; nothing intervenes between her and her Saviour. She leaves husband and children all with the Lord.

Dear old Sister Stephenson is also on the verge of eternity. Go with her, our Father, and light up the valley. Let Thy staff support her. Whisper in her ear, "It is I; be not afraid." [John 6:20.]

Forbid that a cloud should for a moment arise to hide her Lord from her eyes. She has long been Thy servant, and now she leans upon the arm of her Beloved. I will praise Him. "Where shall my wondering soul begin!"

Lord, help me to put away all fear of man, and be ever willing to sow beside all waters. The above hymn is the full outburst of my heart. Jesus, that precious name, it charms away our fears, and makes our sorrows cease.

August 25th 1857
This morning our dear Sister Osborne left us, to be forever with her Saviour, God, to see Him as He is. Oh, may this be the means of doing us all good, that we may as a Church rest not in present attainments.

August 28th 1857
Today Sister Stephenson entered her rest, as a shock of corn fully ripe. And while the tears will flow as one after another leaves us, we are compelled with Wesley to say,

> "Again we lift our voice,
> And shout our solemn joys;
> Cause of highest raptures this
> Raptures that shall never fail;
> See a soul escaped to bliss,
> Keep the Christian Festival."

May her mantle of love fall on us, and may we stand ready girt, with oil in our vessels.

September 9th 1857
Sister Reid was here and told me much about her dear mother, Mrs. Stephenson. She feels her loss so deeply, but I trust this holy life and happy death will be blest to all the family.

She told me she would send me the chair she had bought for her mother, and she hoped I might be able to be lifted up and laid in it, that I might be rested from the bed.

She also said that her dear mother, with almost her last breath, said, "Children, never forget Sister Cooke." Thus I am left as a legacy to that dear family. "Not more than others I deserve, yet God hath given me more."

September 20th 1857

My poor sick neighbor, Mr. Enever, has found the "pearl of great price." Praise the Lord! Prayer is heard, "the malady is removed," as the poor dumb boy said to Charlotte Elizabeth when trying to make her understand that he had found the pearl. The red hand has passed over his heart and made it all clean.

Yes, washed in the blood of the Lamb. Mr. Enever is rejoicing in God his Saviour, waiting till He shall call him to be with Him. Oh, what love. Whosoever will may come; "He that cometh, I will in no wise cast out." [John 6:37.]

Poor man, he would get out of bed and come to my room, leaning on two canes, and when he sat down he gasped out, "I have found it, I have found it. You knew what I needed. Jesus has pardoned my sins. I did not want to be bothered, but you gave me no peace, and I thank you." And he said much more till he was exhausted. Oh, let us be in earnest, bring our sin-sick friends and present them to Jesus.

Monday, October 19th 1857

Since I last wrote, have been very sick with spasms. No one thought I could possibly recover. Dear friends watched with me all night, and again the Lord has spared me and lengthened out this "brittle thread." I found the borderlands near, calm and still, and the Saviour very present.

> "And live I yet by power divine?
> And have I still my course to run?
> Again brought back in its decline,
> The shadows of my setting sun.

> "Wondering I ask, is this the breast,
> Struggling so late and torn with pain;

> The eyes that upward looked for rest,
> And dropped their weary lids again?"

But I rested in the embrace of my beloved Lord.

Had a visit from Rev. J. W. Horne. He has just arrived from Africa where he has been a missionary since 1852. I had a blessed time listening to the Lord's dealings with him in that field of labor. He is very feeble in health. Our cups seemed to run over while comparing the Lord's ways with us. I have daily to say, "Bless the Lord, O my soul, and all that is within me, bless His holy name!" [Psalm 103:1]

November 10th 1857

Mr. Enever has gone to his rest. He died very happy in his first love. A few days before, Brother Osborne gave him the Lord's Supper. Brothers Pullman and Armstrong were present. They told me the sick man's face shone with bliss; the presence of the glory of the Lord filled his soul. Brother Osborne said he did not remember seeing a soul so happy. And thus he continued till his purified spirit took its flight.

I was brought back to this little room on the 1st. It seems to me more like home. I did not see why I was taken from it, but I yielded to the entreaties of Mrs. Enever, and went to the same house and floor with her. Her dear husband has gone to his heavenly home, and she has removed to his people, and I am come home too. "God moves in a mysterious way."

The brethren say they can plainly see why it was, for that poor man was to be brought under the influence of prayer; and he having come to the feet of Jesus and gone to his rest, I was permitted to return to my much-loved little room. If aught has been done through my instrumentality, to God be all the glory.

Chapter 11

New Friends

Blessed is he that considereth the poor. The Lord will preserve him and keep him alive; and he shall be blessed upon the earth (Psalm 41:1-2).

I will speak of the glorious honor of Thy majesty, and of Thy wondrous works (Psalm 145:5).

November 21st 1857

Today have had a call from a new physician, Dr. Sabine. I was very nervous when he introduced himself, and said I thanked him for coming, but I did not wish his services. He said, "Why do you not? You are very feeble."

I replied, "In the first place, I have no money to pay a physician, and I made a vow when my husband died never to go in debt; if I had not money to pay for what I wanted, to go without. In the second place, I had been under so many doctors, and all had said nothing more could be done for me." Besides, it would not be right for me to take his time and attention.

He looked at me and said, "Are you not one of the Lord's children?"

I replied that I felt I could say, "Yes."

Then said he, "So am I; and if He has given me a little more money or knowledge than you, ought you not to be willing to allow me, as His steward, to share it with you?"

I had nothing to say. He said he would be in on Tuesday, and for me to be kept very quiet. Dr. Sabine is a good pious man, but I have no idea anyone but the Great Physician can do anything for me. I am in Thy hand, O my Father. Do with me as Thou wilt: life or death, sickness or health. All is well. Glory! Glory! Help me to show forth Thy praise.

November 24th 1857

Dr. Sabine was here today and talked with me about my circumstances; asked what I had to support me. I told him my dear Hannah could earn about one dollar a week, besides doing the work and taking care of me, and that for the remainder I was supplied as my Father saw best. He asked me if I had got in my winter's coal.

I replied I had some coal. He said that did not answer his question, "Had I my winter's coal laid in?"

A person, Mrs. Marshall, sitting in the room, said, "Well, indeed, I don't think she has much in the cellar at all."

He talked with me some time about my pains and aches, and then said he thought he could help me a little. He could not tell, but there was a new preparation of iron he would like me to try. He wrote the prescription and said I must try and have the best of food, and then left me.

I looked into the paper, and to my great surprise found not only the prescription for medicine to be charged to his account, but also an order for a ton of coal to Messrs. Popham, and to he charged to him. I lay and looked at them. Could I be in my right mind? I was amazed at this kindness from a stranger.

November 26th 1857

Dr. Palmer was here. He is willing for me to try Dr. Sabine, but thinks I should be careful about using strong medicine. How strange, not till Dr. Sabine left me the other day, did I remember that about three weeks ago I dreamed of the doctor coming, and it has turned out just as I dreamed. The very same words were spoken in our conversation that I had heard in my dream. I am very poorly.

December 4th 1857
Dr. Sabine has been here, but declined doing anything. Says I am too weak, and nothing can be done. Directed me to the Great Physician for strength and comfort.

December 24th 1857
Dr. Sabine sent me a turkey and other things. Lord, bless and reward him an hundredfold. He called and sympathized with me. What a man of God he is! He thinks it would be well to put in an issue to relieve the cough and spasms. I said he might do anything he thought best, as I knew he only wanted to do me good.

December 28th 1857
The doctor was here and used the hot iron, and hopes it may relieve me of some of the pain, but is not certain. I must be kept quiet and look to my Father in heaven for strength to suffer and bear His will.

December 29th 1857
Dr. Sabine was here, and desires to bring Dr. Camman to see me. I leave it all with him to do as is best. In all my suffering my prospect is clear and bright. Not one stroke too much; it is from a Father's hand, so I say,

"Trusting as God will,
And in His hottest fire hold still."

December 30th 1857
Dr. Sabine was here with Dr. O., and he is of the same opinion as Dr. S. They may be able to give me a little relief, but no cure. Not one stroke too much, a Father's hand holds the rod. As God will.

December 31st 1857

Thus far the Lord hath led me on to the last day of another year, and I still live. At present He says to me, "Return to thy house and tell what great things the Lord hath done for thee." [Luke 8:39.]

My dear Hannah is dreadfully disappointed. Dear child, her hopes were raised in that the doctor could do something for me, and now she is all cast down – dear, faithful child.

> "When passing thro' the watery deep,
> I ask in faith His promised aid;
> The waves an awful distance keep
> And shrink from my devoted head;
> Fearless their violence I dare,
> They cannot harm, for God is there.
>
> "To Him my eye of faith I turn,
> And through the fire pursue my way;
> The fire forgets its power to burn,
> The lambent flames around me play;
> I own His power, accept the sign,
> And shout to prove the Saviour mine."

To Rev. T. G. Osborne

March 1858

My Dear Pastor,

You will remember that previous to our last love-feast you desired me to give a few items of my experience. I thought much of it, but was too sick even to dictate. But knowing that the love-feast was again appointed, and I being more comfortable, feel it my duty as well as privilege in the fear of the Lord to tell before the great congregation some of His dealings toward me since I last stood up with His people, four years ago.

This body has suffered much, very much, but the mercies and blessings of my Father have far, very far, outstripped them. I can truly say the past four years have been the happiest of my life, for the Lord hath revealed Himself to me in a wonderful manner.

Yea, He hath enabled me to cry out, "Although the fig tree shall not blossom, neither shall there be fruit in the vine, yet I will rejoice in the Lord; I will joy in the God of my salvation." [Habakkuk 3:17.]

Yes, when I look at the way He has led me, I am lost in wonder, love and praise, for "He calls a worm His friend. He calls Himself my God, and He will save me to the end through Jesus' blood."

Yes, for me the Saviour died. I praise Him that His blood is still efficacious, that it sprinkles the throne of grace. I can confidently look up and say, "Abba, Father." And although so unworthy, He is ever saying, "Fear not, I am with thee; I will strengthen thee; yea, I will uphold thee with the right hand of My righteousness." [Isaiah 41:10.]

Praise Him, because my feet are fixed upon the rock, Christ Jesus. Although the winds may blow and the rains descend and beat against the feeble bark, they cannot harm me, for my Father is at the helm.

Sometimes it seems as if I were just in sight of port and about to enter the gate of the Celestial City, when again I am sent back into the world. Still I hear a voice saying, "I will be with thee, I will never leave nor forsake thee, but, lo, I am with you always." [Matthew 28:20.]

Yes, I will praise my Maker while He lends me breath. I know that He to whom I belong is able to keep that which I have committed to Him, [2 Timothy 1:12] and by grace assisting me, I am more determined than ever to "rejoice evermore, pray without ceasing, and in everything give thanks." [1 Thessalonians 5:16-18.]

I know this is His will concerning me. My soul thirsts and pants for more of the mind of Christ, that His image may be so engraven upon my heart that it may shine forth in all my words and actions. There is much I would like to tell of the goodness of my Master. My heart often cries, "Oh, for a trumpet voice on all the world to call," but I know your time is short and I must be brief.

Bella Cooke

Chapter 12

Heavenly places

"When all Thy mercies, O my God,
My rising soul surveys,
Transported with the view I'm lost
In wonder, love, and praise.

"Through all eternity to Thee
A grateful song I'll raise;
But oh, eternity's too short
To utter all Thy praise."

January 1st 1859

The Lord is so good to me, unworthy and unprofitable as I am. Surely it is because His mercies fail not that I am still spared, cared for, and blessed with every temporal blessing. Glory, honor, and praise be to His holy name for His goodness and loving kindnesses.

Through the past year this poor body has been tossed about with disease, and I seemed to be at times near home; but again the Lord hath sent me back. Rest, in prospect, looks very sweet, but the Master hath said, "Return to thine house and tell how great things the Lord hath done for thee." [Mark 5:19.]

Can I cheerfully, joyfully return? Yea, Lord, only Thou be with me; and if 'tis Thy will, though it be three score years and ten, I will, with Thy servant of old, say, "All the days of my appointed time will I wait till my change cometh." [Job 14:14.]

Yes, it will be but as a moment when compared with

eternity; and I feel that it does work for me an eternal weight of glory, while I look not at the things which are seen, but at the things which are eternal. Can I for a moment stagger in my faith, when I have proved Him to be faithful and true to His promises, so long and in so many instances? No, I will trust Him and not be afraid.

My blessed pastor and wife were here today, and we had a profitable time while speaking of the goodness of our Father to us through another year. Yesterday, while friends were here, the Lord was indeed in our midst. Bless and reward them for their work and labor of love to Thy unworthy servant. Dear Sisters Lankford and De Lamater sympathized and comforted me.

> "Not more than others I deserve,
> Yet God hath given me more."

Tuesday, January 4th 1859
Had a letter from Brother Joseph Pullman. He says, "I am the Lord's. The blood of Jesus cleanseth from all sin. I sink into His will and cleansing power, and I must believe the result."

Praise the Lord! I rejoice to hear of the full surrender of this dear youth. Blessed Lord, make him very useful, and give him wisdom and knowledge. Oh, may he be an instrument in Thy hand of saving souls. My soul is resting in the all-atoning merits of my precious Saviour.

> "Give joy or grief, give ease or pain;
> Take life or friends away,"

Only give me the smile of Thy face and all is well. Yes, glory! All is well. "Though Thou slay me, yet will I trust in Thee." [Job 13:15.]

January 6th 1859

Had a visit yesterday from Dr. Bangs, and it was a very profitable time, although not able to converse much. Have had some things of a trying nature to contend with, but was enabled through grace to cast all upon the Lord, who careth for me. I must keep on the watchtower, lest by word or look I should dishonor the cause of my Master, or in any way grieve His spirit.

This poor body has to bear so much; the brain, too, is weak. Oh, my Father, so stamp Thine image upon my heart that the mind which was in Christ may reflect through all my words and actions, that everyone who comes to see me may feel that here Thou delightest to dwell.

Saturday, January 15th 1859

Last evening Brother E. Grogan came in. He has been sorely tempted, but was enabled to overcome. Still the fear of man was before him. We sang the hymn, "Lord, in the strength of grace," and then united in prayer – sweet prayer. Be it ever so simple, there is nothing like prayer – after which he appeared strengthened.

Miss S. was very much melted while we were speaking of the condescension of our blessed Lord and Saviour, and of His great love wherewith He hath loved us, and to think that "the very hairs of our head are numbered." [Luke 12:7.]

Surely it is good to tell of His dealings, and publish abroad the way in which He leadeth us. Yea, His love to us constraineth us to cry out, "Come and hear all ye that fear God, and I will declare what He has done for my soul." [Psalm 66:16.]

"Help me to watch and pray,
And on Thyself rely."

I ask not health or riches, but give me more and more of Thyself. I consecrate myself anew to Thee – body, soul and all my powers – seal me forever Thine.

January 27th 1859
Received a letter from J. P. today. Oh, that the Lord may keep him under the shadow of His wing. Yea, in His pavilion may he trust. Oh, how good is my Heavenly Father to me, ever saying, "Fear not, I am with thee; be not dismayed, I am thy God." [Isaiah 41:10.]

Have been much buffeted by the enemy of souls in various ways, but I remember that the Saviour said, "I have prayed for thee that thy faith fail not." [Luke 22:32.] Help me, my precious Saviour, to look unto Thee in all things. In the day of trouble Thou art and hast been my hiding place.

This feeble frame shall by Thy grace show forth the loving kindness of the Lord, and forbid that by look or word I should for a moment be impatient or murmur at my stay, or wish my sufferings less.

February 5th 1859
Bless the Lord, O my soul, and forget not all His benefits, for He hath done great things for thee. [Psalm 103:2.] Since writing last, the body has suffered much, not only from extreme pain, but excessive weakness, so that at times I thought I would not be able to hold a pencil again. Truly the grasshopper has become a burden [Ecclesiastes 12:5] and the right hand almost lost its cunning. [Psalm 137:5.]

It is now with great difficulty that I write, but my cup is full. "Oh, for a trumpet voice on all the world to call."

Have been sorely assailed by the arch enemy on account of my inability to lead in family worship, trying to make it appear that however feeble, I must do it, making a labor of what has ever been a comfort and delight. But just as soon as I saw from whence the trouble came, and applied to my Father, He brought me off more than conqueror.

February 14th 1859

"Unto whom should I come but unto Thee? Thou hast the words of eternal life." [John 6:68.] Praise the Lord, I can come unto the King of kings and Lord of lords. Thou hast in Thine infinite mercy adopted me into Thy family, and with humble confidence I look up and call Thee *Abba, Father*. My Lord and my God, my Rock and my Tower, whom shall I fear? [Psalm 18:2.]

Again the enemy has been trying to turn my thoughts from my precious Jesus, and I find it is only by simple faith, ever keeping my eye fixed on the atonement, that I can drive him hence, and by the grace of God I can from my heart say,

> "What tho' a thousand hosts engage,
> A thousand worlds my soul to shake,
> I have a shield shall quell their rage,
> And drive the alien armies back.
> Portrayed it bears a bleeding lamb,
> I dare believe on Jesus' name."

Praise the Lord for His goodness, and for His wonderful works to the children of men. My full heart cries out, "Not unto us, not unto us, but unto Thy name be all the glory." [Psalm 115:1.] 'Tis more than an angel tongue can tell, or angel mind conceive.

February 24th 1859

> "If in this feeble flesh I may
> Awhile show forth Thy praise,
> Jesus, support this tottering clay,
> And lengthen out my days."

Yes, blessed Jesus, my times are in Thy hands, and only would I live to bring glory to Thy great and holy name. Therefore purge me, though it be with hyssop; wash me and make me clean. [Psalm 51:7.] Grant that nothing may reign in me but Thy pure love alone. Thy word is very pure, therefore Thy servant loveth it.

Oh, what a perfect Saviour is ours; one who loves us and saves us to the uttermost. Praise the Lord that it was ever written, "The blood of Jesus cleanseth from all sin." [1 John 1:7.] I sink into that cleansing blood, and bathe this weary soul of mine in that fountain which is open in the house of David; for all it is open and free, without money and without price. [Isaiah 55:1.] Glory! Glory! I cannot express what the Lord is doing for me.

"All are too mean to speak His worth,
Too mean to set my Saviour forth."
"I would Thy boundless love proclaim
With every fleeting breath."

March 3rd 1859

"The promised land from Pisgah's top
I now exult to see;
My hope is full, Oh, glorious hope!
Of immortality."

Yes, my hope is full, praise the Lord! Ere long Thou wilt take me to that promised land. There shall be no night, and the Lamb himself shall lead us beside the fountain of living waters. [Revelation 7:17.]

While I am writing, "My soul is leaping to go; this moment for heaven I would leave all below." Yet with Job I can truly say, "All the days of my appointed time will I wait till my change comes." [Job 14:4.]

Yesterday had a visit from dear Dr. Bangs. It seemed while speaking of the goodness and loving-kindness of our Father God, that this spirit "would burst the bonds of clay and soar to realms of bliss."

Sister Platts was also here from Glen Cove, and it rejoiced my heart to hear how the Lord is leading His dear people there. Ride on, Thou mighty conqueror, till all shall be subdued unto Thee, from the least to the greatest.

March 11th 1859

> "Jesus, Thy boundless love to me
> No thought can reach, no tongue declare."

The past few days my soul has been, as it were, in an ocean of love, and "Lost in wonder, love and praise." Infinite condescension of the Lord to me, in view of extreme feebleness and inability to do something for my precious Jesus. I would often be home down, and nature would say, "How long, O Lord, how long?" [Psalm 13:1.]

But praise the Lord, He giveth songs in the night, and is still saying, "I will never leave nor forsake Thee." [Deuteronomy 31:6.] "Yet a little while and He that will come shall come and will not tarry." [Hebrews 10:37.] The *Great I Am*, Jehovah, is our strength. He also is become our salvation. [Isaiah 12:2.]

Monday, March 14th 1859

Had a very profitable day while speaking to Mr. and Mrs. Murray Shipley, of the Society of Friends, of the goodness and loving-kindness of my Father to me, and the way in which He has led me these many years.

March 15th 1859

Yesterday had a very precious melting season. My dear pastor and wife, and Sisters Lankford, Annesley and E. D. Smith, with Brother J. P. were with me when we partook of the Lord's supper, and told of some of His dealings with us. My cup was indeed full. In view of what He had done for me, I was led to ask,

> "Where shall my wondering soul begin?
> A soul redeemed from death and sin –
> A brand plucked from the eternal fire;
> How shall I equal triumphs raise,
> Or sing my great Redeemer's praise?"

This is probably the last time Brother Osborne will meet with us, but by and by if faithful, we will be together above. Hallelujah! We will praise Him.

April 4th 1859

Since writing last have suffered much. Yet, amid all, the still small voice has whispered, "Be thou faithful unto death and I will give thee a crown of life;" [Revelation 2:10] and through temptations and pain I am enabled to say, "Even so, Father, for so it seemeth good in Thy sight." [Matthew 11:26.] For Thou hast said, "Though thou passeth through the fire thou shalt not be burned, nor the waters overflow thee." [Isaiah 43:2.] And here I rest in the arms of my Beloved, learning that He doeth all things well.

Yesterday had my dear pastor and wife to take tea with me. May we meet where the inhabitants shall no more say, "I am sick."

April 17th 1859

The Lord is a sun and shield. How true the promises are, all

Yea and Amen, in Christ Jesus to them that believe. [2 Corinthians 1:20.] In every trial Thou art my sun and shield. [Psalm 84:11.]

May 24th 1859
Have had a sweet visit from my new pastor, Rev. Charles Fletcher, and his wife. I felt perfectly at home with them. Brother F. read the 23rd Psalm, and while beseeching the mercy seat for a continuation of loving kindness, was almost constrained to say, "Let us build tabernacles here." [Matthew 17:4.] "I would Thy boundless love proclaim with every fleeting breath."

June 10th 1859
Many are Thy wonderful works which Thou hast done to us ward. Words and strength fail me to tell of all the blessed work which the Lord, even my God, hath done for me. Not only in spiritual things does He bless me but in temporal things, by giving me dear kind friends who do not tire or grow weary in aiding us.

Among the first is our dear Sister Lankford; and for eleven years has this faithful friend and sister stood by me and mine. In the hours of deepest sorrow she has ever been near my side to cheer and comfort, by day and night, and to supply our wants, and in every way to aid; and continues to be the same untiring friend.

Had a most precious visit from her today. She is not only foster mother to my dear Mary, but to us all. O my Father God, do Thou indeed reward and bless her in this life, but when Thou shalt say, "It is enough," give her an abundant entrance into the land of rest.

Was favored with a melting, cheering season while several were with me who united in reading, singing and prayer. The Lord was in our midst.

"Surely Thou did'st unite
Our kindred spirits here,
That all hereafter might
Before Thy throne appear."

September 25th 1859
Although not permitted to go to the courts of the Lord, where I have sung in sweet and solemn lays, yet He condescends to consecrate a house of prayer in my surrendered heart Glory! Glory be to His name.

January 3rd 1860
It is with deep humility of soul that I would record some of the loving kindness of the *Great I Am*, to unworthy me. Through another year He has preserved me, although in much weakness of body, and, as it were, a broken vessel laid aside.

Yet I rejoice in the Lord, and joy in the God of my salvation. [Habakkuk 3:18.] And though deprived of the privilege of praising His name in the great congregation, as I once delighted to do, yet I can tell of His goodness to my brethren, for He kindly sends many of His dear children of different denominations to see me.

I'll praise Him while He lends me breath. When I look back upon the past year, upon the many mercies that we, as a family, have been blessed with, I am lost in wonder, love and praise.

Death has not entered our circle. We have had food and raiment, and all our returning wants have been supplied. Many dear Christian friends have been raised up to help us along, not only temporally but spiritually. I take all as gifts from Himself to me.

Dear Lord, be pleased to bless each one who has ministered to us. As they have fed us, do Thou feed them with the bread of life, and clothe them with the robe of righteousness, pure and clean, [Revelation 19:8] that they may be made meet for the inheritance of the saints in light. "Sick and ye visited Me," let it be said to them. [Matthew 25:36] It is wonderful – *sick, naked, hungry* and *a stranger*, and all my wants are supplied. It is the Lord, and I will praise Him.

February 4th 1860

> "Pause, my soul, adore and wonder,
> Ask, Oh, why such love to thee?
> Grace hath put me in the number
> Of the Saviour's family."

Hallelujah! Eternal thanks to Thee. The past has been a solemn week, to me and to many. Why such love to me? On Monday had a glorious time, while a few of my Father's dear children met with me in this little room in the breaking of bread. Never, I think, did I realize such a nearness of the Great *Three-in-One*.

It was as if the sky was rent and the heaven opened, and there was my crucified but risen Lord. While each one was telling of the goodness of the Lord, the room seemed filled with the glory of the Most High, like the upper room where the disciples were gathered together when the Saviour appeared and breathed upon them and said, "Receive ye the Holy Ghost." [John 20:22.] He does save to the uttermost all that come unto Him.

> "If such the sweetness of the stream,
> What must the fountain be?"

The body is suffering much, but the promise stands sure,

"I will not leave thee nor forsake thee." [Hebrews 13:5.]

Circumstances seem to call forth a day of humiliation before the Lord by our society, that He would preserve us from the evil in the world, and pardon our transgressions as a Church.

February 10th 1860

I will wash my hands in innocency, so will I compass Thine altar, O Lord! [Psalm 26:6.] My soul doth magnify the Lord. He gives me a word in season to those who visit me, that with humbleness of mind I may tell of His loving kindness.

My soul was wonderfully blessed while conversing with Murray Shipley and Miss Kate, friends who called upon me this morning. Together we wept and praised the Giver of every good and perfect gift [James 1:17], and related the many mercies the Lord had bestowed upon us, and upon me, so unworthy. Yet He deigns to bless.

In the evening, Mr. Shipley returned with his cousin, Samuel Shipley. And, oh, how true it was that wheresoever two or three are met in His name, He will bless. We had a glorious season while Mr. Shipley read from the Word of life and supplicated the throne of grace. Saviour, take the power and glory.

March 16th 1860

Many things seek to distract my mind, but the Lord reigneth. Let the earth rejoice.

I have been asked to resign my dear Hannah to another. Oh, it is a sore trial to me, yet I do not think it would be right to gainsay it or put anything in her way, for the young man is, as far as I know or can find out, all I could wish for my dear child. But I know that now we are a happy little family, and I almost fear to take a step lest it should mar our happiness.

The matter has long been prayed over, for I foresaw what would soon come to pass, and I have long desired and prayed if it would not be for God's glory and our good, some hindrance might be put in the way.

I also spoke with friends who have known him for years, and all seem to favor it. I think I would do wrong to refuse her to him, as there are no just grounds for doing so. And also, if I should soon be taken away, she would have a home. Thus I have allowed her to become engaged. Oh, my poor fluttering heart, be still; thy God still lives.

> "Give to the winds thy fears,
> Hope and be undismayed."

April 11th 1860

> "Here I'll raise my Ebenezer,
> Hither by Thy help I'm come."

Yes, bless the Lord, Thou hast gently led me along and cleared my way. Twelve years since didst Thou show me that narrow path, that way cast up for the ransomed of the Lord. Praise the Lord for the simplicity of the way, by simple faith on the atonement, trusting in the Great Jehovah, who hath said, "I will guide thee with Mine eye," [Psalm 32:8] and "I will hold thee by thy right hand." [Psalm 41:13.]

Oh, how shall I praise Thee, my Father, that Thou hast kept me still in the narrow way? Although I fear that in many things I may have come short, yet I have never lost the evidence, and it is now clear that the blood of Jesus Christ, His dear Son, cleanseth from all sin. [1 John 1:7.] Glory! Glory! The reality of this is almost overpowering for the poor feeble frame.

"Pause, my soul, adore and wonder;
Ask, Oh, why such love to thee?"

My heart cries out, "Draw near, all ye that fear God and hear what He hath done for my soul." [Psalm 66:16.] And now do I again consecrate myself with all my powers to Thee, O Lord.

Chapter 13

Changing Scenes

I know not the way I'm going,
But well do I know my guide;
With a childlike trust I give my hand
To the mighty friend by my side.
The only thing that I say to Him
As he takes it, is "Hold it fast;
Suffer me not to lose my way,
And bring me home at last."

[Hanna's Home]
May 5th 1860
Here I am in a new habitation. Whether for the best or not is unknown, but I trust for the best. I know this, that I am in the Lord's hands, and I have sought to learn His will in this thing, and to be guided by Him.

Friends have been very kind, especially Brother Stephenson, in sending men to move my things and carry me. Last evening they came to see how I bore the moving, and we sang the hymn,

"Thou, Lord, hast blest my going out,
Oh, bless my coming in."

After which we sweetly prayed that nothing should mar our peace, but like the family of Bethany we might have the presence of the Master. And my heart fervently responded "Amen!"

It is not in man to choose his way. In Thee do I put my

trust. Thou art my hiding place. Under Thy pavilion will I rest.

May 31st 1860
Yesterday my dear Hannah pledged her vows to become the partner for life in the joys and sorrows of the young man of her choice, John Paisley. As Thou hast been the guide of my youth and riper years, so guide them.

My dear friends have been very kind in sending Hannah things for her comfort. I have been lost in wonder, love and praise at their kindness; but truly it is of the Lord, and to Him be all the glory.

June 5th 1860
Had a visit from Mrs. Underhill, with a relative. They are attending the yearly meeting. Miss Folwell, from Philadelphia, seems to be very desirous to serve the Lord fully, but is afraid of running before she is sent. Open Thou her understanding, and she will learn Thy will.

June 30th 1860
Dr. Bangs was again to see me. What a soldier of the cross he is! It gives me fresh courage to persevere to the end. It always cheers me to have a visit from him. I think if He has kept his servant so many years, He can also keep me.

Brother Joseph Pullman was here at the same time, and it was food for much thought as they sat side by side – the one just on the steps of the Celestial City, having borne the burden and heat of the day, and the other, in the morning of life, setting out for the battlefield to fight for the kingdom of our Lord.

Make him very humble and faithful; and when Thou hast done with Thine aged servant, grant that he may depart in peace. Dr. Bangs thinks he will not be able to go to camp meeting this year, and it will be the first he has missed in fifty-seven years. What a lesson to others!

Also had a visit from Miss Cromwell, a very sweet young Christian, a Friend. She is seeking *the narrow way*, cast up for the ransomed of the Lord to walk in. O my Father, give her light. I thank Thee that so many of that society are waking up to their privileges and seeking purity of heart. May they come out with more boldness and confidence, and speak more plainly of the Lord's dealings towards them. Yea, be constrained to say, I will praise Thee with my whole heart; with my whole heart will I sing praise unto Thee. [Psalm 138:1.]

Have received back my poor little maid, Kate. Give me wisdom and patience to train her aright, not only for the duties of this life, but for eternity. She is prone to evil. Thou knowest all that is laid to her charge, but Thou canst change the hardest heart. She is under Thy care, as a poor, helpless, orphan child, having never known a mother's loving care.

Mercies

July 13th 1860

This day I am thirty-nine years old. So many years of my life, and how little I have done, and made so little progress. I am lost in wonder that the Lord of the vineyard hath not said, "Cut it down." [Luke 13:7.] Although I have often been weary of life through in-bred sin, yet now can I defy its power and bless the day that I was born.

July 27th 1860

Whom have I in heaven but Thee, my shield and high tower? [Psalm 73:25.] He deigns to bless, to succor and sustain. He will not cast me off; no, for,

"He calls a worm his friend,
He calls himself my God,
And He will save me to the end,
Through Jesus' blood.
"He by himself hath sworn,
I on His oath depend,
I shall on eagle's wings upborne
To heaven ascend."

To Miss Whitall
July 31st 1860
My Dear Sister in Christ,
Yours of the 29th gave me much pleasure, although I suppose you think I have been very remiss in answering it. But this poor, feeble frame was not able, as I often attempted without success.

I often think of your visit, and thank my Heavenly Father for the privilege of conversing with His dear children. Where shall my soul begin to praise Him?

Oh, how I rejoice, dear friend, that you ever set out to seek that way, "cast up for the ransomed of the Lord to walk in." [Isaiah 35:10.] Surely it is a highway, a glorious way, for nothing that is unclean can walk therein.

Praise the Lord! I rejoice with exceeding great joy that you have been enabled to lay hold on Christ as your Redeemer from all sin – to trust in Him, believing that He is able to keep that which you have committed to His care until the day of His coming.

In answer to your inquiry, "Whether we receive the gifts of holiness when we accept Christ as our Saviour from all sin, or not until we are kept in a state entirely pleasing to Him?" I think just as soon as we take Christ as our Saviour *from sin*, and trust and believe that He is not only able, but willing, to receive us and cleanse us from sin by His own precious blood, that then we enter into the way of holiness.

Nor do I think it is left optional with us, for I think we disobey Him if we do not accept His proffered grace, for He has said, "Ask and receive, that your joy may be full," [John 16:24.] and how can joy be full unless we have His smile? Surely He will not smile upon us if we are doubting His word.

I think many of us err in not coming out, if need be, to confess Christ as our Redeemer from all sin before the whole world, but are ever saying by our acts, if not by words, that it is useless for us to attempt to have or seek this beautiful state of Christian experience, as we could not keep it.

It is just what *we need* to keep us. We have, dear friend, a faithful God who will do far more abundantly for us than we ask or think, and all that He requires is that we make a *full surrender* and trust Him implicitly *at all times*. May you ever be able to say, "Take my body, spirit, soul, only Thou possess it whole."

May yours be a living sacrifice, holy and accepted by the Lord; and if at any time you should lack for a moment that clear witness, do not parley with this or that, but look away to the blood of sprinkling, and by faith in the blood you shall be made clean every whit, in a shorter time than it takes me to write it. Remember, dear, that we have not a hard Master, but like as a father pitieth his children, so the Lord pitieth them that fear Him. [Psalm 103:13.]

Though we do many times err through inexperience, want of knowledge, or weakness of body, we have an Advocate with the Father, Jesus Christ, the righteous. To Him, then, let us go, and so live that He will not be ashamed to call us sisters, for He declared whosoever doeth the will of his Father, the same is His mother and sister and brother. [Matthew 12:50.] What a high calling! May we in all things walk worthy of it and adorn it in all things and in all places.

With regard to this poor frail body, I have not much to say. It seems as if I was almost home, just in sight of the pearly gates, and then my Master sends me back for a season.

Ever yours in Jesus,
Bella Cooke

September 10th 1860
Since writing, I have been very near my eternal home, and oh how bright and sweet the prospect! It is so delightful to think of being almost home – angels beckoning me away, just waiting for Jesus to bid me come. But if He says, "Not yet," will I be less joyous? No, if it is His will, gladly will I linger on my three score years and ten. And although rest and home look so desirable, yet my prayer is, "Let me not die before I have done for Thee my earthly work, whatever it may be."

> "Call me not home with missions unfulfilled,
> Nor leave my little spot of ground untilled,
> Impress this truth upon me, that not one
> Can do the portion that I leave undone."

I have heard of the sudden death of a dear friend, Mrs. E. M, and I so frail am still spared. My two kind physicians do all they can. Oh, that Thou wouldst make me very useful this coming winter to any who may come into my little room.

Was greatly blessed while talking to a stranger whom Sister Lankford sent to see me. She is seeking full salvation, and while telling her how the Lord led me, and how great things He had done for me, it seemed as if I was almost carried into the third heaven. Bless to her this conversation, and make her way plain before her, and enable her to take

Thee at Thy word.

Also, a visit from Mrs. E. D. Smith. How kind to come and see me so soon after she came home.

October 7th 1860

Twenty years ago this day I was led to the altar a happy bride, and united to the man of my choice. But during the past twenty years what changes have I seen: four of our wedding party have gone with robes washed white in the blood of the Lamb to meet the Royal Bridegroom and feast at the marriage supper.

Eleven years ago, my dear partner was transferred to his home in heaven, and I, weak and feeble, left in the vale below with the precious little ones committed to my care. How utterly unable did I feel to combat with the world and provide for them, but through grace I was enabled to say, "Even so, Father, for so it seemeth good in Thy sight." [Matthew 11:26.] I am Thine, these are Thine; take us, and do for us as Thou wilt.

He gave me sweet peace, and assured me that He who fed me last would feed me still. He has given me many kind, dear friends, and grace to train my little ones for Him. One, He has safely housed with her father and sister above, and the others, I believe, are earnestly endeavoring to walk in His statutes and judgments and do them, and the little one I have no doubt will be brought into the fold.

Shall I not, in the fullness of my heart, cry out, "Bless the Lord, O my soul, and all that is within me bless His holy name!" [Psalm 103:1.]

The city is a scene of great excitement and bustle in honor of the Prince of Wales, and my whole heart says, God bless the lad, and may he speedily be brought to submit to the Prince of Peace.

What are all the titles and honors of this life compared

with the title held out to us by the King of kings and Lord of lords? We are heirs of God, joint heirs with Jesus Christ. How many would be glad to be called a friend of the young prince, yet they neglect Him who is above all principalities and powers.

November 16th 1860.

Faint, yet pursuing, is my present motto. Hitherto the Lord hath helped me on my eventful journey. In looking back, there some things to mourn over, but so much to be grateful for. Every step of the way the Lord has gently led me and tenderly cared for me.

It is six years this month since He permitted me to bow at the sacramental board in His house and with His people, yet He hath never forsaken me. Thirteen years ago He told me He would never leave or forsake me, and when He hath tried me, I shall come forth as gold.

To Miss Folwell
New York
November 20th 1860
My very dear Friend,
Through the infinite mercy of an all-wise God I am still spared, and was made very glad by your welcome letter so soon after your return home; but, before it came, your kind aunt called with the beautiful book you had left for me. I am much pleased with it, and beg you to accept my thanks.

I greatly rejoice that you have entered into the rest of those who believe. It is a glorious rest. Our Jesus, as you say, is a precious Saviour – One we can run into and find a refuge from everything that would disturb or annoy.

I do thank my blessed Master that He ever enabled me to lay hold on Him by faith and taste of His goodness. He is precious, more than meat and drink, for it takes but little of these to satisfy the poor clay, but I find that momentarily I need and have His aid − His spirit to feed and satisfy this spirit. Praise the Lord!

You ask, my dear sister, if I think it possible to always live resting on Jesus' bosom, or whether it is necessary to have clouds and mists to make us cling to Him by naked faith. I think that it is our Father's will for us ever to live under His smile, or why would our precious Jesus have said, "That My joy might remain in you, and that your joy might be full." [John 15:11.] I cannot see, if our joy be full, how we can be in the mist.

Paul says, "I can do all things through Christ who strengthens me." [Philippians 4:13.] Of ourselves truly we can do nothing, but it is written, "I will put My spirit in you and cause you to walk in My statutes and judgments to do them." [Ezekiel 36:27.] And again, "He led him about, He instructed him, He kept him as the apple of His eye." [Deuteronomy 32:10.]

We may give way to temptation and thus bring mists over our spirits, but I cannot think this is necessary, or in any way pleasing to our Father. It is our privilege to rejoice evermore. Not that we are sufficient of ourselves, for our sufficiency is of God.

Give my love to your dear mother. That peace, joy and love may ever rest upon you and abide with you, is the prayer of yours truly in Christ,

Bella Cooke

December 30th 1860
This is the last Sabbath in the year − a solemn thought that another year is gone. To others it may not appear so, yet I am weaker than this time last year.

"One sweetly solemn thought,
Comes to me o'er and o'er,
I am nearer home today,
Than I have ever been before."

What changes have been in my little home during the year, and we know not what may be in the future, but this I know, my Father hath promised never to forsake me. His promise cannot fail.

January 2nd 1861
The past year has been one of many and great changes, yet Thou hast been our guide, and we know not what is in the future. We received news from our friends in England which troubled us, but the Lord is our Counselor.

I had a few Friends to see me, among whom was Mr. I. Douglass, whom I had not seen for seven years. If seeing our friends gives us so much pleasure, what will it be to meet all around our Father's throne? May we have an abundant entrance.

My room was filled with the power of the living God. I do thank my Heavenly Father for giving me so many dear ones among the Society of Friends.

Miss Shotwell has indeed been as a ministering angel, oftentimes sent with some gift when none but God knew how much I was in need. I have told Him, for although He knows what we need before we ask, yet He hath said, "For all these things will I be inquired of by the house of Israel." [Ezekiel 36:37.]

It is very sweet to go right to Him, as a child to its earthly parent, and tell Him all our wants, and watch Him open the way for us to take our daily food as it were from His own hand, just sent by one of our family. For are we not all of the family of Christ, bound together by one of the strongest ties? Was not the precious blood shed for us all; and is it not declared by Him that we are His sons and daughters?

January 29th 1861
Still give me that sweet, trusting peace, which Thou hast so long vouchsafed to me. Make me pure as Thou art pure; holy, as Thou art holy; so that all with whom I may have converse may feel that I have been with Jesus.

February 4th 1861
Mr. Murray Shipley was here to see me from the West. He is earnestly inquiring after the way cast up for the ransomed of the Lord to walk in. Indeed, I believe he has entered the way, and only needs establishing grace. It humbles me in the dust to think of one like him coming to ask me anything – one so weak and ignorant.

But I know the Lord sometimes uses the most humble to testify of Him, and it is my daily prayer that I may be useful in that which will tend to His glory.

Go with that dear one in all his journey. I have sent him *The Life of Bramwell* and Wesley's *Plain Account*. Oh, that he may be blessed in reading them, and come forth in his society a bright and shining light.

March 1861
Mrs. Butler called, and what a friend she has been to me. She has had a conversation with Mrs. E D. Smith, and they thought I cannot remain here another year [in Hannah's house], as the family is large and the commotion too great. I would rather be alone with Mary, but how can I meet the extra expense?

No one knows how I suffer in having so many about me, but I cast it all upon the Lord. I did not intend to speak of it to anyone, but Mrs. Smith would know how I was supplied.

When both the ladies assured me that I should have all that would make me comfortable, and I should tell Mary to look for a room, and take it as soon as possible. My Father, guide me in all the matter.

July 9th 1861

On the 2nd I was brought back to this dear little old house where so many happy hours have been spent. O Lord, I will praise Thee. Bless my coming in and compass me about, and keep me from sin, that I may show forth Thy praise.

Miss Whitall and several other Friends kindly help me, so that I will be enabled to keep house again. I cannot tell how my poor heart rejoices in the goodness of my Father, that He puts it into the hearts of His dear children to aid and comfort me.

My dear Hannah is removed down to Thirteenth Street. Well, the Lord reigns and we will rejoice. Doubtless it is right, though I may not see her and the dear babe so often, yet she is in the hands of God her Father. While He is with her, He will also be with me. I triumph and adore: my soul sweetly leans upon its Beloved.

While my mind may be taken up in a measure with earthly cares and trials, yet, praise the Lord, my soul sees the King of kings and freely talks with God; for I do feel that the Father, Son and Holy Ghost have come and taken up their abode in my heart. Though poor and unworthy, they deign to dwell with me in this little room. He is mine and I am His. Help me to spread Thy praise abroad and tell Thy wondrous love to me.

September 1st 1861

Since last writing I have been very near home, even in sight of the Celestial City. Suffering and distress of body, with convulsions, have been my lot of late, and the end seemed very near. But above all I could hear the Master's voice, "It is I, be not afraid." [John 6:20.] At such times I have no choice, dare not choose, for I am not my own, and my prayer is, Do as Thou wilt, only let me be Thine, fully Thine.

> "But sometimes, when adown the western sky
> A fiery sunset lingers,
> Its golden gates swing inward noiselessly,
> Unlocked by unseen fingers.

> "And while they stand a moment half ajar,
> Gleams from the inner glory
> Stream brightly through the azure vault afar,
> And half reveal the story.

> "O land unknown! O land of love divine!"

I have been looking through the opened gates. Some friends I would like to have seen, but they were far away, among whom was my dear Sister Lankford, more than a sister to me. But the Lord has spared me a little longer, and afresh on the morning of a new month, I consecrate myself to Thee, body, soul and spirit. Seal me Thine to do or suffer all Thy will.

October 12th 1861
Had a visit from two Friends who are in town from Philadelphia – mother and daughter – Mrs. and Miss Whitall. Both are full of love and good works. I think I never met with a young lady like Miss Whitall, so loving to her mother. She seems ripening for heaven, while here on earth may they win souls for Him.

October 15th 1861

Today had a visit from Dr. Stephen H. Tyng, the first time I have seen him. The almond tree is flourishing, and those that look out of the windows are becoming dim. A great and good man.

I found it a time of refreshing. The Spirit of the Lord was upon him, and we found it good to approach the mercy seat. It matters not by what name we are called, so we belong to Christ. I always find Jesus is so precious while conversing with His children of every name. All one in Christ.

Dr. Tyng presented me with his likeness, which I highly prize. The past week I have found my God to be a stronghold and a present help, while some things which try men's souls have been hurled at me. I rejoice in God; and though an host should encamp against me, in this will I be confident: One thing have I desired of the Lord, that will I seek after, that I may dwell in the house of the Lord for ever. [Psalm 27:4.]

November 1861

My heart was made glad and my spirit was greatly revived to hear of the opening of the Mission School up in Second Avenue by the Society of Friends. The first Sabbath they numbered fifty-seven. All the children are of the poorest, picked out of the streets and brought together to mingle with a few of God's dear children.

Mrs. Ruth Murray and Mrs. A. Tatum were the chief ones to commence this good work. They keep me acquainted with its progress. What shall I render unto Thee, O my Father, for these kind friends? They are so mindful of me. They often send to me just when the oil and meal are exhausted. I daily ask of Him to send me by whom He will; and shall I not take all these blessings from His hand?

Although He knoweth what we have need of before we ask Him, yet He hath said by prayer and supplication with thanksgiving we are to make our requests known. I know that He heareth me, and the skeptic would stand amazed could he know how the Lord hath indulged me – how He hath had compassion on me.

It is very wonderful how I have been cared for and fed all these years, how friend after friend has been raised up. Although in the body I have very much to suffer, yet rejoice in the Lord and joy in the God of my salvation; for He maketh me to mount up as on eagle's wings. "He anointeth my head with oil, my cup runneth over." [Psalm 23:5.] Oh, that men would praise the Lord!

Sunday, November 24th 1861

John says, "I was in the Spirit on the Lord's day." [Revelation 1:10.] May we not also say so, when the Father, Son and Holy Ghost come down and dwell in our hearts?

When with two or three of His dear children we meet in his little room and sing and pray, is it not filled with the glory of God? Such was the case today. Among the rest was Mr. M. Shipley from Cincinnati. Bless them all, and me also, that I may show forth Thy praise.

December 4th 1861

"The desires of the righteous are granted." [Proverbs 10:24.] I must here record a little circumstance to show that the desires of the heart are given to us. On Saturday my dear Mary said, "Now, ma, what shall I get for the dinner tomorrow?"

I said I did not know, but I would like a little piece of roast duck.

She went out and priced them and came back. I said I could not get one; they smelled too much of silver, but if it was best, I should have some soon.

Very early Monday morning, Mrs. A. Tatum and Mrs.

Dickinson called in, and Mrs. Tatum had a plate covered with a napkin. She said, "Bella, we had roast duck for dinner yesterday, and I did want thee to have some while it was warm, but had no one to bring it, so I brought thee some, and hope thee will like it."

"Your heavenly Father knoweth when ye have need of these things."[Matthew 6:32.]

December 27th 1861

I have been almost overwhelmed with the kindness of my dear friends during the past month. They have seemed to be determined I should partake of their share of earthly blessings. We have celebrated another of our Saviour's birthdays.

"He laid His glory by,
He wrapped Him in our clay;
Unmarked by human eye
The latent Godhead lay;
Infant of days He here became,
And bore the mild Immanuel's name.

To Mrs. Whitall
New York
January 19th 1862
My Precious Friend,
Yours of the 10th came to hand all safely. I return you many thanks, dear one. Your letter was a great comfort to me. Love and sympathy from those we love is very sweet, and to have one of those little silent messengers to talk to us and tell us of loved ones far away is very precious. Letters are a great treasure to me.

Your gift adds to my outward comfort. Oh, how kind! May He "whose the earth is and the fullness thereof" ever bless and fill you with His Holy Spirit.

I have not seen Mrs. H. Dickinson lately. She has been so taken up with her numerous duties. I know she is getting along finely in the divine life, going on from strength to strength. I think her a lovely Christian. Mrs. D. asks after you when she comes.

The mission school is progressing nicely. I think a great and good work is begun there, for in that field we have every reason to believe that the seed sown by that faithful few shall in many hearts take root, and bring forth fruit to the honor and glory of Him who died for them.

I am very much rejoiced, dear one, that our Father has been unfolding to you new beauties in His written word. Oh, 'tis sweet to trace out His will in it, and His dealings with those of old; and then to feel that this Great, High and Holy One is ours — our Father and our Friend.

And now you say, "Don't forget to tell me about your poor body." Well, dear, I have only the old story of pain and much weakness. I have had to heal up the old issue, and the doctor had to make a new one in my side. It is about the size of a silver dollar, and, of course, very sore. It makes it very hard to move in the least or use my hand; but perhaps by and by, when I get a little more used to it I will get along better. I have much I would like to say to you but cannot.

I still find the Lord very precious. We have One who pities us as a father pities his children. As one whom his mother comforteth, so will He comfort us, and we all know how tender and kind a mother is to her sick child, yet how much more the Lord is to us! Hannah, her husband, and boy are well. Mary is well and happy. We are very comfortable in our little home. Much love to each of your family, and with many prayers for your welfare.

Ever yours in Christ,
Bella Cooke

August 14th 1862

My Very Dear Friend Mrs. Shipley,

Yours of July 12th came, for which please receive my sincere thanks. I cannot tell you how much good your dear letter did me. I was so glad to hear that you were living so sweetly under the smile of your Heavenly Father. Oh, 'tis sweet to thus dwell under the shadow of His wing. I am glad that you enjoyed yourself so much in our city. The Lord is good, His tender mercies are over all His works. [Psalm 145:9.]

I enjoy very much the visits of our dear band of Christian sisters in Thirtieth Street. They are very, very kind to me, their spirits are so pure. I like to have them sit by my bedside and breathe in that spirit of love which they possess.

Have you heard Mrs. D. is out of town? Mrs. Murray has another little girl. Mrs. Tatum was here the other day; she is very much engaged with the sick and wounded soldiers. I believe she spends two whole days every week with them, and as much more of her time as she can.

I had a visit from Mrs. Whitall on her return from St. John's. She left dear Miss Alice there. I rejoice to hear that she is longing after all the mind which was in Christ. They are pronounced blessed who thus long, for they shall be filled [Matthew 5:6]; this the dear Saviour said, and not one jot or tittle of His word can fall to the ground till all shall be fulfilled. [See Matthew 5:18.]

Go on, my dear sister, yours is a glorious path you have begun to walk in. "No half way work can satisfy you." Blessed be our Lord and Saviour Jesus Christ. He saveth to the uttermost all that come unto God by Him. It is His will, dear one, that you should go forth and be a full possessor of all the promised inheritance.

Satan may try to tell you that you cannot live thus, but you know his character. We don't pretend to believe him. And while nothing short of a full conformity to the divine will can satisfy us, nothing short of this will please Him whose we are and whom we serve.

My poor feeble prayers go up daily for you and dear Miss Abby, that all the will of God may be done in and by you. I have been rather poorly the past week, fainted twice in getting my bed fixed. And now, my dear, I commend you to God and to the word of His grace.

Yours truly in Christ,
Bella Cooke

To Mrs. A. Shipley
November 5th 1862
I fear you will, my dear Mrs. Shipley, think me very tardy in not having before this answered your very kind note by our friend Mrs. Dickinson. It was truly refreshing to me, a few lines from you, and to hear of the Lord's dealings with you. I rejoice that He is leading you step by step into the promised land – that land of corn and wine, that rest of perfect holiness which every true believer pants to see.

Go on, dear friend, turn not to the right nor to the left, but steer a steady course and faint not by the way.

You say truly He would not fail now to destroy all the old inhabitants, after having brought you so far out of Egypt. And He is waiting to fill you with His Spirit's might in the inner man. But we must not forget what He hath told us, that although *He is the One* to blot out all our sins and iniquities, yet He says, "Put Me in remembrance," [Isaiah 43:26] and again, "For all these things I will be inquired of by the house of Israel." [Ezekiel 36:37].

Oh, then, let us come with that living faith which laughs at impossibilities, and cries, "It shall be done." 'Tis sweet to rest in His embrace and know no will but His. I have so often seen and felt that He knows so much better than I what is best for me, that I dare not take my little affairs out of His hands.

I had a sweet and profitable surprise last evening. Mrs. Dickinson, Miss Shotwell and Mrs. Shipley all came to see me. It seemed like heaven below. Jesus, even our Jesus, talked with us by the way. Our hearts were refreshed, we were strengthened, at least I was, and could but praise and adore Him who is so kind.

Well might the psalmist cry out, "Oh, that men would praise the Lord for His goodness and for His wonderful works to the children of men." [Psalm 107:31.] And our hearts echo the same – yes, with our whole hearts will we praise our God.

The ladies were all well, and would send their love if they knew I was writing. I am happy to say Jenny Dickenson is better. Much love to Miss Folwell.

And now, dear friend, may He who is able to keep you faultless, present you without spot at the coming of His Father with exceeding joy, is the earnest prayer of yours, with much affection, in the best of bonds. [Jude 1:24.]

Bella Cooke

November 30th 1862

Thus far the Lord hath led me on. What a world of changes, coming and going, meeting and parting; but by and by we will get home, no more to separate.

A short time ago a young man called and announced himself as George Addy, son of Rev. J. Addy, of Newfoundland. I could not for the moment believe it, as I had not heard anything of them for more than twenty years, and it did not seem possible the son of my dear cousin, who left England twenty-seven years ago as a minister to those wilds in North America, could be standing before me; but so it was.

He is attending lectures at the medical college in this

city, and I am thankful to find that while he is seeking knowledge in his profession he is not unmindful of the God of his father.

The Riot in 1863
"No evil shall come nigh thee."
[Psalm 91:10.]

To Miss Whitall
Second Avenue
August 6th 1863
My Precious Friend,
I was so glad to get a letter from you. You are so kind to me, and I so unworthy; but it is all of the Lord, and to Him shall be all the glory. How can I thank you and your dear mother for your continued kindness to me.

I was well aware that my dear friend would not forget me in the time of trial which our city was passing through in the late riots. We were very mercifully and wonderfully preserved through it all, although the whole block on which we live was threatened to be burned, yet not a hair of our heads was injured.

Although the cannon roared and shook our dwelling, it did not come nigh us. We were hid under the shadow of His wing. Only with our eyes did we behold it. Many were killed in sight and sound of our house.

The people around here attribute our safety to the fact that there were some rebels in the corner liquor store, but I to another cause.

Dear Mary acted very nobly until it was all over. Nor did she falter for a moment in her efforts to keep all calm for me; but when the quiet came, she sank and could scarcely rise from her bed for one or two days.

Dear Miss Alice, I have sent you a card — they say a

picture of myself. How do you like it? I was so tired and nervous in getting ready, and the very effort to throw it off makes me, I think, look silly; but all say it is like me, so it must be right.

Yours, truly,
In Jesus,
Bella Cooke

Chapter 14

The Lighted Pathway

For the promise is unto you and to your children (Acts
2:39).

I long to praise Thee more and yet
This is no care to me,
If Thou shalt fill my mouth with songs
Then I will sing to Thee;
And if my silence praise Thee best
Then silent I will be.

January 9th 1864

Three days ago my dear Mary was married to the Rev.
Joseph Pullman, a young man of deep piety and full of
promise, glad to labor in the Master's vineyard; and God
grant they may both be faithful.

Oh, how lonely my home seems to me without that dear
girl; much as if I had had a funeral. But I believe it is in the
order of Providence that she should be with that young man
to work for souls.

Many friends have contributed to their comfort in
excellent and pretty presents, and I can only say when I look
at all the goodness of the Lord in caring for my dear children
one after another, "What hath God wrought?" [Numbers
23:23.] They are blessed with everything to make them
comfortable and happy. His promises have been yea and
amen, and here I will set up another Ebenezer.

Our dear friend, Rev. Thos. G. Osborne, came to
perform the ceremony at the church. He took dinner with
us, which was prepared and sent by dear Mrs. Taber, so that

I might not be worried with it. After dinner a few friends, Mrs. Lankford and Brother Lankford, with other precious friends came in, among whom was, of course, Brother Stephenson.

They sung the hymn, "All hail the power of Jesus' name." Yes, I did feel that I wanted them to crown Him Lord of all, for He had done everything for me and mine. After this they went around to the church and were united in one, and left for their new home and field of labor.

January 12th 1864
Received letters from my dear children. Their people received them most kindly and affectionately.

To Miss Whitall
Second Avenue
April 9th 1864
My dear Miss Whitall,
I received your welcome letter this morning with your kind gift, for which please accept my warmest thanks. You are so kindly prompt. You speak of thinking it would be better to send or give me the year's money in advance. About this, dear friend, I have nothing to say. It must be left entirely with yourselves.

Shall we see you at yearly meeting? I do hope we will. I hear Miss Abby is coming and perhaps Mrs. Shipley.

I am looking forward to a most blessed time. Not that this is a time of dearth – far from it. The Lord is indeed very good, His mercies fail not. I wonder and adore. Many times I have to cry out, what am I or my father's house that Thou art mindful of me! I have lately been very wonderfully cared for.

I must tell you of what my dear Thirtieth Street friends have been doing. You are aware that in every kind good work, they are among the first. Well, Mrs. Tatum has made many handsome things for the great Sanitary Fair. One is a fancy set of dolls, so made that by turning a pivot or spring they are all set in motion. Some friend suggested it would be well to exhibit it, with an entrance fee, in her parlor for someone's benefit, and it was immediately acted upon. Mrs. T. said she would do it for twenty-five cents each for Bella Cooke's benefit.

This was well received by all. And how much do you think it yielded? Fifteen dollars, twenty cents. Was not this beautiful? I can hardly realize it. Little did I think the Sanitary Fair was to be any help to me. It is providential, for Annie has had no sewing the past two or three weeks, and thus we are cared for. My Father won't let me be anxious. He does supply all my needs, both spiritual and temporal, and to Him shall be the praise.

I have, for the past few weeks, been more poorly than usual, but the Lord is ever with me. He giveth songs in the night season; He leadeth me to rejoice in Him, to trust and not fear; to lie passive in His hands and know no will but His. With many thanks for your kindness, and prayer for your welfare, I remain yours truly,

Bella Cooke

June 20th 1864

The past week I have been near the Celestial City. On the 15th had a severe attack of convulsions, and for some time was unconscious of what was passing. But oh, the goodness of God to me. Truly His mercy faileth not. For twelve years I have been subject to these attacks. The first I had in September 1851, two weeks after the death of my little Josephine.

Friends have been so kind to me in these sufferings that I wonder they don't tire. It is the Lord who disposes their hearts with forbearance and love.

June 27th 1864

This day had the sacrament of the Lord's Supper. My soul seemed to be basking in the rays of the Sun of Righteousness, swimming in an ocean of love. Day by day the Lord unfolds to me new beauties of Jesus, and I feel as it were clothed from above.

> "Jesus, Thy blood and righteousness
> My beauty are, my glorious dress;
> 'Midst flaming worlds in this arrayed,
> With joy shall I lift up my head."

July 6th 1864

Last evening a fire broke out in the cellar of the front house, and the flames were raging for fifteen or twenty minutes before engines could be brought. Brother John Pullman was sitting beside me when the alarm was given. At the first sound he went to lend his aid. I was startled, but in a moment my heart went out to my Father God, and such an inward calm pervaded that I was astonished at myself.

I quietly lay here and gave directions about what was to be saved, and told my dear Annie that the Lord would take care of us, and she must try and keep perfectly calm.

She put up our clothing, in which I placed my Bible, hymnbook and album, then girded the bedspread about me and waited the result, which was that only with my eyes I should behold it, for He gave His angels charge over me.

Brother John Pullman worked very hard, coming in often to see how I was getting along. Many brethren were at the door, but were told it was not best to come in, as Brother Stephenson was with me, and the less commotion there was about me the better. Even the firemen, when asked where the sick woman was, replied, "Oh, we will take care of her, if it takes the whole of us."

I had no fear. This verse was running through my mind all the time,

> "Calm on tumult's wheel I sit,
> 'Midst busy multitudes alone,
> Sweetly waiting at Thy feet,
> 'Till all Thy will be done."

The 91st Psalm was a great comfort to me: "Thou wilt keep him in perfect peace whose mind is stayed on Thee, because he trusteth in Thee."

O Lord, give me a word in season for all who turn in to see me. Let all our conversation be seasoned with grace, and ever be enabled to strengthen each other on our way. Yes, my Father, Thou hast preserved my fatherless children alive; Thou hast dealt bountifully with me and mine.

March 1865

I thank Thee, my Father, that Thou hast granted me my request and permitted me to get for the four past months one dollar per week for Mary Story, a poor afflicted child of Thine. Also many articles of clothing to make her comfortable for the winter. And Thou hast also privileged me to get three dollars per month for poor old Orin Franks, and help her through the past winter.

A little while, and no matter from what clime or color, we will all meet in our Father's house where there will be no chilling winds or fears of rent day. We will all be safely housed in glory.

My dear Joseph wrote to know if it would be well for him to write a note to Mrs. Jaffray and obtain a little help for poor blind Hannah of Middletown, Ct. She is in great need. I sent his note and wrote one also, and received ten dollars for present use, and Mrs. J. will give her five dollars per month for one year. Praise the Lord!

I also made it a subject for prayer, and resolved to ask everyone who came in for a month, except those I had tired out, and those not able to give. My good Dr. Sabine gave me twenty dollars from a friend, Mr. Stephenson five, Mrs. Murray five, and Mrs. W. E. Dodge five. A number of others gave me smaller sums which amount to about seventy dollars. Praise the Lord! He is good and will provide. Yes, His word is truth.

Thanksgiving Day 1865

Poor blind Hannah is again made glad. Mrs. Jaffray continues her kind gift monthly, and, through the goodness of my Heavenly Father I have sent her forty dollars. How blessed to be permitted to do a little for others.

Germantown

January 1st 1866

Dear Bella Cooke,

On this day, the first of the New Year, this day of so many new resolves and turning over of the new leaf, I determined no longer to have to reproach myself with neglect of so dear, patient and forgiving a friend as thyself.

I was especially glad to see thy handwriting again, as but the day or two before I had heard a mysterious report that thy last year on earth had been spent, and thou hadst changed ashes for a crown.

How this arose I cannot say, but Mrs. Shipley heard it from a neighbor of hers. I do not know whether to be glad for thy sake that it is not true, except that I must congratulate that the will of the Lord is being done and fulfilled in and by thy still continuance on this side Jordan. For thou art one who can say, "I worship Thee, sweet will of God, and all Thy ways adore."

What brings quietude and rest to the believing child like

this loving of *God's* will? I cannot boast of loving much, or doing much, but of having been forgiven much I may; and join with thee I do in the song, "Goodness and mercy have followed me all the days of my life," and "I will dwell in the house of the Lord forever."

May this year prove a fruit-bearing year, dear friend, not void of suffering to thee or to me likely, but may honor and praise be brought unto Him, whose we are, and who gave Himself *for us* and has now given Himself *to us*.

I could wish thee could share in some of the good meetings where Mrs. Shipley and I often meet.

I must close my letter and remain thy friend. Mother's affectionate remembrance is to thee.

A. S. F.

1623 Filbert Street
Philadelphia
January 1st 1866
My Dear Friend Bella Cooke,
The first time that I write the date of the New Year is to thee. How my heart reproaches me for my long apparent neglect. Many times have my thoughts turned to thee and dwelt upon the times of refreshing at thy bedside; but there it rested, and I did not write. Indeed, I was so paralyzed with the stunning blow of my father's and mother's deaths, of which perhaps our friend G. Dickinson may have told thee, that I had no energy to write or do anything but exist from day to day.

I have found at last that working for Jesus is the best cure. Although when we first returned to the city, after a summer of so much sorrow, it seemed utterly impossible ever again to go to work. Yet, blessed be His loving kindness and tender mercy, He has at last restored to me the commission, "Feed my lambs," qualifying for His service in my little measure; so I am regaining slowly health and tone of mind and spirit.

But I would not dwell on myself, unless it were to praise God afresh for every turn of His hand upon me, entreating Him to teach me by His Spirit all the lessons He would have me learn in the school of suffering. Thy last letter to A. S. Folwell (December 27) was most unexpected to me.

I had feared I should never see thy handwriting again, for strange to say, there was a rumor here that Jesus had called thee to His everlasting rest. And when I was reproaching myself that I had so long been silent, thinking I should never have another opportunity of telling thee of my loving interest and Christian fellowship in this world, behold thy letter came!

Not yet! Not yet! A little while longer to glorify God in suffering, then to reign with Jesus forever! Knowing the blessed truth that "Whether we live, we live unto the Lord, or whether we die, we die unto the Lord; whether we live or die therefore, we are the Lord's," [Romans 14:8], how little matters it when He calls us home!

One thing is certain, Christians are told to "comfort one another with these words," [1 Thessalonians 4:18] – words of blessed hope and expectation, of looking for and hasting to the day of the Lord's coming with great joy, for we look for new heavens and a new earth wherein dwelleth righteousness.

I was truly rejoiced to hear that thy dear children have been made instrumental in reviving the work of the Lord. Are not prosperity and adversity set one against the other? On the one hand, thou hast the blessedness of seeing thy children not only walking in the truth themselves, but turning many to righteousness. On the other hand, thy faith is sorely tried by the workings of the enemy.

Let patience have its perfect work, and it may be that

even yet thou shalt be able to praise Him for a wonderful salvation where it might be least expected. I need not wish thee "A happy New Year," knowing that as thy times are in His hands who doeth all things well, His will is thy happiness, and the year must be happy.

Abby Folwell is the stay of her aged parents in their declining years, and frequently shows her welcome face with us. We always love to see her come in, and hear her words filled with a holy zeal for the Lord.

I have enjoyed very much this winter the meetings for holiness at Mrs. Longacre's – similar to Mrs. Lankford's. They refresh and feed my soul many a time. Last night we went to watch meeting at Mr. Longacre's church, and had a solemn season. I trust it has strengthened our covenant.

Hoping soon to receive one of thy welcome letters, I bid adieu, commending thee afresh to Him who is the delight and beloved of thy soul.

Thy friend and sister in Christ,
Anna Shipley

To Mrs. A. Shipley
492 Second Avenue
January 22nd 1866
My Dear Mrs. Shipley,
Yours was received, and often I have thought of you in your deep affliction, but felt insufficient to offer you any comfort. But I did earnestly pray the Father to comfort you in the bereavement, and believed you had learned to "go and tell Jesus," and He hath said, "I am the resurrection and the life." [John 11:25.] Blessed assurance, that if we live in Him here we shall reign with Him in glory, when all tears shall be wiped from our eyes, for,

"No lingering look, no parting sigh,
Our future meeting knows;
There glory beams from every eye,
And hope immortal grows."

I was surprised to hear that a rumor was abroad that I had been called "to the land of the living." Not yet hath the Master called me away, but is still saying, "Be thou faithful unto death and I will give thee a crown of life." [Revelation 2:10.]

Is it not worth a little more suffering, toil, perplexities and cares? Oh yes, for we do know that the furnace will never be heated too hot, for the Master sits by and watches the precious metal, and when His image is clearly seen, He will say, "'Tis enough, come up higher."

Oh, I do thank Him for *all* that is past, and am perfectly willing to trust Him for all that is to come, for "when He hath tried me I shall come forth as gold." [Job 23:10.] Oh, the transporting, rapturous scene that rises to my sight!

What a countless company stand before yon dazzling throne. Palms they carry in their hands and crowns of glory on their heads. And if faithful, I, too, shall stand with them who are all in white robes arrayed, and sing the new song unto Him who hath loved us and washed us from our sins in His own blood. [Revelation 1:5.] To Him be glory and dominion forever. Hallelujah!

We will praise Him, for He is worthy. It seems day by day the Lord is enlarging and filling this poor heart, and I cannot praise Him as I would. I want every breath to praise Him. It seems as if everything becomes more beautiful, and my cry is, "Let all that hath breath praise Him." [Psalm 150:6.]

I had a very interesting visit from the gentleman who brought your letter. He seems like a very fine man. How kind of you to write such a good, long letter! I do prize letters so much. They are a great comfort to me. And now, dear friend, I am tired, and commit you to Him who is able to keep that which is committed to His care to the day of His coming.

Kind regards to your husband and children.

Yours in Christ,

Bella Cooke

October 1866

We were about to gather a little sum for poor blind Hannah for Thanksgiving, but she has escaped to bliss, is now set down in her Father's house, seeing and knowing as she is known. Her cares are all fled, her doubts are all slain, and the hour of her triumph is come. And, by and by, Thou wilt take all Thy waiting ones home. Till then, we would Thy praise proclaim.

1623 Filbert Street

Philadelphia

December 24th 1866

My Dear Friend Bella Cooke,

Throughout this long silence thou hast not been forgotten, as thou wilt understand when I explain the gift enclosed. Last summer, when Sister Catherine Shipley came on from Newport, she came to our country home straight from thy sick room, where she told us she had been refreshed in soul and body. She then found us engaged in work for thee, which we intended for the beginning of a children's Christmas Fair for thy benefit.

A kind friend, who had formerly been a boarding school teacher, had started our work by giving us a quantity of material left from her school; and the children were busily engaged making it up. From that time to this we have been devoting our spare time to this; and many sweet and refreshing thoughts of thee and of thy patient endurance of suffering have been mingled with the work.

Our and thy dear friend, Alice Whitall, and family, have also been devoting themselves to helping on the work, and their contributions were so beautiful, I long for thee to see some specimens of their work. Other friends, hearing of it, sent in their contributions; some from Burlington, through Rebecca W. Allison.

Little by little the rills flowed together, forming in time quite too large a collection for our small rooms to display to advantage. On Seventh day last Catherine Shipley kindly lent us her beautiful schoolrooms, and we arranged our fanciful and useful departments: toy table, doll table, art table, etc., for the children.

Our friends, who had been informed of it, poured in, and before noon the prayer I had had in my heart for months was answered, and we had taken in one hundred dollars. How earnestly I gave thanks. Before night, the remainder came in, and with joy I send it to thee for a Christmas present, as a joint gift from many friends to whom the name of Bella Cooke has become a household word; and (through the photographs) her face a memory for life.

Take it directly from thy loving Father's hand. I know thou wilt. He sends it to His faithful servant. Our watchword for the children (about ten were engaged in it) was, "Inasmuch as ye have done it unto one of the least of these, My brethren, ye have done it unto Me." [Matthew 25:40.]

It was beautiful to see how the memory of that text would spur them on to their work when their little hands were weary, or their feet eager to run and play. Is it not sweet to be helped from the Lord through the children?

In haste I send Christian love,

And am thy sister in Christ, Anna Shipley

From Bella Cooke to her brother,
Jas. Beeton, England
New York
December 1866
I am glad to see that you have got the chapel opened. How I wish I could have been there. We received the placard before the day of the opening services, and at family worship, morning and evening of that day, we prayed to that great God who liveth for His people, that He would indeed give His blessing to the services at Beetonville that day, for the building up of His kingdom; and we sung the same hymns. I felt He was indeed the same God in every clime and place. Glory be to His holy name. We will trust and praise Him, for He is worthy.

I tried by allowing for the differences of time to fix the hour when you, my dear brother, should be laying the cornerstone for the new chapel, and have followed along, waiting for the time when it should be opened for services, and am glad I have been spared to hear the glad news.

I shall never see it, but I in thought often travel through the streets you named for us all in Beetonville. By and by we will, I trust, as a family all meet in that city whose Builder and Maker is God. I am glad you gave the ground and brick for it. You will never be any poorer for having done so.

Your loving sister,
Bella Cooke

To Mrs. A. Shipley
March 30th 1867
My Dear Friend,
Your kind note of the 25th of last month was received. I thought it would be best to write to the children first, and this poor body will only allow me to do just so much.

I believe I have answered all the busy bees who have

written to me. If not, please tell me. Their letters will be prized by me as long as I live, they are so sweet and pretty.

You say in yours that you would like something of my history. It is a checkered one, but all mixed up with mercy and boundless love. Oh, my dear friend, it has been all love that marked out my path, and He, my kind and indulgent Father, hath ever walked by my side, guarding me and saying, "This is the way; walk thou in it." [Isaiah 30:21.]

I am perfectly willing, dear friend, to tell any of my friends anything of my former life, but pardon me if I say that during my life, at least at present, I shrink from having it published to the world with my name attached. Sister Lankford years ago, as did also our late Dr. Bangs and others, desired me to make a note of some of the many deliverances the Lord had wrought out for me.

I am not my own, but the Lord's, soul and body. All are His, and if it is right, and will add one tittle to His glory that these things should be known when I shall have gone home, I have nothing more to say about it. Or if He should show me that it is now my duty to have it done, I know He will guide me aright.

His goodness is still the same, boundless and free. Daily He shows me more and more of His love, and oftentimes so weak that I cannot form a prayer, but I just leave myself resting on His bosom. While His left arm is under me, His right hand is over me, and thus I rest, leaning on His bosom as a babe in its mother's arms. Praise the Lord!

And, do you know, when anything turns up that might harass or distress, I look to Him and my heart goes out. Father, I am Thine; save me! And it seems everything, every sharp edge, is taken off, and I can sweetly rest.

His will is mine, and my soul waits for that will. When sometimes things of a very trying nature are thrust at me, they cannot touch me for the armor of my God.

And, my dear friend, those who visit me and to whom I often tell His goodness, cannot but magnify the Lord, as His loving kindness is so strongly manifested in my case. They praise and adore, and it leads them to greater trust. As regards this poor body, it has gone through much suffering, and the frail bark has often trembled in the storm, so that it seemed as if it would founder, but,

> "My failing flesh His rod
> Shall thankfully adore;
> My heart shall vindicate my God
> For evermore."

I know not how to praise Him. It seems sometimes when I dwell on His goodness as if my breath would stop, that goodness is so great. We cannot conceive what He hath in store for us, if we only trust Him and walk with Him. And now, dear friend, praying that our God may ever be to you as a pillar of fire by night and as a cloud by day, leading you just where He would have you go,

Believe me, ever yours,
Affectionately in Christ,
Bella Cooke

To the Same
New York
December 11th 1867
My Dear Mrs. Shipley,
Your very kind and welcome letter of November 11th came duly to hand. I can hardly think a whole month has rolled round since I received it.

I know full well that very many cares are yours, and all the heads of families who try to discharge their duties aright. Could you sit in my room for a week you would find that I too have many duties. Yes, just as much as this feeble body can attend to

The past year I have given out, in Sunday school and at home, about 3,000 pages of tracts; also bought for Dr. Sabine $125 worth, some from the Book Concern and many of the Ashworth tracts. This, of course, takes some care and thought, as I always wish to give a correct account of all money entrusted to my care.

I cannot tell you, my dear friend, how thankful I am to my Heavenly Father that He puts it into the hearts of some of His dear children to let me be the bearer of some of the glad tidings of a Saviour's love. It is so kind in them, and I do praise Him for it. I do indeed find that the way becomes brighter and brighter. My days seem too short to praise Him as I would, and more and more I feel that,

> "His goodness ever nigh,
> His mercy ever free,
> Shall while I live,
> Shall when I die
> Still follow me."

Yes, for,

> "He calls a worm His friend,
> He calls Himself my God,
> And He will save me to the end
> Through Jesus' blood."

Then shall we who are thus cared for, children of a King, ever travel with soiled garments and a wailing cry? Oh, no, we will come before Him with songs of praise. We will appear before our Father with garments washed white in the blood of the Lamb – white as snow, that Lamb slain for us.

Yes, glory to the Lamb! We will with singing to Zion return, for we have a goodly heritage, and we are well able to go up and possess it, for,

> "Courage, your Captain cries,
> Who all your toils foreknew –
> Toils ye shall have, yet all despise;
> I have overcome for you."

But I did not intend to tire you with so much about myself, but pardon me, my pen has run on, for my heart is glad, and had I a thousand tongues I would try and sound my great Redeemer's praise; but, by and by, this stammering tongue will be released, and then,

> "In a nobler, sweeter strain
> I'll sing His power to save."

Give much love to Annie and Susie. Tell them I often pray and think of them, desiring they may be all the Lord's.

Yours truly in Jesus,

Bella Cooke

Chapter 15

Goodness and Mercy

Pure religion and undefiled, before God and the Father, is this: to visit the fatherless and widows in their affliction, and to keep himself unspotted from the world (James 1:27).

Ask God to give thee skill
In comfort's art,
That thou mayest consecrated be
And set apart
Unto a life of sympathy;
For heavy is the weight of ill
In every heart,
And comforters are needed much
Of Christ-like touch.

January 1868

Glory, honor and all praise be given unto Thee, O Lord of Hosts, that through another year Thou hast spared me. Here we are, the living, to praise Thee. Goodness and mercy, yea goodness and mercy, are written upon all our pathway.

Jehovah Jireh, He has provided, and will; for His promises are all yea and amen to them that believe – not maybe – but, blessed be God, are now yea and amen. And we will praise Him with the whole heart.

Many loved ones have been to see me. My returning wants have been supplied, and my Father assures me they shall be, not only this world's need, but He feeds my soul with marrow and fatness. He giveth me songs in the night season, and maketh all my bed, and causeth me to rejoice in His name. Here will I raise my Ebenezer! For hitherto the Lord hath helped me.

February 1868

Glory be to Thee, my Father, that in Thy goodness Thou hast condescended to use my dear children to bring sinners to Jesus. My dear Joseph sends me word that fifty souls have found peace, thirty of them being heads of families, and have raised their family altars.

Praise the Lord! Oh for more souls. We ask not for wealth, or even freedom from pain, but to be useful in Thy vineyard – stars for our crowns. Have just been trying to help a poor old lady, seventy-five years old, a widow whose son followed the sea and was drowned a year ago. For twenty-six years he was a sailor. His daughter lives with her grandmother and earns only fifty cents per day.

The old lady has no use of her hand, having broken her wrist by a fall. Have written a note to Miss Busteed to get some help from the ladies Seaman's Society for her, also a note to Mrs. Clarkson. Mrs. Hunting sent me in some provisions for them. Yes, dear children, while I have breath I will pray for the prosperity of Zion. They say, "Pray on, dear ma; we see the answers to your prayers. You could hardly do more than you are doing if you were up here."

Lord, I thank Thee for this. Thou hast said prayer shall not return void. May my children have mighty faith.

Brethren Mackey and Russell were here today full of zeal in their Master's cause. Brother Irwin is still with my son at Seymour, and souls are coming to Christ. My Lord, I thank Thee that notwithstanding the severity of the winter, Thou has supplied all my returning wants. Thou art my "Jehovah Jireh." [Genesis 22:14.]

All my springs are in Thee. Thou art the life of my delight. The glory of my brightest day and comfort of my nights. Yes, when no eye can see and no ear can hear, Thou givest songs in the night. Thou art my Husband, Brother and Friend, my King and my God.

March 5th 1868

I am thankful for the mercies of another week. Dear Dr. Sabine was here. His visits always do me good – he is so spiritual. We had a good talk about his conversion, his missions, etc., etc. His heart warms on the subject. He is all alive to saving souls – its great importance.

Money seems to be no object with him, so that good is done. He gave me five dollars to give to poor Brother Russell, a dear child of God, an old sailor, who lent five dollars to a fallen brother, and the Dr. thinks he will never get it. On leaving he turned back to say, "Don't tell him I gave it."

Had a visit from Mrs. Onatavia and Miss Elliott. They are members of Dr. Tyng's church, and are true women of God – all alive to spread the truths of the gospel.

Again I must say the Lord has dealt bountifully with me, by enabling me to do something for the poor old woman with the lame wrist, although it is not out of my own pocket. I felt so deeply touched with her case in having lost her son who was all her support.

On Monday I sent Miss Elliott to see her, and she gave her one dollar and fifty cents, and laid the case before a friend of hers, who sent five dollars.

On Tuesday I sent Brother W. L., and he left her three dollars and sent her a ton of coal. In answer to my note to Mrs. Clarkson, I received a ticket for one dollar's worth of food per month. The poor woman is an American and a humble follower of Jesus. Although it is the way of tribulation, Thou wilt bring Thy people through, and wilt not leave them in their distresses.

March 20th 1868

Brother McCreagh was here, and brought a bed quilt belonging to a poor girl in Guildford, Ct., who has lain on her bed for five years with a spinal complaint. She pieces them together and her mother quilts them, and he thought that perhaps I could get more for it here than they could. I will try.

Praise the Lord, I have sold poor Emily's quilt for eighteen dollars, value ten, but I told the circumstances and said I wanted eighteen.

April 10th 1868
Received an answer from Mrs. Jaffray with regard to a note requesting some help for poor old Mrs. Cleveland and E. Kelsey. She will send me five dollars per month for each, for one year. Noble woman, great is thy reward! How these poor hearts will rejoice. What a help it will be for them.

Must try and get Eliza Cleveland something to do to earn her bread. Heavenly Father, direct us. Thou hast said, "Not a sparrow falleth to the ground without Thy notice," and that "the very hairs of our head are all numbered," and we believe it. [Matthew 10:29-30.]

April 14th 1868
Have just parted with my dear Mary and Joseph. They have returned to Seymour, Ct. Am glad of that, as they will be best to nourish the young converts, and may they be more abundantly useful.

April 16th 1868
My dear, good Dr. Sabine was here, and I told him I wanted him to give me two dollars per month for E. K., and he gave me six months in advance.

Praise the Lord! So she will now have seven dollars per month, which will be a great help to her, and I have an order for two more bed quilts at eighteen dollars each. My soul rejoices in the Lord. I feel that He is watering it with the dews of heaven.

Oh, He is so good to me, and I am so unworthy; yet He does not expect strength where it is not given. He knoweth my frame, and remembereth I am dust, therefore He pitieth His feeble child.

May 3rd 1868

Not of works, lest any man should boast, [Ephesians 2:9] yet faith without works is dead. [James 2:17.]

Wrote to Mrs. W. E. Dodge in behalf of E. C. to use her influence to secure her a place of work in the Bible House, and sent Eliza to her pastor for a note, which Mrs. Dodge will indorse.

May 4th 1868

Have a place for E. to work. Praise the Lord! Thou hast a care for Thy children. I will be able to give the old lady four dollars per week until her granddaughter begins to earn something, then I trust to be able to give her two dollars per week, besides the five per month from Mrs. Jaffray for the summer.

May 13th 1868

Have had a letter from Mrs. A. Shipley giving an account of the funeral of our dear departed Miss Alice Whitall. She has gone to reign with her Lord. The last time she was here she brought me some flowers and arranged them on my bedside. Took out two roses, and putting one in my cap and one in my gown, said, "Now, don't thee ever say thou hast not worn flowers."

But they faded, and she is gone to where flowers never fade. Gone to meet her risen Lord where sickness will never pale her face. Gone to the harp and the crown and the welcome, "Well done; inasmuch as ye have done it unto one of the least of these, ye have done it unto Me; enter into the joy of thy Lord." [Matthew 25:40.]

May 21st 1868
Had a call from Mr. H. Lawrence, brother-in-law to Miss Whitall, to tell me something of her last days, and give me twenty-five dollars on account of one hundred she left for me.

Who would have thought when with her soft and quiet step she went forth from my room that her goodbye was the last, and that she would be the first to get home? He doeth all things well. Praise the Lord.

June 9th 1868
Have been much comforted during the past week by the visits of Friends who have been holding their yearly meeting, and many of their prayers of faith and love have gone up from this little room. Sometimes as many as ten or twelve have met here at once, and the Friend, the Most High, met with us, and I was led to exclaim, "It is good to be here!" [Matthew 17:4.]

Bless the Lord that names, sects and parties fall when our blessed Lord reigns in the heart. Thus the prayer of Christ is fulfilled, "That they may be one; as Thou, Father, art in Me and I in Thee, that they may be one in Us." [John 17:21.]

I feel more and more the need of spreading His praise abroad, and this is my greatest comfort – to urge sinners to come to Jesus. I almost wish for a thousand tongues to tell of His wondrous love to me – poor, weak, unprofitable me.

But this is my place, in my little corner, on my bed, and I praise Thee, O my Saviour, that in this little upper room, even here, I know and feel Thee as my companion and friend! Nor would I change for any other place, for by night and by day Thou dost comfort and cheer me, and Thou dost let me lay my weary head on Thy breast, and feel that Thou makest all my bed in my sickness and will never leave me. Yes,

> "Both my arms are clasped around Thee,
> And my head is on Thy breast,
> And my weary soul has found Thee
> Such a perfect, perfect rest;
> Dearest Saviour,
> Now I know that I am blessed."

July 6th 1868

Yesterday, Brother Stephenson brought an Italian brother to see me, who has been converted from Romanism, and he is now studying for the ministry to return to Italy and preach Jesus. He seems to be quite in earnest for a life fully devoted to God.

Many, very many of my dear friends have left the city for the country, but I am left behind – but Jesus goes not from me, but is ever present near my bed and in my heart. I do not feel as I once did when dear ones leave me – no sadness comes over me now. He guides every step of the way, and though it may be up the steep mountainside, He is ever saying, "Fear not, I am thy strength."

This excessive hot weather wilts me down, but even such a little thing as this is noticed by Him who fills the heavens and earth. His words, "Be of good cheer," have often comforted me.

July 15th 1868

Many have gone to the Manheim camp meeting, whither the armies of the Lord are gone up to fight against Satan's kingdom.

> "The praying spirit breathe,
> The watching power impart,
> From all entanglements beneath,
> Call off their peaceful heart."

The enemy has been trying to disturb my peace. How true it is, "Ye are not of the world; if ye were of the world, it would love its own." [John 15:19.] But, glory to the Lamb, He brings us off victorious.

> "No cross, no suffering I decline,
> Only let my whole soul be Thine."

"Give unto him that asketh of thee, and from him that would borrow of thee turn not thou away." [Matthew 5:42.]

Today that text was most powerfully impressed on my mind when one of the Lord's poor children came in, and sitting down began to weep.

"What is the matter?" I said.

She replied, "Oh, tell me no more of rich Christians. I have been to three people this morning to borrow a little money, and they say they don't lend to anyone. I don't want to beg, but I have no money, and my board must be paid. I cannot get work, and what am I to do?"

"Give unto him that asketh thee," etc., rung in my ears. "What do you want to do, and how much do you want?"

"Well," she replied, "I can get books to sell, but I have no money to take me out of the city, or to get anything to eat."

I had ten dollars to see me through the month, and I gave her five.

She wept aloud, "I cannot take it; you cannot spare it. Your daughter is sick, and not able to work. I know you cannot spare it."

"Take it," I said. "I know I shall get along, and don't say

a word against rich Christians. You don't know what they have to try them. 'Judge not, that thou be not judged.'" [Matthew 7:1.]

"Well," she said, "I do not know when I can pay you, perhaps never."

"Very well, I will leave that with my Heavenly Father."

Lord, help us to do all Thy will here, that we may reign with Thee in glory.

July 27th 1868

Jehovah Jireh! Today W. L came in and said, "I have just got a note from Mrs. W. who is in the country. She has sent you five dollars to buy ice cream and fruit this dreadful hot weather." Praise the Lord! "Give unto him that asketh of thee," etc. [Matthew 5:42.] Yes, He knoweth those that trust in Him.

August 2nd 1868

Had a generous gift from a noble brother who is laying up treasure in Heaven. Thus all my returning wants are supplied. He will not suffer us to be tried above what we are able to bear. Glory to the Lamb!

October 7th 1868

Have been very feeble the past two months. My dear Doctor Sabine was astonished after an absence of a few weeks to find me so low, and remarked that I appeared nearly home, that he feared to put in a new issue. He thought I could not bear it, but I begged he would try, and if that does not give me some relief I cannot be long kept from my home in heaven.

No one can ever realize what this poor, frail body suffers, nor can they know how my Father cares for me. Yes, His loving kindness is ever toward me. "His left hand is

under my head, and His right hand doth embrace me."
[Song of Solomon 2:6.]

When reading, "Cast thy burden on the Lord," [Psalm 55:22] I found by the reference it means in the original, "*roll*" thy burden, and so when too feeble to lift and *cast* it, I can *roll* it along at the feet of my beloved Master.

This is my wedding day. Twenty-eight years ago I was married to my dear husband to walk life's pathway together, but he has outstripped me and left me behind. Then the Lord told me that my Maker was my Husband, and truly He hath proved Himself so. For nineteen years He hath kept me sweetly leaning upon Him. As He hath been Husband, Father, King and God to me, I will praise Him.

My dear children have been to Greenwood, the beautiful city of the dead, to visit the resting place of their dear father and little sister. They tell me it is a beautiful spot. Brother Mackey, who gave me the new tomb, also has it kept in order. How indulgent is my Heavenly Father. It is not enough that He should care for my returning wants in life, but permits me to know where this poor piece of clay shall rest until the last trump shall sound.

Brother and Sister Mackey, with my dear children, took tea with me, and the Master was with us and blessed us.

October 16th 1868

My dear children, Joseph and Mary, have gone back to their home. Lord, make them useful in Thy vineyard. Let Thy work revive and precious souls be saved. Give them a single eye to work for Thee.

> "Jesus, all the day long,
> Is my joy and my song."

Praise, my soul, adore and wonder! Ask, Oh why such love to Thee?

November 6th 1868
Am expecting daily to hear of my precious sister's departure. When last she wrote, she told me how much she enjoyed, when here last June, the yearly meeting time. When the Friends visited me, she was in the little room and could hear them pour out their souls at the mercy seat. She said, "It was good to be there, my dear, for they were live prayers and did me good."

It grieves me to hear of so many poor people who are suffering as the cold weather creeps along, and how comfortable my Father in heaven has made me, and so unworthy. How often the hymns of my childhood come before me.

> "Not more than others I deserve,
> Yet God hath given me more,
> For I have bread while others starve
> And beg from door to door."

Like my sister, who writes, "I feel that much of my time has run to waste, and I am perhaps near my home," I have lived too much for self, while there is so much to be done for the Master that I feel it would be just to say to me, "Slothful servant." But I know the sinner's plea: "Mercy!" I take this in my hand and go pleading. It suits my case, for if the Lord should be strict to mark iniquity, who should stand?

November 23rd 1868
My dear sister has passed the trial; the operation has not succeeded to save her. The tumor is so attached that the doctors say they have no hope for her. While they were

getting ready, she took her pen and wrote this to me,
> "Darling Sister, Fear not, only believe the Lord
> reigns; He keeps me in peace; I will not fear;
> blessed be His holy name. The Lord bless you,
> dear little one. Lizzie"

I thank Thee, my Father, that she could, through grace, triumph in view of what she was to undergo. Thy word is true, Thou dost give Thy children grace for every time of need. [Hebrews 4:16.]

Lord, bless her this night, and give her sweet rest through believing, and if it be possible, make her short journey easy by her head leaning on Thy bosom, hearing Thee say, "Be not afraid, it is I."

I being the youngest and smallest, I was generally called little sister or little Bella, and my darling sister in her last effort on earth addressed me by the family pet name.

November 25th 1868
Thanksgiving Day
Last night I felt that my sister was very low. Lord, bless and comfort her, and whisper, "Peace, be still."

November 26th 1868
Annie is home, and my poor sister still lives. They thought she was about to depart on Wednesday night, when I felt she was so near death, but rallied again. "Take life or friends away, but let me find them all again in that eternal day." I leave all with Thee. Thou art loving and kind, and doest all things well.

December 2nd 1868
Yes, precious saint, thy days are ended – all thy mourning days below. Thou hast gone to sit at thy Saviour's feet, to

sing the melodies of heaven clothed in white, and to see Him face to face.

My dearest sister slept in Jesus this morning at five o'clock. Her last words were, "Perfect peace in Jesus." Another gem in my Saviour's crown, another soul in heaven. Yes, from a world of grief and sin, with God forever.

Lord, calm this heaving breast. Thou who didst weep at the grave of Lazarus, Thy friend, wilt not chide these tears when Thou has taken this loved one from us. [John 11:35.] Thou didst comfort the sisters; comfort me. I was not able to go and see the last of that dear one. Abide with me, I am Thine; Thou art my present help in this my time of need.

When the telegram came, I felt what it was, and lifted up my heart to God to sustain me, and He did. He is always true to His word. Lord, strengthen and support her dear husband and son to bear this trial, and sanctify it to the good of their souls, that her faith and patience and almost blameless life may speak to them, that they may meet her at Thy right hand in glory!

She entered into eternal life on the birthday of our mother and sister Hannah. They have hailed her ere this out of a large family, and soon we will gather up our feet and die, and meet our father's God.

My afflicted brother writes, "The monster (tumor) that killed our precious Lizzie I buried in the garden. It was a solid mass, almost like a ham, only more round, no fluid in or about it, and weighed thirty pounds. The seven doctors who attended her, and those at the postmortem examination, never saw its equal." But she is safely beyond its sufferings.

December 25th 1868
Yes, well may I say, "Glory to God in the highest, and on earth peace and good will toward men." [Luke 2:14.] To

think He left the Father's throne and came down to dwell with men. Yes, precious Jesus, we will praise Thee. Thou art all love to Thy children, and may see fit to try our faith, yet we will not fear. Jehovah Jireh!

Some of my dear friends have already brought their kind love offerings: Mrs. Haxton and Miss Naylor some beautiful fruit and flowers, and Mrs. Tatum her annual gift. Yes, the Lord is good, and hath said that water and bread He will give for food, also such things as He sees good, and He indulges me with these delicacies.

Chapter 16

Grace, Mercy and Peace

In the multitude of my thoughts within me, Thy comforts
delight my soul (Psalm 94:19).

> I long to praise Thee more, and yet
> This is no care to me;
> If Thou shalt fill my mouth with songs,
> Then I will sing to Thee,
> And if my silence praise Thee best,
> Then silent I will be.

Yea, Thy comforts delight my soul; they are new every
evening and fresh every morning. Oh, for David's harp or
David's gift of song! Day unto day uttereth speech, and night
unto night showeth knowledge of His majesty and
gentleness, His mighty works and the benignity of His
providences. [Psalm 19:2.] But,

> "If my silence praise Thee best,
> Then silent I will be."

January 2nd 1869
I wrote to Mrs. Jaffray to see if she could help a poor woman
with her rent, and today received an answer, saying she "will
give three dollars per month;" so poor Mary Morrell will be
relieved, praise the Lord!

January 9th 1869
Jehovah Jireh! Yes, the Lord will provide. Faith is being
severely tried. Long standing sources of help are being cut

off; but courage, my soul, on God rely. Deliverance soon will come. All is in His hand, and He will help. He will uphold with the right hand of His power

I will trust Him. My heart goes out with the prophet, "Although the fig tree shall not blossom neither shall fruit be in the vine, the olive shall yield no oil, no herds in the stall, yet I will rejoice in the Lord and joy in the God of my salvation." [Habakkuk 3:17.]

He has cared for me all these years, and will He leave me now? Goodness and mercy shall be my song, and have been allotted me all my days, and trials will only make the crown the brighter. So I say, trusting, "As God will, and in His hottest fire hold still." Praise the Lord!

January 24th 1869
Brother Stephenson was here and sung that good old hymn, "Away my unbelieving fears." I told him I had no fears, but the next verse was my experience, "Although the vine its fruits deny." He said, "Yes," and he felt the last verse was very good, and so it is. I feel every word:

> "In hope believing against hope,
> Jesus, my Lord, my God, I claim."

How sweet to trust Him at all times and in all circumstances. He does all things well. Purge and cleanse me, precious Saviour, if need be; only stand by me. I have heard of the death of my brother's wife in England. She died, as all the rest have done, in the faith and with a hope full of immortality, clinging to the Rock of Ages.

February 6th 1869
All my springs are in Thee. Yes, dear Lord, temporal as well as spiritual.

Thou hast seen fit to try my faith a little, but all is well. Thou knowest my heart, and Thou knowest, though Thou slay me, yet will I trust in Thee. Many sources had seemed to be cut off – friends who had for years sent in their Christmas offerings had failed to do so, and Satan would fain have had me think I was forgotten. But it only made me the more firm, and Habakkuk's faith answered me when I looked upon the empty stall or fruitless vine. I *will* joy in the God of my salvation.

The other day Mr. Lawrence called from Philadelphia, and said Mrs. Whitall had desired him to call and leave me seventy-five dollars, the balance of the one hundred dollars Miss A. W. had left me when she went to her better home. He said Mrs. Whitall thought perhaps I needed it.

Oh, what a condescending Lord! They had said if I needed it any time to send and I should receive it, but the answer always was, "Stand still and see the salvation of God." [Exodus 14:13.] And here it is all explained. Yes, we will trust Him and not fear.

February 10th 1869

The Lord is showing me that He cares for me. My true and long-tried friend, Brother Stephenson, brought me a noble gift. Thus, when He has tried my faith, He honors and will withhold no good thing from us if we walk uprightly. If we walk in the light, we have fellowship one with another, and the blood of Jesus cleanseth us from all sin. [1 John 1:7.]

February 14th 1869

My dear Annie has been very sick, and is still so. Well, the Lord knows best what to do. He does all things well. Therefore, I will praise Him.

Mrs. Haxton and Mrs. E. D. Smith are very kind, doing all they can for us. Mrs. Haxton went to Annie's employer and told him she was ill. He said she should not lose her salary. Mrs. Haxton said if he could not let her have it, she would. He answered it was against the rules, but she should have it. He hath promised, and must perform. Glory be to His holy name. I had no idea of such a thing, nor had I any anxiety about the matter, for He will provide.

May 12th 1869

"I will instruct thee, I will lead thee in the way thou shalt go." [Psalm 32:8.] Blessed promise. How kindly does our Heavenly Father encourage His children to come unto Him. How truly this has been verified to me the past week.

On Sabbath, Brother Stephenson brought Brother Pearsall to see me. "Why," said he, "I thought you had got home long ago." I said, "The Master has left me yet." I had not seen him in some years.

May 16th 1869

Twenty-two years this day since I set my feet on these shores, in this city, and what hath not the Lord brought me through? Goodness and mercy have been my portion − a pathway of love and mercy in green pastures and beside living waters. Oh, "Bless the Lord, O my soul, and forget not all His benefits." [Psalm 103:2.]

Here I am, a monument of grace − abounding grace. How many have been taken from the household band since then: father, mother, husband, children and sisters. These all died in the Lord. Even my little child of seventeen months, with beaming eye, said, as her last words: "See there, my papa, my papa!"

One sister said, "I shall be satisfied when I awake in His likeness." Thus star by star declines till all have passed away. And here I am, the most feeble of the flock and almost the last of the family left.

"God moves in a mysterious way His wonders to perform." He hath kept and brought up my fatherless children, and not one of His promises to me have failed. Yes, with my whole heart will I praise Him.

May 17th 1869

Twenty-two years today since I first met with the church in Twenty-Seventh Street. Precious day. Friends' yearly meeting has been held since I last wrote. Many have been to see me, and our mingled petitions have gone up to the mercy seat.

How preciously the Saviour breathed upon us, and said, "Receive ye the Holy Ghost," [John 20:22], and our hearts were filled to overflowing, while we had to exclaim, "It is good to be here!" He is ever saying, "What is it I shall do for thee?" Ask and receive, that your joy may be full. Yes, we realize it here, a fullness of joy. "Sin, earth and hell I now defy, I lean upon my Saviour's breast."

I have been expecting to hear that my dear Hannah has gone to be forever with the Lord. She has lain for some days on the brink, but the Lord in His infinite mercy has spared her a little longer to us, her husband and children. To His name be all the glory. He will not lay upon us any more than He will give us strength to bear.

How can I fear? Let the storm beat ever so roughly, He is there. His kingly hand is stretched forth and with majestic voice He speaks, "Peace, be still."

June 17th 1869

The Lord has given my dear Joseph and Mary another darling child to nurse for Him. May they, while rejoicing over this their third baby, be more in earnest than ever to live near to God, and thus be enabled to train those precious souls for His glory.

August 3rd 1869

Have had a busy and somewhat anxious time the past two weeks. On the 28th my dear Annie, my youngest, was given in marriage to William H. Hillier, a young man I think every way worthy of her. To say it is no trial would be wrong. It is a great trial, but I have a strong support.

My God is able and does support me in a wonderful manner, and in Him is my trust. But for twenty-eight years I have always had one child to whom to give the goodnight and good morning kiss, and have had the cheery voices around the room; but now all are gone, and I am left alone.

No, not alone, for better than daughters or sons, He has proved Himself to me for the last twenty years. He told me He would be my Husband, Brother, Friend, when He said to that dying saint, "Leave thy fatherless children, I will preserve them alive; let the widow trust in Me." [Jeremiah 49:11.]

Was it an idle tale? No, no, it was said by a faithful God who makes no mistakes, one who never mocks His children, and now I look to Him, and in His embrace I rest.

We had a very pleasant time. A few choice friends met before going to church. Brother Seaman and wife, and Henry and Grace Dickinson, who had just arrived from England, and many others. Brother Stephenson chose the beautiful hymn, "Love divine, all love excelling."

I could say but little. My thoughts went afar off to the marriage supper of the Lamb, as I looked on all my dear children and prayed that as I had them here, I might be able to present them faultless before my Lord, and with him who is gone before stand and say, "Here we are, Lord, and the children Thou hast given us."

He has promised the blessing to our children's children and to all who are afar off, even to as many as the Lord our God shall call. [Acts 2:39.] And well do I remember the prayer offered by the venerable servant of God, my father, for these little ones when he said, "Yes, for the generations to come."

Today I praise my God for such parents. I make not my boast of wealthy parents, as the world calls rich, but of parents passed into the skies.

After the hymn was sung, Brother Stephenson led in prayer, and such a prayer is seldom heard. He went back to the time when as strangers we came to our new home, and brought us all along up to the present time, and I had to exclaim, "Here I will raise my Ebenezer, for hitherto the Lord hath helped us." [1 Samuel 7:12.] The room was filled with the power of God. Jesus was as surely here, as at the marriage feast of Cana. [John 2:1-12.]

After this, they all went to the church, the same to which I went with my dear husband twenty-two years ago when we were strangers in a strange land. My dear Joseph married them, and Brother Stephenson gave her away to another to love and cherish. God grant they may be happy!

All will soon leave me, but the Master of the feast will stay, for He hath said, "I will never leave thee nor forsake thee." [Hebrews 13:5.]

In eight months I have had in my family two births, three deaths, and one marriage. Amen.

Chapter 17

The Shadow of His Wings

Yea, in the shadow of His wings will I make my refuge until these calamities be overpast (Psalm 57:1).

> I do not ask that God shall always make
> My pathway light:
> I only pray that He will hold my hand
> Throughout the night:
> I do not hope to have the thorns removed
> That pierce my feet;
> I only ask to find His blessed arms
> My safe retreat.

January 20th 1870

Goodness and mercy, dear Lord, have followed me all my days, and still are manifested towards me.

The past month has been one of severe suffering, such as I never felt, and never thought could be felt and borne by human being. But in the midst of the hottest fire my Lord was at my right hand, saying, "Fear not, I am with thee; I will be with thee to the end." Praise the Lord, there are no ifs or buts; it is all "*I will!*"

Oh, how the soul rests on this "*I will!*" As I told Dr. Sabine, I had not power *to cling*, all I could do was to rest on this "*I will!*" I could only lie and rest on the everlasting arms which are placed underneath me and round about me. Yes, for His left hand is under my head, while His right hand doth embrace me. [Song of Solomon 2:6.]

Glory be to His holy name; I will trust and not be afraid. When Dr. Sabine came, whom I at last sent for at the earnest desire of Dr. Palmer and others, he felt very badly that I had not sent before. He said he must bring a surgeon and have help. An operation must be performed, and I must take ether or I would surely die. Yet he knew not how I would stand the ether, but they must try.

I said he must do just as he thought best.

On the 31st of December they came. When I saw the instruments and the bottle of ether my soul was kept in peace, and the borderlands were calm and still and solemn as the silent shades. Not a ripple of a wave passed over my peaceful soul, but these beautiful lines were fixed on my mind:

> "Faith lends its realizing light,
> The clouds disperse, the shadows flee;
> The invisible appears in sight,
> And God is seen by mortal eye."

Yea, God is seen by mortal eye – seen in my kind friends ever standing ready to do all that may be done, among whom was dear Mrs. De Lamater, who came every day for nearly two weeks, Miss Elliott who tried to prepare something tempting for me to eat, and many other tried friends.

God is, too, seen in my kind physicians who for years have been ready, by night and day, to give me ease. But above all is He seen in the gift of His Son to die for us in our human form, that He might know what sore temptations mean, what hunger, thirst and fatigue are – that He might sympathize with us and be a more glorious Saviour. Yes, God is seen by mortal eyes. Thanks be unto God for His unspeakable gift.

On Monday, when my good Dr. Sabine came, he was

overjoyed to see me so comfortable, and said, "Your work is not yet done, dear Mrs. Cooke. It is very wonderful how the Lord leaves you with us, and through how much He brings you. It is all of Him.

Now, you must try and eat a little – whatever you like. I know you cannot eat turkey or I would have brought you one. Here is five dollars to get anything you please, which will strengthen the poor body."

Beloved man, thy reward will be great. He has been a friend to me nearly fourteen years. All I can do is to pray for my friends. Would that I could show them what I feel, but my God knows all about it. He has told me that He is not unmindful to forget their labor of love to His little ones.

February 14th 1870

Have had to send for Dr. Sabine again, as Dr. Palmer is worried about me. I have so much suffering and weakness. I have had to use a strong lotion for my issues, which have become very troublesome, the discharge being black and offensive – never so before, although I have had them for twelve years. Dr. Palmer is grieved about it, as he fears the worst results, and Dr. Sabine agrees with him that it all goes to prove the system is very low indeed and in a dreadful state.

Well, the great Master Builder knows best when to take down the tabernacle and set the spirit free, and will in His own time do that which will be for His own glory. They have ordered stimulants, beef tea and eggs. I object to the wine and brandy, but they say it must be taken.

And here I must record some of the Lord's care over me. Dear Mrs. Barney sent me the wine, not having heard that it was ordered, and Mrs. Jaffray fresh eggs. So I am well supplied, and never before from the same friends. So the Lord, through His children, has supplied my increased wants. I am so unworthy. Pause, my soul! Adore and wonder!

Such love in friends of every denomination. Praise the Lord! It is sweet to trust Him. And while He gives me the privilege of doing a little for others of His dear children, He does not suffer me to lack. I have been much impressed with this of late.

On the 6th of the month I had a letter from my sister Evans, saying she had heard from England of an old friend, one with whom we had lived as neighbor when girls, and were at Sabbath school and church together. She has lost the use of her arm from cancer in the breast.

Her husband is dead, and all she had to live upon was half a crown a week. And here I am surrounded with every comfort and such kind friends. The good voice said, "Send Sarah a sovereign."

At first I was a little surprised. Not that I feared to want, but I feel the money is not exactly mine to give away, unless I can so far curtail my expenses that I can save it. Having given a good deal away this winter, for I have many poor coming to me, it seemed a good deal. This was Saturday.

I thought and prayed much over it, and thought of the passage, "Whoso seeth his brother have need and shutteth up his bowels of compassion against him, how dwelleth the love of God in him?" [1 John 3:17.] So the first thing on Monday morning I wrote and sent my seven dollars to poor Sarah, and I was very happy. "There is that scattereth and yet increaseth." [Proverbs 11:24.]

That afternoon Brother Wesley Lyon, a police officer, called to see me and brought with him a gentleman, Mr. G., a Presbyterian who gave me a book of hymns he had aided to compile. We had a pleasant and profitable time in speaking of the love of God in our hearts.

After prayer, Mr. G said, while at prayer, he was

impressed to leave me something, and left a five dollar bill, for which I was thankful, but not a thought of having sent Sarah's.

Next day my friend Murray Shipley called, and after talking awhile said, "Bella, does thee remember a young lady coming with me to see thee in the fall?"

I said, "Yes."

He said, "Well, she desired me to leave thee this." – A five dollar bill.

Still I did not think of the seven dollars until evening. When recounting the mercies of the day, and thanking my Lord for His goodness, the thought flashed through my mind, "You have got your money back." Yes, there it was, three dollars interest for twenty-four hours. How true, "There is that scattereth and yet increaseth." [Proverbs 11:24.]

Bless the Lord! Here He had sent by two, neither of whom I had seen but once, nor had I said a word to either of them of my circumstances.

> "Is thy course of comfort wasting?
> Rise and share it with another;
> And through all the years of famine
> It shall serve thee and thy brother.
> Love divine shall fill thy storehouse
> Or thy handful still renew,
> Scanty fare for one will often
> Make a joyful feast for two."

This I have often proved when dividing my bit with some poor widow; and He is still the same. When Mr. Shipley was going, he said, "Bella, I have come to labor a week or two in New York and Brooklyn, and thought it best to come in here first, that we might ask the blessing of our

Heavenly Father on my labors."

He knelt and poured out his soul to God, as only those used to talking to the King of kings can do, after which we agreed to meet for the coming two weeks at 7 a.m. in prayer for the outpouring of the Holy Spirit, and I felt we will not be disappointed.

17th February 1870

Bless the Lord, "while they are yet calling, I will answer." [Isaiah 65:24.] Today Mrs. Tatum brought a Friend to see me – Benjamin Franklin. After talking a little while, I said I was expecting to hear from Murray Shipley of his success, as I felt there must be some souls converted.

Mrs. Tatum replied, "Perhaps Benjamin can tell thee something about it. He is laboring with Murray."

I was a little surprised, as I had no knowledge of it, nor did I know that he knew Mr. Shipley. But with a beaming face and happy voice he told me how the arm of the Lord had been made bare in the happy conversion of souls while they had labored together.

Glory to God! Who can doubt He hears and answers prayer? We will buckle on the armor afresh, and go to the pulling down of the strongholds of Satan.

February 1870

On last Sabbath, Brother Stephenson brought with him Brother S., and we had a glorious time. The power of the Lord was here. The Saviour did breathe upon us and we were blessed. On Monday, Brother John Pullman and another called, both men of God, and full of love and zeal. Bless the Lord for Christian friends.

February, Tuesday

It was fifteen years since I was in my classroom, that day

Sister Mary Cannon called to see how I was. I said I was going to class. I was bent on that, if it was the last time. And so it proved. She was here this Tuesday evening, and I bade her go and tell them how long it was since I met with them bodily, but that the way grows brighter and brighter, and more glorious appears the mansion prepared for me, and whom my soul loveth – He who is ever near me by night and by day, and careth for me even as a tender mother. "As one whom his mother comforteth, so will I comfort you." [Isaiah 66:13.]

Yesterday many dear friends were in, among them Mrs. B. Haxton. What a happy and pleasant time together. Also Mr. Massey and wife, who brought three new converts and one seeker. They sung and prayed, and God heard us. He is a man of mighty faith and deep love; just the one to lead sinners to Christ.

26th February 1870

Yesterday had Brothers Murray and Samuel Shipley, also Miss Cromwell. We had a most blessed time. It did seem as if the opening heavens around shone with beams of sacred bliss, for Jesus did whisper to our hearts that we are His. They had seen His power displayed in the conversion of many precious souls while laboring the past two weeks. We will exalt the name of the Lord, for Thou art worthy.

Never did I feel more power than I have done the past two weeks, while from seven to eight each morning I met at the mercy seat with God's servant. I had no doubt but he was there at his post, for it seemed as if a multitude of angels were hovering around to join in our petitions to praise Thee our God. Oh, prayer, sweet prayer, it takes us into the pavilion of the Eternal. We soar on eagle's wings. Labor, anointed by prayer, is rest.

This poor, frail body is not good for much. Many times a

day the faint and prostrate spells come on, and my kind physicians urge stimulants. While I must take a little, I cannot use all they think I should. I do not wish to have my mind and brain inflamed or benumbed with opiates, so that when I pray or write I may be clear and ready when the Bridegroom shall call for me, without a spot or wrinkle, with my white robe, my wedding garment. Lord, help me in all my weakness to show forth Thy praise and glory.

Had my dear old friend to see me, Mrs. Dickinson, to tell me of the work done through the labors of Mr. Shipley and herself. It was sweet to listen and, "Now," said she, "will thee join me in prayer before I go in behalf of a precious soul I am going to visit. She cannot take hold of Christ."

We talked with our Father, who has promised that what we ask in the name of Jesus it shall be done. I feel our precious sister shall see the arm of the Lord made bare in the full surrender of this dear one into the Saviour's kingdom.

Had a visit from Mrs. De Lamater and Miss McCauley, two precious souls who cling to me as to a mother. Dear Jesus, give me all the grace needed to set an example worthy of imitation, wisdom and power to lead these precious souls aright.

February 28th 1870

Had a visit from Mrs. Barney and her sister, who brought me some fruit and a bottle of wine; how kind and mindful. What am I that Thou art mindful of me, and that they should sit by my bed and say they derive strength from coming to see me?

Received a letter from Mrs. W. E. Dodge, with a bill enclosed, lamenting that she had been so long unable to come and see me. This is a friendship of nineteen years in sympathy with a helpless one. As long as I could work, she gave me her fine sewing, and when I was laid aside she did not forsake me. Oh, how good the Lord is!

Oh, that I had a trumpet voice on all the world to call and tell of His goodness and loving kindness. Also had a basket of fresh eggs from Mrs. Jaffray. My soul is lost in wonder, love and praise to the Giver of every good and perfect gift. He is so indulgent and knows what I need before I ask Him. He sends by whom He pleases.

March 2nd 1870

Had a visit from Sister Lankford, and Mrs. E. D. Smith, who, I fear, will visit me but a few times more. She seems to be nearing her heavenly home very fast. Her earthly house appears rapidly failing, but she is a ripe shock of corn ready to be gathered into the garner. But, oh, she will be missed; how I will miss her. What a friend she has been to me, no one but my Father in heaven can know.

Sister Lankford brought me ten dollars. It came through Mrs. Wright from Miss Drake, for my poor. Oh, how good Thou art to thus indulge me by letting me do a little for Thee, and influence Thy children who have means to give me some for those they cannot reach. How sweet to watch the ways of the Lord toward His children.

He has told us we shall be abundantly satisfied with the fatness of His house, and that He will make us drink of the river of His pleasures. Yes, well may the children of men put their trust under the shadow of His wings. How excellent is Thy loving-kindness.

Dear, precious Mrs. Haxton was here also, with letters to read to me from her sister, my friend Mrs. Gale, who has been two years in Europe. It is pleasant to be remembered.

April 20th 1870

Have just had the two Misses Smith with me, who have been

to the steamer to bid adieu to their dear mother who has left for Europe in search of health, which I fear it is vain for her to do. She sent me a beautiful bunch of flowers by the young ladies and many expressions of love.

My friend Mrs. Farr is gone with her, and they expect to be gone two years and more. Thus they go, while I stay in my little corner all ready to hear my Master's call, "Come up higher."

I am suffering so much that another operation seems inevitable, and whether it will relieve me I cannot know, but it must be done. If it takes me home or prolongs my life it is all right. On Christ the solid Rock I stand.

With the sainted [Samuel] Rutherford I feel, "How sad a prisoner I would be, if I knew not that my Lord Jesus had the keys of the prison door Himself, and that His death and blood have brought a blessing to crosses as well as to ourselves.

I am sure that troubles have no prevailing right over us if they be but the Lord's sergeants to keep us in ward while we are on this side of heaven. I am persuaded also that they go not over the boundary line nor enter heaven with us, for they find no welcome there, where there is no more death, neither terrors or crying, neither any more pain, therefore we shall leave them behind us."

Yes, He can open and none can shut, and therefore we leave all with Him for time and eternity.

May 4th 1870
My Dear Sister Annesley,
I want to send a few fragments from memory's portfolio, which come to me when dwelling upon my Heavenly Father's providential care over me and mine, when, in 1850, I, with my dear little children, began to keep house again. Many thoughts revolved in my mind; not so much how we

should get bread, but how I might glorify God; how to get to His house and tell the wondrous story of His fatherly care and love.

I resolved, by grace assisting me, that as He and I had covenanted to walk together (for He told me many times to put my right hand in His, and He would gently lead me), if He would preserve my fatherless children that whether my days were many or few, they should all be devoted to Him.

So I determined that nothing should hinder me going to class meeting, that is, no work or company or anything but absolute sickness. Every Tuesday evening I used to take my little ones to spend one half hour at twilight in giving them Bible lessons, or singing with them their Sunday school songs. Then committing them to God in prayer, I put them to bed, locked my door, and ran up to class meeting.

Oh, the strength I then obtained, and I never felt an anxious thought about them, but to no other place did I ever go and leave them at night save to God's house. I had the promise all would go well, and I believed.

One night in January 1851, I went, as usual. Coming home, as I opened the door I found a strong smell of fire. Immediately I got a light. My babies were all asleep, but the fire-board, which was covered with canvas and paper had fallen against the stove. Half of it had burned to a char, and had fallen down and gone out. I stood and looked at it in amazement. I went to the person on the same floor, and asked if she had been in my room.

She said "No, how could she, when I had the key?"

I said, "Come here,."

She looked, and was surprised, and said, "Mrs. Cooke, how could that ever go out?"

I said, "Mrs. Murray, none ever trusted and was confounded. My Master told me He would take care of my little ones, and not a hair of their heads should be injured."

I awoke Hannah and asked her if she knew anything of it. She said, "No, mamma, we went right to sleep when you went out."

Mrs. Murray said, "Will you go again?"

I answered, "Certainly I will. Surely I can trust Him when He has shown such care. The angel of the Lord encampeth round about them that fear Him." [Psalm 34:7.]

Lovingly yours,

Bella Cooke

June 1st 1870

What shall I say? Still spared, still permitted to speak a few words for Jesus. Left to labor and wait. But what a month the past has been! Such suffering and weakness I never remember having passed through.

On the 5th of May, my dear Dr. Sabine came with his son, with the instruments and ether to perform the much-dreaded operation, as Dr. Palmer said he feared if not done soon, it would not be possible for me to rally.

It was all done with great care and skill, when I was laid carefully on the bed, not to be moved at all. I felt perfectly calm, listening to the voice of the Comforter.

I became very faint and found the wound was bleeding. Dr. Sabine came and found me just alive. He took every pillow from my head and fed me with brandy.

Dear Mrs. De Lamater stayed with me, as did also her husband and father till midnight, and left me with Mrs. Hunting and nurse, not expecting to find me alive when they would come in the morning.

As Mr. De Lamater feared I would die before morning, he went to the doctor to ask if anything could be done. He replied, "*Nothing*. He would not be surprised to hear of my passing away any hour."

Friends were exceedingly kind in offering their services

and whatever they thought I might need. The doctor said I must see no one but the two nurses.

In seven days a change took place, and then my dear doctor was perfectly delighted, but would not allow me to be moved in the least. I could not move hand or foot, and many times during those seven days my children, sister and nurses watched me, as they thought, for the last time.

Dear Mrs. De Lamater hardly ever left my side, as also Mrs. Haxton. Why such love to me? Oh, how good the Lord is to me. Truly, goodness and mercy have followed me. I will take the cup of salvation and call upon the name of the Lord. [Psalm 116:13.]

For three weeks I ate nothing; took a little champagne, etc., or a white grape. When my dear Dr. Sabine found me with a better pulse on the seventh day he was perfectly delighted, and said, "Dear Mrs. Cooke, you have hard work to get these poor feet over Jordan, but oh how sweet will that rest be when you do get there!"

I said, "Yes, but you do all you can to keep me here."

"Indeed we will. I don't want you to go before me."

For three weeks I was not able to take any solid food. Then my good Dr. Sabine bought some pigeons, had them cooked and brought me some, and said I must try and eat a little bit. Oh, how kind, how indulgent! What am I, that so many should stand waiting to do something for my comfort?

Willow Brook, Irvington
June 4th 1870
My Dear Mrs. Cooke,
I was very glad to receive your letter of May 28th, but I am sorry to think that you have fatigued yourself in writing to me. You must, I know, be exceedingly weak, and indeed I think your being alive is little short of a miracle.

I must not trouble you, my suffering friend. You have

enough to bear, and it is wonderful to see how you are supported and kept in perfect peace. You see, you preach by your life, and such preaching accomplishes more good than many sermons falling from the lips of God's ministers.

When we of "little faith" see you calm and resigned under all your trials, we reflect that He who does this for you is able also to keep us if we will only trust in Him. He has seen fit to pour out upon me and mine every *temporal* good and great prosperity, and now I want you to ask Him, as I do, to give me *spiritual* blessings in proportion. "Oh, that *my children* might live before Him!"

I wish I could give you one peep of this lovely place this morning, with its flowering shrubs, its sparkling fountains, its graceful willow trees, and let you hear the sweet rural noises, the singing of the birds. One dear little birdie has built a nest upon our piazza, and although we all sit there, the little creature never is frightened away.

Then the beds of geraniums and roses of many varieties are such lovely objects; and beyond all rolls the beautiful Hudson, dotted with pretty white sails. In England the sails are tanned, which spoils their beauty.

Do not be tired of my long letter, dear, good friend. I love to write to you, because I know I have your sympathy. Remember that if you need anything, I am sent to give it to you. I am the fortunate channel through which the gifts are to flow.

With love to your daughters,

I am yours lovingly,

Anna F. Jaffray

June 9th 1870

A week ago today my dear Annie had a lovely daughter. Both are doing well. Lord, give to both parents wisdom and grace to train the little lamb for Thee. Little did I think when her dear father was taken away that I would live to see her a mother. She will shortly leave my neighborhood to live in New Jersey. This is a changing world, but One there is who never leaves us. I feel His promise true.

I am poorly, weak and prostrate, but have a sure resting place. As my doctor said the other day, "It will be a glorious change." Yet, if the Master has anything for me to do, gladly will I linger out my three score and ten, and that twice told, if He abide with me. Blessed be His holy name, He doeth all things well.

June 29th 1870
Mrs. Onatavia, with her three little ones and their governess, Miss Elliott, were here just to say goodbye, as they sail for Europe today. Thus one after another goes away. Yet I am not alone. The Master stays with me all the time. Each of the little ones gave me a five dollar bill with a kiss. How lovely to train these little ones to care for the poor in such a quiet way.

> "Lord, whom winds and seas obey,
> Guide them through the watery way;
> In the hollow of Thy hand
> Hide and bring them safe to land."

I continue feeble, but the Lord is my strength, and I can only feel conscious that I lie in His arms and let Him hold me. All is well, praise the Lord!

August 10th 1870
Had a letter from my precious friends, Smith and Gale, from Lucerne. How kind in them to write to me amid so much hurry and bustle. They seem ever anxious for my welfare and comfort. Who of us can describe or explain the

communion of kindred spirits confined in the body, yet separated by space?

Is there an invisible chain of gold or pearl that binds together hearts that love? A kind of spiritual telegraph that vibrates from one to another when thrilled by the touch of joy, or pressed by the hand of pain and sorrow? Or is it by the ministration of angels, those pure and good beings whom Scripture assures us attend those who shall be heirs of salvation?

Is it when we feel a shade of sadness pass over the spirit without knowing why, the shadow of the angel's wing who has just left the house of mourning or the bed of pain? And when the precious tears of sympathy are shed for another's woe, are they not by these gentle messengers taken and poured upon the wounded, broken heart like a precious balm?

Some very sweet and comforting thoughts were suggested the other day by that passage, "Thinkest thou not that I could now pray to my Father and He would send me twelve legions of angels?" [Matthew 26:53.]

One thought impressed me, that they are sent in answer to prayer. Not that we would pray to them, for that would suppose them to be omnipotent and omniscient, but to our Father whose court in the upper skies is thronged with those holy beings waiting to do His pleasure to His saints in their time of need and danger – or to soothe the sufferings of a poor, sick Lazarus, or finally to catch the freed spirit and bear it away to Abraham's bosom.

Our precious Saviour! He says He will come and receive us to Himself, and will He not bring those happy spirits with Him, or will He present us to them? In any case, it is enough to know, if faithful, we shall be with Him and like Him, for He desires that we behold His glory.

These thoughts seemed to come as I lay thinking of the

sweet communion with my dear friends across the mighty deep, and shall I say with the angel spirit of my darling friend? But I must stop – my poor brain! – Lord, I am Thine. Save me.

Chapter 18

Friends Flitting Away

He giveth His beloved sleep (Psalm 127:2).

> Death is the kiss of God.
> Yes, thou mayst weep, for Jesus shed
> Such tears as those thou sheddest now;
> When for the living or the dead,
> Sorrow lay heavy on His brow.
>
> Jesus Himself will comfort thee,
> In His own time, in His own way;
> And haply more than two or three
> Unite in prayer for thee today.

August 27th 1870

The first time I could trust myself to write of my darling little friend, who one month ago today left us for the mansion prepared for her from the foundation of the world.

What I suffered from the shock no tongue can tell, and every visit from any member of the family since would almost deprive me of reason for two or three days after.

I never had anything affect my nervous system so before. Dear child, how little she thought when she came in the Friday night before, and I chided her for coming, fearing it might tire her too much, that it would be the last time I should see her.

Mary De Lamater said, "I must have another goodnight kiss."

So often after church service she would run in and say, "I will sleep better if I get a kiss. Pa says I ought not to come so late, it makes you too tired. But you are not too tired to see me, are you, Mamma Cooke?" But her race is run, she has gained the victory.

At seven p.m. her husband sent me a note saying, "Our dear Mary was safely delivered of a fine girl at 5.40; both doing well."

At nine, Miss McCauley came to say for me to go to sleep, as Mrs. De Lamater and babe were doing finely. I slept a little while, but then sleep was over, and I lay thinking of the dear one and her benevolent plans for the coming winter, and how I would enjoy her visits again. When lo, at 3 a.m. the Bridegroom came and took her as His ready bride adorned for her Lord. Gone to her beautiful home – our darling is gone before.

"Go to shine before the throne,
Deck the Mediator's crown,
Go His triumphs to adorn;
Made for God, to God return."

At five in the morning I felt so anxious I sent Isabel to see how she was. In a little while she returned with the message, "They are both dead."

I felt a pain inexpressibly severe dart through my whole system, and knew nothing for some time. When I came to myself, I remembered the words of the Psalmist, "I was dumb, I opened not my mouth, because Thou didst it." [Psalm 39:9.]

I felt indeed, "It was the Lord, let Him do what seemeth Him good." [1 Samuel 3:18.] What a blow to her dear parents and husband, and her poor sister who is in a critical state. She does not know it yet.

I sometimes think my head will never be right again. God only knows what I suffer with it, but I am in His hands, still His, in all the afflictions of time. And He has promised I shall reign with Him in glory, that I may behold His brightness. No toil, no grief, no pain can reach my happy home.

September 29th 1870
Have had a very interesting season. Three of my dear grandchildren were dedicated to God in baptism: two of Hannah's, and Annie's little one, Harry B., Frank B. and Annie E. My dear Joseph officiated, and we had a happy time. The Lord is in this little upper room, and here we hold sweet converse with Him.

> "We bring them, Lord, in thankful hands,
> And yield them up to Thee,
> Joyful that we ourselves are Thine;
> Thine lot our offspring be."

October 3rd 1870
I have my maid Fanny back with me. I trust it is of the Lord. How mysterious are His ways; they are past finding out. I thought when I sent for Isabel I was guided by Him, but it has proved a failure. We were much in prayer about it, and so must leave it; but I am glad to get this dear child to be with me again.

I need someone kind and who will not be out at night if even the work is done. She is more like one of my own than a stranger. Oh, how I miss the gentle touch and kind words of my own dear girls, but it is all right. They are in their corner and I am in mine.

October 8th 1870
Today my precious friend Mrs. D. Smith was here. She is very feeble, and I fear I will never see her again in this world. Death seems to be depicted in all her looks and ways.

Her toilsome journey to Europe has done her no good, but friends are satisfied by the trial.

When writing to me a few days ago, she said, "My peace of mind and perfect contentment show me that my Saviour is very near, and His love very precious. If we do not meet again, dear, I know we will meet above."

But she could not rest and must see me once more, and made this great effort, from which I hope she will not suffer. How can I give her up? How can she be spared? Yet our God makes no mistakes, and if He sees best to take her, I trust we will be enabled meekly to bear the loss.

October 14th 1870
Dear Miss Elliott was here again, and brought me six very pretty nightgowns which Mrs. Onatavia brought me from Paris. They were the first to escape from the blockaded city. Three of the seven families are returned. Praise Him for all His goodness.

A Scrap from a Journal
[Writer unidentified]

November 1870
I called on Tuesday to see dear Sister Cooke. She is as cheerful and happy as ever, living her pilgrim days of suffering in close industry for others. Now she has the fair for the Old Ladies' Home on hand, and she showed me some of her beautiful things ready to send. She has made about sixty dollars with her own hands. Marvelous! And the elegant sewing, too. There she has stitched; stitched on her bed until all were finished, and she satisfied herself in doing the best she could.

Besides this, she collected from friends enough with her own work to make a sum of one hundred and thirty dollars for this institution. The expenses of her own work were paid out of her personal self denial. "The secret of the Lord is with them that fear Him." [Psalm 25:14.]

I thought of those words after I left Sister Cooke yesterday. She had related to me so many things she had not spoken of to her own children, and one thing she said: they did not know her extreme necessity after her husband began to meet his severe losses. As often is the case in trouble, one calamity succeeds another. At length she was obliged to leave her pretty, comfortable English home for a venture in a foreign land.

Her husband was too confiding in his integrity, and fell into the hands of the crafty and designing men who swindled him out of one of his lead mines, and out of shares in others, which would have yielded him an abundant competence for his family and the time of old age.

In thinking over all the discipline of Mrs. Cooke's life, with her delicate health and early widowhood in a strange land, and then an effort of a few years to support her children, and in the end become a confirmed invalid for life, one might regard her as one deserted of Providence. But a fuller knowledge shows that she is a chosen vessel to display the grace and power of God to sustain in holy cheerfulness the human soul. She is, indeed, an illustration of the promises of God in the path of obedience.

A page from a journal of Miss M. Annesley which will preface a letter from Mrs. Cooke under the severe bereavements of this year:

December 1870
Dear Sister Cooke feels the loss of her young friend Mrs. De Lamater, and I do not wonder at it. There is a void no one else can fill, for she grew into womanhood under her parents' friendship for Mrs. Cooke, and was as a child to her.

When a special message was to be taken, or something a daughter only could perform, she was ready with her cheerful, loving heart to ease or help in every way their invalid friend. She was feet and hands in time of need.

The shock of her death was terrible, and in Mrs. Cooke's nervous, feeble state we think she was remarkably sustained. She wept and felt her loss, and Jesus wept. He also was comforted by the sympathy of the disciples, and said, "These are they that have been with me in my temptations." [Luke 22;28.]

And now she is anticipating daily the death of her bosom friend and counselor, Mrs. Doremus Smith, who for fourteen years has been the confiding companion of her heart, aiding her in the settlement of her three daughters, matters of great concern to an invalid mother.

She would come in and sit close to the bed, and take her hand and draw out the little questionings about comforts and cares, and listen to everything in which human counsel and control was needed. And thus the little burdens of that household and family were shared by one who knew the pain of sore trials and care of children.

As long as Mrs. D. Smith was able to write notes, she expressed her loving interest in her dear friend, and the other day she wrote, "Do the ends meet?" to which Mrs. Cooke was to send a verbal message. It came by Mrs. Smith's daughter, "Yes, tell ma the ends meet."

That was comforting to the dear friend who was about to enter the heavenly home first, who had pledged herself to be mindful of her trust, Mrs. Cooke's daughters, when it had often been expected that Mrs. Cooke was within immediate reach of the blissful mansion. But God's ways are not as our ways, and the sufferer of years outlives the sufferer of months.

I took up an elegant leather needle-book, partly made,

and said, "What is this for?"

Mrs. Cooke replied, "Oh, that is for the fair at the Old Ladies' Home, and I must get a hundred dollars for the old ladies this year. I think I will, if my Heavenly Father pleases."

492 Second Avenue
December 21st 1870
Dear Sister Annesley,
Jesus has called my precious friend home. He came for her yesterday morning about one o'clock. Precious saint, it is just three weeks since the physicians said nothing more could be done for her. The day before, she wrote me a little note and said, "Do not feel badly, darling. He who loves us both will not leave you. Try to think of me as free from all sin and pain, at rest with my Saviour."

Last Sabbath, when her sister was writing me a little note, she sent her love, and said Jesus was very near to her. She was worn and tired. "Ask Jesus to come and take me home, I am so tired."

What a loss to many, to me a severe one. The past three weeks, I must say, have been full of anxiety. Not that I rebelled, that is not it, dear, for I feel and know my Father doeth all things well. This is surely among the *all things*, and though full of mystery to mortals, it is well. But these two, of all others, were very dear to me.

Mrs. De Lamater was as a dear, tender, loving, affectionate daughter, and Mrs. Smith a bosom companion. A strong, very strong, love bound us together, and it was anguish to rend it. But it is for a little while. It will soon be reunited again, never to be disturbed.

When the word came that my darling was gone, it seemed as if my brain would burst, but on looking up my eyes met the text, "He giveth power to the faint, and to them that have no might he increaseth strength." [Isaiah 40:29] And so my heart, all trembling and bleeding, went up to Him that He would shelter me from the storm and hide me under His pavilion.

The past week has been a solemn time, a marriage company waiting till the bride was fully equipped for her Lord. It seemed as if I could almost hear the Saviour and His attendants approaching to claim His bride.

How sweet the thought: friends may wait, angels beckon, but it is Jesus who comes to take us home. He did not say I will send for you, but I will come again and take you to Myself, that where I am there ye may be also. [John 14:3.]

How strange it looks to mortals as we look back upon the past months over my apparent nearness to the grave. How many times has Mrs. Smith kissed me, as we thought, a final farewell, and would whisper in my ear, "Do not have one anxious thought, darling, for your dear girls. As long as I live they shall be cared for."

Dear Mrs. De Lamater said last spring, when Annie was about to remove, "Don't worry about it, dear Mrs. Cooke. When I get up again I will come every day to see you, and do all I can for you. You know I am your oldest child." But the Master has called them, and left me a little longer to be a care to His dear children.

Dear Mrs. Haxton was in yesterday, and her sister, Mrs. Gale, today, to sympathize with me. How wonderful are Thy ways, O Lord; they are past finding out. Mrs. G. hardly expected to come home this fall, but circumstances called her back, and here she is, and asks to be allowed to take, as far as possible, our friend Mrs. Smith's place: that is, to confide about my little plans, etc., and help me in my little cares.

Oh, what love, what tender sympathy, dear Miss A. I do

not know how to praise Him for all His wondrous works to me. I feel so unworthy such love. But it is all of the Lord, and we will praise Him.

Mrs. G. says she knows no one can ever fill their place to me. No, I do not think they can, but they can fill their own place. We do not want them to root out the love we have for those who are only gone home a little while before. When a child dies, we may have others, but they do not fill the spot that one held in our bosoms. And so no one has been to me the past fourteen years what Mrs. Smith was.

Our minds and hearts seemed blended in one. No one can fill her place. Do not think I wish her back. No, no, I would not bring her to suffer again on this earth; but the human feels its woe, such woe as caused our precious Saviour to weep. The heart trembles with its mortal anguish. But we will try to overcome, and not only sing in the tempest and storm but also in the darkness of night.

And yet again has the angel of death been with us. Brother Wm. Byer, one of our church officials with whom I have been close the past twenty-three years, has gone home. He was all ready, with his lamp trimmed and burning, waiting the Master's call. He was ready for church last Sabbath, but not feeling well, stayed at home. On Monday was worse, and today went home. Thus three of our most prominent members left us in five months.

Lovingly yours,
Bella Cooke

492 Second Avenue
January 12th 1871
My Dear Sister Annesley,
I have been wanting some little time to write to you, but I have been very poorly, suffering keenly. Well, the holidays are over, and my dear Mary, with her little family, are gone

home again. Much as I love them, it is more than my feeble nerves can bear.

Dear child, what a comfort she is to me, beloved by all, and zealous and anxious in the Master's work. Her husband says all the people love her. It seemed when she came to me nearly twenty-eight years ago, that sorrow and trouble came with her. Up to that time, April 1843, our married life had been very prosperous and bright. The only cloud had been the parting with my sisters, who came to New York.

I now, in the commencement of another year, renew my vows to Him who hath done so great things for us. Did I tell you about the beautiful crown I had from the funeral of my darling friend? Before she passed away, she said, "I want you to send the handsomest piece of flowers, after my funeral, to Mrs. Cooke. If a crown, place it at the head of my coffin, and send it as soon as my poor body is laid away. Tell her Jesus was with me all the way through."

Precious soul, she now wears a crown, incorruptible, undefiled, and that fadeth not away. [1 Peter 5:4.] She is with her risen Lord and sees Him as He is. The crown came; it is full of beautiful flowers, and a small cross on the top, fit emblem of the Christian life, for how small the crosses and trials of this life compared with the glory that awaits the finally faithful. Then let us ever keep the blessed end in view.

How very kind my friends have been since her death, for they knew how we loved each other and what a trial it was to part with her. I know and feel He cannot err, and I look to the better land where I soon will be, if faithful, for,

"Whate'er my God ordains is right,
Here will I take my stand –
Though sorrow, need, or death make earth
For me a desert land;

My Father's care is round me there,
He holds me that I shall not fall,
And so to Him I leave it all."

I had a visit from her sister, Miss Lottie Doremus, who told me all about the sickness and death of our precious one. They tried to plan some way to have me taken down to see her, but found it impossible, as the dear one said it would kill me, and it will not be long before we meet, and then I can tell her all.

Come and see me, dear, as soon as you can. My Shepherd has been very kind, indeed, to me these holidays. He has sent by many of His dear ones to supply my need. He gives me very much more than water and bread; He feeds me with the dainties of the land, and I will praise Him while He lends me breath.

Do you know I am surprised at the tender love of some of the Lord's children? They seem to forget that I am a poor, dependent creature, in circumstances so far different from theirs. They love me so tenderly, and get for me everything they can find out that I need. Oh, how much have I to praise God for; "Not more than others I deserve, yet God hath given me more." The Lord bless you, dear.

Yours, lovingly,
Bella Cooke

"Shut in!" did you say, my sisters?
Oh, no! Only led away
Out of the dust and turmoil –
The burden and heat of the day –
Into the cool, green pastures,
By the waters calm and still,
Where I may lie down in quiet,
And yield to my Father's will.

Earth's ministering ones come round me
With faces kind and sweet,
And we sit and learn together
At the loving Saviour's feet;
And we talk of life's holy duties,
Of the crosses that lie in the way,
And they must go out and do them,
While I lie still and pray.

I am not shut in, my sisters.
For the four walls fade away,
And my soul goes out in gladness,
To bask in the glorious day.
This wasting, suffering body,
With its weight of weary pain,
Can never dim my vision,
My spirit cannot restrain.

I wait the rapturous ending –
Or, rather, the entering in
Through the gates that stand wide open.
But admit no pain or sin.
I am only waiting, sisters,
Till the Father calls, "Come home!"
Waiting with my lamp all burning,
Till the blessed Bridegroom come.

RIFTED CLOUDS

PART 2

Chapter 19

Abridged Introduction to Part 2

Words of Friends

A good name is rather to be chosen than great riches, and loving favor rather than silver and gold (Proverbs 22:1).

By her Pastor, W. W. Clark, D.D.
[A short excerpt from the original Introduction. The full Introduction is at the end of the book, page 489]

Sister Cooke's cheerful disposition has ever made her a great attraction to childhood, and none are more welcome to her little room than the children of her friends. To them she is always "at home."

I remember when I first became her pastor she was very anxious to see "the Parsonage boys," as she called my little sons. But they hesitated to accept the invitation, for they thought that a lady who had been so many years confined to her bed must be very gloomy and sad. But after their first visit, the difficulty was to keep them away.

It was always a great treat to them to get permission to see "dear Auntie Cooke."

Chapter 20

With Wings as Eagles

They that wait upon the Lord shall renew their strength; they shall mount up with wings as eagles: they shall run and not be weary, and they shall walk and not faint (Isaiah 40:31).

Be still, and know that I am God (Psalm 46:10).

God doth not need
Either man's work or His own gifts: who best
Bear His mild yoke, they serve Him best. His state
Is kingly. Thousands at His bidding speed,
And post o'er land and ocean without rest:
They also serve who only stand and wait.

Often have I sighed for wings – not the wings for which the Psalmist prayed when "the voice of the enemy and the oppression of the wicked" discouraged him and he longed to "fly away and be at rest," [Psalm 55:6] – but wings to bear me on the errands of my Lord and King. Wings as eagles, that I might carry the savor of His grace to the homes of sadness and the abodes of sin. But "stand still,' was the divine command to Moses, "and see the salvation of the Lord." [Exodus 14:13.]

January 28th 1871
Last evening I had a visit from Murray Shipley, a beloved disciple. Oh, the depth of the love of God in Christ to His

children, even while we were yet sinners. We had a sweet time conversing together.

Brother Shipley feels this love, and while ministering to others is indeed watered himself. It delights me to hear him speak of the work given him to do, and the many he is enabled to gather into the fold.

I felt it to be a very melting time, the glory of the Lord overshadowed us, and we drank largely of the river, the streams whereof make glad the city of our God. [Psalm 46:4.]

Jesus was here, our guest. He came to sup with us, and glad did it make our feast. One little thing connected with this visit goes to show that our Father does grant us the desire of our hearts. When Murray Shipley rose to say goodnight, I took his hand, and from the fullness of my heart said, *"The Lord bless you, Brother Shipley, and make you a blessing to many."*

He replied, "Bella Cooke, I was asking our Father as I sat here, that thou mightest give me thy blessing."

I could only look at the wonderful condescension of our Father in granting his request, as it is a very unusual thing for me to express myself so to gentlemen friends, though not to ladies.

Am poorly, those faint and sinking turns continue. I go to the Great Physician and He gives grace and patience, and for this will I praise Him. I feel sometimes, would that I could go from door to door to publish the glad news of a risen Saviour, a full and perfect Saviour, a willing Saviour, standing saying, "Son, daughter, what wouldst thou that I should do for thee?" But here in this corner is my place, and here will I wait till He bids me come.

Had a call from Mr. Culver, a Friend, who came some time ago with Brother Ladd to talk of the way, he not then having entered into it. Now he says, "I have come to tell thee

I have found the Saviour able to save me."

"Yes, you find Him a perfect Saviour, not only able, but willing."

"Yes, I do."

Praise the Lord, another soul is snatched from Satan's wiles; another soul born into the kingdom of God.

On Sabbath, Brother and Mrs. Dickinson called to say they had seen Mr. Culver and he was rejoicing in the Lord.

From a Friend's Journal
[Writer unidentified]

January 31st 1871

Spent the afternoon with dear Sister Cooke, and as it was raining we had but few interruptions. Even then she had three calls. A little girl who came on her way from school with a message. She had received from Mrs. Cooke a nice bundle of clothing the day before. A poor woman with a sick irrecoverable husband, she received a nice tumbler of jelly and some flannel, etc., for her husband. Poor woman, she has to sit up at night and sew to make out her necessities; but Mrs. Cooke cheered her, and bid her trust in the Lord and want for nothing, but come and tell her when she needed.

Good Mr. Stephenson came in with some errand of kindness, and read us a letter from Sing Mi, who has arrived in San Francisco to labor there among the Chinese. However they may talk about her "little corner," it is impossible for her to be shut up in it. That bed of hers is a wonderfully busy spot, with its movable desk and drawers, and hiding places for letters and valuables; and from it goes out far and wide blessed influence.

I tell her it is her pulpit, but she does so much more than pray and preach that it must also be called her workshop. I do not wonder that the troubled and distressed like to get sitting down in that quiet, sacred spot, and pour out their sorrows, looking into her sweet, sympathizing face. And for every case she has a balm, and some way to help out of difficulty.

February 18th 1871

Had a letter from Miss Cary, a dear young woman who was on here to attend medical lectures and found her way to our little Rose Hill Church. Learned there was a reality in religion which she knew not, as she had for some time attended unscriptural preaching and was unsatisfied. She felt this was the last call of the Holy Spirit.

Brother De Lamater, after some endeavor to enlighten her, sent her to me, and at her second visit she found Him of whom the prophets did write, "Jesus, who saves His people from their sins." [Matthew 1:21.]

Yes, here in this secluded spot, Jesus spoke peace to that weary soul and bade her live. Only think, while amid tears of joy and gratitude we were praising, the angels in heaven were rejoicing over another soul snatched from the burning.

She went home to her people, and writes to me, "I am hungering. I want to sit by your bedside to have the bread broken and to be fed by it."

Jesus, still stand by her and feed her with the bread of life. Give her to drink of that water that shall spring up unto everlasting life.

Pitiful and Merciful

If the Lord in His mercy sends His rain on the evil and the good, and causeth His sun to shine upon the just and the unjust, shall we, poor, ignorant, erring mortals, set up our judgment and say who is worthy and who is not?

This came forcibly to my mind the past week. A poor woman for whom I had obtained a good deal of help, but who gave way to temptation and wasted her money oftentimes in drink, was careless and untidy. She told me she had no shoes, and her feet were wet when she went out.

I knew not what to do. It seemed too bad to do as she was doing, and yet could I know she had no shoes and not buy her a pair? I had no money on hand to give away and did not see my way clear. I took it to the Lord and told Him that if I received any money that week, I would buy the shoes.

Two or three days after, a letter came from a Friend in Philadelphia with five dollars inclosed with a name that never sent me anything before. Here it was plain, and the shoes were bought. Thus the Lord teaches us by His Spirit, and happy are we if we walk in His teachings. Lord, keep us humble and obedient.

A Letter to Mrs. Jaffray
February 25th 1871
My Dear Mrs. J.,
Since you were here with your friend, I have feared that I did not make myself understood as regards my past experience. I did not wish you to think, dear friend, that I did not want to acknowledge what the Lord had done for me. I know that in April 1848, he enabled me to accept Him as a perfect Saviour, one who did save me from sin, and the first Sabbath after that I had a hard struggle.

How could I rise and tell this experience? It seemed like presumption, but the Saviour whispered, "Also I say unto you, whosoever shall confess me before men, him shall the Son of Man also confess before the angels of God." [Matthew 10:32] And, "He that honoreth Me, him will I honor, but he that is ashamed of Me of him will I be ashamed before My Father and His holy angels." [Luke 9:26.]

I could no longer refrain, but rose and told what great

things the Lord had done for me. I said I had found a perfect Saviour, and that He had wrought a perfect work in His child. The snare was broken, and with a "glad heart and free" I have ever since been enabled to rejoice in the God of my salvation.

I know He saved me with a full salvation. Yes, that I was not of the world, but set apart and consecrated to His service, to live and labor for Him. And since then, I have found either to suffer or labor for Him is sweet. I no longer had to say,

"Oh, how wavering is my mind,
Tossed about by every wind;
Oh, how quickly doth my heart
From the living God depart."

But my song was, "My heart is fixed," and thus was I ever willing to tell the great congregation, or in the little room, how the Lord had compassion upon me and healed me. Nor was I beyond temptation, but I was wonderfully kept, and if at any time I looked to the right or left I was enabled, instead of parleying with the tempter, to look right to Jesus and apply the blood of sprinkling. And thus He cleansed me and washed me from all sin.

Nor did I like to say that I was holy, but I could and did say that I knew that Jesus saved me to the uttermost with His full salvation, and that here was a perfect rest to my long tossed and anxious heart. Yes, I was a new creature in Christ Jesus, and still do I rest in His embrace, calmly leaning my head on His bosom.

Yes, He is my Redeemer from all sin, and I must praise Him. But if through weakness or ignorance I err, He knoweth my frame, He remembereth I am dust, and sweetly bears with His feeble child. Oh, 'tis sweet to trust a faithful

God, and He so honors my simple faith that I cannot, dare not, doubt Him.

I delight to watch Him each day unfold leaf after leaf of His great Book, and teach me of the hidden things of God. For you know, dear friend, I cannot get out to learn or be taught in the house of prayer, so He and I hold sweet communion when all is hushed and still.

Yes, "Sees my soul the King of kings, and freely talks with God," and here I obtain strength to speak a word for Him who has done such great things for me. Pardon me in taking so much of your time, and believe me,

Yours truly, in the bonds of Jesus,

Bella Cooke

Blessings and Trials of Faith

February 27th 1871

Last Sabbath was our annual missionary meeting, and the usual amount was raised, over two thousand dollars. God grant much good may be done with it, and may the people, while they give of their means, not forget to send their prayers with it, that those who are sent may indeed be blessed of the Lord.

Have received a letter from my dear Joseph announcing the gift of a little son, for which we return thanks to our God. He says, "What our baby boy's history may be, is hid from us. We will do with him as with the rest, train him up for God our Father and the Lord Jesus Christ. I would like him to be a minister of the New Testament, a strong man in Israel. He is the Lord's as long as he lives.

"The future is hid from us. What will our boy be twenty years from now? What our girls? What their parents? I have no misgivings but that their future will be good, and in the faith of their dear grandma. Our wish is that they grow up good, kind and pious, helpful, industrious, self-respectful and useful. They are God's children, bearing in them many prayers of believing ancestors."

True, although they boast not of forefathers of high estate, they may of men and women of exemplary piety for some generations past. My prayer is that they grow up in the Church of Christ, not a hoof left behind in the march to Canaan. [Numbers 10:28.]

March 8th 1871
Be still, poor fluttering heart, thy God reigns, and His promises are still the same, yea and amen. Therefore will I trust and not fear. Yesterday Willie brought me his baby, and told me that my precious Annie is very low with smallpox. Poor child, she is unconscious of anything that is passing, and so we must keep the baby.

Well, I trust in Him. She is Thine, do with her as Thou wilt. The word today is, "Very low, but little hope." Some friends fear to come and see me, fearing infection, but will do all in their power.

It is *all right*, all right; not as I will, but as Thou wilt. I know Thou wilt never leave or forsake a helpless worm that trusts in Thee. Hannah's two children are sick and Mary is sick.

"Like Moses' bush, I'll mount the higher,
And flourish unconsumed in fire."

March 10th 1871
Dear Dr. Sabine wants me to be vaccinated, and Mrs. Haxton and Gale are afraid I will take it. Willie sent me word they had a fearful night with Annie, but the Doctor thinks if she can be kept over Sunday or Monday, she may rally.

Father, she is in Thy hands, and if Thou seest fit to take her now from the evil to come, I meekly submit. Do as seemeth Thee good. Joseph writes that he and Mary sympathize with you, and pray the dear baby may not take the loathsome disease, for then would your cup be full indeed.

He has promised that He will lay no more on me than He will give me strength to bear. On His word I depend, and should He make earth to me as a desert, I will trust Him. Do as seemeth Thee good.

March 12th 1871

Poor Willie has been here, and Annie is a little better. Knows them, yet very low.

Had a visit from Bro. Stephenson, who deeply sympathizes with me, also Mr. and Mrs. Dickinson and Mr. and Mrs. Culver. He holds fast in a clear and sound conversion. Lord, keep him very near Thy side. He has many severe trials, but Thou art stronger than the strong man armed. He thinks he will have to give up his profession, but I tell him the Lord can keep him, and we need pious lawyers to set a good example.

Our precious babe was so glad to see her papa. She is so good that she is no trouble. Yes, it is all of the Lord, and we will praise Him. How sweetly He keeps me. Some say, "How can you lie quietly on your bed? How can you have any of the family come?"

I tell them one and all I only move and breathe as my Father directs, and at present He says, "Be still and see the salvation of God." [Exodus 14:13.] To the flesh all this is trying, but He keeps me in perfect peace. He gives me sweet words of comfort,

> "Calm on tumult's wheel I sit,
> 'Midst busy multitudes alone,"

quietly listening to the still small voice.

March 14th 1871
Praise the Lord, darling Annie is, we trust, out of danger.
Poor Willie is overjoyed. Yes, the Lord is good; He knoweth
them that trust Him.

Mrs. Haxton kindly sent a girl who has had the disease
to take baby out, and my faithful Fanny has had it too, and
she is very prudent in taking care of the pet. He seems at
times not far from the kingdom. We have precious seasons
at our family worship.

April 1st 1871
Death has been here and stole away a sister from our side.
This afternoon Mrs. Pugh brought me a handsome cross of
flowers from the funeral of her aunt, Mrs. Beatty, a sister of
Mr. Stephenson. Thus the Master is gleaning His children
into His garner. Her end was very triumphant; her lamp was
trimmed and burning.

> "Thus the Christian life adorning,
> Never need we be afraid,
> Should He come at night or morning,
> Early dawn or evening shade."

Am poorly and worn out with the fatigue of the little
one, and trust it will soon be safe for her to be at home No
one can understand what I suffer but the Refiner, and He
supports me in every trial, and bids me be of good cheer.

April 14th 1871
Have received my dear children, Joseph and Mary, from
New Haven. They are appointed to Sixty-First Street, this
city. Praise the Lord; how kind He is. They can often come
and minister to my wants, and be a great comfort to me.
April 29th 1871

My children have just gone to their new home, and I pray they may be very useful in winning souls to Christ.

April 30th 1871
Had a very interesting season. Our little boy, John Stephenson, was dedicated to God in baptism here at my bedside. I found it a precious time. Many friends were present and my pastor officiated.

Some dear friends sent me a beautiful basket of flowers from Mr. Sabine's church, three mottoes on it: *Praying! Working! Giving!* How kind to remember me as I lie in my little corner.

Last Sabbath the Rev. S. H. Tyng sent me a handsome cross of white flowers from his Sunday school anniversary. He has sent one yearly, not only memoirs, but flowers to beautify my little room. Bless the Lord, O my soul, and forget not all His benefits. [Psalm 103:1.]

May 1st 1871
Oh, how good and indulgent the Lord is to those who call upon Him and trust in His word. Heard poor Mrs. Leverich was likely to lose her four dollars a month, and did not know where to get more. I wrote to Mrs. Jaffray to see if she would allow me to transfer three she was giving me for a person who is now able to do without it. Mrs. Jaffray sent me word to do just as I pleased.

I wrote to Mrs. Haxton and Mrs. Barney. They immediately responded with two dollars each a month; and so with these and one from another I will have eight dollars for her every month, which will be a great help. I will feel easier, for I know she will not be in want.

I am suffering very much with pain and utter prostration. It seems as if I can hardly breathe. Pain in my hands and arms, and can hardly hold my pen. They are much swollen, but it is among the all things, and we will trust in the name of the Lord.

Years of Faith

May 16th 1871

Twenty-four years this day I set my feet on the shore of this city, and in looking back, how fraught with mercies and blessings: some cares, some trials, but out of them all the Lord has brought me safely, and kept us by His power. Therefore we will praise Him.

Have sent *The Life of Bramwell* to Brother Kimber, a member of Dr. Cuyler's church, who is seeking full salvation. Oh, that in reading that little book his eyes may be fully opened to find a perfect Saviour who is able to keep us from falling, and present us blameless before Him.

Had a letter from poor Sarah, who is still in the Cancer Hospital in London. Poor thing, her sufferings must be very severe and nothing of this world's comforts, but her trust is in Jesus, and He has promised to supply all her needs.

I sent her a sovereign and hope it will do her good. Gave it to the Lord as a thank-offering for sparing my dear Annie. I sent her letter to my sister, who also sent her one. "He that seeth his brother in need and shutteth up his bowels of compassion against him, how dwelleth the love of God in him?" [1 John 3:17.]

"There is that scattereth and yet increaseth." [Proverbs 11:24.] How many times I have divided my loaf with some poor widow and still I had enough. Yes, bless the Lord, and it has made my heart to rejoice more than when corn and wine increased, for my Lord supplied all my need, and it was sweet to watch Him as He would open one source after another. No lock was too fast or heart too hard for Him.

Today I stand on the solid Rock, all praise and glory to His holy name. And now I am likely to lose my long-tried friend, Mr. Lankford, who is poorly. One after another are called to lay their burdens down and dwell forever at home. I too will hear the call.

Jesus, the Ever-loving Bosom Friend
June 23rd 1871
A kind sister brought me a wreath of immortelles to place on Mrs. De Lamater's picture. One short year since she was called away, and I must sing of goodness and mercy; but home in the distance looks very sweet.

"The end will come and may tomorrow,
When God has done His work in me,
So I say, trusting as God will,
And trusting to the end, hold still."

My soul rests in God and finds a sure hiding place. I have such a nearness to my Saviour as cannot be expressed. It seems like talking to a familiar friend, as if I had been closeted with him asking questions, advice and guidance, then going forth and carrying out just what he thought best.

I do not doubt some of my friends think my actions strange, but I cannot help it. He said, "Ye are not of the world, even as I am not of the world." [John 17:16.] Yet He did not pray that we should be taken out of the world, but kept from the evil; and being kept from the evil, we are commanded to walk with Him and be perfect. Lord, help us.

June 1871
Another dear friend leaving me for the present. Thus the circle becomes very small, but Jesus has promised to be with me to the end. In much pain and weakness, He is *my all in all*. Satan tries to come in various ways to disturb my peace, but I have the one remedy: "It is written." And oh, how

many things are written to help us to put him to flight!

One grand thing he thinks he will do is trying to get me to worry about such and such a thing, or that such a dear friend will be taken from me; or if any new weakness has come upon me, and medicines fail. What, doubt Him who for all these years has stood by me! No, never! Never! His word is gone forth, and I trust in that word. He never will forsake the helpless worm that hangs on Him.

Living Faith

492 Second Avenue

June 23rd 1871

Dear Sister Annesley,

I was so glad to get your kind note, and at the same time sorry to learn that your dear sister is suffering. But by and by our suffering time will all be o'er, and then we shall reign with our Saviour King.

I have been outstripped by another of my fellow-travelers. Brother Brewer has found the rest we toil to find. He was of gentle spirit and sterling integrity.

I had a new lady physician come to me the other day, Dr. Lozier, accompanied by Dr. Barnett. She sat and talked with me a long time, and finally concluded that about all had been done that human skill could devise, and said I must have the best food I could get, etc., etc. She thought I had two or three tumors in addition to everything else. She does not know how I live.

It matters not if I have fifty. I have an arm on which to lean sufficiently strong to bear all my infirmities, and He will lay no more upon me than He will give me strength to bear. Yes, He who has been,

> "My Saviour in distresses past,
> Will not now His servant leave,
> But bring me through at last."

I had Brother and Sister Lankford to see me on Wednesday. Brother L. is very feeble, but I was so glad to see them. Also my good Dr. Sabine. He would be very unwilling to allow anyone to try experiments upon me. I think if he, who has been coming over fourteen years, and Dr. Palmer over twenty, cannot help me, not speaking of others who have come at times, no stranger can aid me.

The girls are well. Yes, dear, it is a great comfort to have my dear Joseph and Mary so near that they can drop in any time.

Yours lovingly in Jesus,
Bella Cooke

A Birthday Gift

Second Avenue
July 14th 1871
To Mrs. Haxton,
Grace, mercy and peace be unto you from our Lord and Saviour Jesus Christ, my dear, dear friend, and that you may be filled with His Spirit is my constant prayer. Tears of joy, gratitude and love filled my eyes after your little daughter and maid left me yesterday, as I looked upon your beautiful gift of fruit and flowers.

My mind traveled back over the past fifty years from my earliest recollection. Always when at home I had some token of love on the 13th. It was made a happy day, as being the youngest of a large family and not being strong, I was very much petted. When married I was idolized by a fond husband, and the day must be kept. My children usually have some little token for me; but, dear Mrs. Haxton, you are the first and only one save those from whom any gift has come on that day.

Twenty-one of those birthdays I have been alone. Those

fond hearts that would fain have sheltered me from every rude assault or anything to grieve, have lain for all these years in the silent grave. But I ought not to say alone, for He who hath created me hath raised up many of His dear children with hearts full of love and tenderness, and He Himself is with me and hath promised to be with me to the end.

Each renewed assurance of your love, dear friend, seems such a cordial to me it sinks away deep down in my heart. The card on the basket will always be kept. Very many times have I put on my glasses to read it over again. Words never can tell what you are to me.

These flowers, basket and card, I value highly – no price could be put upon them. Oh, may your crown in that great day of the Lord be studded with stars, as full as this basket is of its beautiful and various fruits.

I feel I am one of the least of the Lord's children, but He says, "Inasmuch as ye did it to one of the least of these, ye did it unto Me." [Matthew 25:40.]

Bella and Nellie each had brought me a few flowers their mother had plucked out of their garden. Annie, who had been spending the day with Hannah, brought me some pears as she came along, knowing they would be a treat to me. They were here when your kind gift came, and rejoiced with me.

I have been and am still very poorly. It is a great effort to write, and a greater one to spell, my brain is so weak. I seem as if I can hardly spell my name.

I had a letter from dear Mrs. Gale, and will answer it just as soon as I am able.

I hope the word from mother is favorable and that she improves. May I hope to see you, dear, before you leave the city?

Remember me to dear Mrs. Bodstein. I often think of

her. With very many thanks and much love, believe me, yours truly,

Bella Cooke

Faith Cries It Shall be Done

July 20th 1871

Teach me Thy way, O Lord; lead me in a plain path. [Psalm 27:11.] "I will instruct thee, I will teach thee in the way thou shalt go." [Psalm 32:8.] When we ask from a full heart to be taught, and watch for the Spirit's teaching, we shall see clearly what He would have us do, and I have been specially brought to see this the past few weeks.

A poor old woman, Mrs. Smith, seventy-six years old, for whom I was permitted to get some help last winter, fell and broke her arm and two ribs. She is very poor, but has her two little rooms which is a home to her, and for which Mrs. Jaffray and her church pay the rent. She was taken to Bellevue Hospital. When I heard of her accident I felt sad, and wanted to send someone to see if she needed anything.

I asked in prayer that Mr. Gardner, the person by whom Mrs. Jaffray sends her help to the poor, might come. On the third day he called. I asked him why he had come, seeing he never came but the first of the month. He said he did not know, only he felt the past few days that he must come.

"Well," I replied, "the Master sent you. I want you to go to Bellevue Hospital and see Mrs. Smith."

He was greatly surprised, and had not heard that she was hurt. He went and returned. I told him if he would do what he could, I would do the same, as the old lady was going to her home and must be cared for. He said he would. This was Thursday. I laid the case before Him who says, "Let your request be made known unto the Lord." [Philippians 4:6.]

I asked Him to direct me to whom I should make

application to help her. I did not seem to be directed to take any steps but to be still, and see the salvation of God.

On Friday evening Mrs. Haxton called, and before leaving said, "I have brought you the monthly money for that poor woman, Mrs. Leverich, and here are six dollars I brought you to use as you please. I felt I must bring it. I did not know whether you needed it yourself."

I smiled and said I did not need it, but I had a special case, and told her of Mrs. Smith. She answered, "It is strange. I felt I must bring it, so I am satisfied."

I saw my Father's hand in all this, as it was just what His poor crippled, aged child needed. Yes, we will trust and not fear. He leadeth us by a way that we know not.

July 26th 1871
Three days ago I had a noble gift from an old and tried friend, J. S., and when alone, turning it over and over, tears of joy and gratitude to him and my Heavenly Father filled my eyes. I could not but ask, "How shall I thank Thee and praise Thee, O my Father? Why is it Thou art so mindful of me?"

Then I was led aloud to exclaim, "Give unto him that asketh thee, and from him that would borrow of thee turn not thou away." [Matthew 5:42.] I thought for a moment, "Well, I will heed Thee."

Today I received a letter from England, saying that poor Sarah Partridge had been sent from the hospital and was just alive, from cancer which was eating away her life. No money and no home. A poor working woman, acting the part of the good Samaritan, opened her door for her, and is doing all she can to case the poor body.

The case was plain. "Give unto him that asketh thee, and turn not away." [Matthew 5:42.] Nor did I wish to, but heeded the admonition and sent my poor friend, suffering for want of many things, while I have and to spare, one pound ($5.50). May the dear Lord give His blessing to it.

July 27th 1871

A year ago today since my precious friend went to join her risen Lord, and how often it has seemed to me as if the port was just gained when another turn is given to my frail bark, and I am out to sea again. Well, my Father is at the helm; but to the human eye it seems strange so many are taken and I left.

The Hand Has Lost Its Cunning

July 1871

Dear Sister Annesley,

I was glad to get your kind letter, and know you are well.

I am still holding on by faith. As I write this, I can hardly see. Night before last, about eleven, I was seized with a slight stroke of paralysis up my face and neck. It drew my right cheek down to my shoulder, and for some time was very painful.

It has affected my left eye and my mouth, drawing the lips so I can with difficulty take anything out of either a spoon or cup. It also affects my speech a little. But, dear, it does not at present affect my reason, for which I am very thankful.

I feel, dear, as if it may be the far-off noise of the chariot coming for the weary traveler, for soon the Bridegroom will come to meet His bride. I desire to have my garments all pure and clean, without spot or wrinkle.

If it has been necessary for the Master to take so many years to polish the rough stone to prepare it for its place in the temple, it behooves me to be obedient and submissive, that the divine work be not marred. For though He tarry yet,

He will come.

Dear Mary and Joseph, and Annie and Willie, came to see me yesterday and we had tea and worship. Then I had a long talk and told them about publishing my book, how I had prayed over it and been exercised about it, its having been such a trial to have it brought out before the public. But at each time I was brought to the borders of the grave, it stood out before me that I had not done my duty, and each time I promised the Lord if spared I would try.

I have done so, and many, many prayers have gone up with it, and the Lord has helped me wonderfully, and I must send it forth to tell the generations to come what He hath done for me. [*Rifted Clouds Part 1.*]

It has seemed at times while writing as if I was almost lifted up to the third heaven, and then I had to stop and weep with joy at the dealings of my Father, and exclaim, "Glory! Glory to Thee, Thou who art my Husband, Brother, Friend."

(Mary, at Bella's request, finishes the letter.)

Ma was taken so much worse that she was not able to finish, but she is a little easier this morning, and sketched down the last sentence on the slate for me to add to her letter. Her speech was so affected yesterday afternoon that it was with great difficulty we could understand her, and her sufferings were intense.

This morning she seems a little improved, and can say a word or two with great effort. One eye is closed and the other is, we fear, failing too. She has a great deal of pain in it and the sight is very dim. The doctor said yesterday he could tell nothing till today, as he must see how the medicine operated. Ma sends much love.

Yours affectionately,
Mary E. Pullman

"Not Weary in Well Doing"

August 28th 1871

In feebleness extreme would I once more record His loving-kindness, although impossible to make anyone understand what He has done for me. Oh, that I had a trumpet voice, gladly would I employ it to tell of His matchless worth. When not able to speak my heart was saying,

"Above the rest this note shall swell,
My Jesus hath done all things well."

Had a sweet visit from my dear pastor. He is so kind and good, ever ready to do all he can for me. My dear Dr. Palmer also. My friends do not weary over their long care of me. Lord, bless them all. How wonderful that I can again hold a pencil and try to write, which no one twenty days ago ever dreamed I would do again.

September 6th 1871

What a month the past has been, crowned with loving-kindness and tender mercies. Goodness and mercy ever following all I do. I am full of weakness and pain, but I am, as it were, lifted up far above all other earthly things. And while pain and weakness are my lot, my soul "sees the King of kings and freely talks with God."

Though my speech is yet very thick, my sight very dim and feeble, hand trembling as it holds the pen, yet I feel strong in the Lord and in the power of His might. Oh, how glad I am that I can still speak for Jesus, my all-sufficient friend.

Last Sabbath had Communion service here with several dear friends and my dear children, Joseph and Mary. It was a glorious time. The little room was filled with the power of the Most High. Bless the Lord, O my soul, and forget not all His benefits. [Psalm 103:1.]

September 14th 1871

Have been enabled to send Emily Kelsey the last of forty-six dollars for some quilts. Praise the Lord! She writes me in return that she has laid in her coal for the winter and paid for it too, and she rejoiced to have it so.

Oh, what a loving Father we have, ever opening some door whereby His needy children may be provided for, and who enables us to triumph in that which seems in the sight of the world disappointments, feeling as we do that He hides us under the shadow of His hand. There is a close unity between us – Christ and the soul. Surely no evil can befall, while sweetly blessed.

Not yet Beckoned Home

492 Second Avenue,

September 12th 1871

My Dear Miss Annesley,

Five weeks ago I wrote a few lines to you, which, before they were finished, all thought would be my last. But the Lord has sent me back again to mingle with the things of this life, and may He grant that it may add to His glory.

I could not tell you what I have suffered, neither could I tell the holy calm that pervaded my soul as one after another bade me, as they thought, a last farewell. The strong man wept, and many have told me since it seemed a holy place.

I was unable to speak, sight almost gone, almost in an agony of pain a great part of the time. Yet I lay encircled in the arms of my Beloved and was safe. Oh, how I have proved that, "A thousand promises declare His constancy of love." Yes!

'Tis a Rock that cannot move, and on that Rock I stand. We know not, dear sister, why the Master sent me back when so near the rest and home prepared, nor do I wish to seek it out. It is enough He wills me to stay a little longer, and I can truly, with Faber, say,

> "I worship Thee, sweet will of God,
> And all Thy ways adore,
> And every day I live, I seem
> To love Thee more and more."

Friends were very kind; they gave me so much love and tender sympathy. Everybody seems to love me, and I feel so unworthy of it all. Yet I know it is all of the Lord's goodness, and that He influences their hearts to His poor feeble child. The honor and glory are His. Oh wondrous grace! Oh boundless love!

I have much to tell you, dear, but am not able now, as my sight is still very dim. At times I have hard work to get out many words, my tongue still being somewhat stiff. I have begged my kind and faithful Dr. Palmer not to come every day, but he will not leave me more than twenty-four hours. I can only bring him with many others to the mercy seat.

Yours lovingly,
Bella Cooke

September 18th 1871
Kind friends are returning from the country. Some have been in to see me, among whom were Mrs. Onatavia, Mrs. H. V. Butler and Mrs. Dr. Butler. We had a feasting time, and the Master of Assemblies was here and blessed us. Also had a poor crippled soldier in to thank me for getting him a grant to a home for disabled soldiers in Augusta, Me., where he can be well cared for as long as he lives. Poor man, I hope he will there find Jesus, who will give him a better title to a better home when the battle of life is over, if he only gives his heart to Him.

I think things are looking up a little in our Church. Lord, revive us again; make bare Thine arm; wake up every member to diligence; clothe Thy ministering servant with might and power. May he be more than ever in earnest to bring sinners to Christ. Wherever he goes, may they feel that he has been with God. Oh, give us souls; yea, a rich harvest. We feel we must know sinners are brought to God. Time is short and eternity at hand. Lord, help us!

October 9th 1871

Had my beloved pastor and wife, Brother Mackey and wife, and Joseph and Mary to take tea with me, to celebrate the anniversary of my wedding day thirty-one years ago! Twenty-two years of that time my beloved husband has been at rest, praising without any alloy the God whom he loved.

His memory is precious to me still. He was a kind, indulgent husband, and a loving, tender father. There is nothing unpleasant to remember about him, and so I delight to celebrate the day. We had a very pleasant time in singing and prayer. I was very tired.

Had a call from Dr. Barnett, Mrs. Gale, and other friends. How very kind to think of me. Nothing but loving kindness strews my pathway among green pastures and living waters. Praise the Lord!

October 12th 1871

Another year added to this life of confinement. Fifteen long years this day I have lain in this bed, nor have I sat up fifteen hours of that time. How utterly impossible to tell aught of what I have passed through – blistering, burning with nitric acid times out of number; burnings with the red hot iron; cutting with the knife, and many other kinds of treatment to heal or alleviate the sufferings of this poor, feeble body.

Nor has any new remedy been tried, or any new

physician consulted without asking the blessing of the Lord to heal, or give the grace to bear, if He in His wisdom and love saw fit to withhold the healing power. He has indeed given me grace to bear, and rejoice in weakness and pain, so that His word is verified, "My grace is sufficient for thee," for His strength is made perfect in my weakness. [2 Corinthians 12:9.]

Most gladly therefore, will I rather glory in mine infirmities, that the power of Christ may rest upon me. Little did I think when years ago I could walk from eight to ten miles at once, could go six miles to hear a sermon from Billy Dawson, or ride forty miles in a light wagon and walk eight the same day to hear James Caughey, that these poor feet and limbs would lie idle and useless for so many years. Nor did I for years believe what physicians told me, that I would not be able to walk or sit up again.

I would think, perhaps I shall at such and such a time. But I have long since ceased to think anything about it, and only try to do what I can for my Lord, and wait His coming. For while I keep my lamp trimmed and burning, what need have I to fear? He has kept me all these years, and He will not leave me now.

Add to the fifteen, one year in the hospital and five years of severe suffering which caused Dr. Sims and Dr. Jenkins, when they saw me in 1855, to say they knew not how I lived, nor had they seen such a case. Still, by the mercy of God I am spared, and my almost daily prayer is,

"Lord, give me patience to abide
The unknown workings of Thy will."

I praise Him, that I can speak a word for Him, recommend my Saviour to all who may come. I praise Him for my reason. I praise Him for my sight, dim as it is; for my hearing, and the use of my hands. Yes, and for all His unbounded goodness and mercy to me all the days of my life. Yes,

> "I'll praise my maker while I've breath,
> And when my voice is lost in death
> Praise shall employ my nobler powers.
> My days of praise shall ne'er be passed
> While life or thought or being last,
> Or immortality endures."

October 20th 1871

Bless the Lord, He does give us the desire of our hearts. Last Sabbath a good sister came and told me of a poor American woman, Mary Pierson, who was very destitute of everything, had buried her husband and only son who was her support. I told her to send the dear woman to see me.

She came, and as I looked at her bowed down with grief, I could only think of the words, "The only son of his mother, and she was a widow." [Luke 7:12.] Jesus thought tenderly of the widow.

I said I would try to do what I could for her. I thought everyone seemed to be sending to Chicago, the burned city; [The Chicago Fire of 1871 burned from October 8 to October 10, destroyed thousands of buildings, and killed an estimated 300 people] but I took the case to my Lord and told Him all about it, and I was directed to write to two friends.

Mrs. Jaffray sent fifty dollars to give her by installments of four dollars per month; Mrs. Haxton two dollars; Mrs. Barney two dollars; Mrs. McCauley sent a new dress and bonnet; Miss H. a waterproof cloak and a shawl; myself, two flannel skirts. Thus the widow's heart was made to sing for joy, and we were the happier in being permitted to be the instruments.

Oh, how good the Lord is. None ever trusted Him and were ashamed. I am suffering so much, but my Father knows, and will be with me to the end. The church has engaged Miss C. to visit and urge the people to church. Give her all needed grace.

Provision for the Needy

November 1871

This poor man cried unto the Lord, and He delivered him out of all his troubles (Psalm 34:6).

He is faithful who hath promised (Hebrews 10:23).

Sold for Mary Pierson ten and one-half dozens of little brushes, ten dollars and fifty cents.

November 14th 1871

"His goodness ever nigh,
His mercy ever free,
Shall while I live, shall when I die,
Still follow me."

These words came so sweet today while thinking of His great love to me, so boundless, so free. Goodness and mercy all the way through. Had a visit from Mrs. Phebe Palmer to see if I had all my wants supplied, as she had heard from an over-anxious friend that they feared that they were not.

It was very kind of her, as she was only told of it yesterday. Thus does He put good into the hearts of His dear children. But I told her that not one of His precious promises could fail, for He said bread should be given and water should be sure. [Isaiah 33:6.]

Faith might be tried at times, but I always come off victorious. The One who stands by me is so much greater than the host which may encamp against me. So I stand upheld by the arm of omnipotent love, which not all earth or hell can pull down.

We also had the class meet here. My dear pastor tonight brought them round, and we met and talked to one another. The Lord hearkened and heard and we were blessed. We found it sweet to tell of His dealings with us. We had a great feast.

Sunshine within

Sabbath eve
December 9th 1871
A rainy day without, but that does not detract any joy from the children of God. The Sun of Righteousness shines with all his beauty and glory, and illuminates the inner man. We can truly say, "December is as pleasant as May," for we see Jesus and talk with Him, and our converse is sweet.

Sabbath, December 10th 1871
Blessed Sabbath, sweet day of rest, how I love thy stillness. How I feel the incense going up from thousands and thousands of hearts to the mercy seat, in and from the temples set apart to worship the Lord God of Hosts, and Thou art no less here, precious Saviour.

Just as much do I feel Thy lovely presence here as did the sisters of Bethany. Amid many otherwise lonely hours I talk with Thee, and feel Thee very near. Season after season rolls on, year after year passes away, and still I am spared. Many, young and old, are called away and I am left behind.

How gladly would I flee away and be at rest, were it the Master's will, but at this time He wills that I should stay. Lord, give me patience to abide the unknown workings of Thy will.

Rest from pain, nervousness and care looks very sweet.

My soul longs for more holy love and more of the fullness of the Godhead. The body is exceedingly weak and tired, but the Master Builder knows all about the frail tenement.

Had my old, tried and faithful friend, Brother Stephenson, to see me, and we had a pleasant visit, though I was very weak. Could not control my feelings and wept, which is very unusual with me; but the Father in heaven "knoweth our frame." [Psalm 103:14.]

We were talking of the wonderful care of my Great Provider. I was feeling that friends were about to get some kind of a new bed, and it was too much to spend on one thing, and I may not need it long, or I may live on and on some time. But I must leave it all with Him who says, "Your Heavenly Father knoweth you have need of these things. [Matthew 6:32.]

> "Good when He gives, supremely good,
> Nor less when He denies."

December 22nd 1871

Death has been here and taken away our lovely boy, Harry Paisley. He was taken from us by a few hours' illness, to with the angels stand. Lord, let it be sanctified to those dear parents, who feel sorely stricken; and may it please Thee to spare the other two: two on earth and two in heaven. Oh, grant that they may feel that Thou doest all things well.

Had a visit from Mrs. Tatum, who brought me fifteen dollars for the poor. I am so thankful, as I was wondering where I could look for some ready money for these poor people. How indulgent our Father is to His children.

I am very feeble. A great effort to write. Such dreadful sinkings, but oh, the oneness with God, the power with which He comes to His feeble ones, such fullness, such glory.

This little upper room seems sometimes illuminated, and the great Three-in-One having taken up His abode here. 'Tis little short of heaven, for the veil is rent and we can talk with Him who is invisible to mortal sight, but who reveals Himself to His humble children.

December 25th 1871

Glory to God in the highest, peace on earth and good will to men! Amid the excitement of the expected death of an earthly prince, comes ringing in our ears the song of the angels, He whose name is wonderful the Mighty God. His name shall be called Jesus, for He shall save His people from their sins. [Matthew 1:21.]

Yes, He does save us, and that to the uttermost. [Hebrews 7:25.] Blessed be His name. It is a full salvation, and we will go forward and trust Him to the end. My grandchildren are all happy. One dear little thing said, "It is Jesus' birthday."

I had five of the dear little things to come in early this morning to wish me a merry Christmas, and their little presents from grandma made them all so joyous and glad.

Kind friends are not slack, but all contributed something to supply my need and make me feel happy. Presents of money from three. From my dear Dr. Sabine his usual gift of turkey, etc., for the Christmas dinner. I have many tokens of love, among which is a very beautiful mosaic musical album from Mrs. Jaffray, which she brought from the falls of the Rhine. Goodness and mercy all the way through, and we will praise Him!

Chapter 21

Lead Thou Me On

Thou hast dealt well with Thy servant, O Lord, according unto Thy word (Psalm 119:65).

> Lead Thou me on! Keep Thou my feet;
> I do not ask to see the distant scene;
> One step enough for me.
>
> So long Thy power hath blessed me, sure it still
> Will lead me on
> O'er moor and fen, o'er crag and torrent, till
> The night is gone,
> And with the morn those angel faces smile
> Which I have loved long since and lost awhile.

January 2nd 1872

Another year has fled – another year is come. The past has been one of many blessings. How many during the year have been called to exchange worlds, but we are spared. How near we have seemed to be to the better land. Still we are left, a wonder to many, but none can know in how much nervousness and pain. But the apostle Paul says, "Those members of the body which seem to be more feeble are necessary." [1 Corinthians 2:22.] So I will try and fill the place the Master has given me, and faithfully toil in converting barren into fruitful soil.

January 26th 1872

My Dear Sister Annesley,

It is a long time since I wrote to you, and a long time since I heard from you, and my heart goes out after you every day, and wonders how you are and what the tidings of the day. Your heart all alive to the Master, your hands employed, and thus your life glides away calm as a summer evening. I have longed so much to see you, and yet I know that you are no doubt in the place where your Heavenly Father wishes you to be.

I am journeying on, dear, to the New Jerusalem, the city of our God. I feel as if I had passed quite a number of milestones, and by and by I will reach the city whose builder and maker is God.

I have been very poorly, dear, and suffered much more since my illness in August last, and still at times am threatened with a relapse, but it is all well, well, well! I rejoice in the will of my God, because that will is sweet.

I am not able to sleep at all without chloral every night. I kept from it just as long as I could, but the fearful nervousness that follows paralysis is beyond description, and without this medicine I pass very painful, sleepless nights. The Lord has been very gracious and merciful to me, dear. He supplies all my need and keeps me in a wealthy place. I do joy in the God of my salvation, for He hath dealt bountifully with me.

Hannah's baby passed away after a few hours' illness. He was a lovely child, sixteen months old; but his mother will never fear or care for him. Another safely housed.

Joseph and Mary are well, and having a gracious time in their little church. Meetings almost every night. Some have found the pearl of great price. Oh, it is joyful news, a soul saved from sin, washed in the blood of the Lamb.

Joseph had a fast-day last week in order that the

members may feel the full importance of the work, and we are all praying that many, many precious souls may be born of God.

We are not having any stir in our church. We have a good visitor now who works very faithfully among all classes. She goes from house to house, and is doing a deal of good.

I have been able to do very little writing since August except to some friends, and some notes about my poor.

Now, dear, I must say goodbye, and may the blessing of a triune God ever rest upon you, is the prayer of

Your loving sister in Christ,

Bella Cooke

To Miss A. Annesley

March 1872

Well, dear, we have just been surprising my dear, faithful Dr. Miles Palmer. On the 16th of this month it will be twenty-one years that he has been attending me and my children until they left my home for their own.

In the summer, a lady, Mrs. Haxton, was with me a great deal during my severe illness, and hearing that it would this spring be that length of time, and seeing the doctor's increasing attention to me, said that if I lived until spring some memento must be gotten for him.

So last month they decided to get a mantel set, and an elegant clock with ornaments was purchased, costing $230. The clock is surmounted by a bronze statue of an eminent Italian surgeon, and on the back of the bronze chair is inscribed,

Miles W. Palmer, M. D.
From Friends and Children of Bella Cooke.
A tribute to kindness and voluntary professional
attendance during twenty-one years.

April 16th 1872
I invited, to be present at the presentation, Bro. Stephenson, Mrs. Haxton and Mrs. Gale, Joseph and the three girls, the doctor, his wife and Mrs. Adams. Bro. S. made the presentation, after which we had a little ice cream and cake and some pleasant conversation, when we sang that beautiful hymn, "Thou God of truth and love."

Joseph led in prayer, and then the dear friends left. It was a grand and joyous time. Everyone was happy, and those who received were *surprised* and delighted.

Was it not noble in friends? Mrs. Jaffray, Mrs. Haxton, and Mrs. Barney were the principal ladies in it, with Bro. Stephenson, my children, and a few others. Dear Dr. Palmer has a large heart, and deserves far more than that.

As ever,
Bella Cooke

A Love-feast Testimony
492 Second Avenue
October 6th 1872
Dear Brethren and Sisters,
Having heard that you were to have a reunion love-feast, I longed to be with you, that I too might speak for Jesus. But as I cannot go to you, it occurred to me I might write a few lines and have them read, if it was thought best.

"To many of you I am a stranger, to some known only as an invalid at home, to others I was known in more active life, but these are becoming very few. But you are all very dear to me as members of Christ's body and co-laborers in His vineyard, and it is this which prompts me, although in much pain, to join with you on this glad day the reopening of our church, and a fresh dedication of ourselves to God and His cause.

"It is almost eighteen years since I knelt with you in the house of prayer, but I have not been left to perish. My Father and your Father has been very gracious to me and has done great things for me, wherefore my soul rejoices in Him and my heart is made glad at the mention of His name. Yes, it is a name high over all. It is dear to us above every name; it charms our fears and bids our sorrows cease.

"I feel I am not the less one of you because I cannot be with you, but am interested in everything which relates to the welfare of our Zion. Her very walls are dear to me. I meet you in spirit at every session. At Sabbath school, preaching of the word, and at prayer meeting, and at my class meeting, my thoughts follow you.

> "You sing His deeds, as I have sung
> In sweet and solemn lays;
> Were I among you my glad tongue
> Might learn new themes of praise.

"But my Master has seen fit to place me in a corner, and I praise Him for His ways toward me. They have been love and mercy all the way through. Yes, here I'll raise my Ebenezer.

"God has been very gracious to me, and His tender mercies are nearer in every trial and sorrow. The everlasting arms have been felt in time of untold suffering, and His voice has been heard, 'It is I; be not afraid.' Yes, blessed be His holy name.

"I will praise Him for all that is past, and, by grace assisting me, trust Him for all that is to come. Oh, let us as a church arise and shake ourselves from our lethargy, and buckle on the whole armor of God and do the Lord's work."

I am unable to write more. The Lord bless you all, and

keep you unspotted from the world, is the prayer of your sister in Christ,

Bella Cooke

December 30th 1872

Dear Miss A.,

I want to tell you of a new token of my Father's goodness. Mrs. Onatavia has just been trying to make me more comfortable by getting me a new kind of bedstead. It has three kinds of movements, one by which the head and shoulders are raised, one to raise the knees and the other to raise the feet.

Then there is an arrangement by which the patient can be raised in a canvas the height of two feet, so the mattress can be turned over and dusted, without annoying the patient on the canvas.

I told Dr. McLean I did not wish Mrs. Onatavia to get any such thing, as I did not wish her to spend so much money, for I might live but a very short time, then it would be a pity; and that if I lingered on I would perhaps need what was used for it.

I was told Mrs. O. did not ask me whether I wanted it or not. She was going to get it, and no matter how short a time I needed it. If I could be made more comfortable, I should have it.

And so the man brought it. The bedstead alone cost, I believe, eighty dollars. Just think, all that spent for me to lie on. Well, dear, I am on it, and I think it is going to be just splendid. Was it not very kind?

The girls are well. I have not seen Sister L. since they went to board in New Jersey. Mr. L. still lingers on the shores of time, with sails already set for the skies. Oh, what a glorious company will be there; songs of joy will be ours. We are ready to say, "Lord, hasten the day."

Yours lovingly in Jesus,

Bella Cooke

Samuel Bettle

I often think of the first visit I had from Mr. Samuel Bettle, a minister in the Society of Friends, a man esteemed for his rare gift of discernment of character as well as his uniform piety.

Early in June 1865, on a lovely Sabbath morning about nine o'clock, Mrs. Sarah Underhill called with Mr. Bettle. They had just left the breakfast table of Mrs. Tatum's. He did not know where he was going or who he was going to see.

When they entered the room I could not but notice what a sad, solemn face Mr. B. had. He asked me a few questions, which I answered, and told of the loving-kindness of my God.

He was silent for a while, and at last said, "Well, Bella, we must be careful that we do not take the oil of joy for mourning and the garment of praise for the spirit of heaviness." [Suggesting Bella should refuse the promise in Isaiah 61:3.]

I replied, "Mr. Bettle, I cannot help rejoicing. I have had so much done for me by my Heavenly Father that I must and will praise Him."

Mr. Bettle said, "Sarah, I would be going."

Mrs. Underhill said, "Samuel, it is too soon for meeting."

"Well," he replied, "I would see the clerk of the meeting," to which she replied that he would not be there.

I was deeply moved, and felt there was something more to be done. I said, "Mr. Bettle, shall we not have prayer before you go? There is time, is there not?"

He put down his hat and stood leaning against the

bedpost. The Master greatly helped me, and I fervently prayed for our brother, and for God's presence and power to rest upon the meeting.

While at prayer I heard Mr. B. slide down on his knees, and the moment I closed he began, and poured out his soul in prayer. It was a solemn time.

Then he arose and said, while holding my hand, "Bella Cooke, the Lord has shown thee all my heart as no one else knows it, not even my wife; and God has blessed me under thy supplication."

The tears ran down his cheeks, while his countenance was very bright. He was in no hurry to be gone. It seemed as though he could not leave.

At last Mrs. Underhill, who had been a silent listener, said, "Samuel, we must go. I had feared that I was going to be disappointed in thy visit here, but I am not," so they left.

I was afterwards told that his friends who had breakfasted with him, said, "Where has Samuel Bettle been to?" and the answer was, "He has been to Bella Cooke's."

An article in the New York *Evening Post* of the next day, in giving an account of the meeting, said that an aged minister, Samuel Bettle, spoke with great fervor and power, and his face seemed to shine.

On Tuesday Mr. B. came again, and told me how wonderfully the Lord had blessed him on Sunday morning here, and he was glad I had dealt so faithfully with him. He wanted a copy of the words of my prayer, but that was impossible.

In after years he always loved to speak of that time, and said how differently he had seen things of a spiritual nature since then. He has been a kind friend in things spiritual and temporal, aiding me to procure things needful for the comfort of this poor body. Many of the Society of Friends will remember with pleasure these facts.

A New Tomb

To Miss A.,

"And the field and the cave that is therein were made sure unto Abraham for a possession of a burying-place by the sons of Heth." [Genesis 23:20.]

And now I must tell you another piece of indulgence from my Husband, Brother, Friend. It was not enough that this body should be fed and clothed and my little ones brought up, but still farther does He go, and permits me to know where this poor clay shall lie.

In the summer of 1866 I was very ill and lay a long time in spasms. It seemed as if I would not be long on this earth. Sister Lankford was here and asked me where I would like to be laid when the Master should call me home. I said I would like to be laid with the remains of my dear husband and baby, but it was so far away that the children could not visit the place as often as they would like. But any place would do.

She replied, "Well, dear, I have thought much about it, and I have decided to have you laid in my lot in Greenwood by my side. I do not know of anyone I would rather have laid there than you."

I was very weak, and could say but little. My heart was too full for utterance. I could only wonder and adore. I related it to some friends who came in, not that the subject had troubled me at all, but now that my kind Master had gone before me in my expectations, I must thank Him and tell it to His praise.

In a few days Brother Mackey came in, and I told it to him. He said it did not seem to him just the thing. I thought it beautiful, but could not make him think so.

In a few days more he came in and said, "Sister Cooke, I believe the Lord wants me to buy you a lot in Greenwood."

I replied, "I do not know about that. You had better be

sure before you do anything about it. Besides, I would not like to displease Sister Lankford, and it would be like throwing away her kindness."

"I will make it all right."

So off he went to see Sister L., and said he understood that she had said she would like Sister Cooke to be laid in her lot.

She said, "Yes."

"I believe the Lord means that I should buy her one."

"Praise the Lord, Brother Mackey, I will be very glad to have you do so, but while she had no lot, I wished her to be laid in mine."

Then away he went, bought a nice little lot, had it fenced in, a gate put up with my name upon it, and brought me the deed and bills receipted. Was it not a noble deed? Thus the Lord indulges His children.

But all was not yet complete. Dear Sister Lankford could not rest. She must have something to do with it, so in October she went to Peekskill and had the remains of my dear husband and babe taken up and brought down to the city, and left in an undertaker's for him to bury them in my new tomb.

Strange to say, it was Saturday when they were brought here, and had to remain until Monday. The Sabbath day that intervened was the twenty-sixth anniversary of our wedding day. I knew that at some time she intended to do so.

I had by trifles saved about fifty dollars to pay my funeral expenses, and I gave it to her to pay their expenses, but she brought it back to me, and said, "My dear, I want you to spend this in things you need for your comfort. I will bear all this myself. It is my part. I wanted Brother Cooke and baby to be laid here, and then you can be all together."

Goodness and mercy are all the time about my path. Well might the Psalmist say he had "Never seen the righteous forsaken or his seed begging bread." {Psalm 27:35.]

Oh, for a thousand-seraph tongues
To bless the incarnate Word;
Oh, for a thousand thankful songs
In honor of my Lord.

Come, tune afresh your golden lyres,
Ye angels round the throne;
Ye saints in all your sacred choirs,
Adore the Eternal Son.

Chapter 22

The King's Work

They that feared the Lord spake often one to another (Malachi 3:16).

> We were talking about the King
> And our elder Brother,
> As we were used often to speak
> One to another.
>
> The Lord standing quietly by
> In the shadows dim,
> Smiling, perhaps, in the dark to hear
> Our sweet, sweet talk of Him.

March 12 1873

My Dear Sister A.,

For some days I have been trying to get nerve enough to write to you, that I might acknowledge the kindness of your delightful letter.

Our precious friend Thomas Lankford has gone to the bosom of his God. He sweetly slept and breathed out his mortal life after lying with closed eyes for two weeks. Once only did he open them, and looking at Mrs. L., he put up his poor hands and drawing down her head he kissed her many times, and told her over and over how he loved her. Then his work was done.

"When he had said this he fell asleep." [Acts 7:60.] Oh,

the mystery and strength of human affections. He was very patient all the way through, and finished his course with joy one of the kindest and best men I have ever known. Mrs. L. is very much broken. I feel for her very much; but as you say, it brings heaven very near us. I love to think of it.

The leaflet is beautiful. When I lay so low with paralysis that all thought I was going, the Saviour's words were my comfort. I felt He would say, "She hath done what she could." [Mark 14:8.] I have thought frequently that I have indeed done all I could, and many have told me far more than the Lord wanted me to do.

I must tell you how signally the Lord blessed one of our little enterprises. On the 18th of last month Mrs. Jaffray wrote me a note saying that a few ladies of the Christian Union were trying to open a sort of temporary home, just to give a night's lodging to the homeless.

She wrote, "We are trying to get as many one dollar subscribers as possible, that many may be interested. Pray for us, dear, that our treasury may be filled."

I prayed to the Master about it, and He led me to resolve to ask all who might come to see me for the next two weeks. I did so, and He sent many who had not been for months, and the result was fifty dollars, for which I thank my Heavenly Father.

I sent it with great joy to Mrs. J. She was very glad, and said she had been praying so earnestly that the Lord would give it favor in the sight of the people, and here was an answer. Some gave me one dollar for themselves, and one for each member of their families.

Well, dear, now I have opened a second subscription list for our new Home, and hope to get a little more, for when I think of my cosy home and good bed I am grieved for the homeless wanderers and children of sorrow. It is done as unto the Lord, a thank-offering to Him for His great love and care over me. Not more than others I deserve, yet God hath given me more.

March 13th 1873

I have had a sweet visit from dear Sister Lankford. She tries to bear up nobly, and is supported by Him who says, "Fear not, I will hold thee by thy right hand," [Isaiah 41:13] and she is indeed letting Him hold her up. Praise the Lord! We both wept freely, but our Saviour did not chide us. They were not tears of rebellion, but of tender, loving submission.

Yours very lovingly,

Bella Cooke

From Anna F. Jaffray

615 Fifth Avenue, N.Y.

March 1873.

My Dearest Mrs. Cooke,

How much pleasure you have given me I cannot express! It is wonderful that lying on a bed of suffering you are enabled to *do so much* for the good of others. I thank you, and love you more than ever. I find only forty-seven dollars subscribed, not forty-eight. I say *only*, because you fancy that you ought to send forty-eight, and I received your second note with the enclosed three dollars today.

I think I must just return you the list, dear friend, and when you feel well enough you can look it over and return it to me. I have prayed our Lord will incline the hearts of many to think well of this "Temporary Home," and this is an answer to my prayer. I am so delighted.

Just think, so much money from you, my dear Mrs. Cooke. Why, it is just lovely. You say, "Mrs. Barney regrets that we do not receive larger subscriptions." We do, when we can get them, but we think it a good plan to obtain as many dollar subscribers as possible. This plan gives us so many friends, and everyone can give one dollar, when many could not give more. Don't you see, dear? Many thanks for the tracts, which I hope soon to read.

Yours, with much love,
Anna F. Jaffray

492 Second Avenue
June 17 1873
Dear Sister A.,
It is a long time since I have written to you, but, darling sister, I have no strength, and have tried again and again, but am so tired.

I have lately had a very direct answer to prayer, which I must tell you. The 2nd of May I wrote to my precious Mrs. Jaffray to see if she could give me some steady help for a poor Scotch woman, seventy-eight years old. Her father, grandfather, and brother were preachers, and she supported herself until now by teaching.

On the 8th, Mrs. J. sent her maid to say she would give me five dollars per month, but did not send it for May. The girl told me that Mrs. J. said she knew I would keep praying for it till I got an answer. Three or four weeks before this, Mr. Gardner, a person who is engaged by several rich ladies to do errands of mercy, called and said he had met with a very poor family, sick, and could I get anything for them?

I said, "No! We were just having to pay the funeral expenses of a poor man whom we had been caring for all winter."

Then it came with great force to pray for help for that poor family. Meanwhile I had been asking my Father to send me the five dollars from Mrs. J. for poor Miss MacFarland. Thus these cases passed on till the 21st, when Mr. Gardner came and brought me the five dollars I wanted.

I said, "What about the C. family?"

"Oh," he replied, "they are very needy. Cannot you ask some of your ladies for help?"

I said, "No, I cannot. The Lord shows me no light on the subject at all. We must pray and wait. When it is right it will come, but I can ask no more."

About four hours after, two ladies called. One said, "Sister Cooke, are you praying for anybody?"

I said, "Yes; a good many bodies."

"Well, but any particular one?"

I asked, "Temporally or spiritually?"

"Temporally," she said.

I replied, "I am, but get no light."

"Well, I have brought it. A gentleman belonging to Bedford Street Church has seen you *once*, and yesterday he said, 'Sister Lovejoy, I am impressed that Sister Cooke needs some money, and I want to send her twenty-five dollars. Tell her to use it just as she pleases.'"

I could only exclaim, "Bless the Lord, O my soul, and forget not all His benefits." [Psalm 103:1] My soul was so joyful in God in that He had deigned to hear my prayer, and answer so speedily. So I sent for Mr. Gardner. We rejoiced together at the goodness of God, and the poor family was relieved.

From certain of my friends who delight to "lend to the Lord" through His poor, I had heard nothing, and was almost ready to think I would not have all I wanted, but I have had twenty dollars more given me by a lovely lady, so I thank God and take courage.

You know, dear, the societies close, and the people of means nearly all leave the city, so the poor suffer in the summer as well as in the winter. "Blessed is he that considereth the poor, the Lord will deliver him in time of trouble." [Psalm 41:1.]

To the Same
June 19th 1873
Were you here I could slowly and quietly tell you much of interest, but it is so difficult to put anything on paper. Some little notes I write must be written over by another, which is never satisfactory.

My precious friend Mrs. Jaffray has had her daughter, Miss Ada, married. The week before the ceremony, the dear child came to see me; she is a lovely Christian. I had an invitation, and after the wedding, cake and the bride's bouquet were sent to me. Was it not very kind?

And so the dear Lord mixes me in with the rich and the poor, and He is the Maker of us all. Oh, how many links there are to His great chain of Providences. How one and another are brought to me, till my clusters of friends seem like love-bunches of flowers culled from the gardens of paradise. And, so wonderful, my humble circumstances never seem to give them a thought. It is all of the Lord, and I will praise Him.

The God of all grace be with and bless you.
Your loving sister in Jesus,
Bella Cooke

A New Friend

July 1873
In the latter part of the winter 1873, dear Mrs. Bodstein had often talked to me about a young married lady, one of her pupils in singing. She had also brought me grapes several times from this friend, and a little book, *Thoughts for Weary Hours*.

On one of her calls, Mrs. B. showed me a photograph of her friend. It was a lovely face, and I said, "It is beautiful, but I suppose I shall never see her." A few months passed and I heard this friend had been called to part with a beloved sister very suddenly, shortly after which Mrs. B. brought her to see me. Her name is Virginia Field.

I was much pleased with her. We had a long talk about divine things and the strange providences of my life, but nothing was said of my circumstances. When they went downstairs, Mrs. F. said to Mrs. B., "Do you think Mrs. Cooke would feel displeased if I sent her this?" handing Mrs. B. a ten dollar bill.

Mrs. B. brought it up to me, and in that unexpected kindness I saw the hand of God. I had saved ten dollars for the summer's ice, but knew it was no use beginning to take ice until I had a new box.

I spoke to my daughter Mary about it, and she said, "Ma, you would better get the box, and the ice will come."

I had done so and had the box, but no ice. The ice dealer had called twice to know when I would begin to take ice, and was asked to call on the next Monday for an answer.

It was Saturday when the ladies called, and here was the ten dollars sent by this new friend for the ice for the summer. "The silver is Mine, and the gold is Mine, saith the Lord of hosts." [Haggai 2:8.]

From that time, Mrs. F. and her sister, Miss Helen B. Hamersley, have visited me steadily. Their brother also has called to see me. Thus I am blessed. Dear Mrs. B, she is so kind. One day she brought me a beautiful vase containing a wax cross, with fine vines and flowers twining all about it.

I said, "Why did you bring me this elegant thing?"

She answered, "Because, dear, I thought you would enjoy it, and I can get out to see the pretty things." She has a lovely family, so tender and kind.

"By this shall all men know that ye are My disciples, if ye have love one to another." [John 13:35.] And surely these things are more than "a cup of cold water," which we are told shall not lose its reward.

A Broken-Hearted Mother

In July of 1873 a person, Mrs. Montgomery, was sent to me for help. I saw a fine-looking, intelligent Irish lady, who plainly in other years had been in better circumstances. She had four daughters, three of whom were well educated, interesting young women. The fourth was a weak-minded girl of about twenty years. I aided them to the best of my ability, helping two of the young women to situations in stores, and the other obtained a situation as governess.

I felt that Mrs. M. acted strangely, but attributed this to her changed circumstances and poverty, for they had been in favored conditions in Ireland. Mrs. M. wished to become a lady's nurse.

I sent her to Dr. Sabine, who said if she could go to the Women's College, Eighth Street, Second Avenue, under Miss Blackwell's care for four months, he would be able to give her plenty to do.

We could get her into the college free, but where was her board to come from? I thought it over and decided to raise the money by shares of ten dollars each. I wrote to several ladies. Sixty-four dollars was needed for board, besides the expense of providing for the youngest girl. Mrs. Jaffray wanted to meet it all, but others willingly came forward to help.

Mrs. Field was here one day and took a share, and, going home, wrote me at once, "My husband wishes to take a share in your stock, so I send $10 for him also.

Mrs. M. entered the college, but by her constant daily visits to me I found her mind was impaired, and later on I found that the cause was a broken heart. At that very time a son of hers was awaiting execution for the murder of the cashier of a bank in the city of Armagh, Ireland. His aged, broken-hearted mother, having spent all her fortune in his defense, had fled the country with her children.

He had stolen the funds of the bank, and the murder of the cashier was needed to cover the footsteps of the theft.

It is no wonder that her poor brain had lost its balance. She fancied that she was the daughter of King William IV. That she was the rightful heir to the British crown; that Victoria was a usurper; that all her daughters were princesses. She was indignant that they must come to a strange country to work for bread, for she had been the wife of Prince Frederick of Prussia.

One morning a New York daily paper gave an account of the day set for the execution of her son, and this account was read aloud in the house where Mrs. M. was boarding. The poor old mother, who happened to be sitting by, heard the terrible news at the breakfast table. She silently arose, left the company with a bursting heart and came to me.

I knew what had brought her. She put her arms around my neck and sobbed out, "My heart is broken; you don't know."

I said, "Yes, dear, I know all about it."

She was amazed. "Do you? How long have you known?"

I told her, since soon after her first visit to me.

"And you never named it?"

"No, I could not wound you by doing so."

She cried out in a sobbing cry, "Thank God for one friend. What shall I do? I cannot go back to that boardinghouse. Let me stay here."

I was then caring for her half imbecile daughter in my little home. I thought it over, and decided if possible to keep and shelter her all I could. I sent to Mrs. Haxton to see if she could lend me a cot and mattress. Then I hired a small room from the person upstairs and had it put in order for her.

The days wore on, and at last the day of execution came. The agony of that aged mother as she watched the clock, went again and again into the bedroom to agonize with God in prayer, then returned to me wringing her poor hands and crying, "Oh, Mrs. Cooke, my boy, my poor boy!"

Such agony in that tearless face few have ever witnessed, and may God grant none may ever experience. It was a terrible day. But this poor Rizpah [see 2 Samuel 21:1-14] must be cared for. For a while we provided a place for her in the Unsectarian Home, but they refused to keep her.

At length it seemed to her daughters desirable to get her back to her relatives in Ireland. We secured her a passage ticket, and one of my lady friends saw her aboard the steamer. For a year after her return I sent her $5 per month according to a promise made to her before she sailed.

492 Second Avenue
September 23rd 1873
My dear Sister,
I have so much to say to you, that I don't know where to begin. It has been a busy summer with me, you know.

I have had brought to me a dear lady, Mrs. Field, who was very tender from having lost a sister a few weeks before. Mrs. F. is wealthy in the world's sense of the word, but has heretofore known chiefly the theory of the plan of salvation.

She watched me and listened attentively, and very prayerfully did I counsel with her, as step by step I tried to lead her to the feet of her precious Saviour.

The Master was with us, and she now rejoices in the God of her salvation. She has composed some verses of which I send you a copy. She does not know what to do or to get for me. Sister Lankford has met her twice.

Now let me tell you that my dear children, Joseph and Mary, have resolved to be all the Lord's, and have been blessed with a fresh baptism of His grace. And such a change! When I got the enclosed letter from them I wept and praised God.

Joseph is giving no uncertain sound to his people. Now the Scriptures are all life and light and power through the Holy Spirit. Praise the Lord! It is goodness and mercy all the way through.

I have been poorly, dear, having had an attack of pneumonia which weakened me very much, and my new friend so kindly came every day and cared for me. She has bought material for six new gowns, also linen for sheets and pillowcases. Then she bought me an eiderdown silk quilt for winter, with many other little things.

Why, dear, I am just amazed at it all, and almost tremble at the goodness of God to me through that dear child. Mrs. F. also bought me a little [clockwork] machine to stand on my table and fan me; it is called, Indian Zephyrion.

Joseph said, "Why, ma, are they going to send you to heaven on flowery beds of ease?"

They cannot do that, but they are certainly making my pathway as easy as they can. "A thousand promises declare His constancy of love."

Another dear friend, Mrs. Haxton, on my last birthday sent me a dollar for every year of my life, fifty-two dollars, and a beautiful lamp. For all these things I can only say, "Bless the Lord, O my soul, and forget not all His benefits." [Psalm 103:1.]

Now I have to tell you a sad story. My dear Mrs. Jaffray has lost her eldest daughter, Mrs. Hurst. She had her fourth child and they were all so joyous and happy, when a fever set in and the dear one was taken from friends on earth to friends in heaven. Without doubt she is with her Lord. Pray, dear, that my dear Mrs. J. may be comforted and sustained amid it all.

And now, my dear, I must leave you. Would that I had a thousand tongues to tell my great Redeemer's praise. I send you some of the little books I have been distributing of late.

Yours lovingly in Jesus,
Bella Cooke

To Mrs. Haxton
November 26th 1873
My Precious Friend,
Here I lie, hardly knowing how to contain myself, whether in the body or out of it, with my twenty-eight turkeys on the dining table close up to my bed, awaiting their distribution to the poor and needy. I have written a verse of Scripture appropriate to each case, and they are pinned on each one of them. Mrs. Douglass was here, and greatly rejoiced over her turkey, coal and grocery order.

You have obeyed, dear one, the command, "Thou shalt open thine hand wide unto thy brother, to thy poor." [Deuteronomy 15:11.]

Miss Callender was here, also Mrs. Field, and were astonished at the sight. "Blessed be the Lord, who daily loadeth us with benefits." [Psalm 68:19.]

Yes, yours will indeed be a joyful thanksgiving, for you have made many hearts glad. Annie is here assisting, and preparing the baskets. I was greatly disappointed yesterday, for I wanted a long talk with you; but as we cannot control these things, we must endure them.

Your loving but humble friend,
Bella Cooke

To Miss A.
December 16th 1873
Beloved Sister,
You will think it strange I have not answered your very kind and welcome note of love and greeting. But I have so many poor days that I cannot do anything but endure. Then I have

been so busy.

I did have a good time during the session of the Evangelical Alliance, for although none of the visiting strangers, with one exception, called, yet many of our own people who came to the city came with my dear Joseph. You know he likes to bring his friends to see ma.

I read in the papers the reports of their doings, and the great speeches. On the 17th of November, John Ashworth, of Rochdale, England, the great tract writer, was brought to see me. He came with Mrs. McCready. I was amused by the way they came. Mrs. McC. spoke out while on the stairs, "Does my beloved hear my voice?"

John Stephenson was here, and as they were introduced, I could but think, as I saw the two big-hearted Christian men standing together, how few such useful men and of such small pretensions! Mr. A. left me to visit the Bookroom with Joseph. He sailed for home on the 19th.

Well, dear, you say that I cannot be spared this winter, but were it the Lord's will, how gladly would I hie me to that home where the weary are at rest. I am so unable to bear any movement at all, notwithstanding all my bed improvements. But by and by, there will be no sickness, no toil, no night, no weary wasting of mortal frame. And yet amid all, I have had a very happy autumn.

One of my ladies sat beside me one day and listened as I told her of a family in sore distress and sickness. I had no money on hand to give, and was forced to borrow five dollars from Mrs. Jaffrey's fund, for it was an urgent case. The lady went home, and organized what she was pleased to call the "Bella Cooke Bank" for the poor.

During the past month the "Bank" has furnished sixty-five dollars, and relieved twenty-eight cases of suffering and distress.

It was good Mrs. Susan C. Haxton into whose kind heart

the Lord put this happy thought.

Well, dear, I gave away for Thanksgiving thirty turkeys and four pairs of chickens, and now I am asking the ladies who come to me to give me pairs of chickens for the poor people's Christmas dinner. And I will get them, too. I never expect to he denied, because I always ask my Father to touch their hearts, and He does it.

There is a poor woman near here who is quite sick with consumption. I asked the Master to put it into the heart of Dr. P. to go and see her, and on his next visit he asked me, "Has that sick friend of yours a physician?"

I said, "No."

"Well, I will go and see her." And he is now attending her.

As things look now, Mary and Joseph will leave New York, and I shall miss them. But I gave them to the Master and His work, not to dictate where they shall labor, but anywhere to be most useful. "Good when He gives, supremely good, nor less when He denies." Love to Mrs. Root, and a large share for your own dear self.

From your loving sister in Jesus,
Bella Cooke

Chapter 23

The Resting Place

Now there was leaning on Jesus' bosom, one of His disciples, whom Jesus loved (John 13:23).

And evermore beside him on his way
The unseen Christ shall move,
That he may lean upon His arm and say,
"Dost thou, dear Lord, approve?"

O holy trust! O endless sense of rest!
Like the beloved John,
To lay his head upon the Saviour's breast
And thus to journey on.

To Miss Annesley
January 2nd 1874
Dear Sister in Jesus,
On this second day of a new year I want to talk with you a little while. As I was writing just now, a line or two which my dear mother used to sing came floating through my mind.

"If thy heart be as mine,
If for Jesus it pine,
Come up into the chariot of love."

That tongue has been silent in the tomb for twenty years. A happy, joyful Christian she was, and she is now singing the new song. And by and by, dear, we too shall join our song with those venerated parents in the home of the saints. I would not be impatient to be gone, nor unmindful of the mercies of a gracious Providence.

He has given me bread and raiment, a work to do, friends to love and return my love. He has given me my dear children and grandchildren, and my own dear little home. Besides all these, He has put into my heart the "peace that passeth all understanding," [Philippians 4:7] and, despite trials and constant pain, "they that believe do enter into rest. With the devout Faber I can say,

> "I know not what it is to doubt;
> My heart is ever gay."

Joseph is having good meetings four evenings in the week in his church, and souls are being saved. I stay by the stuff, and every little while send up a little ammunition in the form of cards and little tracts which are distributed in the congregation and in the neighborhood. I also keep our own little church supplied. Praise the Lord for the privilege.

You ask me, "What about the Christmas dinner for the poor people?" Well, I did what I could. I sent turkeys or chickens to twenty-one families, one or two chickens as the case demanded, and to the sick ones, chickens.

For New Year's Day I have spent already for food and coal, thirty dollars. One poor, sick woman had four sheets and four pillowcases, another a bed quilt. Half were supplied from my own stock, the others I begged. I sent a woman to whitewash and clean the rooms for one poor soul, so I know she is clean and comfortable, with plenty of food and fire.

Thus, dear, I try to fill out my days in doing what I can for Him who hath done so much for me. I long to hear the words "Come home," but although in so much suffering and pain I still feel "all the days of my appointed time will I wait till my change comes." [Job 14:14.]

Now, dear, I must say goodbye, and I continually pray

that all the blessings our Father has in store may be yours. With love to Mrs. R. and dearest love to your own dear self.

Yours truly in Jesus,
Bella Cooke

January 26th 1874
Have been much interested in helping a worthy Christian woman, the widow of a former missionary among seamen, Mrs. Byrne, who is sick with consumption. A friend who visited her at my request found her in need of bedding, and I have written to Mrs. Jaffray for blankets. Dr. Palmer is kindly attending her.

January 27th 1874
Mrs. Jaffrey's coachman has been, and brought a splendid pair of blankets for Mrs. B. Praise the Lord, He teaches me where to go. Now the dear woman can sleep warm. A sister of Mrs. B., who is also sick and poor, is soon to be confined. On the advice of Dr. P., I have arranged that she shall be cared for at the Ladies' College. She has four children in St. John's Home. Received also ten dollars from Mrs. Jaffray to buy clothing for them.

January 31st 1874
A neighbor, whom I had never seen, came in and told me a Mr. Maynard was in great distress. I asked how it was.

She replied, "You know he has been very sick with inflammatory rheumatism. He says you have been very kind in sending coal, etc., to him, but his wife was confined last Monday, and this morning his little girl, two years and a half old, died. They are very destitute, and I have come here, unknown to them.

I gave her a chicken to make some broth for Mrs. M. Closed my eyes and asked my rich Father to whom of His children I should go. He told me. I wrote to my dear Mrs. Field, stated the case also to Mrs. Haxton. They are ever ready to help with every good work. At one p.m. I sent my girl with the notes.

Before four o clock, Mrs. F. brought me nineteen dollars. Mrs. H. sent me twenty. Mr. Stephenson also sent me five. On Monday Mrs. F. sent me nineteen more, from some members of her family.

Spoke to Mr. Blossett, missionary at Castle Garden. As Mr. M. had only been about a year in the country, he sent a commissioner who found his statements fine, and sent him twenty dollars.

Thus the Lord hears our prayers and directs our steps. Joseph went in and talked and prayed with them. The lamb is in the fold above.

March 20th 1874
Dear Sister Annesley,
I was very glad to receive yours, and thank you for all the words of comfort.

Pain and weariness have pressed hard upon me for some time, and to such an extent as I could not describe. But it seems as if the glory of the Only Begotten of the Father also beamed upon me, and with His left hand under my head and His right hand encircling me, what matter? My Beloved is mine, and I am His, and we are one – praise the Lord! [Song of Solomon 2:16.]

I have had a very busy winter, and it has borne heavily upon me. But I love to work for Him, either by talking by the hour to loved ones or strangers; telling of the rich things of Jesus, as revealed to me by His great love, or in helping the poor to coal, clothing or food.

By the way, I have given about thirty tons of coal this winter – twenty-two by money and the rest by orders from

Assistant Sick Society, through Mrs. Hunting. I have distributed nearly one hundred new garments, besides many old ones; many of these from dear Mrs. Field.

The Lord has greatly indulged me, and I praise Him. Often and often come the lines to me,

> One more day's work for Jesus,
> One less of life for me;
> But heaven is nearer,
> And Christ is dearer
> Than yesterday to me.
> His love and light
> Fill all my soul tonight.

Oh yes, 'tis joy, not duty, to tell of His wonderful grace and glory, love and care. Eternity will only be sufficient for all His praise. The Lord fill you full of His love.

Yours,

Bella Cooke

To Miss Annesley

May 7th 1874

Dear Sister Annesley,

I was glad to receive yours. Yes, dear one, I am joyous in hope, feeling that ere long I shall escape to my Home where there will be no more pain or nervousness. I cannot tell you how very weary this ponderous, cumbrous clay is, but they that endure to the end, the same shall be saved. [Matthew 24:13.]

We have had a trying month. On the 7th, Joseph Olden, Mary's youngest boy, was taken to rest with his Saviour. He died after seven days' struggling with membranous croup. Poor Mary and Joseph felt this, their first great sorrow, very keenly; but a friend said to me, "I only wish some people, who do not know the help of grace, could step in and see those two watching the struggles of that lovely boy, and the sustaining grace vouchsafed to them."

Yes, dear, the promise is still the same, "Underneath are the everlasting arms," and we still praise our God. [Deuteronomy 33:27.]

They have gone to their new charge in Birmingham, Ct., where everything is bright and pleasant. I felt their leaving me very much, but it is all right. I wish their labor spent where they may be most useful, but I know of no parting, since that of leaving my dear mother, equal to it. They have been very much to me the past three years: the little ones coming down to take tea with grandma, and bringing something new mama had made, or a bunch of flowers, or a little plant.

I shall miss the quick step and hearty kiss of papa as he ran in on his way from the Bookroom; their Friday night tea with grandma – all, all is missed; but all is well. A little while and, "I, too, shall gather up my feet and die, my father's God to meet." [Hymn from Genesis 49:33.]

I suffer terribly with the lumps in the spine, right in the back of my neck. I never could have believed such suffering could be, and reason retained, but He doeth all things well.

I have been very prostrate for some time from overwork, and have very little strength. My friends are annoyed at my trying to do anything, but while I can, I must, for the night cometh when no man can work.

Yesterday a stranger came in and told me he had "just come to look" at me, that he had heard so much of me. He lives in Harlem. I asked who had spoken to him of me.

"Oh," he said, "you are known all over for your faith and good works." He left no name. How these things humble me and fill me with a sense of my short-comings.

20th

Since writing the above I have been very sick, and your letter has had to wait. This morning I had a very profitable visit from brothers Samuel and William Bettle, of Philadelphia. Truly the bread was broken to us, and we were fed with the hidden manna.

It was good to be here, for we received the grace of the promises. They are dear men of God. Samuel has long been a useful minister among the Friends.

I came across a piece of poetry that pleased me, of which I must send you a stanza, although my pastor, Rev. W. H. Wardell, has told me that while the poetry is pretty, it does not describe my case.

> "I can do nothing but pray,
> Laying here, useless, day by day,
> Tired feet, that no more may go
> On my Master's errands to and fro;
> Languid hands that perforce are still,
> Folded, inactive at His will;
> The long, slow hours pass away,
> Able only to pray."

Lovingly,
Bella Cooke

To Miss Annesley
November 11th/12th 1874
Dear Precious Friend,
A long silence it has been, but the old story is the excuse: so feeble. Well, dear sister, I am in the hands of the Great Refiner, and He is Master of His work; and when it is completed, then He will stay His hand.

It has been a time of great suffering and feebleness, all

summer and fall. Still He has kept me, the waters have not overwhelmed; no,

> "Like Moses' bush, I'll mount the higher,
> And flourish unconsumed in fire."

I am greatly troubled, as you know, with partial paralysis. Besides, I had pleurisy and slight pneumonia, which made me very sick. My faithful doctor came twice a day. Still the Master says, "Not yet."

I have had some terribly trying things to contend with from quarters where I least expected it, and have learned to sympathize with the Psalmist for his words in the 55th Psalm 12th and 13th verses. I commit it all to Him who careth for me:

[For it is not an enemy who reproaches me; then I could bear it. Nor is it one who hates me who has exalted himself against me; then I could hide from him. But it was you, a man my equal, my companion and my acquaintance.]

You see our dear sister, Phoebe Palmer, has outstripped us and is safe, safe at home, gathered to the bosom of her God. How much the church will miss her! Dr. W. C. feels it deeply, and many fear that he will sink under it.

Two days before, Mrs. P., one of my poor people died, a widow. About an hour or two before she passed away, a friend called to see her, when she said, "Tell dear Mrs. Cooke that I am sweetly resting in Jesus, and have no anxiety for time or eternity. I leave my children with Him. I have only one ungratified wish, that is, I wanted to see Mrs. Cooke. No one knows how much she has added to my comfort, how much she has done for me."

A year ago her case was brought to me, and I did all I could for her. She could not afford to pay a doctor, and I laid it before the Master that He might influence my good doctor to offer his assistance. She was a consumptive. I had spoken of her to him, but could not ask him to visit her, as I had sent him to so many who could not pay.

But one morning he said to me, "You spoke of a sick woman near here. Has she a doctor?"

I said, "No, I believe not."

He answered, "Well, I will go if you say so, and do what I can for her."

He went, and kindly attended her to the last, just as if she was paying him. I told him he would have to look to the Lord for pay. He said that was all right.

When they both passed away so near each other, Mrs. Palmer and Mrs. Byrne, I said to the doctor that the Father was coming and taking them all home before me, and leaving me still in school. He replied that He had a little more work for me to do. I will try and wait all the days of my appointed time, and trust and labor still.

Do you know I have over sixty names on my list, all of whom need help to support the poor bodies, and to all of whom, while giving them food to eat, I may be enabled to reach forth a little of that bread that perisheth not. Then, dear, I need so much discretion, for I have more than one hundred dollars entrusted to me to give away monthly, besides my tracts and clothing.

Most of all do I need grace and help to meet those in high positions in life who come, and oh, how many, that I may be faithful and honest with them, and use even the probe and knife if needful. Pray for me, dear sister, that all grace may be given, that having done all I may stand fast.

The Lord is my refuge and strength, He is my shield and buckler, I trust and am not afraid, and by grace I shall overcome by the blood of the Lamb and the word of my testimony. Praise the Lord! [See Revelation 12:11.]

Oh the glory that awaits the finally faithful! I feel it all, in body and in soul. It fills me with overwhelming Hallelujahs!

Your loving sister in Jesus,
Bella Cooke

Chapter 24

Faint Yet Pursuing

And let us not be weary in well-doing; for in due season we shall reap, if we faint not. ... As we have therefore opportunity, let us do good unto all men (Galatians 6:9-10).

> When pain o'er my weak flesh prevails,
> With lamb-like patience arm my breast;
> When grief my wounded soul assails,
> In lowly meekness may I rest.
>
> Close by Thy side still may I keep,
> Howe'er life's various currents flow;
> With steadfast eye mark every step,
> And follow Thee where'er Thou go.

To Miss Annesley
March 8th 1875
My Beloved Sister in Jesus,
On this lovely morning I will try to pen a few lines to you. I would have done so long ago, but a busy winter and a suffering body have been my excuse. The pain in the upper part of the spine has just been all I could possibly bear; then the continual threatening of a return of paralysis gives me much trouble.

Well, is it not a gracious favor that my dear Lord gives me something to do? As the dear doctor says, "If I did not have company, I could not live and endure all I have to bear. The brain would give way."

Why, dear, in January I had one hundred and seventy-three calls, in February one hundred and eighty-five, not counting any of my poor people. Last month I collected and gave out two hundred and sixty-five dollars, besides help from two societies.

So you may know I have not had much idle time, and always in severe pain, only able, as I told the doctor, to withstand crying aloud. But underneath are the everlasting arms, and resting my head on the bosom of my Beloved I travel on, knowing that by and by He will say, "It is enough; come up higher."

I have been greatly encouraged by the wonderfully rapid growth of my precious Mrs. Field. She is making a great stir among her own class of people, trying to bring them to the stature of men and women in Christ Jesus, and leading them to the full liberty of the children of God. She accepts fully all the plan of full salvation − a perfect trust in a perfect Saviour. I do thank God for such a gift as she is. She takes many to the Tuesday meeting, and if any are unable to walk she takes them in her carriage.

My heart rejoices in God for her, and I earnestly pray that she may be more and more as a city set on a hill that cannot be hid. [Matthew 5:14.]

I sink in humility before God, and rejoice that He brings to this little room so many friends who by social position and culture are able to wield great influence over others.

Oh, my precious sister, the glory revealed cannot be told. It is very far above all we either ask, or think to have done, while we rest implicitly in His will. His truth shall triumph and we will rejoice, yea with our whole heart we will joy in the God of our salvation.

This morning Mrs. Field brought Rev. W. McVickar and sister, of Philadelphia. We had about two hours and a half talk and prayer − a blessed time. Mrs. J. has been to the Tuesday meeting. You must help me praise Him from whom all blessings flow.

I have had some trials the past six months. These come to all, as shadows in the presence of the sun, but the Divine Friend gives wisdom and grace.

But I must close; very tired.

The Lord bless and keep you under the shadow of His wings,

Yours lovingly,
Bella Cooke

To Miss Annesley
From Annie E. Hillier
April 21st 1875
Dear Friend,

Mother wishes me to write you about her illness. A week ago yesterday, she was taken with a severe chill and high fever, and on Wednesday the erysipelas began on the right side of her face and head, and until Monday morning the doctor gave us but very little hope. He was afraid it would go to her brain.

The pain in her head and face is, and has been, beyond description. No one can imagine the agony she has been in. Her whole face is as large again as it ought to be. The doctor says her hair must be cut off.

Mother has had very little sleep, and only by snatches for a few moments at a time, and in those moments she twitches and starts. The doctor allows no one to talk to her, and orders perfect quietness. She is very weak, having taken nothing but her medicine and ice water for a week, when a little beef tea was given her.

She rested a little better last night, and is easier this morning, but the pain is severe in her head.

Mother desires me to say that on Sunday it seemed as if the warrior was going to lay down his armor; but now a new order has come and the armor is to be taken again for a little while.

Since ma has been so ill, Mr. Stephenson asked if there was anything she wished to have done. He received her answer, and they waited for God's will; but our dear ma is not to leave us yet.

Respectfully,

Annie E. Hillier

A Card

July 12th 1875

No dear, my "Society" keeps open all the year. No vacation, for there are rents to pay, sick to care for, the hungry to feed, the naked to clothe, and words to be spoken for the precious Master. His mercies fail not, and shall I say I am too tired, and cannot do this or that?

He forgot His hunger and weariness by Sychar's well. [John 4.] Oh no, I must do with my might what the dear Lord sends me to do. The resting time will come by and by. May I be found at my post. Suffering, you ask. Yes, suffering much, but leaning on the bosom of my Beloved. Praise the Lord! 'Tis sweet to suffer on and do His will.

Lovingly,

Bella

I received a note from Mrs. Prentiss, as follow:

Dear Mrs. Cooke,

Shortly before leaving town for the summer, your friend Mrs. Collins gave me a hymn which she said was a favorite with you. It at once occurred to me that you might find something in verses of mine, many of which grew out of suffering. Some call it a sad book, but I do not think you will, for you know that to suffer and to rejoice are not inconsistent with each other.

I am not willing to describe my life as a sad one, for it

has been full of Christ, and on your couch of pain you have felt His presence, and love, and sympathy, and know Him, as He is rarely, if ever, known to the well and prosperous. May He give you more of this soul-satisfying experience.

Your friend,

E. Prentiss

You will receive the book soon.

It came, and was well named *Golden Hours*. I have enjoyed it greatly. Many things in it express my own feelings as I could not have expressed them.

I also had from my little granddaughter, Annie Hillier, a book of poems, *Compensation*, by Miss Havergal. These I shall enjoy, for I think of her as one of the purest of spirits.

Like myself, she had traveled long before she found that rest in Christ which the Christian may quickly find through faith. Yet perhaps it is permitted that some of us should thus wander, that we may teach others a shorter way.

Dear Mrs. Lankford Palmer has many times said, "Dear, it seems as though the Lord had given you a taste of almost every kind of trial, in order that you would be able to comfort others." In fact I have often thought when listening to others' trials and perplexities and saying, "Yes, I know all about it," that it might be thought it was a habit to say so. But it was not thus, for I have passed through strange varieties and depths of trial.

Work for Jesus

July 18th 1875

My Precious Sister in Jesus,

I have enjoyed the sweet cards of message which from time to time come to me from you – sweet words of love and encouragement. And although my strength is perfect weakness, yet He indulges me by opening my way to a little usefulness.

The past was a hard winter, many sick and many suffering, and work very scarce. I gave in halves and quarters over forty tons of coal, besides food and clothing. You may know, dear, when I tell you I received and spent about one hundred dollars per month, and in the month of February about two hundred and fifty dollars.

Have sent three families back to Ireland, begged the money for four, with a few pounds extra when they should get there. Have helped two others to go to England. Last week got a poor sick man into The Consumptive's Rest, at Tremont. This week am planning to get a poor woman into some home.

Add to all this, on an average two hundred visitors each month, besides my poor. Then do you think it any wonder I am tired? But the theme of most of my visitors is, "Tell me of the better way." And so I tell them of the way my precious Lord hath led me, and how He has had compassion upon me.

Miss Warner tells my thoughts better than I am able:

> "One more day's work for Jesus,
> How sweet the work has been,
> To tell the story, to show the glory
> Where Christ's flock enter in.
> How it did shine
> In this poor heart of mine."

My precious Mrs. Field is growing most beautifully. I do not remember ever to have had a friend grow faster or more surely in the divine life. She has got into correspondence with Sister Lankford, and is acquainted with Mrs. Jaffray and Mrs. W. E. Dodge, for which I am very glad.

Mrs. F. has begun a Bible class at her country home, to

learn the way more perfectly with her friends and neighbors; and in that class of society where it is so much needed, for as a general thing the rich are a neglected people. Ministers are afraid to speak plainly to them, and Bible-readers have no chance to get at them; but the Father has raised up this dear lovely young woman to teach a living Christ, a full, present, abiding Saviour.

They have just been fixing up my room: new paper, carpet, oilcloth, etc. It looks very grand. It would seem as though there is another winter's campaign before me. How it would gladden my heart to see you again. Hallelujah! The Lord God Omnipotent reigneth. The Lord bless and keep you.

Yours lovingly,
Bella Cooke

Chapter 25

Faith, Hope, Charity

Send portions unto them for whom nothing is prepared
(Nehemiah 8:10).

> Give! as the morning that flows out of heaven;
> Give! as the waves when the channel is riven;
> Give! as the free air and sunshine are given;
> Lavishly, utterly, joyfully give.
>
> Not the waste drops of thy cup overflowing,
> Not the faint sparks of thy hearth ever glowing.
> Not a pale bud from the June roses blowing,
> Give! as He gave thee, who gave thee to live.

To Miss Annesley
January 15th 1876
My Dear Sister in Jesus,
The beautiful Christmas cards have been received and are a comfort to me. I had intended to write you before, but could not. The exhaustion from my Christmas work keeps me down for some time. Well, dear, the Master is very gracious. He opens up our way most wonderfully.

I have had a very busy season. So many poor, and so small the funds from the public charities, so many failures and suspensions. Yet I have no fear. Blessed be His Holy Name, I still feel that,

> "His goodness ever nigh,
> His mercies ever free,

Shall while I live, shall when I die,
Still follow me."

Oh yes, for all this I have fully proved.

"Faithful, O Lord, Thy mercies are,
A rock that cannot move,
A thousand promises declare
Thy constancy of love."

I praise, dear sister, that He lets me do a little of something for Him. My dear ladies are very kind. At Christmas I gave to forty-seven poor families their dinners, which consisted of half a peck of potatoes, three and a half pounds of flour, two quarts of apples, and one or two chickens, according to their families. Thus they all had good dinners on the Redeemer's natal day.

At Thanksgiving I gave out fifty-one turkeys, and a large card with illuminated Scripture to hang in their rooms, that having been fed with the bread that perisheth they might also feed upon the Living Bread.

I have been very feeble, dear, and after those busy days am hardly able to raise my hand or keep my eyes open. When callers come for bread, or to ask about the Bread of Life, I rouse up and talk with them, only to sink down again.

Well, dear, it is all right, just what I want to do for my blessed Master, though Sister Lankford thinks I should not do it. I do want to be at work and watching when the Lord shall come, and the watching and the waiting have their comforts in my little room.

I had a request the other day to find a housekeeper for our evangelists, Moody and Sankey, while they are at work in the city. Well, anything that serves or comforts.

My precious Mrs. Field still goes from grace to grace in

the higher life. Her Bible class continues and she goes right along, blessed child. She runs in frequently to see "Mama Cooke."

Goodbye, dear sister, by and by we shall meet to part no more.

Lovingly,
Bella Cooke

A Card
February 9th 1876
To Miss A.,
Where are you, dear? Have been longing to hear from you. 'Tis a busy time, and the poor body rebels at so much to do, but the spirit triumphs, and thus I am borne along day by day, wondering at what is accomplished, and at the tender charities of the stewards of the Lord.

There is a power that reaches heaven and brings an answer down; that power is prayer. Ask and it is given, spiritual and temporal. All glory to Him who sitteth in the heavens and dispenseth to His creatures.

Oh, darling, my soul sings of His mighty love night and day, and it seems as if I must burst the bonds of clay and go to meet my Beloved.

Yours in our blessed Jesus,
Bella

April 1876
Had a visit from my long-tried and faithful, loving friend, Mrs. Lankford Palmer, who on the 18th of last month was joined in marriage to our esteemed friend Dr. W. C. Palmer. I doubt not it will be a very happy union the few years they may be spared to each other, genial spirits both spending their lives in the service of their Master.

The Lord bless their going out and their coming in from

this time forth and for evermore.

Praise! Praise!

To Miss Annesley
May 30th 1876
My precious Sister in Jesus,
Your little weekly visitors are a great comfort to me and are
hailed with joy. Well, dear, we are still suffering much in
body, but the spirit is upheld.

> "The fire forgets its power to burn,
> The lambent flames around me play."

Oh the blessedness of being wholly given up to Him, our
Lord and our God. He has permitted me to see some souls
step into the liberty of the children of God: some of the
inquirers from Mr. Moody's meetings at the Hippodrome,
and some from other places. God met them and blessed
them in this "little upper chamber."

Mrs. W. E. Dodge brought Mrs. S., and Mrs. Field
brought others. Oh how sweet the work is, to tell the story
how Christ's love entered into our hearts. Though it
exhausts me, still I could not have one less come, either the
rich who come to ask the way of life, or the poor who come
for bread. All, all are welcome. This is all I can do, and with
my latest strength and breath I want to point to the
Redeemer.

It is most difficult to get my breath, on account of the
terribly enlarged liver which presses up against the
diaphragm and lungs, and it seems at times that breathing
must cease. Then comes the severe inflammation of the
membranous coverings of the spine and partial paralysis,
also the sciatica.

So you see, dear, I have considerable to contend with.

"But when I am weak then am I strong." [2 Corinthians 12:10.] Praise the Lord, a present help, a God nigh at hand, ever ready to attend my cry.

Dear Sister L. Palmer gets to see me every week, and we have sweet counsel together with the Lord. Praise His name!

My dear Mrs. Field has had great success with her Bible class in the city the past winter, and will resume the class at her country home this summer.

The children are all well. Pray for dear H. I must stop, am *very tired*.

Yours lovingly in Jesus,
Bella Cooke

A Card
August 22nd 1876
Dear one, I am still left amid heat and suffering. Our Father calls others home from school. Well, 'tis well to stay, to go is best. Home and rest look sweet. Still, if there are any to comfort, any to help, I am willing to give many more days' work for Jesus.

I have been very ill − suffered greatly from heat and pain, but abounding grace prevails. Praise the Lord! We serve a faithful God. Your messages to H. comfort her greatly; nothing too hard for God.

B. C.

September 22nd 1876
Dear Sister Annesley,
I am always glad to get a line from you. Yes, our dear Bishop Janes has run his race and joined the loved one whom he mourned. Although this body is so very weak that it seems difficult to keep alive in it, yet I would not be jealous of those who step in before me.

I have to take one and a half pounds of beef tea every

twenty-four hours, besides wine and brandy stimulants, which latter I have fought against all these years, but have to come to it now. Such sinking, fainting turns come over me from this enlarged liver, and, as I am told, tumor.

The stomach is so crowded that but little food can be taken, as the weight of the liver or tumor rests upon it. Well, dear, I am willing to stay all the days of my appointed time, for in His own good time He will come and take me home to my long-sought rest.

Last Saturday Mrs. Field brought the choir of young ladies from her church in Tarrytown to see me, eight in number, and we had a delightful time. They sang for me, and we talked together. After this I led in prayer, and then spoke with each one alone, and they were one and all affected to tears. It was, indeed, a precious time. Let us pray that the seed may bring forth much fruit.

My winter's work is begun. Many of the ladies are coming home, and the poor, whose wants are many, increase; but strength for the day is promised.

Joseph and Mary are greatly pleased with their home in Birmingham, and the promise is that they will be made very useful. God grant they may.

Amid all the severity of times, dear sister, it is wonderful how the Lord has cared for me. Among those who were raised up to take the place of former friends, are two brothers named Bettle, from Philadelphia. The Lord told them of my needs, for I did not, and they said that they must leave something with me.

I was amazed at the goodness of God, and yet why should I be? Is it not just like Him? Have any of all His promises during twenty-seven years of widowhood failed me? Hath He not indeed and of a truth been a Husband and a Father? Yea, verily, and as I said to one of these two gentlemen eleven years ago when he first saw me, "I *must and will* praise Him."

But I am so tired.

Well, dear, we shall meet one day never to part. The Lord bless and keep you as ever.

Yours lovingly,

Bella Cooke

From Sarah M. Schieffelin

Paris

December 2nd 1876

My Dear Mrs. Cooke,

Your two precious letters came safely, and were welcomed with a joy which I cannot describe. I have many correspondents whose letters are a great delight to me, but I can truly say that none has given me more pleasure than yours. I read and reread them with renewed interest, and, I hope, profit.

How can I thank you enough for your kind thought to send me your photograph, which I value more than I can express. They do not, indeed, do justice to your sweet face with its bright varying expression, but they recall your dear features, and bring to mind that patient touching attitude which suffering has enforced for so many years.

I, with your other friends, cannot be sufficiently grateful for the effort you made, with so much pain, to gratify us. I am so thankful to God that He has kept you through the summer's dreadful heat and raised you again from a dangerous illness.

May it be His holy will to spare your life, and to give not only peace and rest to your soul, but great comfort to that poor, frail body, that temple of the Holy Ghost.

I pray for you earnestly, dear friend, and I trust that a merciful Saviour will answer all my requests for you. And do you, dear Mrs. Cooke, still remember me in your daily petitions? It would be such a heartfelt satisfaction to know that I have a continual place in your prayers.

Your account of the interview with Mrs. Field's class is most touching. May Jesus impress upon those youthful hearts the lessons that they received that day!

How blessed are you in being thus Christ's chosen instrument in gaining souls for Him.

I am always yours,

Sarah M. Schieffelin

Alone, but not Alone

[To an unnamed friend]

December 8th 1876

My Beloved Sister in Jesus,

Your cards, messengers of love, come to me as bright stars that comfort and light me on the weary path. I would have written earlier, but the past two or three weeks I have been so very busy getting ready to give my poor people a dinner that I had to let all writing go I possibly could.

Well, dear, I gave a turkey or chicken and some potatoes to sixty-three families, also a large card with one or two Scripture texts in large letters to hang up in their rooms, so that long after the turkey is gone they could feast on the Word of life.

Last year there were two souls brought to Christ by similar ones. Praise the Lord! "We know not which shall prosper, this or that, or if both shall be alike fruitful," and we will sow beside all waters and pray for the increase.

15th

I must tell you, dear sister, of a great loss we have sustained since I began this letter. I was so tired after I had written the first part, and then I had to get my bedstead fixed, which upset me entirely.

On Monday our dear old faithful and tried friend, John Pullman, died. On the preceding Sabbath he had been at church, Sunday school and prayer meeting. He had visited the sick in the afternoon, as was his habit, and seemed as well as usual. On Monday morning he swept the snow from the stoop, went into the back parlor, took out the morning paper, and so far as we can tell, sat down to read and slipped down on the carpet and died.

Mrs. P. went up to the parlors before ringing the breakfast bell, and found him with the spirit fled. She had seen him on the stoop not ten minutes before. He was ready for the call, fully equipped for an abundant entrance. But oh, how we shall miss him!

Almost the first thought, when I heard it, was, Am I to be left alone? Are all those old and dear friends with whom I took sweet counsel, to leave me, and escape to bliss before me?

Only one of the many dear brethren who were in the church when I joined, thirty years ago, remains. All dead or removed, and here I am left almost alone. The years move on, the solemn, silent years. Yet One abides who has said, "I will never leave nor forsake thee." [Hebrews 13:5.]

On the 16th of May 1847, Mr. Pullman called to see us. It was the day after we landed, and he said, "Child, don't you want to go to church?"

I said, "Yes, I am very hungry."

He replied, "Get on your hat," and away we went, he, my husband and I.

A true friend he has ever been, and for a number of years has called upon me every other Saturday evening. But he will come no more. They come not back, but I will go to them. He was a just man and full of modest charities; one about whom the Saviour's words of Nathaniel might be spoken, "An Israelite indeed in whom is no guile." [John 1:47.]

It was sudden glory to him, but on whom will his mantle fall? Dear Hannah and Joseph feel it very much. He was Hannah's class leader.

Good by, dear one.

Yours, very lovingly,

Bella Cooke

Giving up Chloral

In 1872 chloral had been prescribed for me by three physicians, so that I might sleep. Having used it constantly for four years, the feeling came to me that if I would leave this world with clear intellect, I must give it up. In my Father's name I resolved to give it up.

The physicians thought this could not be done, for I was then taking sixty to seventy grains a night, and they feared the consequences. My answer was, "It is my duty; and while I cannot in my own strength, He who has helped me in all the past will help me still."

I set about it with a will, and with fervent prayer for help. The first two nights the agony was something terrible. The third night I took a little of the drug, then I went without it four nights, fighting my battle for escape; and on the following night took a little more. That was the last. The snare was broken, and from that time till the present hour I have not tasted it.

But I could not make anyone understand what I went through during those days and nights. My physicians looked on in wonder, but the Lord helped me and it was done. I bless Him for giving me strength for the struggle, for I was becoming a slave to it, and no one can tell where it might have led me. "He always causeth us to triumph." [2 Corinthians 2:14.]

Chapter 26

Clouds, Rain and Sunshine

And I said, this is my infirmity; but I will remember the years of the right hand of the most High (Psalm 77:10).

> "I see not a step before me
> As I tread on another year,
> But the past is still in God's keeping,
> The future His mercy shall clear:
> And what looks dark in the distance
> May brighten as I draw near."

Letter to Mrs. Annesley
492 Second Avenue
January 9th 1877
My dear Sister in Jesus,
Another year, and we are spared to glorify Him whom not having seen, we love. When I look at the wondrous love the Father hath had toward me through another year, I am lost in wonder and adoration. Darling, I feel my unworthiness so deeply, and His mercies, love and care so great, that I am amazed at His gracious constancy.

At the beginning of the year, as regarded temporal things, it looked as if all human helps were failing me, but my soul triumphed greatly. I have known somewhat of the "open vision" and the "fellowship" spoken of in the holy book. My soul has seen the King of kings and freely talked with God. The year has passed, and I have been wonderfully taken care of, enough and always something for a poor brother or sister at my door.

How shall I praise Him! Then, dear, to think of so many

of His precious children who come to see me, and the glorious times we have while talking of Him by the way. Oh, I cannot explain or express it. 'Tis just wonderful, wonderful!

Then, too, they help me so with my poor. I sent to dear Mrs. Jaffray and asked her to give me a little more for my poor. She sends me nearly fifty dollars per month. Nehemiah on one occasion bade his people rejoice: "Mourn not, nor weep." [Nehemiah 8:9.]

My dear friends may take that word of cheer to themselves, inasmuch as they have kept Nehemiah's counsel, "Go your way, eat the fat, and drink the sweet, and *send portions unto them for whom nothing is prepared*; neither be ye sorry, for the Lord is your strength." [Nehemiah 8:10.]

I am not rested from Thanksgiving and Christmas. So tired, so tired, but home and rest will come by and by. At times my soul is in haste to be gone, to see Him face to face, and faith seems almost lost in sight. The Invisible appears in view, the rent veil is seen through into the inner temple, and the soul leaps, the heart flutters, and the rustlings of the garments are heard of Him who said, "I will come again and receive you unto Myself, that where I am there ye may be also." [John 14:3.]

And this God is our God, worthy of adoring gratitude.

Very lovingly,

Bella Cooke

P.S. You might like to know the dry goods I have begged and given out this winter, thus far: Three hundred and two yards of muslin; one hundred and seventy yards of calico; ninety-eight yards of flannel, red and canton; fourteen pairs of stockings, blankets, skirts, shirts, etc., besides much half-worn clothing. B. C.

February 15th 1877

They have laid away the remains of my much loved Mrs. Onatavia. She did not tarry long behind her beloved husband. They have both gone to reap the reward of their abundant charities and devout labors, for they loved to work for the Lord.

Kind, gentle and sympathetic towards all they were, and I shall greatly miss their kindness and love. This bed, which their bounty provided, has brought during the past few years more comfort to me than I could possibly tell. As Drs. Palmer and Sabine said, the Lord knew when this was needed, and sent it.

Yes, "Your Heavenly Father knoweth that ye have need of these things," and "No good thing will He withhold from them that walk uprightly." [Matthew 6:8 and Psalm 84:11.]

Mr. Onatavia's acts of kindness can never be forgotten. Unsolicited by anyone, he sent the last three Thanksgiving Days a half barrel of cut sugar, and Mrs. Onatavia never went away without sending all the little ones with Miss Elliott, each having a gift of money for Auntie Cooke.

Yet much as I shall miss all this, more, far more shall I miss their genial visits and words of love and cheerfulness. The last visit dear Mrs. Onatavia made only a few weeks before she left us, she told me what a blessing she had ever found in coming to this little upper room. Also how the children would at any time rather come to see Auntie Cooke than go to a party or take a drive in the park.

She also told me how much our dear Miss Elliott was to them, and that if she were taken away she did not wish anyone to have the care of the children but Miss Elliott, for all they were, she had made them.

Little did we think it would be her last visit to me, but our God doeth all things well, and these four little orphans are as His especial care, for has He not said, "Leave thy

fatherless children, and I will preserve them alive."
[Jeremiah 49:11.]Yes, dear Lord, we have found all Thy
promises, yea and amen.

He gathers home His children one by one. He knows
their names and calls them each in his turn. He is honored
when we wait cheerfully.

> "I lift my head to watch the door and ask
> If He is come;
> And the angel answers sweetly
> In my home:
> Only a few more shadows
> And He will come."

Even so, come, Lord Jesus.

Submission to the Will of God

September 18th 1877
My Dear Sister Annesley,
Since you were here I have been very, very poorly. I suffered
intensely with my head in particular, but I have still, as
through many years, found all the promises yea and amen in
Christ Jesus.

Three weeks ago I said to Dr. Palmer that I did not know
what was the matter with my head. I had thought it was
weakness, but it gets worse and worse. He questioned me
closely, and said he was very sorry I had not told him
sooner.

A few days after, Hannah was here when he called, and
he said he must speak plainly, that there was every
indication of softening of the brain, but he hoped to arrest it

My mind was full of this prayer – Oh, that God would
spare my reason and allow me to cease [suffering] at once,
to work and live.

For this I besought Him oftener than Paul for the thorn in the flesh, and the answer was that He would never leave me. This was enough, and from my heart I spoke the Redeemer's words, "Nevertheless, not my will but Thine be done." [Luke 22:42.]

If I can glorify Thee more as a helpless imbecile, so let it be. I asked my pastor Joseph and others, to wait upon the Lord about it, and they said they believed God would spare my reason to the last.

Dear Sister Lankford Palmer was here, and I told her all that was in my heart. She knelt in prayer, and when she rose, said, "I believe we have the answer. God will let you at once cease [suffering] to work and live."

Praise the Lord! But if He should otherwise ordain, I know He will help my loved ones to bow at His command, and acknowledge that He doeth all things well.

Last Sabbath my dear doctor was more hopeful, and felt now that he might conquer the disease. He would scold very hard if he knew I had written all this, as I am forbidden to write or think.

The Lord bless and keep you.

Yours lovingly in Jesus,

Bella Cooke

November 17th 1877

My Dear Sister Annesley,

You no doubt think it strange that I am so silent, but again I have been very sick. A heavy cold settled upon my lungs and larynx and was very bad. My breathing could be heard at the front door. If the wind blows upon me I take cold, and have yet a bad cough and hoarseness which is very troublesome.

My ear has also been very painful, and these added to my chronic ailments were pretty severe. The doctor was much worried, but the Master says, Not yet, stay a little longer; a few more pleading prayers to offer, a few more sorrowing hearts to soothe.

Well, dear, as God wills; I have nothing to say. I find Him just as precious in storm as calm.

Let the furnace be heated ever so hot, He sits beside and watches, oh how tenderly, each spark.

Yes, I have read the letter in the New Orleans paper about me, but it is too flowery, has too much gilt on. I prefer plain dress. Mrs. Field read it and is in raptures over it. Well, that is something over which I must be silent. If it can in any wise do any good, so be it.

Oh yes, dear, I must feed my hungry poor with good things, that they may have melody in their hearts and give thanks to God. It is little use to tell people with empty cupboards and empty stomachs to sing praise and give thanks. When God undertook to cure Elijah's despondency, He first fed him well, then let him sleep, and then fed him again. Afterwards, He showed him His power, and not till then could poor Elijah hear "the still, small voice." [1 Kings 19:12.]

The doctor has ceased to tell me not to do this or that, because I shall, just as long as God gives me sense and enables me to get the means. The ladies do not deny me. They look on me as a spoiled child that must be humored with what I ask.

He only cries out about the windows. He told me this morning that if I wished to live, the windows must be kept shut. I wonder he does not get tired bothering with me.

I will send you word after Christmas about how much I have given this past year – if spared. Well, dear, I must stop. God bless and keep you and make you more useful than ever.

Your loving sister in Jesus,
Bella Cooke

Chapter 27

The Fiery Furnace

I, the Lord thy God, will hold thy right hand, saying unto thee, "Fear not; I will help thee" (Isaiah 41:13).

> Oh, teach us henceforth, Lord, to see
> That human want and human woe
> Point out where Thou would'st have us go;
> That wrecks of souls along life's sands
> Show where Thy work needs loving hands;
> And when we start dismayed
> To see some shadow in the path,
> Say soft, "Oh ye of little faith,
> 'Tis I, be not afraid."

6 a.m. January 14th 1878

Dear Sister Annesley,

Through the mercy of our God we are spared to the commencement of another year. Mercies and blessings, clouds, and trials, have mingled in our experience during the old year, but the enemy has not been permitted to triumph over us.

Again will we raise our Ebenezer, and in fresh courage take up the work appointed us, and go forward in the name of our Christ Jesus.

He giveth songs in the night, and though my nights would be called terribly bad, yet the Comforter has brought up the things of God, a precious promise or a lovely hymn, and by these I have been encouraged.

The past, although a year of great weakness and pain has been a busy one. I have had two thousand eight hundred and ninety-four visitors, besides visits of my poor, and I received and gave away two thousand and twenty-four dollars, all the recipients coming to me personally, in order that I may know them well and hold out to them the Bread of Life. I also gave nearly three hundred new garments, besides a large number of half-worn ones for children and others.

It would be impossible to tell you, dear, the excessive nervousness and pain in which it has been done, as it would also be to tell the joy of doing it. Then too, dear, I have to praise Him for the loving kindness His dear children have shown me, each one trying in some way to add to my comfort in messages of love, fruits, flowers, and needed aid.

Paul's promise to ancient saints is still true: "My God shall supply all your need according to the riches of His glory." [Philippians 4:19.]

Oh, He is good, and His mercy endureth forever.

Much love,

Bella Cooke

Sweet Communion

Second Avenue

February 11th 1878

On the 5th I had a little prayer meeting in my room, and it seemed little short of heaven's gate. The presence of the Mighty One was plainly felt, yea, we might say,

> "The clouds dispersed, the shadows fly,
> The Invisible appeared in sight,
> And God was seen by mortal eye."

The following friends were present: Mrs. Jaffray, Mrs. Shank, Mrs. Field, Mrs. Bottome, Miss McCauley, Miss Wilson, Mrs. B., and Hannah. Mrs. Lankford Palmer could not be here, as it was Tuesday, meeting day.

I have been very poorly, such suffering as few can understand, but my strength is in the living God. Poor H. is in trouble, and she seems at times to be ready to cry out, "How long, O Lord, how long?"

Lovingly in Jesus,
Bella Cooke

Second Avenue
April 28th 1878
My Dear Sister A.,
This has been so far a year of great suffering and constant labor. I have had two widows to provide for, who have just lost their husbands, and bring through their confinements. Seven orphan children in one family, the youngest only one month old, are also on my hands.

Mrs. Jaffray and her blessed daughter, Mrs. McVickar, gave me clothing, coal and money for the widows. The other family was cared for chiefly by Mrs. Kingsland, who besides providing for the larger children secured a place for the baby in the Child's Nursery.

Another family I have rescued from the very borders of starvation. Dr. Palmer went to visit the woman and returned to tell me it was food they needed more than doctors.

I raised her up with beef tea and light food for two weeks, having also fed the husband and three children. Then I clothed them all and paid their way to Boston, their former home. They are good Christian people.

Then I had another family of five to get back to England who were much in the same condition – no money, no food, no anything. I obtained one steamship fare from St. George's Society, begged another, clothed them all, and the man worked his passage on the steamer.

Two children went for one fare and the infant free. I also

gave them five dollars to take them from Liverpool to Newcastle-on-Tyne, a basket of provisions, a Bible and my blessing, and shipped them off. God go with them. Besides these, my steady poor are very numerous.

This poor body is so weary, so tired, not of the work and waiting, but of constant nervousness and weakness.

> "It is not that I am weary of pain,
> Or impatient of trial or care;
> But I know that to die would be gain,
> And I long, oh, I long, to be there."

I want more and more to glorify Christ, and hold Him up to rich and poor as the One altogether lovely, the great I Am, our Redeemer. Our wonderful Saviour who saves His people from their sins, our Counselor, the Prince of Peace. Yes, He is all this to me, even to me, one of the least of His children. Praise His name!

I had many beautiful things for Easter. What a wonder my blessed friends do not get tired of me; but then it is all of the Lord, and I will thank them and praise Him.

I think I never felt my littleness, my weakness and insignificance more than at the present time, but my trust is in God. Sometimes in the hush of night the query comes, "Will He count me worthy? Oh, darling, to stand before the King of kings is a serious thing, and yet the grace of Calvary!

> "Jesus, Thy blood and righteousness
> My beauty are, my glorious dress."

I bring nothing to merit His favor; it is all free grace and boundless love. Pray for me and write soon. The Lord bless thee and keep thee.

Yours very lovingly in Jesus, Bella Cooke

P.S. I have just received a letter from a missionary in India who visited me before she left. The God of all grace be with the advanced guard who man the outposts of the Everlasting Kingdom.

From Miss M. McCauley to Miss Annesley
August 13th 1878
Dear Miss A.,
At dear Mrs. Cooke's bedside, your postal card is before me. Our precious friend has been very near the "better land" since you heard from her. The heat of early summer greatly prostrated her; then came hemorrhage of the bowels, leaving her very weak.

Two weeks today, inflammation of the stomach came on, since which time she has lived entirely on brandy and medicine. This morning the doctor tried a small quantity of beef tea. It has not made her sick, which greatly encourages us.

For two weeks she has had watchers every night, and medicine or brandy every five minutes for days together. Last Sabbath morning a week ago she had a fearful convulsion, followed by spasms throughout the day, and we certainly thought she would pass away.

Her sister and children were telegraphed. Mary remained a week, and returned home with Mr. Pullman and baby yesterday morning.

On that Sabbath our darling was rarely conscious. Once she looked up in my face, smiled and repeated a line from the hymn, "Jesus leads me all the way." Very wonderfully she is sustained, and in all her suffering she rejoices in her Rock and Saviour.

Hannah is better than one month ago, but deeply anxious for her dear mother. Annie, her husband and child, all have had malarial fever, and this a little retards Mrs.

Cooke's recovery, but she patiently and sweetly rests in the assurance that our Father doeth all things well.

She sends love to you, and says she will attend that business just as soon as she has strength.

Two weeks tonight, the doctor was called at midnight, and for two hours he sat beside her trying to relieve her terrible suffering. Her faithful doctor will have a glorious reward.

It was very touching to see her so deeply anxious, not only about their friend, but also as to what would become of them if she were taken away. We see no reason now to doubt her recovery; and we so long for it, if our Father sees best.

With kind love,
Your friend,
M. McCauley

From the Same
August 19th 1878
My dear Miss A.,
You will be anxious to hear of our precious Mrs. Cooke, and I am very glad to say she seems slowly regaining her usual condition, yet very slowly. More than three weeks of intense suffering leaves her greatly exhausted, patient and gentle, and amid it all attending to her poor.

Going to her bedside this morning, as is my great privilege many times in the week, your letter was handed to me to answer with many others. I wrote nearly two hours, and brought yours off to the quiet of my home where I could more easily collect my thoughts; for no matter how ill our precious one may be, the stream of friends and poor flow on.

Up and down the little stairway such anxious faces, and when they may not enter, we hear the earnest, "How is she?" "Will she live?" "May I just look at her one minute?" "What shall I do if she is taken away?" – until our heart aches and our sympathies are all aroused for the poor people whose very lives seem to depend on her benefactions.

One day last week, when so ill they could not be admitted, an old woman stood in the yard looking up at the window with the tears streaming down her face, and her hands clasped in prayer. It seemed as if she could not leave the place.

At one time when she was so ill that we thought she must pass away, two poor people came whom she sometimes assisted. We knew the funds were overdrawn, and sent them away. She heard of it after a while and reproached herself that she had failed to apply for more funds to meet the need. "Write to Mrs. Kingsland for money;" the response came. The wants were met and then she rested.

In a long lifetime we may never meet such another spirit. It would seem very difficult to suffer pain every hour of one's life, and always have a sweet smile and word of welcome for dear friends. And in great suffering to listen to the sad stories of the poor, the wants, the privations, the details of cares and purposes, hopes and fears of the lowly ones. To be always ready to console, to enter into their plans, advise, assist and encourage − it would seem to require an angel's heart.

And in this way her days and years are spent. In more than twenty-five years of closest intimacy I have never detected a shade of annoyance at the frequent visits of the poor, or the slightest impatience at their often untimely calls.

Thus, day by day, we see the divine power so transforming her nature that we are led "to wonder and adore," and only eternity will reveal the influences that have gone out from that "little upper room."

Purposes are there formed for a new life. Weak,

trembling ones are strengthened; discouraged ones led into new and brighter paths; dark minds pointed to the Sun of Righteousness, and sinners led to Jesus.

During all her recent sufferings, with unusual family cares pressing on her, I have never seen Mrs. Cooke so gloriously upheld. Truly, her "peace flows as a river, her righteousness as the waves of the sea," [Isaiah 48:18], and when dear ones have been grieved at her sufferings, she would smile and say, "It is all right; Jesus knows best. I am perfectly satisfied."

Mrs. Cooke sends her sincere love to you. She loves you very fondly, and will write as soon as well enough.

This is the twenty-ninth anniversary of the death of her husband, and the twenty-seventh of the translation of her little daughter, but there is no gloom attached to her thoughts of them. They are safe, safe at home, and thither she is journeying.

At Mrs. C.'s this morning I met Mrs. Haxton, Mrs. Field, Miss Wilson and others. So they cluster around our dear one with love and sympathy. Goodbye.

Yours,

M. McCauley

October 26th 1878

Precious One,

Did I ever tell you of a little incident which occurred about a year ago? I was very poorly one day, and my dear Joseph was sitting beside me and took up a little book, *Chamber of Peace*, and turned to a piece in it: "So tired." He read it for me, and I said, "Yes, dear, so tired."

At that moment a knock at the door, and Mrs. Haxton's waiter came in with a parcel. Joseph opened it, and there was a beautiful picture of flowers with the words, "I will give thee rest." To the casual observer it might seem as nothing, but to me it was a great deal, even a message fresh from Him who has said, "I will give thee rest." [Matthew 11:28.]

It was as a cooling drink to the way-worn pilgrim who is parched on the weary road. And thus I drink by the way, a sip from this and a sip from that; but all from His wells of living water. How wonderfully have I proved His love and care the past three months.

My expenses were great. It has cost me more than two hundred dollars extra. Eighty-six night watchers at one dollar per night, twenty-one of which I paid one dollar and twenty-five cents per night, besides extra help in the day, as I was unable to take the medicine or help myself. Yet it came from my old *true* and *tried* friends, Mrs. Haxton, Mrs. Jaffray, Miss Elliott, and others.

Some came from abroad, as Mr. Bettle of Philadelphia; also from other sources that I had no idea of. How true, "His mercies fail not." [Lamentations 3:22.] Oh how good the Lord has been to me, and how sweet it is to see those dear ladies tire not, but cluster around me with all the love and affection possible.

Truly it is the Lord, and we will praise Him. I would not wonder if they did grow tired as year after year I am left a care and expense to them. I often think, did ever anyone see or know so much of the loving care and sympathy of God and His dear children? Do you wonder that I want to cry out, "Bless the Lord, O my soul, and all that is within me bless His holy name?" [Psalm 103:1.]

While I have my being, will I bless Him; and when my voice is lost in death, praise shall employ my nobler powers. I often think when I want to sing and cannot: never mind, by and by, in a nobler, sweeter strain I'll sing His power to save.

I can write no more. God bless you and give you peace.

Yours lovingly in Jesus,

Bella Cooke

Abounding Privileges

December 13th 1878

Beloved Sister in Jesus,

Your two cards were most welcome; thanks for them. Yes, dear, I am the Lord's, and I leave all, and rest in Him and His will.

Many come to me about faith healing, but as I told Mrs. M. D. James last week, I do not believe God intends to heal me here, and I have nothing to do with it. Living or dying, sick or well, I am the Lord's, and all is well. Yes, dear, I have been very *tired*, but happy in the Lord and could sing,

> "One more day's work for Jesus,
> How sweet the work has been."

At Thanksgiving I gave dinners of turkeys and chickens, potatoes and apples; and to the aged, tea and sugar. To ninety-two families almost six hundredweight of poultry, two and a half barrels of potatoes, and two of apples.

I do feel so thankful to God that He gives me favor in the sight of the ladies who so kindly give me the means to buy these things. I take them as from the hands of the Saviour, as did the disciples of old, and distribute to the multitude.

The text which I wrote for each was sewed on the neck of the fowl. It was, "O, give thanks unto the Lord for He is good; for His mercy endureth for ever." [Psalm 107:1.] Then they had their large Scripture text cards to hang up, also a paper, *Words of Life*; and I was just as happy as I could be this side of heaven.

I have been collecting money to enlarge our Old People's Home in Forty-Second Street, and have succeeded to the amount of about sixty dollars.

Now I am getting up a little Christmas for each of the infant class of our Lott's Creek Sunday school, near Fort

Dodge, Iowa. A few years ago my friend, Miss McCauley, started a Sunday school at Lott's Creek. To help the good work I sent them three dozen Bibles, about twenty hymnals as rewards for catechism recitations, and over one hundred library books.

Besides, I have the Christmas dinners for the sick and aged ones. So you see, amid my weakness and pain I am kept busy. And all my ladies must have a New Year's greeting, and my grandchildren some little thing. But how I love the work, none can tell. Permitted to do anything for Jesus is a privilege.

I am not as strong, dear, as I was before my last illness, but He increaseth my strength in Him day and night. Praise His name, for it is life and health and peace.

One of my ladies has had to stop a part of her contributions for the poor, so I was fifty dollars short. Thus I had to try and beg from others, which with the more than one hundred necessary to raise for Thanksgiving caused a good deal of writing, and that increases my pain; but, dear, the joy to see all those poor people happy.

What a happy lot is mine! I often wish you could see us on Sabbath afternoons when my six or seven boys are here, ranging from seventeen to twenty-two or three. They come regularly to sing for me, and either one of them or I lead in prayer.

Last Saturday I had sixty ginger cakes made and sent to the Hopper Home for discharged prisoners, and the poor things are so glad to get a little change from the poor fare. Miss Doremus visits them every Saturday. So, dear, you find we are all kept pretty busy.

The Lord help and bless you to the end.

Yours very lovingly,

Bella Cooke

Chapter 28

Rich, Not Poor

As poor, yet making many rich; as having nothing and yet possessing all things (2 Corinthians 6:10).

> Call me not poor; I nothing lack,
> For lo! a voice divine
> Has made me feel that I am His,
> And told me He is mine.

> Weep not that on this weary bed
> I long must droop and pine;
> Here I have learned the peace of God,
> And know that He is mine.

January 1st 1879

Another year of mercies and blessings. While many have been called to mourn the loss of near and dear friends, we have an unbroken circle. How thickly strewn have been the blessings of my God to us year by year! He hath kept me in the corner, having clipped my wings on purpose, that I might see His providing care. May my spared life show forth His praise more than ever. I sing with Wesley,

> "Come, let us anew our journey pursue,
> Roll round with the year,
> And never stand still till the Master appear.
> His adorable will let us gladly fulfill,
> And our talents improve
> By the patience of hope and the labor of love.

That at last, having done and suffered all His righteous will, I may hear the glad word,

"Well and faithfully done!
Enter into My joy, and sit down on My throne!"

Have had very much love and kindness shown to me the past year by my friends, for which I do thank and bless my dear Lord. Surely though the thorns may at times bruise the feet along the rugged pathway, and we may say as we look to Him with humble confidence, "Is this the way, my Father?" Yet we feel His hand gently and carefully leading us, and we can sing,

"Above the rest this note shall swell,
My Jesus hath done all things well."

Many poor cluster around me for help, and friends are very kind; but it takes labor and thought and much prayer to find coal, food and clothing to give even a little to each. But the gold and the silver is Thine, the work also is Thine, and we leave it all with Thee.

January 12th 1879
Had a call from my old and faithful friend, Mr. Henry Dickinson. For nearly fifty years a strong friendship has existed between Mr. and Mrs. D. and myself. A truly devoted couple, constantly at work in the Lord's vineyard.

Had a visit from Mrs. Schieffelin and Brother Stephenson, with many other dear ones, and we held sweet communion with our Lord.

Mrs. Henry Clewes and Mrs. Brewster called today.

February 1879

"I will extol Thee, my King and my God, I will bless Thy name for ever and ever. Every day will I bless Thee, and I will praise Thy name for ever and ever." [Psalm 145:1.]

My dear sister has been to see me, and we had a precious time. The sacrament of the Lord's Supper was administered, and we realized His presence as we gathered around the Lord's Table. I had with me to share the feast my dear sister, Mrs. Glover, Mrs. McKennell, Miss McCauley, my leader and Pastor Glover.

> "I would Thy boundless love proclaim
> With every fleeting breath;
> So shall the music of Thy name
> Refresh my soul in death."

Had a visit from my late pastor, W. W. Clark. While recounting the mercies and blessings of our Father, I find they very far outweigh the trials, though these to the observer seem very great. But while the great I AM stands by me and says, "Fear not, be not dismayed; I will be with Thee, I am Thy God," [Isaiah 41:10] how can I fear?

My heart is hungry for souls. Lord. Revive Thy work in our little church. Bless the efforts put forth for a Pentecostal shower. Make bare Thine arm; bring many to bow to the mild scepter of Jesus. Give to our dear pastor and leaders strength to wrestle with Thee in mighty faith, that Thy name may be glorified. Send the power, O Lord; send the power to a preached word, and give us a mighty blessing.

March 1879

Another month gone into eternity, and we are spared.

"When all Thy mercies, O my God,
My rising soul surveys,
Transported with the view I'm lost
In wonder, love and praise.

Dr. Cullis of Boston was here to see me with two ladies, to entreat of the Lord to heal this poor body. He spoke with me at length, assured me I must be healed, that I had lain here long enough, and that I must believe in the healing of the body, for I could do more good if I were up and around.

I told him I was willing to be healed or not, just as pleased my God. Sickness and health I left with Him, glad to be healed or glad to be on my bed in pain, only to be where I could glorify Him best.

He said, "Yes, you are too passive."

I told him when I had asked for healing, the answer given to Paul was given to me, "My grace is sufficient for thee." [2 Corinthians 12:9.]

He said I did not know that Paul was not healed of his infirmity. He then read in James, "Is any sick among you? Let him call for the elders of the church; and let them pray over him, anointing him with oil in the name of the Lord." [James 5:14.]

Having asked me if I believed God's word, he prayed, laid his hands upon me and anointed me with oil. It was a very solemn time.

He then asked me if I were healed, and bade me get up and walk.

I answered that I could not.

He then told me that I must have faith, and believe I was healed. But how could I, with all the pain and weakness? I asked him to teach me how to believe. I would do anything I could, but did not know what to do, and could not do impossibilities. I had no lights on the subject at all.

He asked me if I did not feel the healing power.

I said, "I do not know. I feel the sacred awe that dares not move."

Dr. Cullis turned to the ladies, and said, "Come, in three days' time she will walk."

I trembled all over, and was greatly exercised. I begged of the Lord to teach me what and how to believe, to help my unbelief. None can know what I felt. I was ready to ask, had I ever had any faith, or what was the matter with me?

I promised the Lord if it were His will to heal me, I would devote all my time and strength to Him. I knew if it were His will that I should lie here and suffer, He would not desert me, but still give strength to labor and to wait.

I did not dare to speak of it to anyone but my kind physician, who said none would be more glad than he to see me well. I feared if I spoke of it and were not healed, I would bring discredit on the faith of these good people and injure their usefulness.

Thus it went on till the second night, when almost distracted I begged of the Lord to return my peace of mind, and, as often before, I left myself again in His hands to do what seemed good to Him. Healed or not healed, I was His — soul and body. All my will was His, and His will was mine. Then peace and rest came back to me.

None can tell what I have suffered in mind and body by well meaning and devout people on this subject of faith healing.

They come and assure me that God had sent them to heal me, that I had no faith, and thus I was a stumbling block to many. All this has made me so nervous that I have been ready to think I must be either doing something wrong, or leaving undone some great Christian duty.

Not until I was enabled to cast it all from me, to lay it down as a burden not to be carried, and had taken refuge in the care of the everlasting arms, was my old peace and rest restored to me. Praise the Lord for a hiding place. I tell them God has not revealed Himself to me in this particular, and I can do nothing until He does.

Give me patience, dear Lord, and teach me Thy way, and lead me in a plain path. All the praise shall be Thine; the glory shall be Thine now and evermore.

March 31st 1879

"How precious are Thy thoughts unto me, O God! How great is the sum of them! If I could count them they are more in number than the sands of the sea; when I awake I am still with Thee." [Psalm 139:17.]

On the third day after Dr. Cullis was here, Miss Bailey came again and asked me if I had been up and walked yet. I told her no, I could not, but if my Father took away the enlarged liver and other ailments, that same power would put strength into the spine, and then I could walk.

She replied that I should not worry about it; that perhaps I could do more for God as I was. I said I felt I was just where God would have me be.

A Mrs. Hughes has also been here. She told me that the Lord had sent her, and that she was so full of the Holy Ghost that she could hardly stand.

She took off her gloves and put one hand on my chest and one on my spine, and groaned and prayed and pronounced me healed. She gave me no chance to converse with her, but hastened away, saying, "You are healed. You have served Satan long enough; get up and glorify God."

April 1879

Conference is over, and my dear children are sent to West Winsted, Conn. We had hoped they would have been sent near to me, so I could have had the pleasure and comfort of their company; but they are Thine, my Father, and I am Thine. Take them, do with them as Thou wilt. If they can serve Thee better there in the distance, amen.

These dear ones are all Thine and Thy promises are still the same. "Leave thy fatherless children, I will preserve them alive, and let thy widows trust in me." [Jeremiah 49:11.]

> "All my trust on Thee is stayed,
> All my help from Thee I bring;
> Cover my defenseless head
> With the shadow of Thy wing."

May 30th 1879

The Lord is my light and my salvation, whom shall I fear? The Lord is the strength of my life, of whom shall I be afraid? [Psalm 27:1.]

I have passed through severe ordeals. Oh, the terrible wickedness of man when he forsakes his God.

Though ten thousand foes my soul or body assail, greater is He that is for me than all that are against me. He has promised, and I trust His word.

July 14th 1879

Another milestone passed. Friends still so kind. Dear Mrs. Haxton was here with her birthday gift, and the luxuries for our little party. It is indeed very beautiful. Many other dear ones come with gifts to cheer me by the way. Oh, what blessings, how richly they abound!

A great strain and duty has been put on me, and it called for money. Never before in my thirty years of widowhood had I asked anyone for help, as I made a resolution when my dear husband died neither to go in debt nor ask for help, but to look to my Heavenly Father. But on June 16th we had to raise two hundred and fifty dollars.

I took it to the Lord. I slept on it, then the next morning I wrote to two friends. Each sent me one hundred dollars. In six hours I had returned half of it; I did not need it.

Did my Lord fail me in my extremity? No, a thousand times no, for a thousand promises declare His constancy of love. None ever trusted and was put to shame. Faith was tried, deliverance came. Praise the Lord. Many stand amazed at His goodness to me, but,

> "His goodness ever nigh,
> His mercy ever free,
> Shall while I live, shall when I die
> Still follow me."

My dear Joseph and Mary came down and stood by me a great part of the time, as did also my pastor, Mr. Glover, Brother Stephenson and others, all of whom wondered at the strength given.

"If thou seest the oppression of the poor, the violent perverting of judgment and justice in a province, marvel not at the matter, for He that is higher than the highest regardeth, and there be higher than they." [Ecclesiastes 5:8.] And while He, my God, is near, I need not fear. No, "Though an host should encamp against me, my heart shall not fear." [Psalm 27:3.]

August 1879

I have had a very weak and suffering time of late, so much trouble with sick stomach and prostration. But "He giveth power to the faint, and to them that have no might He increaseth strength." [Isaiah 40:29.]

Thirty years have passed since we laid away the remains of my beloved husband. Thirty years of bliss to him, thirty years of unnumbered mercies and blessings to me.

How shall I praise Him?

> "In want, my plentiful supply;
> In weakness, my almighty power;
> In bonds, my perfect liberty;
> My light in Satan's darkest hour;
> In grief my joy unspeakable;
> My life in death, my all in all."

September 10th 1879

Sister Louise called today to say she had at last found a house that would answer her purpose. She had long been wanting to organize a Free Home for poor, respectable Protestant women and children. There had been some old furniture given, one month's rent promised, and she had come to me for the first donation.

I said, "Sister Louise, I have no money to give you. What I have is all appropriated, and of my own I have given all I can."

She replied, "I have felt all along that you must give the first donation with your blessing, and the Home will prosper."

I said, "Well, I have a three-dollar gold piece that I had given me to keep. I will give you that with my blessing."

She answered, "With that we shall open the Home."

Sister Louise is a deaconess of the Episcopal Church. She was brought to me about a year ago by Dr. Headley, a man full of faith and good works. Sister L. is a great worker amongst the poor, and has given her life to that work. May her efforts be blessed.

In her first report she says, "We waited for one year, during which time we received, from one who has rested upon a bed of incurable sickness for over twenty-five years, the cornerstone of our Home in a three-dollar gold piece. This, with a sufficient sum for one month's rent, enabled us to begin the work."

October 1879

I have been very poorly since I last wrote. Such utter prostration. But as the cool breezes come, we hope, if it be the Lord's will, that I may be a little stronger. Many loved friends are coming back from the country. Oh, the precious privilege of communing with His children!

How many changes since I last wrote, among them the sickness and translation of our beloved friend and sister, Miss Annesley. She was a bright and shining light. Our Father was very good to her. She always dreaded pain, and He took down the earthly tabernacle without any pain. She sweetly slept and sank away.

How little we thought that she would be taken, and I left. She desired, if it were the Lord's will, to be permitted to give to the world the little jottings I had made from time to time of the Lord's dealings with me. But she is gone and I am left to still receive of His goodness here, and tell of His wondrous works.

Her niece, Miss Gray, writes that often when her dear aunt would arouse she would say, "I must write to Sister Cooke."

Thus her thoughts followed us to the edge of the Border Land while any consciousness was left. How I shall miss her kindly visits, her bright and cheery laugh, her little bits of pleasantry and her earnest prayer at parting, after which she would often say, "Now, you lie there and preach from your pulpit, and I shall run around doing the Lord's will as He shall send me."

How her heart would rejoice to hear of a soul being blessed and brought to the Lord at this bedside! But she has gone to rest, and we are left to labor and wait and suffer still. 'Tis well,

> I linger on my three score years
> Till my Deliverer come,
> And wipe away His servant's tears,
> And take His exile home.
>
> Give joy or grief, give ease or pain,
> Take lilts or friends away,
> But let me find them all again
> In that eternal day.

The Master had need of our dear one to swell the great throng in singing the new song. Thus our close union of twenty-six years of Christian friendship is broken; but patience, my soul.

November 10th 1879
"My soul followeth hard after Thee, Thy right hand upholdeth me." [Psalm 63:8.]

Have got the promise of help for my poor as usual for Thanksgiving. From Mrs. Haxton fifty dollars, and other amounts from a number of others, so my soul is glad. I now begin to make ready for the feast.

Give me strength, dear Father, that I may do all with an eye single to Thy glory. Tell me what is Thy will and where to go. Still, if it please Thee, give me favor in the sight of Thy children. Much money is needed for food, coal and clothing for the poor, besides the money for the dinners at Thanksgiving.

November 30th 1879
Have had a very busy month. *Very tired.* Again have kind

friends rallied around this room and given me funds by which I provided good things for dinners for ninety-eight families, all of whom would have had very little to make a Thanksgiving Day.

I often wish the ladies could see the happy faces and the hearty "Thank you" from many, while some are so full that they can only look their thanks through tearful eyes.

Thus another Thanksgiving Day is gone. May the truths given in tracts and Scripture cards, and the seed sown yield much fruit. Nor while thinking and planning for others was I forgotten. Dear ones sent, as usual, a bountiful supply for my own use.

December 30th 1879

Again a busy month, and still tired. Oh, so tired, yet the work is sweet. On the 23rd gave to fifty poor aged and sick ones a basket full of good things for Christmas dinner. The weather is cold; coal and clothing are needed.

I have already drawn largely on Mr. Blake for coal from the city funds. Dear Mrs. Jaffray has sent me her usual donation of clothing for the poor. Blessed woman! Many kind ladies come to my help.

Praise the Lord! The gold and silver are His, and He has the hearts of all men in His hands. My Christmas Day was made very bright by kind gifts from many dear ones.

I wonder they do not get tired, since I stay so long; but no, no signs of that. They seem to vie with each other, not only to supply all my needs, but to gratify me in things of beauty as well as of use.

I cannot find words to express the goodness of God to me; it is past finding out. He fills my soul so full that when alone and in the hush of night, I cannot but cry out in praise and adoration; and as the Comforter takes up the things of God and reveals them unto me, our converse is very sweet.

Another year has come to its close. Have I been as faithful as I might have been; as tender and gentle to the wayward ones; as full of love as I ought to be? I fear I have left undone many things I ought to have done, missed opportunities of speaking a word for Thee. Blot out, I pray Thee, every sin of omission and of commission, every unworthy act or thought or unconscious sin, and thoroughly cleanse this soul that clings to Thee. Afresh I do give all I have and am to Thee. Do with me as Thou wilt.

> "In full and glad surrender
> I give myself to Thee,
> Thine utterly and only
> And evermore to be.
> O Son of God, who loved me,
> I will be Thine alone,
> And all I have and all I am
> Shall henceforth be Thine own."
> Amen.

Calls received during 1879: 3,526. Moneys received and given to the poor during the year: $1,681.25.

By Miss Mary H. Doremus

My beloved mother, the late Mrs. Thos. C. Doremus, became acquainted with Mrs. Bella Cooke nearly thirty years ago. The friendship thus commenced has been an inheritance in the family, who have esteemed the influence of her powerful character as a benediction.

When, in 1855, The Woman's Hospital was established in New York, Mrs. Cooke was one of the first patients. But when after some time her case was found to be incurable, several ladies, appreciating her worth, engaged rooms for her with suitable comforts, feeling this afflicted child of God was especially their care.

While at the hospital she commenced the first religious services conducted in its walls, each morning and evening singing a hymn, reading the Holy Scriptures and praying. Many heard there for the first time the comforting words of the blessed volume.

Thus Mrs. Cooke was at the hospital a remarkable instrument for good, as she has ever been outside of its walls. No one can look upon her lovely countenance without being drawn to a better and holier frame of mind. In this, her personal magnetism has greatly aided. Her cheerful obedience to her Heavenly Father's will, in laying her aside from the usual duties of life and its activities, has always been a great example to others.

Not only has her influence been felt among her especial circle, but among the rich and fashionable who, being led to comfort and minister to her, received from her lips a double blessing for their souls. Many of these "daughters" for whom her prayers have been heard will be given to her as sparkling jewels in her "crown of life."

Mary H. Doremus
New York

Chapter 29

Joys of Friendship

A friend loveth at all times, and a brother is born for adversity (Proverbs 17:7).

There is a friend that sticketh closer than a brother (Proverbs 18:24).

> Much beautiful, and excellent, and fair
> Was seen beneath the sun; but naught was seen
> More beautiful, or excellent, or fair
> Than face of faithful friend; fairest when seen
> In darkest day.

January 1st 1880

The friendships to which my indulgent Father has introduced me have, next to the fellowship divine, been the joy and blessing of my life. These beautiful friends, who from love measure not their kindness to me, they know not, and can never know the sunshine they have thrown about this poor heart.

I have read somewhere of the blessing it is to have friends to whom one's deepest or one's most foolish thoughts might be intrusted safely, and I have known the comfort of feeling safe with friends, having neither to weigh thought or measure words, but certain that a love which knows no suspicion will sift my poor speech and keep what is worth keeping, and throw the rest away.

With many such friends, I renew my covenant on the morning of another New Year's Day.

January 18th 1880

Dr. Palmer brought to my notice a poor old couple, brother and sister, aged eighty-two and eighty-four, both sick and helpless. I sent to Mrs. J. Crosby Brown, Mrs. Field and Mrs. Kingsland and received liberally from each of them, and then sent food and a nurse to care for them. I fear they do not honor their Lord and Master as they should. Lord, prepare them for the great change that awaits them.

I have sent to Mr. Blake for coal for twenty poor families from the city funds. He is very kind, and responds to my requests with great promptness. Blessed privilege to give for the healing of human woes!

Although the weather is not as severe as some winters are, yet there is great suffering amongst the poor. Many dear ones come to see me, and some young people to sing for me.

February 8th 1880

Have had a glorious day, although very feeble in body. The Lord is my strength and will be my portion forever.

Had a visit from my old and esteemed friends, Mr. and Mrs. Murray Shipley, of Cincinnati. For more than twenty years he has been coming to see me in this little home, a man of God, earnest, zealous, "a scribe instructed unto the kingdom of heaven." [Matthew 13:52] A willing laborer in the vineyard, preaching the word, visiting the sick and pointing them to the cleansing blood of Christ.

We have had many precious seasons in this upper room where the Christ, the Son of the Living God, has met with us. "That they may be one; as Thou, Father, art in Me and I in Thee, that they may be one in Us." [John 17:21.]

March 26th 1880

Good Friday

A. solemn day is beautiful Good Friday. Our hearts and eyes

o'erflow as we think of the hour when for us the Saviour died. I have been with Him in the garden, and have felt afresh that mysterious sorrow, and heard His unfathomable cry about the cup when His sweat was as great drops of blood.

I have beheld Him in the palace of the high priest crowned with thorns, and as He stood forth, king-like, before the Roman in the hall of judgment. I have followed Him to Calvary and heard His gracious prayer, "Father, forgive them, they know not what they do;" [Luke 23:34], and we know that for us He died. He bore our sins in His own body on the tree.

> "I, I alone, have done the deed,
> 'Tis I, thy sacred flesh have torn;
> My sins have caused Thee, Lord, to bleed,
> Pointed the nail and fixed the thorn.

> "My Saviour, how shall I proclaim,
> How pay the mighty debt I owe?
> Let all I have and all I am,
> Ceaseless to all Thy glory show."

> *Easter Morn*
> "Break off your tears, ye saints, and tell
> How high your great Deliverer reigns.

"He is not here, for He is risen," was the angel's salutation. And then was our poor humanity transfigured in the light eternal. We shall live forever! Glory! My soul rejoices. How shall I praise Him? Tears of joy my eyes o'erflow. "He ever lives above for me to intercede." Yes. "He rose; He burst the bars of death and triumphed o'er the grave."

Many beautiful flowers have been sent to me by Miss

Haxton, Mrs. Field and Mrs. McVickar. Also very many lovely Easter cards. Bless and reward them, my Father.

My dear sister was here with me to enjoy these great feasts of the Christian year, and by and by we shall be where parting is unknown.

April 2nd 1880
Very sick. Dr. Palmer here twice yesterday.

> "When pain o'er my weak flesh prevails,
> With lamb-like patience arm my breast."

I praise Thee, my Father, that all, all is known to Thee. Oh, sanctify every stroke. Give me patience to listen to the sad stories of the poor, and help me to be eyes to the blind and feet to the lame. Send *whom* Thou pleasest and *when* Thou pleasest. Give me patience with the selfish and perverse. May I remember how Thou hast borne with me, and give me a word in season for them that are weary.

Many things of a trying nature have lately presented themselves, but I try to look above for wisdom and strength. Oh, for the great victory of Paul in the matchless outburst with which he closed the eighth chapter of Romans. [For I am persuaded, that neither death, nor life, nor angels, nor principalities, nor powers, nor things present, nor things to come, nor height, nor depth, nor any other creature, shall be able to separate us from the love of God, which is in Christ Jesus our Lord.]

April 14th 1880
My dear Mary and her daughter Nellie came today from Winsted, Conn. They are preparing [Mary's daughter] Bella to visit her Uncle Thomas Pullman in Ireland, who wishes her to spend a year with them. God grant it may be for the

best. If not, O Lord, thwart the preparations.

April 24th 1880
They have all gone to see the dear child Bella Beeton
Pullman off on the steamer *Devonia*. I feel it greatly. O
Father, Thou who holdest the winds and waves in Thy hand,
guide her safely; cover her with Thy feathers; permit no evil
to befall her; keep her amid all temptations and deliver her.
May the same spiritual strength be given her as was given to
her great-great-grandmother Smawfield, who in the earliest
days of Methodism received stripes for Christ's sake.

Let me tell the story. My grandmother with a neighbor
had been attending religious meetings, although their
husbands, who were farmers, were godless men. The worthy
farmers talked it over, and decided that their wives should
not disgrace them by attending the meetings. So they agreed
to tell them that if they went again, on their return they
should be horsewhipped.

Our grandmother heard the mandate, and asked her
husband if she had neglected her home duties? No. If she
had been a less dutiful wife because of her religion? No.

"Very well then, by the help of the Lord, I shall go."

She went and had a good meeting. On her return her
sturdy husband met her with the greeting, "Now, Betsy, you
have had your way, I will have mine."

He took the whip from behind the door, and whipped
her till he was weary, if not ashamed.

She asked him if he had done. He said yes.

When undressing at bedtime she looked at her shoulders
and arms, and seeing them all black and in ridges from the
whip, she said, "Praise the Lord, stripes for Christ's sake."

It touched her husband's heart, and he fell on his knees
and begged her to forgive him. She replied, "You have not
offended me, but you have offended my Saviour. Ask Him to

forgive you."

He did this, and with great contrition sought the divine mercy. He obtained mercy, because he did it ignorantly in unbelief, and became an earnest Christian for the rest of his life. Thus the Lord works, and none can hinder.

My dear Mrs. Stillman was here and gave me money with instructions to buy a new carpet for my room. "He maketh me to lie down in green pastures."

A Friend Gathered Home

May 17th 1880

Had a visit from Mr. Wm. Bettle, a kind and true friend who for many years has been coming to see me, and by words of cheer and prayer has often brightened my pathway. He tells me with tears and faltering voice that his dear brother Samuel will never come to see me again, for in January last he finished his course, and heard his Saviour's welcome.

He was a most earnest, faithful man of God. How I shall miss him! These two brothers have helped greatly to keep the barrel of meal, and cruise of oil supplied. William told me that only the day before his brother entered into rest, he said, "Brother William, I want to go and see Bella Cooke and Theodore Cuyler before I pass away." But the Master called, and he was all ready.

> "Another gem in the Saviour's crown.
> Another soul in Heaven."

May 31st 1880

Another month gone, in which I have had as usual many dear friends. It has been filled with mercies and blessings innumerable. Dear Mrs. Wood has sent me two beautiful rugs and new oilcloth for my room. She also sent a man to paint it.

Many dear ones have been to say goodbye, as they are going to different places for the summer, and among them was Mrs. Jaffray. Also dear Mrs. Stuyvesant, with one dozen cambric handkerchiefs marked B. C., made for me in Paris.

Letters from our darling Bella tell us of her safe arrival in Belfast, and hearty welcome. Praise the Lord. Mrs. Crosby Brown and one of the children came to say goodbye. Go, we beseech Thee, with one and all, and may their health be precious in Thy sight.

June 17th 1880

Mrs. Brewster was here on the 14th to tell me about her approaching wedding. She sent me a beautiful copy of *The Land and the Book* by Dr. Thompson, also fifteen dollars for poor Mrs. Lilley's rent for three months – one of my poor widows whom Mrs. Brewster was greatly interested in. Mrs. B. also sent ice cream and cake to all the inmates of Roosevelt Hospital, that they might all rejoice with her on her wedding day. God grant it may be a very happy union, both spiritually and socially.

June 30th 1880

Have been very feeble the past month, the weather has been so hot. Well, by and by I shall, if faithful, be where no sun shall light upon me, nor any heat.

Again many have been to say goodbye, amongst whom was Mrs. F. W. Vanderbilt and Mrs. McVickar, who brought me Dr. Wm. Taylor's book, *Peter the Apostle*. I know I shall like it, for Dr. Taylor's *Elijah* and *David* are grand.

Dear Miss Hamersley with Mrs. Schieffelin also came with their kind gifts, so that while they are away I may lack nothing. Dear Miss H. with her father and brother leave for Europe.

"Lord, whom winds and seas obey,
Guide them through the watery way;
In the hollow of Thy hand
Hide and bring them safe to land."

July 13th 1880
Fifty-nine years old! Dear Mrs. Haxton cannot be with us today; she is sick at Staten Island. Goodness and mercy have followed me all my days, and still His banner over me is love. [Song of Solomon 2:4.]

Very feeble from gastric troubles, but God is my strength and my portion forever.

July 20th 1880
Had my dear pastor in. He is in trouble. Has to raise five hundred dollars toward repairs in our dear old church. He showed me some names and asked me what I thought he would get from them.

I told him that I would not be willing to give him seventy-five dollars for them.

"Why," he said, "I hoped to get four hundred dollars. You have knocked all the breath out of me."

I promised to raise him one hundred dollars by the middle of September. He was delighted, and said that he had now a foundation to work on.

August 3rd 1880
Very hot. Had dear Mrs. Field here to tea. We had a very pleasant time. She sang, and played her guitar for me.

Had a call from Mrs. Fletcher Harper, and felt the presence of the Lord while we talked of His goodness and His power to save. Thus, one and another of the noble women of our city come to this little upper room and sit and talk with me, and as Doctor Sabine once said, bring me,

"Out of Second Avenue into Fifth." But His saints are one in Christ Jesus.

Had a visit from a lady whom Mrs. F. W. Vanderbilt sent to see what I needed to make my room look cheerful and comfortable. I sent word: Nothing, I had all I wished.

Mrs. V. sent a letter saying, "Get new muslin for window curtains and bright new ribbons to tie them. Also a new stair carpet. Send the bill to me." My cup runneth over. [Psalm 23:5.]

> "Not more than others I deserve,
> Yet God has given me more."

August 26th 1880

My dear class leader laid away the remains of his wife today; a good wife, a faithful, devoted daughter, a loving mother. Bless and comfort them all, and may they find a resting place in Thee.

Brother Stephenson and many others called after the funeral services. Thus, "friend after friend departs."

August 28th 1880

Have just received all the little ones back home from Bath, where they have been for six days to enjoy the fresh air and sea bathing and good, wholesome food. I have sent twenty poor children to the seaside this summer.

It is a lovely sight when they are starting off. All have to come here and get a goodbye kiss. Their bright, happy faces do me good. Happy, happy childhood! How I love to see them and help them along; then, too, it helps their mothers, most of whom are widows.

September 9th 1880

Miss Kilmer was here to ask help for a poor woman who is in

a terrible condition, having fallen down the hatchway of a steamer coming from England, and is fearfully hurt. She is a devout Christian, and as it is not at all likely she can live long, we must do all we can for her.

September 19th 1880
Have had a blessed day, blessed Sabbath, sweet day of rest. Had my dear Mrs. Congdon to see me today for the first time since her precious sister, Miss Elizabeth Smith, was taken to be forever with the Lord.

Years of watching that precious one had made the parting very painful. Well, she too, will by and by go to meet her Lord and dwell with Christ at home.

Dear Miss S. S. Murray was with her. Miss Murray thinks she can get Mrs. Abblet's daughter a position in the coffee house. Also had a visit from Brother Mackey that cheered us.

A Happy Pastor
September 23rd 1880
Had my dear pastor, Mr. Glover, in, and handed him the $100 I promised him for the church.

1 said, "I promised to raise you this sum by this time, and have kept my promise."

I wrote to several ladies (not any of them were Methodists), and told them we were having needed repairs done in our little church – the church I came to as a stranger, where I had two of my children baptized, where one was buried and three were married. A church very dear to me.

They all responded heartily, and some said if enough was not raised, to write again and they would help more. Among them were Mrs. Jaffray, Miss Hamersley, Mrs. Field, Mrs. Stuyvesant, Mrs. Stillman, Mrs. McVickar and others, all of whom ever stand ready to help me. My pastor was amazed and greatly encouraged.

September 30th 1880
Have been able to get considerable help for the poor woman who fell down the hatchway, Mrs. Abblet. I find she is from Hull and knew my dear brother, and had lived in one of his houses in Beetonsville and heard him preach. She knew his likeness in my album, also those of his daughters and grandsons. Mr. Abblet had worked for my nephew at the brush business in Hull.

October 13th 1880
My darling granddaughter Bella, and great-niece Mary W. Beeton, arrived safely on the 10th from England after a pleasant voyage. How I thank Thee, my Father, for bringing those dear girls safe across the mighty deep.

How very strange, my nephew's child bearing my maiden name, the full name of my beloved eldest sister, Mary Beeton. How fresh and near it brings the dear child, and what memories it awakens of other days and loved ones gone before. May it be the supreme blessing of her life to come among us.

October 17th 1880
Had sacrament of the Lord's Supper; a blessed time. Surely He was in our midst.

> "Too soon we rise: the symbols disappear,
> The feast, but not the love, is passed and gone;
> The bread and wine remove, but Thou art here,
> Nearer than ever – still my shield and sun."

October 20th 1880

My kind friend Brother Stephenson has succeeded in placing rubbers under my bed to relieve me from the vibration caused by the Elevated Railway. Dr. Palmer said something must be done, or I must be removed. He feared the moving and the vibration and noise, but Mr. Stephenson came to our rescue.

Thank God for kind friends. Several ladies, as well as my daughters, looked for rooms, but none could be found that would do. Mrs. Wm. Kingsland and Miss Callender said they would meet an increase of rent if a place could be found to suit me. But the rubber fixing answers admirably, and here I am in the same old corner still, and where I hope to remain until called home, for many have been blessed and brought to Christ in this little upper room.

October 26th 1880

Many dear friends have come back from the country, and have been to see me: Mrs. Wood, Mrs. Schieffelin, Mrs. Hunting, Mrs. Rutherford, and others.

Had a little visit from Mrs. Sarah Holmes of New Bedford, and two of her daughters, both lambs of the fold of Christ. It was she who first brought Samuel Bettle, of precious memory, to see me. If we have such sweet communion here, what will it be when we meet in the many mansions?

> "If such the sweetness of the stream,
> What will the fountain be
> When saints and angels draw their bliss
> Directly, Lord, from Thee?"

October 28th 1880

Class night. Had my dear Miss McCauley here to tea. Read

Colossians 1, and felt while at prayer that we were indeed risen with Christ, and are seeking those things which are above: kindness, humbleness of mind, meekness, long suffering, and, above all, charity, which is the bond of perfectness.

My class leader also called. It has been his custom for a long time to call on his way to class and ask me what hymn they should sing. Tonight I gave them, "Come ye that love the Lord," for it is full of joy and brightness.

Had a call from my much loved and valued friend, Sister Lankford Palmer. She does not like my having resigned as a manager of the Convalescent Home, but I think it best, as others can serve with more efficiency than I.

My work is with the poor of this neighborhood, given to me of the Lord. May He help me to be faithful to the grace given. I cannot beg for every cause, and I do not want a name to work and be an idler.

October 29th 1880

Had a pleasant visit from Rev. Mr. Bray, of Providence Conference, sent by Sister L. Palmer.

In conversation he asked me what I thought of healing by faith, and said he was cured of cancer in the nose by faith. I told him I had not had any light on the subject. God had not yet given me the gift of faith to the healing of this body, but I had ever found grace according to my day.

Lord, give me faith to do just what Thou wouldst have me do. Teach me Thy way. Mould and fashion me as Thou wilt. Endow me with the gift as well as the grace of faith, if for *Thy glory*. Oh help me to believe to the healing of this body, if it be Thy blessed will, by medicine or without; or if Thou seest I can best glorify Thee here, Amen. But should the furnace be yet more heated and the years lengthened, all is well.

Mr. Bray told me of Lizzie O. Smith, another prisoner of the Lord, who is unable to feed herself or move. I am better off than she.

Dear Mrs. Haxton was here, and made me happy by giving me something for my poor, and promised me her annual donation of fifty dollars for Thanksgiving dinners. Mrs. Abblet is still very sick, but ready to go or stay, as her Divine Master sees best.

Had Miss Elliott to tea, who for more than twenty years has been to me as a dear, tender daughter, doing great things in every way to add to my comfort, and smooth my pathway. Never the least break in harmony of our Christian love.

November 7th 1880

Another six days' work is done, another Sabbath is begun. Lord, grant it may be a foretaste of the eternal Sabbath. Each returning day of rest is a fresh blessing; fifty-two springs on life's journey, where we may drink and be refreshed.

My two poor women are very low.. Seem to be nearing the end, and ready and willing that the Lord's will should be done. Dear Miss Wood and others have given me much to make them comfortable.

November 10th 1880

Dear Mrs. Schieffelin was here today. We had a great time of refreshing, while recounting the mercies of our God. What a sweet, Christian spirit is hers. Amid all the comforts this world can give, she, her husband and dear daughters find their greatest joy in the work and service of our God: a home where God delights to dwell.

Mrs. Wood gave me $10 for a nurse for Mrs. Salmon; Mrs. Jaffray $20 for a nurse for Mrs. Abblet. Mrs. Field and

Mrs. Kingsland both help largely.

Had six ladies from Franklin Street Church to sing for me. Very feeble, yet sweetly trusting and resting on the arm of my Beloved.

November 14th 1880

Had a call from Mrs. Dimmick, of Honesdale, Pa. She is a faithful worker in the Lord's vineyard. She has a large Bible class of young men, and is seeking for more light and knowledge to train and guide them.

Happy Thanksgiving

My dear niece came back this evening from Connecticut to help me with my Thanksgiving work. May she be blessed while here. Show her, my Father, what she is by nature, and what she can be by grace.

Funds come in nicely. Hope to be able to give to all that come.

November 27th 1880

Have had a very hard week, and gave well-filled baskets to one hundred and eight families. Tears of joy and thanksgiving filled many eyes as they tried to utter thanks.

Each one had a turkey or chicken, according to the number in the family, with potatoes and apples; and to the aged tea and sugar, with a Scripture card, a copy of *Guide to Holiness* and *Words of Life*.

Mrs. Kingsland came to see the sight, and bring her liberal gift toward defraying the expenses.

Mrs. W. E. Dodge paid me her regular visit with kind gifts; also Mrs. Congdon, who is still very feeble and cannot seem to recruit from the anxious care and long watching of her beloved sister. It has almost proved too much for her frail body, but we cannot spare her − the poor need her, we all need her, and earnestly pray the Father to restore her to her usual health.

I wrote to Mr. C. Vanderbilt to ask a donation for my poor, and he kindly sent me $20. May he find a rich reward in the eternal habitations.

My dear niece was a great help to me. It was a novel sight to her to see my quiet room turned, as she expressed it, into a house of merchandise, for on one side stood a table with fifty turkeys, on another a table with sixty chickens, another table with bread, a large tray with tea and sugar. In the hall, a barrel of potatoes and one of apples; but they were soon gone, and quiet restored.

But, oh, I suffered greatly, and for two days could not take any food, although I had the usual cooked turkey from Mrs. Haxton. But it is a blessed privilege to be permitted to make so many happy. "Inasmuch as ye have done it unto one of the least of these My brethren, ye have done it unto Me." [Matthew 25:40.]

December 1st 1880

Had a visit from Mrs. J. Crosby Brown to ask if I would like some toys, books, etc., for my poor children for Christmas. She had interested herself in getting the people, young and old, in Orange Valley Church and Sunday school to make or buy with their spending money something for poor children in New York City. She wished me to have them for my children.

This was their first attempt at anything of the kind, and many were quite poor, but she thought it would do them good to try and give of their small means to those with less. I told her I would be delighted. Mrs. B. also said that her children would buy and fill twelve pairs of little stockings for the little ones' "Santa Claus." Praise the Lord! I shall be rich.

Mr. Wm. Bettle, of Philadelphia, was here today. He

misses his brother Samuel greatly, for they were so strongly bound together. Nor can anyone fill that good man's place for me. It is painful to see the tearful eye and quivering lips of this dear aged friend. I feel as though I shall not have him long, which would be a great loss to me in every way. Surely they have been to me as brothers beloved in the Lord ever since June 1865.

December 8th 1880
Had a call from Dr. Newcombe, an earnest worker for Jesus amongst the poor. He, with my own Dr. Palmer, thinks I ought not to try to do anything at Christmas for my poor, as I am very poorly. But the work is the Lord's, and He can give strength according to our day.

Had many dear ones to see me.

December 17th 1880
Had a call from Rev. Mr. Whittaker, pastor of the church of Orange Valley, N. J. He came to tell me about the things they are getting ready to send me for the poor children. He, with Mrs. Brown, feels that the people will be blessed by giving to those more needy. Yes, for it is written, "Blessed is he that considers the poor." [Psalm 41:1.]

Mr. W.'s conversation was profitable and cheering. He seems deeply interested in his work. Lord, make him very useful amid his flock, and a faithful shepherd.

A Merry Christmas

I am trying to gather up strength so as to be ready for Christmas.

December 20th 1880
Miss – – was here and brought me forty-nine boxes of candy, and twenty cornucopias of candy, from the small children of

her school. The other day Miss E. Skinner was here with her dear mother. They found me putting pictures on some old ice cream boxes I had begged, in order to fill them with candy for some of my poor children who would otherwise have none.

The dear child caught the idea, and afterwards asked her teacher if she might do some for me. Miss –– was pleased, and told the little children if they would like to do so with their own money, they might ask their mamas to allow them, and she would bring them to me.

They were delighted, and gave a goodly number of boxes of every conceivable shape all well filled with good candies. God bless the little givers! These things are great riches to me, for what sparkling eyes and happy hearts when these pretty and well filled boxes are given.

My doctor wants me to give up doing anything more for Christmas, but I tell him my invitations are all given out, and I must receive my company. God will give me strength this time. The work is His and He giveth power to the faint, and to them that have no might He increaseth strength. [Isaiah 40:29.] They look to me, and if I fail them, what will they do?

December 28th 1880

What a busy week the past has been – receiving and giving. What a luxury it is to give! On the 23rd I gave well-filled baskets to forty-eight poor families. Chickens, tea, sugar, bread, potatoes and turnips; and all were made very happy. Mr. Whittaker and Miss Eider came to tell me that the barrel of things was on its way.

On Friday my dear niece unpacked it and arranged the toys and gifts, putting the names on them as I dictated. Dear Miss Keteltas and Miss Callender were here, also Mrs. Stillman and Mrs. Thomas, with gifts, beautiful gifts for me.

Mrs. Field, Mrs. Wood, and others sent lovely gifts.

At evening, mothers came for the filled Santa Claus stockings: twelve pairs from Mrs. Brown's children and six pair from my dear niece.

My beloved sister and her husband came to spend Christmas with me. Christmas morning from ten to twelve o'clock, I had my children come. As they came in, they would stand and gaze as though they had come to fairyland; such sparkling eyes, such smiles. Oh, it was just grand. I asked them as they would stand beside me, why we called this Christmas, and why we gave presents.

Several little ones lisped, "Because it is Jesus' birthday." One boy of eleven years did not know, and when we told him the "old, old story," he stood with open mouth and eyes, and said, "A boy like me?"

"Yes, he was once just your size."

"Did you say he was born in a stable, and lay in a manger?"

It was all strange to the little fellow. I think we need more home missionaries. Well, they each had a present of a toy or a doll, book, or clothing, some both, besides a box of candy. And thus my children were made inexpressibly happy.

I also sent a Christmas pillow letter to each of Sister Louise's inmates in her Home for Incurables, that these poor suffering ones might also sing, "Glory to God in the highest, peace on earth, good will to man." These last I ordered from England, and they were very pretty and good.

In the early morning, Mrs. J. C. Brown's servant-man brought me a lovely Christmas tree, all filled with pretty things for myself, their own gift to me. On the Sabbath I rested. Monday morning found me busy with the remainder of the little ones, for although it was very stormy, they all came from ten to twelve o'clock.

I can never describe the sight. How they would hug their dolls, peep into their books, try on their nice warm mitts; it was grand. One little one said, "Mama, didn't I tell you if you would leave the stove lids off, Santa Claus would come? You see, he brought me all these nice things in my stocking. Last year you shut them down and he could not get in." Happy simplicity of childhood.

Nearly all the sixty-seven little ones were fatherless. Many said mama could not buy them anything. It was to me a splendid time, and well I wished that those who had sent the beautiful things could have seen the children's joy.

My special interest just now is for the conversion of my dear niece [Mary Beeton] She comes of a pious ancestry, and is the child of many prayers offered by those who have long since finished their course with joy. I think her more thoughtful than when she first came among us. Help her to see her only hope in Thee.

Thus another year of mercies and blessings has come to a close, and here I am, a monument of saving grace, purchased and saved by blood divine. I thank Thee for all the way Thou hast led me. I thank Thee alike for trials and blessings, for when Thou hast tried me, I shall come forth as gold.

Received from my kind friends for the poor, and distributed among them during the past year, $1,732.50. Had during the past year 2,990 calls; sent 25 children to the seaside for one week in August; received from Mrs. Hunting for the poor 12 garments and one ton of coal; from Mrs. Jaffray and Mrs. McVickar, their usual donation of dry goods, muslins, flannels and calicoes. Collected for Convalescent Home, $74. Collected for Sister Louise's Free Home for Incurables, $40, besides garments, coal, etc.

Received for my poor 14 tons of coal from Mr. Blake, from city funds.

Chapter 30

The Onward March

I will strengthen them in the Lord; and they shall walk up and down in His name, saith the Lord (Zechariah 10:12).

> "Strong Son of God, immortal love,
> Whom we that have not seen Thy face,
> By faith, and faith alone embrace,
> Believing, where we cannot prove!
>
> Thou seemest human and divine,
> The highest, holiest manhood Thou:
> Our wills are ours, we know not how;
> Our wills are ours, to make them Thine."

January 3rd 1881

Yesterday we were comforted and strengthened in the Breaking of Bread. It is a solemn privilege to show forth our Lord's death in His Supper, and it is fitting that with the vows of the Holy Communion we should begin another year.

Little Nellie Cornell was baptized at my bedside. The old year is gone, with its hopes and fears, its lights and shadows, and it was a good year to me.

> "And looking backward through the year,
> Along the way my feet have pressed,
> I see sweet places everywhere,
> Sweet places where my soul had rest."

It was a grief to me that my dear niece would not receive the sacrament with us, but, Lord, she is in Thy hands and we feel she must come to Thee.

I sent New Year Bible class mottoes to Mrs. Hunting's Bible class, also to Mrs. Dimmick's at Honesdale, Pa., and to all the Bible classes in our Twenty-Seventh Street Church.

May the seed thus sown take root in good soil. Help us, dear Lord, to sow beside all waters, and give Thou the increase.

January 15th 1881

Have been very poorly, so prostrate and full of pain, but I look to Him whom a look or sigh can reach.

Have had many dear friends this month. My dear and long tried friend, Brother Stephenson with his kindly gift, dear Mrs. Jaffray, Mrs. McVickar, Miss Callender, Mrs. Haxton, have all kindly continued their contributions to my poor. Besides these, there is a cluster of ladies who respond to calls for new cases.

My soul has been going out in one long thanksgiving psalm today, for prayer has been so beautifully answered. I had all day yesterday been asking, where shall I go for funds for my poor? If our dear Saviour were on earth, both cold and hungry, how gladly would we go and feed and warm and clothe Him, but He says, "Inasmuch as ye have done it unto one of the least of these, My brethren, ye have done it unto Me." [Matthew 25:40.]

Oh how happy it makes me when I have plenty to give. Well, last evening my dear niece got up from her chair and, without a word having been said by me, said, "Here, Auntie, give this to the poor," and handed me half a sovereign, with tears and kisses.

I said, "God bless you, darling. He will make it up to you."

In a letter received today, Mrs. Congdon writes me from Philadelphia, "I enclose ten dollars, dear Bella, for Mrs. Abblet, which thee will please use for her."

About noon a messenger boy came with a note from Mrs. McVickar. "Please find enclosed ten dollars for coal for your poor people. Papa gave me one hundred dollars for a Christmas gift; I send you one-tenth."

Praise the Lord, the gold and the silver are His and the cattle on a thousand hills. [Psalm 50:10.] Lord, bless these dear ones who are striving to work for Thee.

January 17th 1881

My dear niece seems very thoughtful. We must have this dear one brought to acknowledge Christ as her Lord and God. Hasten the time when she shall bow to Thy scepter, precious Saviour.

Had a visit from Miss Prow, recently returned from India, where she has been at work for her divine Master. Impaired health has sent her home. She expects to go back in the fall and take a life companion with her. What a noble work!

When I was young it was a burning desire of my heart to go to a foreign field to labor for God, but He answered my prayer by putting me in the corner on the bed, and bade me work for Him there. This is not what I would have chosen, but "It is not in man that walketh to direct his steps." [Jeremiah 10:23.]

"Let God do His own work," said Robertson when dying. I wanted the world for my parish, but instead of that I have been shut up in this little upper room. Yes,

> "Shut in with the Spirit to comfort and cheer,
> To guide me in duty and make the way clear."

January 24th 1881

Had a lovely visit from Mrs. Wood and Mrs. Dahlgren, sweet, precious friends and noble women. Mrs. Wood left some funds for my poor, and Mrs. D. is to send me *The Life of Miss Havergal*, who is one of my favorites among writers and disciples.

I have requested my children and several friends in the city to join me in prayer, that my dear niece may find the pearl of great price. How little the dear girl realizes that we are all besieging the throne in her behalf. But although she does not say anything, I know she is coming nearer. Hasten the joyful day, O Lord, when there shall be joy in heaven over this precious one's being brought into the family of the living God.

January 31st 1881

> "O wondrous power of faithful prayer,
> What tongue can tell the almighty grace?"

O glorious day! There is joy in heaven. Our cup is full – no words can express the joy we feel. Dear Mrs. Field came this a.m. with a young lady, Miss Price, from Troy, who was seeking the Saviour. Mrs. Field asked me to relate a little of my experience: how I wandered from my Lord, and how He brought me back again.

My dear niece listened eagerly as I went over those memories of past years. After much talking and prayer, Miss P. and my niece made a full surrender and found peace through believing in God their Saviour; but I will give my niece's own words from her diary:

"A day long to be remembered by Miss P., Mrs. Field, Aunty and myself, for I have given my heart to Christ, and taken

Him to be my guide. It was quite strange. This morning Mrs. Field and Miss P. called to see Aunty. I was writing and I usually keep on writing when anybody comes in, but this morning I shut my book and laid by my pen.

"Mrs. Field asked Aunty to tell a little of her early life to Miss P., as that young lady wanted to come to the Saviour, but did not see her way clear to do so. Aunty talked to her a good deal, and I listened and thought some things that were said suited me exactly, but I did not say so.

"At last, Mrs. Field said she thought Aunty had better pray. Aunty prayed and gave us both most earnestly to Jesus, asking Him to take us just as we were.

"I gave myself to Him while on my knees. Then Mrs. Field prayed, and when we rose up Aunty asked Miss P. if she would not come to Jesus now. She answered 'I will try.' 'Oh but you must not say I will try, you must say, I will come now; now is the accepted time.'

"After talking a little while, she said, 'I will, I do come to Jesus now.' Then as Aunty was telling how good Jesus was and how glad to receive her as His child, Mrs. Field turned to me and said, 'Will you not come too?'

"I said, 'I will try,' but recalling Aunty's words, I said, 'I will come now.' Then we sang 'Tis done, the great transaction's done; I am my Lord's and He is mine.'

"I shall never forget this day. I cannot write half strong enough. How happy I am, and how glad dear Aunty is! She said to me, 'Oh my dear child, your good old great grandmother's God still lives. He is not dead, and her prayers will be answered. The grandchild of one of her children has come to Christ. Praise Him, my darling child; Praise the Lord. There is joy in heaven.'"

In a letter to her cousin Bella, my niece wrote, "You told me, dear Bella, that it would pay me to come from England to

New York to see Aunty. It has paid me, for I have found my Saviour, the pearl of great price."
February 8th 1881

> "When all Thy mercies, O my God,
> My rising soul surveys,
> Transported with the view I'm lost
> In wonder, love and praise."

Goodness and mercy, dear Lord, goodness and mercy all the way through. Today was greatly comforted while telling Mrs. Lawrence, Mrs. Hunting and Dr. Pinkney some of the Lord's doings.

My dear niece is at Tuesday meeting; may she be fed with hidden manna. She is greatly exercised about a poor German whom she found at Ward's Island Hospital. He cannot speak English, and was glad to find a lady visitor who could speak in his own tongue. Poor man, he has no hope either in this world or the world to come. My niece is asking the prayers of the meeting in his behalf.

February 10th 1881
Had Miss Field and Miss Hamersley. Dear, dear friends, they are so very kind.

Mrs. Wood and Mrs. Hunting were here to lunch. We had a very nice time, after which my niece went with them to Bellevue Hospital.

Mrs. Lawrence called and brought me, to my great surprise, a present from a friend. Sent Mrs. Abblet a new wrapper. She is much better, and may live long to show forth the power of God. This has been a happy day to me.

February 12th 1881
Blessed Sabbath, sweet foretaste of our eternal home. The

tribes of Israel have gone up to the courts of God to keep
"holy day," while I stay home to pray for the peace of
Jerusalem. "To each his work." It is mine to remain in my
corner.

Breathe, Lord, upon the assemblies of Thy saints. Anoint
afresh the sons of Levi; send grace upon Thy heritage.

Dr. Barnett came to take my niece down to Jerry
McCauley's Mission. She marvels at the power of God as
manifested in those poor men and women from the lowest
classes, and loves to hear them tell of His grace. Rich and
poor, as "one family we dwell in Him." Praise the Lord, joint
heirs with Christ Jesus.

About nine o'clock my niece came hurrying upstairs and
said, "Aunty, can I bring Mr. Kerr upstairs?"

I said, "Certainly."

They sat down, when she said, "Mr. Kerr, may I tell
Aunty the good news?"

He said, "Yes."

He had pledged himself to be on the Lord's side. We
talked, and I urged him not to rest in present attainments.
At prayer, I had great liberty in bringing him to our precious
Saviour.

February 14th 1881
Monday
Sister L. Palmer was here. What a blessed spirit is hers.
What a great comfort she has been to me ever since the
memorable April 1847.

February 15th
Tuesday
My dear Annie and niece were at Tuesday's meeting, and
enjoyed it very much. Mary went to see the Regans and
found them very poor but clean. She took a pair of shoes for

one of the children and bought a pair for each of the other two, comforted them all she could, and pointed them to the Saviour.

Have had calls from Mrs. Field, Mrs. Lowry, Mrs. McCabe and Mrs. Murphy. They had all been to Tuesday meeting. I tried to tell them how I was brought into the light. I love to tell the story.

I wrote to Mrs. Wood and Mrs. Clapp for help for the Regans, and both responded immediately. Praise the Lord.

February 17th 1881

The past two days have been quiet days. Mrs. Kingsland was here and gave me something for my poor. I have given poor Mrs. Regan into Mrs. K.'s care. Mrs. Marie was here also, and she kindly promised me something for the poor family.

In a note to me she says, "Perhaps it would be a pleasure to you to know that the peaceful influence which you shed abroad from your little room and sickbed has been with me ever since I saw you. You see you have the privilege of dispensing all kinds of blessings to all kinds of people. Your little room is like an oasis in a desert."

Mrs. Haxton sent me some clothes for the Regan children. My dear niece was down again last night and took some food and garments for them.

February 18th 1881

Felt great liberty at family worship this a.m. Have had few calls. It is very cold. Another letter with ten dollars from dear Mrs. McVickar for coal for God's poor.

Dr. Douglass was here, and kindly authorized me to call on him for professional service for my poor. He would like to help me with them. Thus the Lord raises up one and another to help along.

This a.m. my niece said, "Aunty, you do not know what I

did at class last evening."

I said, "No, dear. Did you witness for Jesus?"

"Yes, Aunty. I tried several times to rise, but I did at last, and told them that from this time forth, by the help of God, I would give up theaters, dancing, and card playing."

I had had a talk with her the other night on the theater question, when she said she did not see it wrong. I told her the blessed Saviour and the Holy Spirit would show it all to her.

After some moments in silence she said, "Aunty, I know I shall come to your way of thinking. You win people so. You do not scold them into religion."

I said, "No, darling, why should I scold? All I say is in love, for God is love, and he that dwelleth in God dwelleth in love." [1 John 4:16.]

To her dear mother in England she wrote, "I felt like a black sheep in Aunty's quiet little room. Everything was so different, and I had to yield to the influence."

March 21st 1881

Poor Mr. Regan has died, and the afflicted wife cannot last many weeks. Mrs. Kingsland has been very kind, as also Mrs. Bond, with food, money, and clothes. Had an unexpected call from a Miss Patterson, the daughter of an English missionary to India.

March 26th 1881

Had a visit from Miss Jennie Smith, Mrs. Grant, and Mrs. Sherman. Dear girl, she is all alive to work for her Lord. She is about to open a home for the Master's tired workers, where they may turn aside and rest awhile.

This is what the compassionate Saviour did when the multitude had worn out His disciples. He was ever mindful of the physical as well as spiritual needs of that chosen band.

The question was raised in our conversation: As Jennie had been healed, why not I? To which I answered that God had not given me any light or faith on that subject at all.

Jennie said, "I have no liberty in asking that Sister Cooke shall be healed. I believe that God has a work for her to do that she could not do if she were on her feet."

How little friends know how much it pains me to be questioned on this subject. Do they fancy that I have determined to keep my bed and enjoy lying here? If my Father should speak the word, how gladly would I quit this corner, repair to His house, and sing of His mighty works in the assemblies of His saints; how gladly go from house to house and urge the sinner to Christ, or sit by the sickbed and tell them of redeeming love.

But I know it is not His will, and therefore I bow at His command and wait for those whom He may send. In the course of a year I speak to more than two thousand souls. I have an average of from three to four thousand calls a year, and more than half have to hear of my Father's loving care to me. Yes,

> "I'll praise Him while He lends me breath,
> And when my voice is lost in death,
> Praise shall employ my nobler powers;
> My days of praise shall ne'er be past,
> While life and thought and being last,
> Or immortality endures."

March 29th 1881
Yesterday I was surprised by a visit from Mrs. Abblet, whom all winter we have been expecting to die. It seemed like one raised from the dead. When Miss Kitching brought her in I could not but exclaim, "What hath God wrought!" [Numbers 23:23.]

Have had many friends in today. Had an earnest talk with dear Mrs. Ruggles on the vanity and emptiness of this world without Christ. Open Thou our eyes, dear Lord, and we shall behold wondrous things in Thy law. [Psalm 119:18.] Prevent us by Thy grace that the beautiful gifts of Thy providence prove not a snare. Keep us from that spirit of worldliness which dulls the vision for divine beauties, and closes the ear against the music of heaven. Keep Thou our feet, for it is easy to go astray.

Last evening our people gave a pleasant surprise to our dear pastor, Rev. C. E. Glover and his wife who, having labored with us the past three years, go to another field. We have had a pleasant and prosperous time during his pastorate, but now we must separate.

These uprootings are painful, and teach us that this is not our rest. One after another comes and goes, but One has said "I will never leave thee nor forsake thee." [Hebrews 13:5.]

April 4th 1881
A glorious morning in beautiful spring.

> "I wait Thy will to do
> As angels do in heaven."

As our earth drinks in the sunshine of the spring, and responds in buds and flowers, so my soul basks in the beams of the Sun of Righteousness, my King and my God.

I felt through the last night as though I must almost say, "Stay Thy hand," so overwhelming was the sense of the great Three-in-One.

Yesterday a few of us met to commemorate the feast of His dying love. "Christ our Passover is sacrificed for us, therefore let us keep the feast;" [1 Corinthians 5:7-8] and He broke the bread and fed us.

"Heaven came down our souls to greet,
While glory crowned the mercy seat."

It was the last Sabbath our dear Pastor Glover would be here. He seemed too full for utterance. We have had many precious seasons during the past three years, but the best wine was kept until now. We felt the smart of parting. Earnest, kind, gentle, sympathetic in all his ways; thus he leaves us. Lord, go Thou with him and bless him.

I had with me dear sister L. Palmer, who thirty-three years since took me by the hand and taught me the way more perfectly. There was also with me a little band of faithful friends who have stood by me in many storms of suffering and trial, some over thirty years, others for a quarter of a century.

But this brings other thoughts. Some who have knelt in this little room are now on "the sea of glass mingled with fire," [Revelation 15:2] and have drank of the new wine in the kingdom of our God. Soon our turn, for we too shall be there, and see the King in His beauty in the land that is afar off.

May 11th 1881
Have just received my dear cousin, Rev. John S. Addy and wife, from St. John, New Brunswick. I had not seen him since the day, forty-five years ago, when we bade him farewell on his leaving England for Newfoundland as a pioneer missionary.

Our Father, God, has been with him and blessed his labors, and now he has come to see the remnant of the old family. When I saw him, venerable in mien and with the old gentleness in his manners, as he entered my room I could but exclaim,

> "And are we yet alive,
> And see each other's face?
> Glory and praise to Jesus give
> For His redeeming grace."

What memories have been awakened by this visit after forty-five years' separation! Yes, varied have been our experiences during those years: marriages, births, deaths, many labors and trials, yet out of all, the Lord hath brought us, and here will we raise our Ebenezer. For hitherto the Lord hath helped us.

As a family, He has done great and marvelous things for us, and as individuals He has held us up when it seemed as though the waters would overwhelm us. Surely He has been our hiding place for generations past and will be to the end. The words I learned to sing at my mother's knee I still sing:

> "Glory, honor, praise and power
> Be unto the Lamb forever,
> Jesus Christ is our redeemer,
> Hallelujah, hallelujah, praise the Lord."

May 19th 1881

Mr. George Muller and wife, Mrs. Field, and Miss Hamersley were here today. Mr. M. leaves for his home, Bristol, England, on Saturday. For forty-five years he has been working for the great Master, and the orphan houses, schools, and colleges in Bristol are the monuments of the faithfulness of our God. He is a peculiar man [old meaning can include private], but full of faith − the faith that laughs at impossibilities, and cries, "It shall be done." He read and explained the third Psalm, and prayed.

May 28th 1881

Another farewell, another parting with a dear one. Be still, my trembling heart, for there shall be no parting yonder. My beloved grand-niece, Mary Beeton, left me today. Eight months ago she came a stranger, now a most loved and loving child.

Here in this little room she entered into the covenant of God's dear people, and took Him for her God. We do so thank Thee for the grace given. Go with her and make her a bright and shining light, and may she sing,

> "I'm not ashamed to own my Lord,
> Or to defend His cause."

June 7th 1881

Today had a call from Edwin Jay, a son of Allen Jay of Indiana. There is a singular bond between us of tender sympathy. Some six years ago his mother came to see me in great distress. She had left this son with a physician for treatment for spinal trouble, and was given to believe that the lad would be a cripple for life.

We talked together about him and had prayer, during which I was greatly drawn out to ask that this boy should be cured of the disease. When his mother rose to go, I told her I believed her boy would be cured, for I had felt the power of God while at player, and was assured that our petition was answered.

Some time afterward I received a letter from that mother, with the tidings that her boy was well. He is now to all appearances a strong and healthy youth, and acknowledges the hand of God in his cure.

His family were almost as much surprised as delighted at his speedy recovery. About a year after, a lady called and told me she had brought to me a little girl from the West, sick and crippled with spinal disease, that through my faith and prayer Allen Jay's boy was cured, and would I not plead for her child too.

I answered that I could not foreknow about these things, that the Lord had especially blessed me in praying for the cure of that boy, but I did not dare to say that her child would be healed by my intercession.

My heart goes out after this youth, that he may be a man of God, mighty in faith and prayer to the pulling down the strongholds of Satan, for surely his life and strength are given him for some special purpose.

June 28th 1881

Have sent four happy children to Sing-Sing for three weeks to get the benefit of country air. Happy childhood! Each had to come and kiss me goodbye. God, bless the little children.

Chapter 31

The Flood of Years

And thou shalt remember all the way the Lord thy God led thee (Deuteronomy 8:2).

> "O Father, in whose mighty hand
> The boundless years and ages lie,
> Teach us Thy boon of life to prize,
> And use the moments as they fly.
>
> "To crowd the narrow span of life
> With wise designs and virtuous deeds:
> So shall we wake from death's dark night,
> To share the glory that succeeds."

July 14th 1881

Another birthday, another milestone passed. Sixty years old! I can hardly realize it. Sixty years of loving kindness and tender mercies. This ceaseless onflowing of time greatly impresses me. The flood of years that knows neither rest nor change, but changes all things in its course!

Gone are the friends and scenes of my childhood, far away is the dear land of my birth and home of my forefathers. Those early days, how they come back to me! The moors of Derbyshire, the haymakers in the meadows, the lark singing in the sky, the silvery Derwent and the old bridge, and, more than all, those venerated parents – that blessed mother.

We could not have my dear Mrs. Haxton to tea, as she is out of the city, but she kindly sent me her beautiful gifts.

Had pretty presents from my dear children and grandchildren and others, and a lovely tribute of love and esteem in a letter from my dear Joseph.

Had my pastor, Rev. J. Dickinson, my dear sister, Miss McCauley, and my daughters to tea.

"With thanks I rejoice in Thy Fatherly choice
Of my state and condition below,
If of parents I came who honored Thy name,
'Twas Thy wisdom appointed it so.

"I sing of Thy grace from my earliest days,
Ever near to allure and defend,
Hitherto Thou hast been my preserver from sin,
And I trust Thou wilt save to the end."

From Mrs. Cooke's Son-in-law [Joseph Pullman]
West Winsted, Ct.
July 1881
Dear Grandma,
The years roll on. Time, like an ever-rolling stream, bears all its sons away. It is well for us that our vision is not bounded by the grave, and that the Word speaks of Paradise as well as Hades. Sixty years old! Sixty years since in the English home, there was joy to greet the little intruder.

How dependent we are, how hedged up and helpless. You had gifts and qualities which might have produced all and more than Florence Nightingale did with her soldiers, or Una with her paupers. But like Job, to whom "light" had been given, your way was "hedged up," and events came to pass which you would have used every effort to prevent.

And yet, you have proved this, that despite circumstances, in the teeth of fate ("I speak as a man"), your pound has brought forth ten pounds; and in the Gospel I believe *that* faithful servant received unqualified praise.

I am hopeful of something being done for the Master's kingdom by my children. I can't do much, having reached the measure of my abilities, except that at this pace I may plod on for many days to come halting, Jacob-like, upon my thigh. But the children will have a better start than I, besides having a dash of the fine blood of "dear old grandmother," the soldier's wife.

My hope is that the children will do something for "the kingdom," and for this reason I would wish to give them a good education. The advantages of the University at Middletown as a school impressed me very much when I was there on the Examining Committee two weeks ago, and though I don't know where the money will come from to pay expenses, yet I am convinced of the duty of educating them. Mary thinks Johnny is too fit for business to waste time on books. Perhaps so; we will see.

The inclosed picture, painted by an artist of our town, the children send for your birthday, with the wish that you may live till its flowers fade, to which devout wish their parents say Amen!

And now before I end up, let me say that we have a happy home here, with neither suspicions nor discontents, but lots of love and thankfulness. As Muller, of Bristol, said, "He is a kind Master."

Our church needs a Pentecost – greatly needs it. This would make an excellent ending for our life in Winsted, and would put us under a heavy debt of gratitude to Him whose we are and whom we serve.

Can you give me a Testament or Psalms with large print, not heavy, for a poor bed-ridden women of eighty, who needs such a book?

With love and wishes of "many returns," affectionately,
Joseph

July 20th 1881

Very hot, very feeble, and much care. Have had a very sad case. Mrs. Perine, a very poor woman, just from Connecticut and about to be confined, has six children. The selectmen of her town would not allow her to remain, as she, with her coming babe, might become a charge to the county. So she had to break up her home and come to the city where her dissipated and worthless husband had been for some months.

She has two empty rooms, but no food, clothing or money. She had traveled all day, was footsore and weary, her heart almost broken, had had no food all day, and did not know where to go. I was low in funds, but did not dare turn her away, for my Father holds all the gold and silver.

July 26th 1881

Another sad case. A young woman came to me, having been sent by St. George's Society. She, with her husband Mr. Chamberlin, came from England some months ago. Had bad advisers, had been sick in two hospitals; her husband and she had become estranged. She expected a little stranger, but had nothing to put on it when it should arrive; had been to Marian Street Home, but they were full.

I heard her sad, sad story, gave her a little change, sent her to her stopping place and provided clothing. I shall see her through her trouble.

I was amused today. I sent to the store for some ice. The young man said, "Oh yes, I know who it is for — the reform lady."

The person I sent said, "What do you mean, Charlie?"

"Oh," he said, "the lady who reforms people."

"Then are you afraid she will reform you?"

He said, "I don't know."

This reminds me of a little boy who lived in this block.

Some little boys came into the yard to play. He said, "Boys, don't make a noise. The good Samaritan lives there, and she is sick."

August 5th 1881
Very hot the past few days, and I have been very feeble. Had a letter from dear Mrs. Stillman, also from dear Mrs. Schieffelin in Europe, inclosing a kind gift to myself. I just had to close my eyes, the tears of gratitude would come. To think that these dear ones do not forget me while far away in search of health in a foreign land. I sing,

> "Jesus, Thy boundless love to me
> No thought can reach, no tongue declare."

Dear Mrs. Schieffelin, after regretting her inability to call and see me before leaving the city, wrote, "You cannot know how dearly I enjoy my visits to you, or how much benefit I derive from your conversation, and what a deprivation it is to lose both. Remember, dear friend, that I pray for you just as constantly as if I were with you every day. Pray for us without intermission."

I do thank Thee, my Father, for the love of Thy dear children: those who are so far above me in this world's comforts, yet they come to my humble position and thus fulfill the Saviour's prayer, "That they all may be one." [John 17:21.]

August 8th 1881
A lovely morning. Twenty-five dear little children came at seven a.m. to be sent to the country for a week, so bright and happy. God bless them and give them a happy time. I had them sing, after which we had prayer, and I committed them to the Saviour. Happy, happy childhood! How they will

enjoy the bathing, the great sea, and the liberty of the fields.

August 14th 1881

I was surprised to see the young wife come in with her babe ten days old. She said, "I have nowhere to go. The landlord has put the woman with whom I am stopping out on the street, for rent. What shall I do?"

I told her to sit down. She seemed as though she would faint. I gave her some food and sent her to lie down and sleep. I sent again for her husband and for Mr. Hutchinson of the St. George's Society. Had a long and plain talk with them. The husband again said, "Marie does not want me, does not care for me."

I sent her and her babe up to the Convalescent Home, and in a few days urged her husband to go up and see her and his babe. Prevailed on him to go again and be present at its baptism. But the wife wanted to go home to England, and so I got things all ready for herself and babe, for she had nothing. Secured her passage ticket and then sent for her husband and Mr. Hutchinson.

Her husband agreed to send her ten dollars a month to England. I had seen their marriage certificate. The husband was of a rich family, and now he could not dig; to beg he was ashamed. Their trunks had been kept for board, and they were both in distress. He was now working in a restaurant on four dollars a week and board. He was too proud to let his people know he had married, or his destitution.

August 17th 1881

> "Close by Thy side still may I keep,
> Howe'er life's various currents flow."

Hear me, O Lord, for Thy loving kindness is good; turn

unto me, according to the multitude of Thy tender mercies; hide not Thy face from Thy servant, for I am in trouble. [Psalm 69:16-17.]

My faithful physician is very ill. Has been so for a week. There is but faint hope of his recovery. None can know the bond of Christian friendship that has bound us together for the past thirty-one years of continued medical care. If it be possible, if at all consistent with Thy will, spare Thy servant, O Lord, for further usefulness. Turn this cup of sorrow aside and let it pass from us.

August 19th 1881

Thirty-two years since my beloved husband went to his better home: all those years of bliss before the throne. Thy blessings to me have been thickly strewn, but yet there is a void nothing can fill.

I murmur not. I often seem to hear that cheerful whistle, and the happy voice seems to ring in my ears. Well, if faithful, I shall go to him, and we shall together adore Him who was the author of our love and Saviour of our souls. All the days of my appointed time will I wait till my change comes.

August 20th 1881

Dear Doctor Palmer still very ill. His son was here with medicine. Wants to send Doctor McMurray, but I want no other doctors.

Mrs. Chamberlin, the young mother, has sailed with her babe for her mother's home in England. Before leaving, she called on me, and with her baby in her arms, standing in the middle of the room, she spoke as follows. "Mrs. Cooke, it is a great thing to save a poor body from ruin is it not?"

I said, "Yes."

"Well," she said, "you have saved a soul and body from

ruin and death, for I had promised that stranger who came to see you, that after my babe was born I would leave George and baby and go with him. But your kindness in doing for me and keeping me all night, that prayer and that talk, then sending me to that home has saved me.

"When I left you, and you sent George to me and made me promise to have my baby baptized, I felt I could not do as I had promised. Yes, you have saved me, soul and body, and my husband from despair, for I know he loves me; but I must go home. That man follows me everywhere, but I am an honest woman. I have been true to George."

It was a scene for a painter. We prayed, and I bade her goodbye, giving her money to pay her fare from Liverpool to Norwich. The baby had been christened Edward Cooke.

After her arrival in England I received letters from her and also from her mother, in which they showed great gratitude. Her mother wrote, "I cannot thank you enough for your great kindness to my child, and I thank God that He raised her friends in a strange land, and that she was kept from doing what would have been a great sin before God and man. Dear madam, I hope you will not think me intruding if I ask you to write to her."

From Mrs. Laura Hunting
Hotel Byron
Villeneuve, Lac-de-Geneva
Switzerland
September 6th 1881
My Precious Friend,
How can I tell you the real joy your last letter gave me. I read and re-read it, and felt homesick to come to your bedside at once, and hold that dear hand and hear the voice that has ever made me feel stronger for the battles of everyday trials.

I have been in Switzerland the past five weeks, surrounded by mountains which have always been my delight, and here we have them in such perfection. Have had plenty of time for meditation, and never have found Israel's God nearer.

I hear from my Sunday school scholars often. The hours spent at your bedside have done much to strengthen their faith in the Christian life. Each one sends their love. I cannot think your face, without any line of care or time, indicates the sixty years of life, your heart and manners seem so young.

Accept a heart full of love from,

Laura Hunting

September 9th 1881

So feeble. Doctor P. is a little better, praise the Lord! His dear wife brought a box of medicines that the doctor had put up for me, with directions how to use them.

She told me the dear doctor said he had taken great comfort from a text motto I once sent them. For when too ill to talk or read, he could, when conscious, look at it as it hung at the foot of his bed.

September 26th 1881

Have just heard of the death, which occurred two months ago, of Dr. James D. Fitch, an old physician and Christian friend, who when he heard of the death of my dear husband, came and kindly offered his services free for any medical treatment I might need.

He had been my physician in 1850, when he and Doctor Cooper said it was no use giving me any more medicine as I was incurable; that I could only live a few months; that I should have the best of care, and be made as comfortable as possible.

It was at this time Sister Lankford asked Doctor M. W. Palmer to visit me, and he also told me that he could not cure me, but might be able to relieve present suffering. He has faithfully done so, and yet has ever been willing to stand aside and let other physicians try whom ladies would send, but the while quietly watching lest any wrong treatment should be used.

October 7th 1881
My wedding day, a lovely day, and made more bright by seeing Doctor Palmer enter my room once more, but to see him walking with a cane and measured step brought the tears. He is very feeble.

I shall be better now. I told him not to come more than once a week.

November 1st 1881
Since last writing I have been very very ill. On the 16th of last month I wrenched myself in reaching, and during the day was thought by three dear friends to have passed away. They sent word to Doctor Palmer that such was the case.

He came, though very feeble, having had a relapse, and sat with me till I came to consciousness after two hours. Then suffered intensely, and my feet were as black as flesh could be, and swollen out of shape.

Have night watchers still, as the doctor is unwilling to have me left alone, nor am I able to attend to my medicine. Again kind friends rallied around me and did all they could for my comfort, and again am I sent forth to tell of His power to save, yea to save to the *uttermost*. [Hebrews 7:25.]

November 29th 1881
Have had a pretty hard two weeks getting ready for my poor. Again have friends come to my help, and I have been

enabled to give a basket full of provisions to the needy ones. One hundred and fifteen families were fed.

We distributed turkeys, chickens, potatoes, turnips, apples and bread. Thirty-five old ladies had tea and sugar. All had tracts and picture text cards. All were very happy, but disappointed because I could not have them upstairs.

My daughters waited on them downstairs, and all were supplied. Nor was I forgotten, for dear Mrs. Jaffray, Mrs. Haxton, Mrs. W. E. Dodge, and Mrs. Stillman all sent kind gifts to me, that I with my own dear children might have a happy time. In feeding ye are fed, in blessing ye are blessed.

December 29th 1881

Again we have celebrated the birth of our precious Saviour; He whose coming the prophets foretold; He who laid aside His glory and humbled Himself to bring us to God. We may well sing,

> "Come and worship,
> Worship Christ, the new born King."

On the twenty-fourth had many friends bring their mementos to the Lord's prisoner: Mrs. Kingsland, Wood, Stillman, Keteltas and other ladies. Dr. W. C. Palmer and Brother Stephenson and my dear Dr. M. W. Palmer all met here and we had a happy time, although very tired, for I had given dinners to about fifty aged and sick ones; and toys, stockings, mitts, fruit, books and candy to about one hundred children.

The candy came from the infant class of a private school. Beautiful books, cornucopias, toys, dolls, etc., from Mrs. Stillman, and a barrel full of toys from the St. Cloud Sunday school, in Orange, N. J. I do wish the donors could see and hear the happy little children.

It was a very cold day, but they came from all quarters. My maid said, "Oh, Mrs. Cooke, it would seem so much like home, and I would be so happy if you would have two big Christmas candles burning;"

I said, "Very well, go and buy two, and light them."

She did so, and the poor girl was delighted beyond measure. Poor girl, far away from all her kin, she sat and watched them burn, every little while, "It is so much like home – they have candles tonight."

And when I would say, "These are Ellen's candles," her face would light up to the music of a merry laugh.

Yes, I knew the heart of a stranger, for I had been a stranger in a strange land, and it was a little thing to give so much pleasure.

I have sent New Year Bible class mottoes to our Bible classes and teachers, also to Mrs. Dimmick's at Honesdale, Pa., and to Mrs. Hunting's. Also "Christmas letters" to the Free Home for Incurables, and Convalescent Home, and to over fifty of my lady friends.

Thus another year's work is done, and I thank my Heavenly Father for all His goodness to me in permitting me to do a little for Him, for the bodies as well as the souls of many. The angel fed Elijah in the wilderness, when want and defeat had discouraged him.

Collected through the year from Mrs. Jaffray, $562, also one piece of muslin, one of red flannel, one of canton flannel and one of calico. From Mrs. McVickar, $166.00; from Mrs. Haxton, $144.00; from Miss Callender, $120.00; from Miss Barney, $36.00. Collected for Sister Louise's Home, through the year, cash, $57.00, two tons of coal, one piece of muslin from Mrs. McVickar, one niece of muslin from Miss Barney. Cash collected for Convalescent Home, $60.00; also 12 tons of coal for poor from city funds.

Moneys received during the year from the above and

other ladies, $1,482.00, all of which was prayerfully distributed to the poor. Praise the Lord. Had during the year 3,210 calls, besides those of my poor.

Chapter 32

Tender Mercies

For as the heaven is high above the earth, so great is His mercy toward them that fear Him. As far as the East is from the West, so far hath He removed our transgressions from us (Psalm 103:11-12).

There's a wideness in God's mercy,
Like the wideness of the sea;
There's a kindness in His justice
Which is more than liberty.

There is no place where earth's sorrows
Are more felt than up in heaven;
There is no place where earth's failings
Have such kindly judgments given.

January 6th 1882

Another year has come and we are still spared; mercies and blessings all the way. We take the clean new book of 1882 and ask our divine Lord to give us grace to love and serve Him with renewed vigor and faithfulness, that no stain may mar it when the volume is closed.

Many dear friends have been to see me and wish me a happy New Year. Mr. and Mrs. Frow were here to say goodbye. They leave for India, whither they go to proclaim the world's Redeemer. Lord, give them health and strength to labor for Thee with clean hands and pure hearts, and prosper Thou Thine own works.

Again my kind friends continue their means for the poor and the needy, and give me the pleasure of feeding them with daily and spiritual bread. Like Job, I would be eyes to the blind and feet to the lame, and the cause that I know not would I search out. [Job 29:15-16.]

March 7th 1882

After many days of anxious watching and prayer, dear Mrs. Hunting got safely home. The machinery of the ship broke and they were detained more than a week, but He who holds the wind and waves in His hand brought them safe to land, and we rejoice in His mercy and love.

How sweet to meet our loved ones after so long a separation, but what will it be when all the ship's company meet in the haven above – what joy and victory!

March 15th 1882

Had a visit from a Mr. Power, an English gentleman who came from England on the steamer with Mrs. Hunting. He has come to see our schools, day and Sunday schools; also the Young Men's Christian Associations of this country.

We had a very pleasant talk. Mr. P. is the brother of Rev. Mr. Power, who has written *The Oil Feather* series of tracts for the working classes in England.

We each spoke of the work our Father had given us to do, and of the great love wherewith He hath loved us. Mr. Power told me that his wife and he had bought a number of cottages to be homes for aged women who were too respectable to go to the workhouse. They gave to each two rooms, and charged them two pence a week in order that they might maintain a certain degree of independence, and also so that if they did not do right they could be removed.

He said that the old people were very happy, ever expressing their gratitude to God and to them. What a wonderful thing the religion of our blessed Lord is; how it brings goodwill to men.

Surely its foes who revile it know not what they do. "By this shall all men know that ye are My disciples if ye have love one to another." [John 13:35.]

Mr. P. gave me ten dollars for my poor, and after prayer, left me to go to Chicago.

April 3rd 1882

Had a very profitable call from my late Pastor, Rev. W. W. Clark, a man full of love to God and his fellow men. My soul longs for more and more of the image of the Perfect One, that every look and word and act may be born of God.

> "Thou art spring of all my joys,
> The life of my delights,
> The glory of my brightest days
> And comfort of my nights."

This blessed "fellowship with the Father and with His Son Jesus Christ." [1 John 1:3.] I have often to call myself away from holy communion to attend to the duties of life and the wants of others, and then my soul seems in haste to be gone.

April 5th 1882

Mr. Power was in to say goodbye; he sails for his English home tomorrow. He is well pleased with his visit to the States, and has found many earnest Christians with whom he has been fed. He promised me an account of his journey, which is to be printed for the Sunday schools.

It is not likely we shall meet again on earth, but I doubt not that we shall meet when all the King's workers are gathered on the banks of the River of Life.

April 15th 1882

Jerry McCauley with Mr. Mackey was here today. He has been made a vessel fitted for the Master's use, unlettered though he is. He has learned the language of Zion, and can tell of the beauties of the religion of the meek and lowly Jesus.

Very, very feeble, but when I am weak then am I strong. Praise the Lord.

May 4th 1882

Mr. Wm. Bettle, of Philadelphia, came to say goodbye as he sails for Europe in a few days. For many years he has been very kind to me. May the Lord bless and reward him abundantly and bring him safely home again.

Dear Mrs. Wood and Mrs. Hunting were here to lunch. How kind in them to come to my little room and eat and drink with me. By and by we shall meet in our Father's house, where we shall never have to part, and shall drink the new wine in His kingdom.

May 11th 1882

Had dear Mrs. Field, Mrs. Dahlgren, Miss Hamersley and Mrs. Ruggles to tea, with my dear sister and Annie. They are kind and gentle friends, all style and formality are laid aside and we are of one heart and mind. Praise the Lord for kind loving friends.

May 13th 1882

Another dear one, Mrs. Stillman, came to take a cup of tea with me before going away; and thus they throw light on the weary path.

May 30th 1882

The past week has been one of many farewells. Dear Mrs.

Wood and Miss G. Wendell are to sail on the *Bothnia*. Dear Miss Leo Smith on the *City of Richmond* goes to Italy to her sister. Shall I ever see them again?

We had a precious time as I committed them to our Father God. In the hollow of Thy hand, hide and bring them safe to land. Dear Mrs. Stillman also came to say goodbye. Oh, how I miss them all when gone. Keep them and me close to Thy side, that if we meet not on earth we shall meet in Paradise.

June 28th 1882
I have been very poorly the past month and able to do very little, but crowned with tender mercies and loving kindness.

Had dear Mrs. Haxton and Mrs. Bodstein to tea, and a very pleasant time. Two faithful loving friends, their attachment to me is something very wonderful. May the Lord reward and bless them.

July 6th 1882

> "In each event of life, how clear
> Thy ruling hand I see;
> Each blessing to my soul more dear
> Because conferred by Thee."

Had my old tried and true friend Brother Stephenson to see me; for so many years a counselor and guide, a friend and brother. Great will be thy reward, for thou has been a friend to many. All have found in thee a kind word and a helping hand in trial and need.

From Joseph Pullman, Mrs. Cooke's Son-in-law
43 Fleet St.
Brooklyn
July 1882
Dear Grandma,

As you have nine years yet to live according to the permission of the ninetieth Psalm, it is fitting that you and friends should be full of thankfulness on this, your sixty-first birthday. I send my greetings and congratulations, and wish that you may at least fill up the full Scripture time.

We have been leaning on you so long that it would be perilous to be thrown back on ourselves. "Late may you return to Heaven," was an ancient way of praising the good, which we repeat, and we fervently hope that "the kind doctor" will continue to beat in the hand-to-hand encounter, all "the diseases to which flesh is heir" (barring a diseased heart and brain), as he has done for the last thirty years.

With much love,
Joseph

July 14th 1882
Passed another milestone of my life. Had my dear children and some of my grandchildren to dinner and tea. Another year of mercies and blessings. Many pretty gifts were brought me, and among them was *The Life and Letters of Mrs. Prentiss*, from Joseph. I wanted it much, for I had long admired her writings. *Stepping Heavenward* has been one of my favorites. I had the copy once owned by dear Mrs. De Lamater, and it was well marked.

August 2nd 1882
Sister Louise was here with four of her little incurable girls. What an untiring little body she is! Ever busy to help in suffering. My Doctor Palmer is also untiring in his labors at

the Home for Incurables, to relieve their ailments and thus make life more endurable. I hear good news also from our Convalescent Home.

August 12th 1882

A new physician was here today, Doctor Avery. He came ostensibly to ask if I knew anything more of Doctor Newcomb. I only knew that the dear man is in the Insane Asylum, where I fear he will spend the remainder of his days. What a sorrow for his poor wife.

Doctor A. asked me many questions about myself. He said he had often wished to see me, having heard so much about me. He felt my pulse, carefully examined me, and then said, "Well, this is a very remarkable case. I have not seen anything like it – why, I cannot find any pulse. How do you live?"

I said I live by the power of the grace of God. I believe he is an unbeliever. God grant it may be as a nail in a sure place.

Doctor Gale was here also. Dear young man, I have known him from a little boy. He was very desirous to invent something to make me more comfortable. Came to talk with me about some poor people.

August 19th 1882

Another year of blessedness for my darling husband, while still I wait outside the golden gate. But as time rolls along I never forget the day he went home, and his words, "I am going home today, dear," ring in my ears and the tears still flow afresh. I miss his kind and gentle words, his tenderness over me, his sweet songs of praise, his fervent prayers. Yes, when all my loved ones are away, my heart turns to those happy days.

Nothing he could get was too good for me, nothing he

could do was too much. But I am satisfied, my Jesus hath done all things well. I would not have him back, for it would be a living death to him to have seen me suffer all these years. Yes, dear Lord, it is well.

August 23rd 1882
Death has been here and stolen away a brother from our side. Yesterday my dear Annie came home and told me that my brother Evans was very sick, and she feared he would not live.

This a.m. the dear child came over and told me she had a telegram that Uncle Evans was dying, and that she must go at once. Mary and she left by the 11 a.m. train for Meriden, only to find that he had passed away about 9 a.m.

Poor, dear sister, after living together forty-seven years they are called to part; but it cannot be for long; soon must another message come. Be a comfort to her in this loneliness, O Lord, and may she too realize that Thou art a Husband to the widow.

August 26th 1882
This evening I received my poor, sorely stricken sister, and my three dear girls. They came right from the graveyard which is situated on a beautiful hill near Meriden, Ct., where they laid to rest the remains of our dear Brother Evans till the resurrection morn.

Little did we think when he was here last May that it was the last time we should see him on earth, but so it is. We feel it keenly after a friendship of fifty years. My poor sister is greatly broken up; but Thou, Lord, art the healer of the broken-hearted. Comfort and support her, we pray Thee, as one whom his mother comforteth.

September 13th 1882

My dear sister went home today to her lovely but lonely house. I am very thankful that my dear children can be with her.

Dr. White, of our church, was in. After some talk on church matters, he felt my pulse and examined the enlarged liver, when he exclaimed, "Why, Sister Cooke, I had no idea that you were in this condition."

I said, "No, few of you realize it. I try not to complain or look sad. He is the health of my countenance and my God."

September 23rd 1882

One said, "Christ's cross is the sweetest burden I ever bore; it is such a burden as wings are to a bird, or sails to a ship, to carry me forward to my home." Many of my loved friends write me from Europe, "We feel your prayers are with us." Oh that I may prevail in their behalf.

September 28th 1882

Have three extreme cases of distress: sickness, want of work, new babies coming, nothing to eat, no rent, no clothes. But my kind ladies come to my relief. Mrs. Stillman, Mrs. Jaffray, Mrs. Field, Mrs. Vanderbilt, Mrs. Congdon, and Mrs. McVickar have sent me help for them in money and dry goods and clothing.

Praise the Lord; He holdeth the hearts of all men in His hands, and it is very wonderful how these ladies answer my appeals, for it takes a great deal to keep the wolf from the doors of the poor. Food, rent, clothing, fuel, medical aid: all these take much labor and money.

One of my old pensioners of twelve years' standing, the widow of a physician, came and said, "Well, Mrs. Cooke, I am trying to get money to take me to Chicago. Can you help me? I have sold everything I had, bit by bit to live on, and now have nothing left. My granddaughter sent word if I could get there, she would give me shelter and my bit of food. What shall I do? Can you help me?"

I gave her six dollars. She was earnest in her thanks for what had been done for her all these past years. "Bear ye one another's burdens, and so fulfill the law of Christ." [Galatians 6:2.]

October 10th 1882
My soul sweetly rests on Him whom I adore and love. He is the One altogether lovely. I hold sweet communion night and day, for often, "He holdeth mine eyes waking," and then I feed with Him. How restful and sweet.

Had a visit from Miss Eddie, a missionary from Syria. She has come on for treatment for her eyes. I was greatly interested in hearing of the work she and her father are doing in that far-off land. She told me of her school, the pleasure they felt when Mrs. Wood kindly sent them my picture; but now she could tell them of the sustaining grace given me, having seen and talked with me. Miss E. seems to be a very lovely Christian young woman.

October 15th 1882
Have had a feast of fat things today. A few friends, with my pastor, Rev. J. Dickinson, met me here and we commemorated the sufferings and death of our precious Saviour. My class leader was one of that little band of faithful friends, and we were richly fed with heavenly bread.

Thus we gather strength to go forward and take up the battles of life, ever realizing that He who is for us is far more than all that are against us.

Dear friends are coming home again, for the autumn winds are blowing and the north is sending back its cold. The wants of the poor are increasing, and help needed for both soul and body.

From a Little Friend in Europe
Vienna
Sunday October 30 1882
Dear Mrs. Cooke,
I should not have written till November, because May and I take turns writing. She writes one month and I the next, and as she has written this month, I am afraid you will get no letter dated November.

We are very comfortably settled here, much more so than we dared to hope, but now our lessons and everything are satisfactorily arranged. It was so kind in you to think of writing me such a lovely long letter, especially after you have had such a sick summer.

Our parlor is all fixed up and decorated with all sorts of pictures of home, and of the home people. Yours is also up, so you see that you are not forgotten. You would have no reason to think so, anyway, but now we cannot forget you. Mama has told Miss Russell, a lady friend of hers to whom she is going to send all our flowers this winter, to bring you some several times during the winter.

It snowed today for the first time this fall, but perhaps you know that we had quite a hard storm at St. Moritz in August. I suppose it would have been very welcome if it had been in New York. Please do take care of yourself this winter, and don't work too hard.

Please do not feel obliged to answer my letters, for I know that it is such an effort for you to do so. I would rather have you take the time for resting, which you hardly ever do.

With much love from Mama, May, and especially from myself,
I remain, your loving friend,
Bessie Brown

November 1st 1882
Dear Mrs. Schieffelin was here today with two friends, Mrs. Douglas and Mrs. Young from Chicago, to see me. We had a very precious season, the Lord was with us. I was much pleased to hear of the work done in that city for the Master of the vineyard.

Miss Sabine and Miss Hamersley were also here. "One family we dwell in Him." How kind in them all to visit me.

November 26th 1882
Very feeble, but I believe strength will be given me to go through with the work for the needy ones. Have got nearly all the money collected and the good things ordered for Thanksgiving.

Miss Ellis was here today with the little twins, Mary and Alice, daughters of Lord Mandeville. Dear little tots, how little they know of all the pomp and grandeur that awaits them if they live; but what a blessing they have so good a teacher and guide in their governess. May she long be spared to train them and lead them to the Saviour who died for rich and poor. He is no respecter of persons.

December 8th 1882
So tired! Shall the road wind uphill all the way? Yet the working and waiting have their sweetness, and we can still sing,

> "One more day's work for Jesus:
> How sweet the work has been."

We had a busy day on the 29th. My dear Mary and granddaughters Dora and Annie were here, and gave a filled basket to more than one hundred families: of turkeys or chickens, bread, potatoes, turnips, rice, tea, and sugar,

Scripture texts and religious papers. May they all feed on the bread that perisheth not.

Oh, the happy faces, the bright cheerful "thank you" of most of them. There were some of a less thankful nature, but He maketh His sun to shine upon the evil and the good, His rain to fall on the just and the unjust. [Matthew 5:45.]

May our dear Father bless and reward all the dear friends who send the means to procure the good things for the poor. We send the things to some who are too old or feeble to come for them.

Miss G. Wendell, Mrs. Field, and Miss Hamersley were here today.

December 28th 1882

Another week's work is done, and soon another year will close. Who shall do this work next year, we cannot tell. May we all stand ready so that when our Lord shall come we may be ready to go forth to meet Him.

We gave a basketful of food to fifty poor and feeble old women on the morning of the 24th, with which they were all greatly pleased. Many dear ones came with many pretty and useful gifts to me. Others sent dainties of many kinds.

A large box and barrel came from the St. Cloud Sunday School of Orange, N. J., with toys, dolls, and useful things for my poor children, all of which were very acceptable and will make many hearts glad.

One hundred and ten boxes of candy, large and small, came from the small children of a select day school. Mrs. J. C. Brown's children sent the usual Christmas tree all dressed for me.

On Wednesday the children came and we had a grand time. Such exclamations, such smiling faces, such bright eyes. Oh, it is worth all the trouble, care and pain it causes.

I wish the donors could see them, for it would repay

them for all the expense. Toys, books, candy, oranges, apples, stockings, gloves, mittens – all, all, were acceptable, and all used up.

On Christmas Eve, after the old women had been supplied, Miss C. said to me, "Are there any more you would like to send to?"

I said yes.

Miss C. said, "Well, take this, and use it as you like."

So I sent a bag of flour and bushel of potatoes to five more poor families. One little boy seeing the potatoes said, "Mamma, may I have one to eat?"

She said, "Not till they are cooked," and turning to my maid the mother said, "They have not had anything to eat today."

My own dear grandchildren came on Christmas morning, each bringing some little present to Grandma.

> "Not more than others I deserve
> Yet God has given me more."

Praise the Lord, Amen and Amen.

Have collected and given away through the past year about two thousand and sixty-two dollars. Have had two thousand nine hundred and eighty-seven calls, not including those of the poor. Mrs. Field took three of my large families, and with her sewing and Sunday school classes of young ladies, supplied them with goodies, books, garments and food.

Much has been given through the year by the ladies: dry goods from Mrs. Jaffray, Mrs. McVickar, Mrs. Stillman and others; food from the N. Y. Association; coal from the city funds. For all of which we give thanks and praise to our God, for He is worthy.

All this has caused many sleepless nights and weary

days, but the work is very sweet, and we are very happy, and what avails all this unless it is done in alight spirit, done for the Master?

We earnestly ask to be given the right and best words for each, rich or poor, to bring them into a closer union with the precious Jesus, or to lead those who know Him not, to His feet who is ever ready to bless all who come unto Him.

Beautiful words: "This man receiveth sinners and eateth with them." [Luke 15:2.]

Chapter 33

Great and Precious Promises

Thou wilt show me the path of life: in Thy presence is fullness of joy; at Thy right hand are pleasures for evermore (Psalm 16:11).

As the deep blue of heaven brightens into stars,
So God's great love shines forth in promises,
Which, falling softly through our prison bars,
Daze not our eyes, but with their soft light bless.
Ladders of light God sets against the skies,
Upon whose golden rungs we step by step arise,
Until we tread the halls of Paradise.

January 3rd 1883

Often I lie here on my bed and think of the wanderer who found God in his dreams, and beheld a ladder that reached to heaven. [Genesis 28:12.] Jacob's troubled and penitent heart yearned for the protection of Abraham's God, and lo, God was with him, and the "wilderness and solitary place was glad." [Isaiah 55:1] And he called the place Bethel, the house of God.

My little home is Bethel unto me, for often have I seen the ladder in sleeping and in waking hours. One by one have the promises risen up before me as a ladder reaching to the skies, grace above grace, comfort above comfort, assurance above assurance; a golden stairway radiant with mercy, and above all my gracious and compassionate Redeemer bidding me faint not, nor grow weary. Those blessed promises! They are new every evening, and fresh every morning.

"Upon their golden rungs we step by step arise,
Until we tread the halls of paradise."

I am at the dawn of another year, and here, my Father, like Jacob of old, I fain would make a new covenant with Thee. Through another year, oh, take my hand and guide me. Darkness and thorns may lie along the path. Come Thou, and all shall be well. And if death this year shall end Thy pilgrim's journey, this only I ask: that Thou be with me in the valley and the shadow.

"Do what thou wilt! Yes only do
What seemeth good to Thee,
Thou art so loving, wise and true
It must be best for me."

"Send what Thou wilt, or beating shower,
Soft dews or brilliant sun;
Alike in still or stormy hour,
My Lord, Thy will be done."

January 6th 1883
So tired. The past two months have been months of trial and suffering both in mind and body. "When He hath tried me I shall come forth as gold." [Job 23:10.] But I shrink from none of these things, and only ask that the promised grace be given. We are only secure and peaceful while constantly looking to the King and listening to His voice.

I have not had as much sweet communion with dear friends as usual. All have been so busy. Sometimes I think they fancy that the "shut-in ones" have no temptations, and that a compassionate tempter lets them alone. But they are mistaken, for temptations come into this upper room.

"Satan hath desired to have you that he may sift you

as wheat." [Luke 22:31.] We know what those words mean, but we also know that One, even our Jehovah Jesus, hath prayed for us that our faith fail not. He ever lives above for us to intercede. Blessed, thrice blessed be His holy name.

> "His blood atones for all our race,
> And sprinkles now the throne of grace."

January 8th 1883
Many kind letters and verbal messages have been received, telling me of spiritual help and comfort obtained in this little room the past year. But I fail to find one soul that has been turned from darkness into light, and this grieves me and has been a great source of temptation.

Is it that the Master sees best that we should not see the fruit of all that we do? It is ours to so sow beside all waters, His to give the increase.

January 10th 1883
Yesterday I had all my dear children to dinner in honor of the golden wedding of our old and valued friends, Mr. and Mrs. John Stephenson. We had a very pleasant time. Who would have thought I would have lived to see this event? Wonderful are Thy ways, O Lord, Thou King of saints. [Revelation 15:3.]

Have been made very happy. Mr. McV. has kindly increased his subscription for the poor, and Mrs. McV. has also commenced to contribute monthly to the same cause. Lord, bless and reward this young couple, and may they become more and more like Thee. How these added funds will gladden the hearts of many who are starving for bread.

Mrs. Jaffray, Miss Callender, Mrs. Haxton, Mrs. Wood, Miss Barney, Mrs. Stillman, all continue their monthly contributions through the year.

January 20th 1883

Letters from Italy with Christmas gifts from my darling Miss L. Smith. She assures me that she will return ere the hot days of summer come. My heart yearns for her. She has ever been as a dear, faithful, loving child since her sainted mother on her dying bed committed me to her care. God grant her the peace of the gospel in that land where Paul preached it, and in due time a safe voyage home.

January 25th 1883

For the past few cold days and nights I have been at a loss to know how to get bedclothes for many poor people who are suffering for want of them.

While thinking and asking where shall I apply, Mr. Jaffrey's name came right up before me. I hesitated, knowing how much he and his dear wife were doing for the poor, yet I could not get rid of the name.

So I wrote a short note telling Mr. Jaffray that bed clothing was needed, and that it was the Master's work. Well, at 5 p.m. that day I had six pairs of blankets, and when the bundle was opened I shouted for joy. Two pair were distributed that night and the rest the next day, and to my surprise and joy, that evening two pair more came. "While they yet call I will answer." [Isaiah 65:24.]

Allelujah, for the Lord God omnipotent reigneth. Oh how those needy ones rejoiced in their new treasure to keep them and their little ones warm through winter's cold.

February 5th 1883

Had a call from my late pastor, Rev. C. E. Glover. My old pastors do not forget the little room in the rear house.

Just received a present of a lovely shawl brought by a

young lady from London. Also a very pretty table cover embroidered with my name, from a young friend in Munich. Thus from many parts of the world dear ones think of me and send pretty little tokens of love.

February 8th 1883

Good news reaches me of a full church and good meetings from my dear children at Fleet Street Church, Brooklyn. They tell me many are forward for prayers. Mr. P. wants something to put in the hands of the new converts, and thinks *My King*, by Miss Havergal, will be good.

My heart pleads for a great triumph. Lord, revive Thy work still more and more, make bare Thine arm, and may the slain of the Lord be many.

February 12th 1883

> "Unveil thy bosom, faithful tomb,
> Take this new treasure to thy trust."

A great and good man has left us to join the spirits of the just made perfect. Mr. W. E. Dodge is just being taken to his resting place to await the great resurrection morn. What a loss to this city in example, in admonition, in Christian benefaction. All, all will miss him, a kind, genial man of sterling integrity, and a devoted Christian.

He with his wife, whom I have known for twenty-four years, called on me on the 29th of November last. Mr. Dodge came into my room with a smiling face, carrying a turkey under his arm for me. After talking in a very pleasant, jovial way for some time, he said, "Child, why do you have that window open at your side?"

I replied that it was such hard work to breathe with it shut. The day was very cold. He said, "I will give you a text for this year," and repeated slowly, "In your, *our* Father's house are many mansions; Jesus said, I go to prepare a place for *you*, and if I go and prepare a place for *you* I will come again and receive *you* unto myself, that where I am there *you* may be also." [John 14:2.]

"There will be one for *you* and one for me, and there will not need to be any windows open there." He greatly emphasized the you each time; then turning around, and seeing the table full of poultry for the poor, spoke playfully about them, and asked where I got them and what I was going to do with them.

My dear Mary said, "Ma, has Mr. Dodge written in your birthday album?"

I answered No, and then he kindly wrote his name; and when Mrs. Dodge wrote hers, he playfully said, "Now my dear, put down your age as I have mine."

He was full of life and vigor then − but he is only gone a little while before, and we shall meet again where the many mansions be. A prince and a great man has fallen in Israel.

My long-tried and faithful friend Mrs. L Palmer, also Mrs. McVickar were here. Of course our converse was of the great and good man who had so suddenly gone from us to be for ever with the Lord.

Have had a very busy week with the poor. So many sick ones needing help; so many new babies with their mothers need so much care.

Dear Mrs. Stillman wrote me, saying, "Dear Auntie, tomorrow is my birthday. I expect to go downstairs for the first time in six weeks. They are making great preparation for it. I send you ten dollars for you to get up a nice dinner for you and your children, also ten to give a dinner to some of your poor, to surprise them and help me to keep my birthday. Will you do it? Do anything you like with the money. If you spend it in goodies, so much the better."

I sent dinners to six families – meat, vegetables, pies and fruit, and they were very, very happy. They blessed the giver and thanked God. Ladies do not realize how much good they do, or how many prayers they bring down on their heads by such gifts.

February 18th 1883
Had sacrament of the Lord's Supper; a refreshing time from the Lord.

> "We need not now go up to heaven
> To bring the long-sought Saviour down;
> Thou art to all already given;
> Thou dost e'en now Thy banquet crown."

A few faithful friends were present with my pastor, Rev. J. Dickenson, and class leader. If such the sweetness of the stream, what must the fountain be?
Very feeble.

March 26th 1883
Easter morning
Once more has it been my privilege to recall the last days of my Lord's life on earth, and the great tragedy of Calvary. Once more have I been with Him in the garden and at the cross. Divine Friend and gracious Redeemer, accept our sympathy as the incense of sincere gratitude. We adore Thee for the grace of Thy healing sorrows.

> "O sacred head, now wounded,
> With grief and shame bowed down;
> Now scornfully surrounded
> With thorns, Thine only crown.
> O sacred head, what glory,

What bliss till now was Thine!
Yet though despised and gory,
I joy to call Thee mine."

But the grave could not contain Him. "He is not here, for He is risen." [Matthew 28:6.] And on this Easter morning let me follow Him to the right hand of the majesty in the heavens, where He superintends the Everlasting Kingdom and listens to the prayers of His people.

"O risen Christ! Thou art the door,
The ever-shining way,
The blessed Easter-gate of life,
That opens to the day."

Many beautiful lilies, fair emblems of Easter brightness, have been sent to me by loving friends.

April 15th 1883
A new pastor is sent to our church, and we trust he is sent of God, for much prayer has gone up for this. Oh, that he may be a live coal to kindle a great flame, so imbued with the spirit of his Master that he will set us all afire with the love which constrains men to be reconciled to God.

Brothers Lavery and McKennell brought the new pastor, Rev. C. J. North, in to see me.

April 16th 1883
Had a very pleasing incident today. A few days ago I was led to write a business letter to a gentleman whom I had never seen, at the close of which I added a few words of the loving Master, and that I wrote as I lay on my back in bed where I had lain many years.

The next day the gentleman called to see me. We

conversed on the loving kindness and the long suffering of our God. He related to me his experience, how he had again and again wandered from the fold, and how gently the Lord had rebuked him and brought him back; how at this time he was on the verge of despair, but was moved to afresh consecrate himself to God.

I since heard that the Lord had used our interview to defeat the enemy and give him a fresh baptism of the Holy Spirit, and he is giving the glory to God. This he related in a public service.

Very feeble, but He giveth power to the faint, and to them that have no might He increaseth strength. [Isaiah 40:29.] Hallelujah!

O Lord, give me to stand before Thee in uprightness of heart. Take from me any inclination to turn to the right or to the left, and establish me upon the eternal basis of Thy grace.

April 23rd 1883
Very, very sick. Doctor here twice. Lord, prepare me for whatever Thou shalt see fit to lay upon me. If now fresh suffering is to come to me, help to move the closer to Thee.

From Mr. Samuel B. Power
Gloucester House
Swansea, England
May 18th 1883
Dear Mrs. Cooke,
I suppose you can hardly expect much relief from your long life of suffering, but you may look for that supply of patience under it which our Heavenly Father will give. The inclosed little leaflet (*Reality*) may interest you from the fact that it was given to me last Saturday by Miss Havergal's sister, upon whom I called. She lives near here.

I sometimes picture you to myself in your nice room, the picture of neatness, and also of long-suffering patience. I only wish something might happen to give me another trip across the Atlantic to have the pleasure of seeing you again.

But we shall meet in the sweet by and by.

Believe me yours very sincerely,

Samuel B. Power

(Mr. P. is brother to Rev. Mr. Power, author of *The Oil Feather Tracts* in England.)

Letter to Bella Cooke's daughter, Mary Pullman
Irvington-on-Hudson
May 22nd 1883
Dear Mrs. Pullman,
I am stunned by the intelligence you sent me about your dear, dear mother. What shall I do when she is gone? No one can know what she has been to me the ten years it has been my privilege to know and love her personally.

Tell her how I love her, and long to be like her in her Christian life. And if indeed God does call her first, I know that when life's fitful fever is over she will be waiting and watching for me.

Of course I will continue my money for her poor while life and means are spared to me.

Anything else that I can do for her I will do gladly. I shall wait anxiously to hear further from you, and remain

Your sincere friend,

A. J. McVickar

May 23rd 1883
My Dear Mrs. Pullman,
Having today received your note, I hasten to beg you to tell dear Mrs. Cooke that I shall send the money for her poor

people just as she desires to have me, but I hope God may yet spare so useful and valuable a life for some time to come.

I know it does not seem kind to pray that she may be kept from her Heavenly Home, and her crown, and her Saviour's presence, but we do not want to lose so loving and precious a friend as your dear sweet mother is to so many of us, and so we must ask her Father to bless the remedies used for her recovery.

With very much love for her,

I am, yours sincerely,

A. F. Jaffray

To Bella Cooke

From Mrs. S. M. Schieffelin

My Dear, Dear Friend,

Will you very kindly let someone write to me how you are? I was so very sorry not to be able to go and give you one kiss before we left town, but it was impossible.

I am praying for you, dear, and I still hope that God will give you back to all who love you so fondly.

Is it very selfish to wish to keep you here? I know it is, but is there another to take your place, should God call you to Himself? And how can we live without you? May God bless you now and always.

Your loving friend,

S. M. Schieffelin

June 3rd 1883

Dear Miss Callender called. I was very ill. After a kind greeting she asked me about the expense of night nurses and other things, and then said, "Now, Mrs. Cooke, I was looking over my accounts yesterday, and I said to myself, 'Now, May Callender, you are not giving enough to the Lord. You just go and take fifty dollars to Mrs. Cooke,' and so I filled out a check, and here it is."

I did not know what to say. Yes, "Before they call I will answer, and while they are yet speaking I will hear." [Isaiah 65:24.]

Our dear aged friend, Mrs. McCauley, was very ill, and it seemed hard to tell which would get home first; but she outstripped me, and was first to gain the prize.

> "'Tis good at Thy word to be here;
> 'Tis better in Thee to be gone."

Through thirty years of suffering I have prayed for grace to stay till the end of the day. Father, hear still that prayer.

> "Let me not die before I've done for Thee
> My earthly work, whatever it may be;
> Call me not hence with mission unfulfilled,
> Let me not leave my space of ground untilled;
> Impress this truth upon me, that not one
> Can do the portion that I leave undone."

From Mrs. A. R. Dahlgren
Hart Cottage, Newport
June 6th 1883
Dear Mrs. Cooke,
As I take my pen for a little talk with you this beautiful morning, your gentle, sweet face looks at me from its place on my toilet table.

How I wish I could have you here, that I might show you the ocean, glittering in the sunlight, as if it were a sea of glass. Last Sunday how I thought of you when we drove out to St. Mary's, where my dear mother rests.

Nothing on earth can be more lovely than that beautiful churchyard, with the little ivy-covered church standing on a gentle slope; just above it and beyond, green fields stretching out to the river which runs back from the ocean.

I never go there without thinking of the "green pastures beside the still waters," and you would love it, because it is more like England than any landscape I have ever seen.

Dear friend, though we may not look upon the same scenes together in this world, we know that in the "better country," that "land of pure delight," we shall together look upon beauty of which the heart of man may not conceive. There, "sweet fields beyond the swelling flood, stand dressed in living green," and where we shall never say, "I am sick."

When you are able to write, dear Mrs. Cooke, I shall be glad to hear from you, but you must obey your good doctor and not attempt too much. Only remember me in your prayers, that I may be thankful enough for all my blessings, and that your example, like that of the still Higher One you have so closely followed, may be blessed to me.

That the Lord may bless thee, and keep thee, and make His face to shine upon thee is the prayer of,

Yours always,

A. E. Dahlgren

To Bella Cooke
From Mrs. S. M. Wood
Seabright
June 7th 1883
My dear Friend,
Those who have been ill must receive first attention, although many letters are waiting to be answered; and I cannot tell you how rejoiced I am at your recovery from that terrible illness.

The direct finger of God is in it. He has work still for you to perform, of which we know not. We only know that He is very good to spare you to us still longer.

These past few warm days, dear friend, must be most trying to you in that little "upper chamber." How much I wish it might be possible to bottle up some of these cool breezes from the ocean and send you, or that I could bring you down here.

With best love, yours,
Sarah M. Wood

July 8th 1883

> "If in this feeble flesh I may
> Awhile show forth Thy praise;
> Jesus, support this tottering clay
> And lengthen out my days."

Since I last wrote, I have been very ill. I think I never was *so ill for so long a time.* My kind Dr. P. was here two and three times a day. On the 10th of May he was here two hours in the night. All thought I would pass away. The Doctor said I must not be left without one of my daughters, besides a nurse and my maid.

I was very low one Saturday. The dear children, Mrs. Field, Mrs. Bodstein, pastor and wife, all were here. They sang and prayed with me. Then again in June I reached a point when the flickering flame was ready to go out, and all thought that the end had come.

Dear Mrs. Field, Mrs. Schieffelin, Miss Barney, Miss Hamersley, were here on the Sabbath. All wept, thinking the hour was come. Mrs. Haxton hastened to Mrs. Bodstein's and told them if they wished to see me they must come at once.

My dear sister came twice in May from Meriden. Medicine, beef tea, and stimulants were given me every fifteen minutes, night and day, for seven weeks, as the doctor ordered. My class leader brought old Father Brown, age eighty-four, to say goodbye.

The dear old man prayed and committed me to the Father's care, and spoke of my beloved husband, once a member of his class, as having been so many years at rest before

Oh, the peace, perfect, perfect peace. I seemed to talk face to face with God. Not a ripple of a wave troubled me; *it was perfect peace* and *rest of mind*. I seemed cut loose from everything of earth, and feasting with the King of kings.

July 11th 1883

I had all things arranged for my poor dear people; how I love them. Mrs. Jaffray, Miss Callender, Mrs. Haxton, Mrs. McVickar and others said they certainly would continue their monthly contributions for the poor when I was gone, and my dear Annie was to take charge of it.

I was much gratified that this could be done, but the miscellaneous giving would be difficult for another to take up, as it had grown with me. The begging of funds and clothing, and the distribution of the same, the Thanksgiving and Christmas festivals for the children, would all be very difficult for another to manage.

Rev. Mr. Elmore was here, pastor of Thirtieth Street Presbyterian Church. He said he wanted to thank me for the interest I had taken in his people, that I had lifted many burdens from his shoulders by the help, temporal and spiritual, I had rendered them. Words like these encourage me.

Chapter 34

At Evening Time, Light

At evening time it shall be light (Zechariah 14:7).

> Beyond the smiling and the weeping,
> I shall be soon.
> Beyond the waking and the sleeping,
> Beyond the sowing and the reaping,
> I shall be soon.
> Love, rest and home! Sweet hope!
> Lord, tarry not, but come.
>
> Beyond the parting and the meeting
> I shall be soon.
> Beyond the farewell and the greeting,
> Beyond this pulse's fever beating,
> I shall be soon.
> Love, rest and home! Sweet hope!
> Lord, tarry not, but come.

July 14th 1883
Another birthday! Sixty-two years old! Sixty-two years of loving kindness and tender mercies. Surely it was a way that I knew not, and the world would say, not a journey to be envied; but they know not the secret comforts that come to pilgrims when Jesus walks by their side. "Did not our heart burn within us, while He talked with us by the way, and while He opened to us the Scriptures?" [Luke 24:32.]

It has pleased my Father that sore trials and deep distresses should come to me along the way. Trials that mortals may not know and words would fail to portray, but concerning those trials one and all this is my testimony, that *there was supernatural aid in time of need*, and that no human friend could furnish.

When swooning as into very death, angel arms were under me to bear me up. When this poor body was racked and broken in agony of pain till reason fled, a divine hand was on my brow and a sweet voice quieted me. Oh, He has kept His promises; He is a covenant keeping God.

But the end cannot now be far off. "Now is our salvation nearer than when we believed." [Romans 13:11.] He will soon be here.

So I am watching quietly every day,
Whenever the sun shines brightly, I rise and say,
"Surely it is the shining of His face!"
And look into the gates of His high place beyond the sea;
For I know He is coming shortly to summon me.
And when a shadow falls across the window of my room,
I lift my head to watch the door and ask if He is come;
And the angel answers sweetly in my home:
"Only a few more shadows, and He will come."

My children and grandchildren celebrated my birthday by taking tea with me, and they and others brought me birthday gifts. Mr. Pullman gave me *The Life of Sir John Lawrence*, India's great Christian statesman, and I shall enjoy reading it when able. Thus I am cheered on the way.

How much I enjoy my dear grandchildren. They make me young again. I love to see them with their merry eyes and sweet ways, to hear them sing and enjoy their merry laugh subdued for fear it will make grandma sick. All the little ones save up their pennies to buy something for grandma. Surely I am blessed.

July 26th 1883
One week ago our valued friend, Dr. W. O. Palmer, entered into rest. Surely it was sudden death and sudden glory. Like Barnabas, he was a son of consolation. "He was a good man and full of the Holy Ghost and of faith, and much people was added to the Lord." [Acts 11:24.]

May our dear sister be upheld and sustained! She writes me that when the message came, and the dear doctor was saying, "I fear no evil, Thou art with me, *Thou art mine!*" her soul was so full she had to shout aloud, "Glory! Glory!" What triumphs of faith are ours when trusting in the King of kings! What a glorious translation was his!

Oh, that we may be found as ready and as fitted for the change as this dear servant of God!

My kind physician feels the loss of his brother very much. They had been closely united so many years.

July 28th 1883
Have heard from Miss Stokes, who is at the Adirondacks. The result is that seven happy children have gone to Hillsdale, N. J., for two weeks. Also Mrs. McVickar has taken five others to Camden, N. Y., for two weeks. They all had to come and get a goodbye kiss. Happy children, God bless them.

August 8th 1883
Have had word that I could send eight more little ones to Hillsdale, and they are gone.

August 19th 1883
Another year has gone, and afresh it brings to mind the

removal of my loved ones. Thirty-four years of unalloyed bliss has been his, while I have been traveling on here below: he with the two little ones, I with the three. How often the dear girls have said, "Ma, how we would have enjoyed it if we could have had father with us."

Yes, and how proud he would have been of his children and grandchildren. But our God doeth all things well; and so it is well with my husband, it is well with my children;

> "Far from a world of grief and sin,
> With God eternally shut in."

From Miss R. Polhemus
Stamford
August 15th 1883
My dear Mrs. Cooke,
How I wish I was by your bedside this afternoon. I think of you so often, wondering how you are these warm days.

We well people wander off trying to find a cool spot, while you, who are so patient, are still in the same "little corner," so many, many years. Oh, what a lesson this is to us all.

Your sweet face comes up to me so often, and then the thought of your suffering so all the time, enduring it all so lovingly and patiently for your Heavenly Father.

Now, dear Mrs. Cooke, I hope to hear from you; but do not write yourself, for I know it pains you so much to do so. With so much love to you, believe me,

Yours very affectionately,
Ramona Polhemus

September 24th 1883
After an absence of three years spent abroad, I have just got

back my dear friend Mrs. Gale. The Lord has spared her and hers, and blessed them with a safe return. Other dear friends have returned also: Mrs. Haxton, Mrs. Field, and Mrs. Bodstein, all of whom have been to see me.

Dear Mrs. Field is full of the spirit of her Master, and very desirous that I should be healed by faith. She attends Mr. Simpson's meetings, where this subject is held forth.

I tell the dear one I dare not say or doubt that others are not healed, but I say I have not as yet had any light on the subject. I am asking and waiting to hear the Master's voice. When He shall speak I shall surely be healed.

Mrs. F. urges this with a devout earnestness, as she thinks I would be a much more efficient worker for Jesus if I were up and around. I tell her God keeps me here for a purpose of His own, and on my couch I try not to be idle.

It is now thirty-three years since Doctors Fitch and Cooper pronounced me incurable, twenty-eight of which I have passed on my bed. But all the promises of God have been yea and amen in Christ Jesus. He hath surely been my Husband, Brother, Friend, and,

> "In loftiest songs of sweetest praise
> I would to everlasting days
> Make all His glories known."

October 23rd 1883

The past month the angel death was here and bore away some valued friends. First, Rev. S. Kristellar, one of our preachers; then came the word that Rev. C. E. Glover had entered into rest. I had not known of his illness. It seemed like a heavy crash of thunder on a bright summer day. I shall hear that cheerful voice and hearty laugh no more, nor see his genial smile.

All the three years he was with us in Twenty-Seventh

Street Church, he was a kind and faithful pastor and friend, ever ready to do anything for my comfort or that of my dear children. He was a devout Christian, a pure and upright man, and all who knew him felt that he walked with God.

Then came the tidings that Sister Mary D. James had been called to her reward. And great will be her reward, for she was an "elect lady"; few to compare with her. I love to think of that gentle spirit the loving touch, the sweet, soft word, the heavenly smile; but she too has gone to swell the chorus unto Him that hath loved us.

October 24th 1883

Such a night as I had last night has rarely been granted me. Sleep was holden from my eyes, but it was to see the glory and hold sweet converse with the great "Three-in-One." It would be impossible to tell it. My soul was full, full of glory. I had to shout and sing and weep for joy. It seemed I was not of earth. The little room seemed filled with the bodily presence of my God.

Today I had a visit from Mrs. Rev. J. Carter from El Paso, Western Texas, where her husband is pastor of M. E. Church.

October 25th 1883

Daily we have word that our dear old church is looking up; souls are coming to Christ. Our pastor and wife are putting forth every effort to save souls and quicken believers. He is setting all to work who can, and I in my corner would not be left behind. I often think of my childhood hymn by Watts,

> "I have been there and still would go,
> 'Tis like a little heaven below."

This church, truly a little vine of His right hand planting, is now budding and blossoming, and we look for great results. She is very dear to us; we love her very walls. Ever since we reached this land, travel-stained and weary, distressed in soul and body in 1847, we have found there a home, a Bethel.

Lord, indue Thy servant the pastor and the flock with living, mighty faith. The rams' horns were not warlike weapons, but with obedience and perseverance they brought down the walls of Jericho, and then followed the shout of the people. "Then shalt thou call and the Lord shall answer; thou shalt cry and He shall say, here I am." [Isaiah 58:9.]

October 26th 1883

Had a letter from Mrs. Jaffray. Among other kind things, she says, "Dearest friend, I long to see you and talk with you. God has His own good purpose to serve with you on earth, and we are glad to have you spared to comfort us and help the poor."

Dear, dear friend, for twenty-two years she has been very, very helpful to both me and my poor, contributing largely of her means for my needs constantly, and always responding to my appeals for others. May the God of all grace bless her and hers abundantly.

The poor seem to increase. I wrote to Mr. McVickar for a piece of white muslin and a piece of white flannel to clothe infant children, and I was answered at once by a full piece of each from him.

One poor woman, a widow with eight children, came to beg of me to put her youngest child into the nursery, that she might go out to work. She has struggled for sixteen months to keep them together. Her husband was killed; we have helped her all we could.

When these cases are fresh, many are touched and give help; but in a little while the interest lags and they suffer, for their wants continue. This poor woman is being put out for rent, but as soon as the babe is cared for she will do better. Mrs. Townsend receives the baby to the nursery.

October 27th 1883
Another comes from help. She is sick and a widow with two children, infants. Still another comes for help from Widows' Society; has six small children and no work. My heart goes out for these poor widows. Another for clothes for sick daughter who is weak minded. They have no home, but the mother is trying to find one for the daughter, then she can care for herself. Gave help to all.

An "in memoriam" card came today from Dublin, in memory of Miss Mary Scheckleton, secretary of Invalids' Prayer Union, of which I have been a member some time. Thus,

> "Friend after friend departs;
> Who hath not lost a friend?"

Those lines of Montgomery take me back to my childhood when I used to look with reverence at the little old man as he moved about among us on Whit-Monday when the Sunday school children met on the green outside of Sheffield – many thousand children. And when the circle was formed, he was the chief figure in the center, and sang with us the hymns written by himself for the occasion.

November 1st 1883
And yet another has passed away, gone to the mansion prepared for all who love His appearing: Dr. Gale, a young man full of promise, whom I have known from a little child. He was a true friend to the poor, who will miss him very much.

He often came to me to ask the best way of helping them for their best good. The last time he was here he was trying to plan something by which I could see the setting sun or the moon by reflection in mirrors, something I have not seen for many years.

November 20th 1883
Many dear friends have kindly sent in their donations for Thanksgiving without being asked, which I take as a token that it is my duty to get the poor their dinner.

December 5th 1883
On Thanksgiving Day, my dear children had the people downstairs and attended to them, giving well-filled baskets of provisions to 117 families. I was not able to see any of them, but I knew that they had the food, and I thank God that means were sent to get it. Sixty-four of the women were widows.

So tired. I have settled up all my bills, and have a little left for the poor for Christmas.

December 10th 1883
Again hath He called, and another dear one has gone to the realms above to take possession of her heavenly home. On the 6th my beloved and long-tried friend, Miss Mary A. Cannon, left us to dwell with Jesus. Thirty-six years we have been as two with a single heart. Cemented by the love of Christ, we felt and spoke the same.

Many days and nights in my early widowhood we spent together. Together we went to the house of prayer; together we visited the sick and dying in homes and hospitals; together we knelt in class. When I could no longer go with her, she came to me and spent her Sabbath evenings here while my girls went to church, and our converse of our

Redeemer was sweet. We were strengthened, she for her labors and cares, I for the waiting and suffering.

She was one of the few who loved my poor, and new applicants I could safely intrust to her. These she visited, and then would send them to me. Thus, year after year, I was blessed with her companionship until she became too feeble to come out evenings. Then she would come in the daytime until a very few weeks before the Master came for her, and at last she finished the race before me.

Thus one after another is taken, and I remain. In the past five months eight of my friends have been taken: Dr. W. C. Palmer, Mr. Henry Quinan, Rev. S. Kristella, Rev. C. E. Glover, Mrs. James, Dr. Sims, Dr. Gale, and Miss Cannon. With all these I have taken sweet counsel, and "these all died in the faith." [Hebrews 11:13.]

Collected and distributed this year two thousand and twenty-five dollars; had three thousand calls besides my poor. I have made up my mind to have my son, Rev. Jos. Pullman, prepare the papers I have written for publication, so that should I soon be called away, they may be ready.

Dear Sister Palmer was to have done this, but many duties and labors, besides the preparing a memoir of the Doctor, have interfered. So I prefer Mr. Pullman to prepare the manuscript for publication. He knows me better than anyone else, and will give a truthful account. It is a great trial to have so much of my life made public, but it is for the glory of Him who has done so much for me.

It has been written in great pain – how much, *none can ever know* – and with much prayer that the blessing of God may go with it, and that it may prove a blessing to many.

Should my friends publish the volume before I reach my better home, or after that blessed hour, I fervently pray God to bless it to every reader. And if it bring but one soul to Christ, it will richly repay all the pain and weariness it has caused.

Now follow several memories of Bella Cooke requested by her daughter, Mary Pullman, for publication in this book [*Rifted Clouds Part 2*].

From her Pastor
Rev. Thomas G. Osborne
Spring 1884
In the spring of 1857 I was stationed by Bishop Morris at the East Twenty-Seventh Street Methodist Episcopal Church, familiarly known among the members as "Rose Hill." It was then a flourishing society of five hundred members, many of whom were successful businessmen as well as active Christians. The congregation consisted chiefly of energetic young men and women, several of whom have since achieved eminent success in life.

Soon after my arrival I was informed of a very intelligent and devoted lady who had been confined for months and years to her bed of suffering. I called upon her in company with John Stephenson, Esq., who was then and always has been to her a generous friend and sympathizer. I was at once struck with her remarkable cheerfulness under her multiplied afflictions.

She suffered at times intensely from spinal disease and other complicated ailments, which sufferings were often increased by surgical operations, made with the hope of eradicating the disease and affording permanent relief.

During the whole period of my ministry in that church, and in my frequent pastoral calls, I never heard a murmur or impatient word escape her lips. Her little chamber was not merely the abode of resignation, but the home of cheerfulness and even joy.

Mrs. Cooke always felt and manifested great interest in

the prosperity of the Christian Church. Her Christianity was too broad to be confined to one sect. Intelligent and wealthy ladies from the Episcopal, Presbyterian, and Baptist churches, as well as from the Society of Friends, I have frequently found, while visiting her, in her room.

These devoted Christian women visited her not merely from a sense of duty to a fellow sufferer, but for aid and encouragement in their work of faith and labor of love. She cheerfully gave them counsel and sympathy, and above all, bore them to the throne of grace in her prayers.

I have often felt reproved for my want of faith when I have witnessed such sublime faith in her. What was this poor, helpless widow, confined for years to a bed of suffering, and with these children dependent upon her for support, to do? She could do nothing but cast her burden upon the Lord. She did so, and was wonderfully sustained.

On more than one occasion, while I was her pastor, she seemed to be nearing the gates of death. At the time I took down some memoranda, attesting her strong faith and even triumphant rapture, in view of what she and we thought her approaching change. These notes, made beside her sickbed, were cherished for years, but have now disappeared amid the losses incident to the itinerant life.

In her own church she felt a special interest, for she was personally acquainted with many of the members and their children. It was then a time of great religious awakening. Many of the advanced scholars in the Bible classes and some of the teachers in the public schools, who had been accustomed to visit her, were found at the altar seeking salvation. She greatly rejoiced in this outpouring of the Holy Spirit.

Doubtless many of these seekers received abiding religious impressions while conversing, as they were accustomed to do, in her little room. I shall always remember with gratitude her prayers for her pastor's success in that Rose Hill Church. Never shall I forget her counsel and sympathy in trouble, and her heartfelt rejoicing when lost sinners were coming home to God.

In that little chamber I have witnessed in this suffering woman a faith and peace which kings in vain might envy and rich men give their gold to buy. There, ministers have been helped to preach, and businessmen have learned fortitude and patience amid the trials and struggles of life.

Twenty-seven years have passed away since I first called on Sister Bella Cooke, and during that time no one but herself knows her sufferings in the furnace of affliction. She still survives, a monument of patience and suffering, a beautiful illustration of the sustaining power of divine grace.

Who can tell how much consolation she has imparted to the afflicted in all these years? How much instruction to the inexperienced, how much sympathy and good cheer to all Christian workers who have known her! In yonder room, where she has lain so many years, I have witnessed a Faith,

> "That will not murmur or complain
> Beneath the chast'ning rod,
> But in the hour of grief or pain
> Will lean upon its God."

[Letter to Mary Pullman, Bella Cooke's daughter]
Willow Brook
Irvington
May 22nd 1884
My dear Mrs. Pullman,
I received the pictures of the room in which I have often held sweet communion with your dear mother, who is to me so precious a friend. I am delighted with the photograph, which faithfully portrays each object in that chamber, to me

hallowed by most tender associations, and the likeness of dear Mrs. Cooke, although not a flattering one, is still sufficiently like her to be easily recognized.

I can hardly realize that it was in 1861 that my friend, Mrs. Henry V. Butler, introduced me to your mother, as she has changed very little during the years that have gone since that time, notwithstanding the suffering through which she has been passing.

With love to her from Mrs. McVicker and myself,

I am yours most sincerely,

Anna F. Jaffray

From Mrs. A. H. De Guynon
May 1884
My Dear Friend,
More than twenty-five years ago, when I was residing on Bergen Heights, I became deeply interested in the accounts frequently given me by Grandma Cooper of a lady, a member of the same church with herself, who was undergoing terrible physical suffering. It was not thought possible for her to live long, and friends gathered around her expecting, almost longing, for her to receive a speedy release.

Dr. Cooper was one of the many physicians and surgeons who considered death inevitable, but dear Mrs. Cooke is living yet, a "bush burning but not consumed." I became personally acquainted with this elect lady in 1874. I must allude slightly to myself in order to tell you how we met.

I had been for a long time a semi-invalid, with a strong probability of becoming a couch-bound prisoner for the remainder of my life. A mutual friend mentioned me to Mrs. Cooke, and at once her great heart embraced the ease, as it embraces all cases of suffering, with longings to extend relief to the sufferer.

Mrs. Cooke's home is not one of wealth, far from it. Her apartment is not spacious, only I think about twenty feet by fifteen, with a ceiling not over nine feet high. I can scarcely give you an accurate idea of its immaculate sweetness and neatness.

If the tiniest cloud of dust ever ventures within the shining portals, I never met it. Her little range shines like a metallic mirror, and gives not the slightest indication that all the year round, in heat of August, and in December's cold, it accomplishes the cooking for herself, her one servant, and her frequent guests.

It stands in the same small room with her bed – think of that, Beth, when you are fleeing from the heat of summer to mountain air and ocean breezes. Her tea kettle never boils over as other kettles do, but just sits and sings a dreamy lullaby, like the never-to-be forgotten cricket on the hearth. No broiling or frying ever thinks of defacing the polished brightness of that marvelous stove.

The four walls from floor to ceiling are a rare mosaic of engravings, mottoes, portraits and painted panels. The old often giving place to new, which loving friends delight in placing there. The spotless white drapery of the two windows opening westward, is tied back with bright ribbons.

In one corner stands the narrow bed (I would like to say throne), with the head to the south, thus it has a window at the left side. As the hall or entrance door is on the north, the first thing that greets you as you enter, is the sunny face of the room's presiding genius.

Ah, how can I paint for you that face! I have watched it in hours of keenest suffering; when death seemed surely drawing near; through weeks and months of terrible trial; in seasons when daily household cares accumulated. Yet never have I seen it anxious or too much concerned, never without its patient, beautiful smile of content and trust.

I once took a friend of mine to see Mrs. Cooke, a person of unusual discernment, one whose opinions have great weight with others, and who is somewhat incredulous as to high spiritual attainments, and I was so impressed with a remark she made when coming away that I shall ever remember it in connection with my dear friend. She said, "1 have at last met a thoroughly healthy Christian."

Our dear Mrs. Cooke is a lady of rare executive ability. Her charitable work is as skillfully organized and executed as by a regular society. Without loss of time, or wasted preliminaries, she at once reaches and aids her army of worthy poor. I do not know that she has ever been deceived, so clear is her insight into human nature. I do know that both men and women, of "high degree" as well as lowly, come to her for counsel; and seldom, if ever, has her quick sympathy and unerring judgment failed to see just what ought to be said or done.

To look upon my friend's bright face, never without its credential of pain, resting upon its bank of snowy pillows, always meeting you with a smile of welcome, I confess I feel when I step into her little room, as if I were standing on holy ground. She has no words of sorrow wherewith to greet you, but glad words of praise.

I am the friend of your youth,

A. H. de Guynon

Memories from Virginia H. Field

21 Madison Square, North

May 1884

Eleven years ago I paid my first visit to dear Mrs. Cooke in the little upper room, which has proved such a blessed spot to me. I had heard of Mrs. Cooke some time before this, and through the interest that was awakened in me, had purposed at some time to see her.

It was only, however, after a sad bereavement that this idea was carried into effect, and that God in His infinite mercy and love led my steps thither.

For several years ere this He had been teaching me that things of earth, apart from Himself, could not satisfy; that our desires could not always be realized and that His will must be done.

I was learning the lessons slowly, and had been looking to Him to make up to me what I lacked, for my precious mother's early teachings had shown me where to go for comfort.

Thus, seeking the light, I found it beside the bedside of my invalid friend, where for eighteen long years she had lain, praising, rejoicing and trusting in God in spite of almost continual bodily pain and testings of various descriptions.

I found her in the room she now occupies, in the same corner upon her snowy pillows, everything spotless in its purity around her; an expression so happy and peaceful resting on her face such as one finds nowhere where God is not.

I was so pleased with my visit that I went to see her several times before leaving town. My sojourn in the country lasted but a short time, and on my return I resumed my visits, which soon became almost daily.

I was in deep mourning, with a heart in an impressionable condition, hence all my interest ere long centered in the new spiritual life which Mrs. Cooke's words, as she told me day after day of God's dealings with her, awakened in me.

She recounted to me her early conversion, her zeal in God's service when a child, which deepened in her girlhood; her heart's longings for a deeper work of grace, lessening after her marriage, to return with greater ardor subsequently as she realized how far short she was of the heights and depths which were her privilege as God's child.

She rehearsed to me her sad trials and afflictions in England and in America, her pride and rebellion, until in a little village on the western shore of our own beautiful Hudson she entered into the rest of faith and joy in her Lord, whom she had so long sought, after yielding up her will to Him through the ministrations of a lovely, faithful friend.

She still rejoiced in the same loving Saviour when God in His providence graciously took me to her to be taught the same sweet lesson. Years have passed since that first interview, and many a friend have I taken to see this saintly woman, to whom she has told precious portions of her life's history. Would she might be to them what she has been to me!

How I should rejoice to see her as well in body as she is in soul. I hope and pray that this may yet be to the honor and praise of Him, "Who forgiveth all our sins and healeth our diseases." [Psalm 103:3.] Many have been the valued Christian friends whom God has brought to me as I needed them, and rich have been the blessed experiences I have enjoyed, and glorious the revelations of truth from God's own word during this period.

Yet, as I date my spiritual life from my acquaintance with Mrs. Cooke, anything I have learned in this "life hid with Christ in God," [Colossians 3:3] or have been enabled to do in His service, I trace back to this good friend who by God's grace proved so great an influence in my life. Thus God hearkens when in moments of need we seek Him, and raises up for us the human instruments best suited to our necessities.

Let us, who have been so kindly dealt with, stand ready

in our turn to be used by Him among the weary and heavy laden of earth, to tell them of the love, power and faithfulness of our God as we have opportunity, "till He come" or our labor on earth ended, we shall be called to depart hence and be "forever with the Lord." [1 Thessalonians 4:17]

To Bella Cooke's daughter Mary
From Mrs. S. M. Schieffelin
New York
My dear Mrs. Pullman,
It has been my pleasure to know your mother, Bella Cooke, for over eight years, and during that time I have always esteemed it a blessed privilege to be numbered among her friends. I believe that she is one of God's chosen saints whom He has allowed to suffer so long, that in her wonderful patience and submission His faithfulness might be manifested.

Tried in innumerable ways, she has never been found wanting. In extreme want, her faith has never failed, and her dependence upon her Heavenly Father has never been in vain. It has always seemed to me that in her glowing love to the Saviour, she equals many of the martyrs who held not their lives dear for His sake.

All her sufferings appear to her as nothing, compared with the *Divine* sufferings which have wrought for her this rest and peace in Jesus. This remarkable life in Christ has been used of God to attract many sinners to Him. Until the last great day no one can know how many souls have been brought from darkness to light through her instrumentality.

In closing, let me add that the thought of her unwavering trust in God, and of her daily and hourly resignation to His will, has, since I first saw her, been to me one of the strongest incentives to growth in grace.

Praying that God will still prolong her life for usefulness in His service, and for the happiness of her large circle of friends,

I am yours very truly,

S. M. Schieffelin

[To Bella Cooke's daughter Mary]
From Mrs. M. E. Brown
September 1884
My dear Mrs. Pullman,
Absence from home has caused delay in answering your letter. I think it a great privilege to have known your dear mother. If one were to be told the story of her life without seeing her, it would be difficult to credit it, and yet it is more wonderful than can be told. Her power and influence over children are very great, and they always enjoy going to see her and connect nothing but pleasure with her sickroom.

Of her work among the poor it is unnecessary to speak, for all who know her must have heard of it. I can only say that I believe she has accomplished more than any well woman I know in her work for the suffering and needy, while at the same time suffering intensely herself.

Yours sincerely,

Mary E. Brown

From Miss Helen R. Hamersley
Newport, R. I.
September 1884
Dear Mrs. Cooke,
Enclosed you will find ——, which please accept toward the publishing of the book about your dear self. Nina sent me word in regard to it. I hope it will be speedily published, and I am sure its mission will be a blessed one.

That the book may do as much good to others as the witness of the reality has done for me, is the sincere wish and prayer of,

Yours lovingly,

Helen R. Hamersley

From Mrs. Anna F. Taler

New York

October 15th 1884

My dear Mary,

I am very glad to hear that there is a prospect of your mother's life being published, for it has been such a remarkable manifestation of divine grace that I hope to see it a blessing to many who will never have the privilege of her personal acquaintance.

In all the years that have passed since my acquaintance with her commenced, her sweet placid face has taught me precious lessons, and her cheerful faith in the midst of close trials and great suffering has helped me in many an hour of depression. I hope you may be able to convey some idea of her joyous spirit, of her ability to fit herself to the characters of those about her.

Old and young, poor and rich, the sad and the joyful alike, find in Bella Cooke a genial companion or sympathizing friend. The simple fact that she is at leisure from herself gives an indescribable charm to one's association with her. But more than all, while she must know that God has done wonders for her, and given her great victories, there is not a particle of spiritual pride to mar the beauty of her life.

Always the humble Christian, she claims nothing for herself, fulfilling more than anyone ever knew the injunction to let your light so shine before men that they may see your

good works and *glorify your Father which is in Heaven.*
[Matthew 5:16.]

    Affectionately,

    Anna F. Taber

PART 3

The Life Story of
Bella Cooke Concluded

By Mary Pullman, Bella Cooke's daughter

First Published 1909

(Considerably abridged by White Tree Publishing.
See *Publisher's Note* page iii.)

Chapter 35

Concluding Diary
By Mary Pullman, Bella Cooke's daughter

Since the publication of Volume 2 of *Rifted Clouds* [in 1884], Mrs. Cooke has each year become less able to bear exertion, and it was often with great effort that she attended to the necessary daily routine. This accounts for the fact that she kept no account of her work as in former years, which will no doubt be a great disappointment to the multitude of her friends all over the world.

It had become more and more difficult, as Mrs. Cooke had grown much more feeble, for her to continue her diary, and among her papers but few pages have been found. Only an occasional day, when she felt a little stronger or some peculiar circumstance had occurred, is noted in a few lines.

The visits of her numerous friends had not been of less interest or been less frequent, neither were the number of strangers calling from all parts of the world fewer. But the effort to keep note of these visits became a burden. Often after visitors left, Mrs. Cooke had to rest for hours.

Strangers most frequently came with the introduction, "I have read your book *Rifted Clouds,* and want to be assured there is such a person as Bella Cooke!"

After being with her a little while they left, feeling that all they had read or heard about her was fully exemplified in her. Thousands have testified that her room was a Bethel, and they could never lose the influence of the spirit that was manifested there.

The work for the poor has been as great as in former years. In fact, Mrs. Cooke has said repeatedly, "Every year the distressing cases seem to increase."

She could do but little for many of them and daily refused others, as she had not help to give. Never was as much coal given by her, usually a quarter, sometimes a half ton at a time, to help a family when work was scarce or there was sickness.

As had been her custom for years, she always had ready the outfit for the newborn infant, and bed garments for the sick of all ages. Many friends remembered her when renewing their wardrobes, others sent new flannel and goods to be made into suitable garments, thus furnishing sewing to some of the poor women.

Though very weak, Mrs. Cooke was never too feeble or too tired to listen to the tale of distress and want that was heard and relieved so often in that little room, where she had spent so many years. Often, when so very ill that friends could not be permitted to see her, she would be alert to catch the first intimation that her poor were not being cared for, and would try to give directions as to what should be done for them.

When, at various times, it was believed that Mrs. Cooke could not recover her usual health, though she was never free from pain, it was pitiful to look into the little yard and see the poor, needy creatures standing, and often kneeling on the pavement, offering up a prayer for her.

One might say it was one for her and two for themselves, as they would cry and bemoan their wretched condition, saying no one would care for them when she was gone. They felt they had no friend but her. They seemed to think by coming and gazing up at Mrs. Cooke's window, virtue and help would come to them.

Dr. Palmer has often said, when she would rally, after getting quite down to the river's brink, "The poor prayed her back."

Mrs. Cooke's heart was always very full of tenderest

sympathy for the aged poor, who came to her, or of whom she heard as being crippled by disease, or too feeble to get about, and for the widow with a family of little helpless children. Most of the pensioners she had, belonged to these two classes.

June 19th 1899

During the past two weeks I have enjoyed a number of calls from my dear friend, Miss Billbrough, of England. She has traveled extensively to observe various methods of work in which to advance the Master's kingdom, and to enable her to more wisely and efficiently work for this end.

She has just come from visiting her sister in Canada, who supports and conducts a home there for little waifs, gathered from the streets of London.

She is a marvelous woman of marked ability. Miss B. first came to see me fifteen years ago, and a strong bond of Christian fellowship was formed, which has strengthened with the years, and will continue to do so till we meet in our Father's house above.

July 13th 1899

Another year has gone, and I have reached another milestone, entering my seventy-ninth year. How wonderful has been the goodness and mercy of God through these years! It is true I have had to pass over some rough places, and the adversary is not always absent from my little room. Still the Strong Arm has ever been mine to lean upon, and grace has always been sufficient.

When my path seemed hedged up, that voice has spoken to me, saying, "It is I, be not afraid." [John 6:20.] Thus I have been strengthened and new beauties have been revealed to me in the promises to the faithful, and I have been enabled to walk with joy in the way my Lord led me.

Joseph and the three girls took dinner with me today. I have grown more feeble and soon become weary, and am not able to have the dear grandchildren take lunch with me, as in former years, on my birthday, but they each send me some little love token.

Mr. and Mrs. Hamilton called, also Miss Upham and a friend, and we had some sweet songs. Miss U. accompanying on the little organ, the gift of Mr. and Mrs. H. five years ago. We all sang,

> "And I shall see Him face to face,
> And tell the story, saved by grace,"

after which we were refreshed with a sweet season of communion with God.

The afternoon mail brought three letters of congratulation from friends in England, who had read *Rifted Clouds*, but whom I had never seen. Also a letter from a dear friend traveling in Germany. This is one way my Father blesses me, giving me a place in the hearts of His children.

To us as a family, the past year has been one of blessing, though my dear grandson, Joseph Cooke Pullman, has been ill and is now in Colorado in search of health. I fear he will never be strong again and that he will not be able to come East to live.

An interesting letter from my dear Mrs. Wood who is in Syria, and has spent so much money and given so much time and strength to spread the Master's name and kingdom, has come with birthday greetings.

August days are quite trying to me, yet I am happy in being busy. Two of my dear ladies, Mrs. and Miss Bliss, purchase and send here large quantities of dry goods every summer, which I have cut into garments and given out to be made by some of the neat and capable poor women, who in summer find it so difficult to find work.

The articles, when finished, go to the nursery of Grace Church. In this way many are blessed, and the dear benefactors will have their reward. These ladies also pay for the making.

How often I recall the dear sweet face and spirit of Miss Bliss's sister, who was very dear to me, called home in early womanhood! She seemed to get way down into my heart, and it was a severe shock to me when she was taken suddenly from us.

I have been interested in reading an article by Dr. Packard, on Daniel in the lions' den. He says, "In our own commonplace trials and testings, of patience and faith, it is for us to remember that the way in which we endure may make a contribution to the coming of the Kingdom of God. Others may take note of our cheerfulness and submission, or of our power to rise out of ourselves into joyful service for others; and so it may be seen in the end that others were more in the mind of God than we were, when the pain and loss were allowed to come upon us."

Let us seek the fullness of God's spirit within our own heart; then we shall be ready for whatever may come.

From Mrs. C. Palk
Auckland, New Zealand
September 1st 1899
Dear Sister Cooke,
This is not the first letter you have received from a stranger. My love for you is so sincere and deep that, although distance separates us, and we have never seen each other face to face, yet I feel I know you. Your book, *Rifted Clouds*, I purchased about twelve years ago. I was wonderfully uplifted as I perused its pages. I at once felt that the book

should be placed in the hands of invalids.

Sister Cooke, I cannot tell you the comfort and blessing the contents of the book have given me. How your holy submission to your heavenly Father's will has filled me with sweet assurance. Your God and my God knows what is best, and in every sorrow of the heart, eternal mercy takes a part.

My husband is a home missionary in the Methodist Church. We love the work, and pray that God may bless our efforts. A few weeks ago we saw an article which delighted us very much. It mentioned a conversation you had with some visitors in May, this year. We both had the idea that years ago you had gone home to the celestial city, away from the weary body with all its pain.

You truly are a miracle of God's power to save and keep. My dear husband joins me in sincere good wishes and Christian love.

I am sending you six cards of mounted New Zealand ferns, the work of my husband, and trust you will receive them in good order. May I express one wish, and that is how much we would prize a few lines from you, in any form?

Yours very sincerely,

Mrs. C. Palk

Letter to a Friend

Dear Friend,

Your letter was duly received, and I am thankful that the reading of my simple life story has been made a blessing to you. It is an unvarnished story of our Lord's keeping power, of one of His feeble ones, and with Wesley, I sing,

"In blessing Thee with grateful songs,
My happy life shall glide away;
The praise which to Thy name belongs,
Hourly with lifted heart 1'll pay."

Yes, for He hath done and is continually doing such great things for me, that my soul doth magnify the Lord. When I think that His great heart of love is yearning over me – yes, even me – surely tears of love and joy my eyes overflow. And as I lay awake in the silent watches and commune with my Elder Brother, the veil seems rent at the top, and I have a glimpse into the inner temple, and behold the glory of my Saviour as He sits at the Father's right hand, interceding for me.

It is at these sacred times that the unity that He prayed the Father to grant to us, is mine, and He abides with me, and I scarcely know whether I am here on a bed of pain, or freed from it all and at home with Him. Well, e'er long,

> "I shall behold His face,
> I shall His power adore,
> And sing the wonders of His grace,
> For evermore."

Yours in Him,
Bella Cooke

To Mr. Wills
Mrs. Cooke's Class leader
Dear Brother Wills,
As you requested, I send a few words for the class tonight. My testimony is that great is the loving kindness of God, which calls for praise and thanksgiving. Surely no one has proved His loving kindness more than I; hence, no one has more cause for praise and thanksgiving.

My heart says, "I will praise Thee, my God and King; and I will bless Thy name for ever and ever. Every day will I bless Thee, and I will praise Thy name for ever and ever." [Psalm 145:1.] Yes, He hath done great things for me, and His love toward me has been boundless.

Amid great pain and weariness, the everlasting arms have been round about me, and I have heard those precious words, "I have redeemed thee; I have called thee by thy name; thou art Mine." [Isaiah 43:1.]

Rapturous thought! Redeemed by the precious blood of Jesus Christ, saved by the King of Kings; and I realize that, only as I am washed from my sins in His own precious blood, can I be accepted of Him. Not by aught that I have done, or can do, but by His abounding grace, and still He giveth more grace, even to the end.

Your fellow classmate,

Bella Cooke

Mrs. Cooke wrote the following article for *The Guide to Holiness*

Dear Brother Hughes,

At the close of another year, I would add a few words of testimony to the faithfulness of my God. "The Lord is nigh unto all they that call upon Him, to all that call upon Him in truth. He will fulfill the desire of them that fear Him; He also will hear their cry and will save them." [Psalm 145:18-19.]

These words have surely been verified in my life of seventy-eight years, but never more than during the year just drawing to a close. It has been goodness and mercy all the way through. Even amid great pain and feebleness I have proved the immensity of His love.

He has made me to lie down in green pastures, when faint and weary. He has led me beside the still waters, restoring my soul, and giving me to drink from the living fountain.

Again and again has it seemed as though the chariot was at the door to convey me to the mansions my Elder Brother has prepared for me, and yet again comes the word, "Return to thine house and tell what great things the Lord has done for thee." [Mark 5:19.]

He has put a new song into my mouth,

> "Jesus, Lover of my Soul,"
> Bids me in His bosom stay,
> And though billows round me roll,
> I am safely hid away;
> For He holds me in His arms,
> Quite beyond the tempest's reach,
> And He whispers to my heart
> Words unknown to human speech.

> "Other refuge have I none,"
> He my habitation is;
> Here no evil can befall,
> I am kept in perfect peace.
> I am covered all day long
> With the shadow of His wing;
> Dwell in safety through the night,
> Waking, this is what I sing:

> "Thou, O Christ, art all I want,"
> Rests my helpless soul on Thee;
> Thou wilt never leave alone,
> Nor forget to comfort me.
> Thou hast saved my soul from death,
> Thou hast scattered doubts and fears,
> And the sunshine of Thy face
> Sweetly drieth all my tears.

> "Thou of life the fountain art,"
> Thou dost wash me white as snow;

> I'm content to dwell apart,
> From all else, Thy love to know.
> Blessed Sun of Righteousness,
> I so love to look on Thee,
> That my eyes are growing blind
> To the things once dear to me.

Yours in Christ,
Bella Cooke

January 1900
A new year has opened to me, and I ask that it may be one of service, and that I may perfectly fulfill God's will in me.

January 22nd 1900
Word has come that my dear grandson, Cooke Pullman, is failing. The doctor has written, unknown to him, that his mother had better come out to Colorado. He has been bravely fighting alone, in that Western city, Pueblo. How we wish he were home!

February 1900
My dear Mary is busy, getting ready to go to her sick boy, and arranging plans for the dear ones at home in Stamford.

February 14th 1900
Mary has been to say goodbye as she starts on her sad journey. Our Father, keep her under the shadow of His wings, and may she reach the dear boy in safely.

Undated
I have received a letter from Mary. She had a safe journey, and found Cooke very feeble, but able to be about if he kept very quiet. The least exertion sends the temperature up.

When she spoke to him about coming home, he begged her not to ask him, as he was not ready to give up the fight, and going home would mean he would have to do so.

March 1900
The letters from the West bring words of increasing feebleness, and my dear Mary longs to bring her boy home. She fears he will become too weak to take the journey.

Have had delightful seasons of communion with several of my dear Father's dear children, and,

> "The King of Heaven His table spreads,
> And blessings crown the board;
> Not Paradise, with all its joys,
> Could such delight afford."

The glorious Easter season is here, and we rejoice in our risen Lord.

Worship, honor, power and blessing, Thou art worthy to receive.

> Loudest praises, without ceasing,
> Meet it is for us to give.
> Help, ye bright angelic spirits,
> Bring your sweetest, noblest lays;
> Help to sing our Saviour's merits,
> Help to chant Immanuel's praise!

During the past week I have received very precious letters from friends abroad. One might think, when the time is so occupied sightseeing, they would forget the one laid aside in her little corner, but I receive frequent letters from most of my friends who are in distant lands.

Earth is awakening from her winter's nap, and soon the

trees will put on their refreshing green and the birds will return with song.

April 18th 1900
The annual conference is over, and my dear Joseph has been elected a delegate to the General Conference to be held in Chicago during the month of May. He will probably go the latter part of the month to Pueblo to see his dear wife and son.

Dr. Robert Lauder, my granddaughter's husband, has been appointed a lay delegate to the same conference.

April 28th 1900
Dr. Pullman and his son-in-law have been in to bid me goodbye, as they start for the Conference at Chicago.

Word has come to me that the sick boy is ready to come home, and Mary has telegraphed for tickets. He is impatient now to get here.

May 3rd 1900
The dear ones have started, and are to stop off at Topeka and visit Mrs. Lakin in order that the feeble one may rest. Their plan then is to come on to Chicago, spend a week there with Joseph who has not seen his boy for sixteen months, and then come directly home.

May 11th 1900
We are having intensely hot weather, which always prostrates me. The ice bags to my spine are a great relief when my bed seems all on fire, and there is such burning of my spine and feet.

I cannot describe what I suffer with my feet, and how many the remedies I have tried to relieve them, but generally come back to cold water as the most effectual. Still

He giveth songs in the night and feeds me with hidden manna.

May 14th 1900

This has been a very memorable day. My dear granddaughter, Bella, has a little daughter, the first girl. She has two fine boys. May both mother and babe do well and may this new life bring great comfort and love to the parents' hearts.

About two o'clock the dear travelers arrived, and came to see me before taking the train for home. What a change in the dear boy! Very thin, and so feeble, his voice almost gone, only able to speak in a whisper. I was glad to find him cheerful. His brothers met them at the train, and John has gone home with them.

May 16th 1900

Mary writes from Stamford that on their arrival some of the kind friends had a carriage waiting for them, and on reaching the Elderage (Dr. Pullman was Presiding Elder of the New York District), they found the house beautifully and bountifully supplied with flowers and food, and a most comfortable couch for the sick one.

So the Lord cares for His own. May He grant the dear boy great peace. As the body grows feebler, may his trust and love grow stronger. I presume I shall never see him again in this life, but we shall meet where the inhabitants never say, "I am sick."

July 13th 1900

Another year has been added to my life, and I am still here to praise and pray. Most of my ladies are out of town, and so my visitors are few. Quite a number of my poor are sick, and several babies will have hard work to live through the hot weather.

I almost always ask the kind Father to take them, their lives so often prove to be lives of want and suffering, and many of the poor mothers know so little about caring for the children.

The Summer Sewing is progressing nicely and will be finished early, as I have found a couple of very worthy people who are capable and neat. I often have to tell some of those I help that "cleanliness is next to Godliness" and give them soap to help them. Mr. Pyle supplies me with soap and pearline which I can use to great advantage.

August 19th 1900

The past few days I have been suffering keenly, but great is the peace given me amid it all, for He, my Lord, holdeth mine eyes waking, and He Himself keeps me company in the night.

This is the fifty-first anniversary of the entrance into life eternal of my dear husband, and as each day passes I feel that I am a little nearer laying aside the weary frame and going to join the glorious company of those who are singing the new song, and, above all, nearer seeing Him Who is to present me blameless to the Father – and to be with Him and like Him. Lord, help me so to live that this shall be my portion! Amen and amen!

September 25th 1900

The summer is slipping away, and I will welcome the cooler weather.

There is a good deal of sickness among the children, and several broken-hearted mothers have come in their trouble to get help to bury the little ones.

It is wonderful how much help has been given from this little room to lay away many, both old and young. Generally

I send for the undertaker and arrange with him about the expense, and his bill is sent to me for part or full payment. In this way I know the money is rightly used.

When at times I am so very feeble it seems I cannot have any more added care, and the daily routine seems so great a tax that I almost wish to be at rest, the lines of a godly woman come to me,

"Not now; for I have loved ones sad and weary;
Wilt Thou not cheer them, with a kindly smile?
Sick ones, who need Thee in their lonely sorrow;
Wilt Thou not tend them yet a little while?

"Not now; for wounded hearts are sorely bleeding,
And Thou must teach those widowed hearts to sing:
Not now; for orphans' tears are quickly falling,
They must be gathered 'neath some sheltering wing."

My heart responds, "Gladly will I be spent in the service of my Lord"; and daily I prove that His "strength is made perfect in weakness." [2 Corinthians 12:9.]

When friends say to me I should not tax my strength doing so much for the poor when so feeble, I tell them if my Father did not wish and expect me to care for those less fortunate than I of His children, He would not send me the means to use for their relief. No, I cannot give up the work while I have any strength to do it.

Many times, when a specially necessitous case is brought to me, I take it to Him to whom belong all the gold and silver and the cattle upon a thousand hills [Haggai 2:8], and know that help will come. At times I will be impressed to write to some particular friend; at others I feel I am to just wait patiently and the necessary funds will come: and it always does come in time to give the needed help.

Often a friend from whom I have not heard in some time will write and say they were impressed to send me something for my work, or one will call and say they felt they must come and give me help for my poor. "He that hath pity upon the poor lendeth to the Lord." [Proverbs 19:17.]

I am trying to get ready for my winter work. It will not be long before Thanksgiving week is here, and there is much writing and planning to be done for that.

When a day comes that I feel able, some of the cards are written that are tied on the necks of the turkeys or chickens. On each is a text of Scripture, the name of the family, the hour the card is to be presented, and across the corner the size of family, so that each will receive a proper portion.

The week before Thanksgiving a duplicate paper is sent or given to each family to be helped, which they present on the Wednesday. In this way confusion is avoided, as only a limited number come at the same hour. Since I have become less able to bear the commotion, the food has been dispensed downstairs.

I have about two hundred families to supply this year. It does not require much time for the tidings to spread, that at 492 Second Avenue dinners for Thanksgiving are given out. I am sure each year there are over one hundred who come and try to prevail on me to give them a ticket. Gladly would I do so if I could.

It is always hard for me to refuse any who seem needy, but I have not unlimited funds; not nearly so much as in former years, as many who used to send me large checks have died.

The past few days I have had several of the Lord's dear ones visit me, and to me the communion of saints is always precious. Our Father leads us in such varied paths, yet all tend toward His kingdom and the experiences help to fit us for His use.

"Father, I thank Thee that I cannot trace
The path Thou hast in love marked out for me;
For every day I bless the wondrous grace
That keeps my soul in sweet security.

"Resting in Thee there is no room for care;
I know Thy grace sufficient is, and free,
I know Thy love is with me everywhere,
Thy strength alone supports my frailty.

"Though led in devious paths, all strange, unknown,
Trusting I walk, nor fear though trials come,
Since 'tis Thy hand that guides me, Thine alone,
I know, whate'er betides, it leads me home."

Daily I thank my Father for the wonderful way in which He has led me, for the host of His children He has brought to this little room, and the wealth of affection He has permitted to grow between us. I ask Him to make me worthy of all this love and confidence, and keep me filled with His Spirit, that the needed and most helpful message may be given me for each.

November 12th 1900
Word comes from Stamford that our boy who has tried in vain to fight the disease is steadily failing. He has strong willpower and will not give up till compelled. He is too feeble to walk around, but sits up most of the day.

He has a kind Christian physician whose service is one of love, who spends quite a little time twice a day in cheery talk with him. A strong attachment has sprung up between them, and his mother writes me he always watches the clock, wishing for the hour when the doctor will come.

How often have I proved the blessing of being

ministered unto by kind Christian physicians. I have had a number, but most I owe to the one who for half a century has visited me almost daily. Verily, they will receive their reward.

November 23rd 1900
The changes of weather have caused me to have a severe cold, and the coughing takes my strength and tires me very much.

There have been a number of poor in asking for coal. As the winter comes on I trust the dear Lord will put it into the hearts of some of His stewards to send me money for coal. I have again received the two hundred dollars from The Haven Fund. This is always to be used for special cases.

Today is my sick boy's twenty-fifth birthday. Once so active and hopeful of life, today just waiting for the call to enter into rest; oppressed with weariness, too tired longer to struggle. How well I understand what this weariness means. Often the mere existing seems a burden.

During this week I have had one hundred and seventy-eight come for their order for next Wednesday. From now till then I shall be kept busy, and also sad, as it always hurts me to refuse the poor women who come and beg for a Thanksgiving dinner.

December 1900
Have been very poorly and feel I am growing old. I don't get rested and able to go on with my work after a few days of quiet as I used to, but the weary days and nights lengthen.

Yet, more than ever I feel I must "work while it is day" [John 9:4]; and I have this promise, "He giveth power to the faint; and to them that have no might He increaseth strength." [Isaiah 40:29.]

I will continue to praise Him, that He permits me to

work for Him.

December 15th 1900
Joseph sent me a telegram telling me our precious boy, Joseph Cooke, left us at one-thirty this morning; and later a letter telling of the great desire the dear one had to be at rest, and of his perfect trust in his heavenly Father.

Though with great difficulty, he could speak a word at a time. He thanked Dr. Pearson who had attended him so faithfully since he came home for his great kindness, then with great effort he appealed to the dear ones, "Shall I meet you all there?" to which his mother replied, "Yes, dear, we shall all meet you there."

How strange it seems that one in young manhood is cut down, and I, in my extreme feebleness and old age, am left! "My thoughts are not your thoughts, neither are your ways my ways, saith the Lord." [Isaiah 55:8.]

December 18th 1900
Today they have laid our dear one away in Greenwood, and on the way home to Stamford called to tell me about the beautiful service for him.

My dear Mary is almost worn out with the constant watching and care for the dear boy who was so tenderly devoted to his mother. He could not bear to have her out of his sight, he was so dependent upon her. I know how saddened her heart is, though his great suffering and exhaustion led them all to ask that the release might come.

"Though today we're filled with mourning,
Mercy still is on the throne;
With Thy smiles of love returning,
We can sing, 'Thy Will be done.'

> "By Thy hands the boon was given;
> Thou hast taken but Thine own;
> Lord of earth, and God of Heaven,
> Evermore, 'Thy Will be done.'"

The Christmas time will be less joyous, as the vacant chair will be there; but then we all rejoice that the sufferings are ended and he has entered the haven of eternal life and rest.

December 20th 1900

These December days are full of work. My little rooms are being filled with Christmas gifts for my poor. The barrel has come from the St. Cloud Presbyterian Sunday School at South Orange; the box from the Circle of Kings Daughters at Mamaroneck, and Mr. Selchow's boxes of dolls; several dozen beautifully dressed dolls from Mrs. Stickney and another dear lady; together with quantities of handmade hoods, and boxes of stockings, mittens, woolen scarfs and handkerchiefs from Miss Bliss which will soon arrive.

These gifts have been coming annually for years, so I am always able to plan ahead what I will do with them. Beside these, there is always much sent in from unexpected sources: old and new clothing, books, toys, and canned goods, with some money with which I send Christmas dinners to my old people and a little coal to a number of poor widows with children.

My heart rejoices as I think of the happy hearts and beaming faces I shall see when the mothers and children come for their gifts. I formerly had all the children come, but now I am so feeble I have one child come and get the package put up for the family.

December 27th 1900

Mrs. Hunt, my postman's wife, brought their little cripple girl to see me today. She has spinal trouble and has been strapped to a board for over a year. She is a very sweet child and loves to come, and I enjoy having them bring her, as it gives them comfort.

She wanted them to bring her so that she could tell me how she loved the beautiful doll I sent her for Christmas, also the little story books. This dear child has always been ill, and since the trouble has developed in the spine, though much is being done for her, I feel she will always be a sufferer, and I am specially interested in her.

Christmas time brings many beautiful and useful gifts to me for my personal use. Mrs. Field and Mrs. Charles Stickney sent the new supply of exquisite embroidery and fine linen for my pillow cases. They have furnished these every Christmas since Mrs. Townsend left us. She took great pleasure in supplying these for years.

Miss Bliss, Miss Callender, and a host of others have remembered me in sending so many beautiful things. I say sometimes my Heavenly Father is too indulgent to me, and daily I thank Him for the large place He has given me in the hearts of so many of His children.

February 25th 1901

Holy, Holy, O Lord of hosts art Thou this blessed Sabbath: All is hushed and still. While I am shut in with my Lord, I am thinking of the multitudes who have gone up to the Sanctuary to worship, and the promise comes to me, "I will be to them as a little Sanctuary." [Ezekiel 11:16.]

The communion is sweet we have together in my little room, where so often I have found my Lord very near. A number of friends called this afternoon, among them my late class leader, Mr. Wills, and as we talked of our Father's dealings with us, my heart was filled and I was constrained to say, "O magnify the Lord with me, and let us exalt His name together." [Psalm 34:3.]

While we sang, one of the ladies played the little organ given me several years ago by my kind friends, Mr. and Mrs. Hamilton.

Kept By the Power of God
The New York Weekly Witness
1901

A few days ago I paid a visit to Mrs. Bella Cooke, "the good Samaritan," "the kind sick lady," as the people in the neighborhood call her, and whose life story John Stephenson described as a marvelous life of physical disability and suffering, mingled with peace, joy and usefulness, seemingly combining the extremes of human possibilities.

Mrs. Cooke lives in the rear of 492 Second Avenue, in a modest three-story brick structure. Her little home is hemmed in on every side by tall buildings, and from her upper windows the only view she has is a stone-paved yard, the rear entrance of a saloon, and the narrow, dark passageway leading to the street.

In answer to my ring at the bell, the door opened noiselessly. I was just about to enter when I found the right-of-way contested by a huge bay horse which I had noticed being unharnessed as I walked up the street. As the hall was too narrow for both of us, I stepped aside while the horse trotted briskly through.

"Don't be scared, it's all right. If you want to see Mrs. Cooke you just follow the horse. He won't hurt you. And then you go upstairs to the second floor in the rear house," said a voice from somewhere.

I obeyed instructions, and passing through another doorway, like the horse, I found myself in the yard where a dozen or more chickens were cackling. The horse turned to the right into a neat one-story stable which stands between the front and rear buildings, while I went up a pair of neatly oil-clothed stairs and knocked at a lattice door covered with a green baize curtain.

A low, sweet voice bade me, "Come in," and I entered the room. Mrs. Cooke's bed is directly opposite the door, and the visitor is greeted by a warm smile of welcome and a cheery, "How do you do?" from the invalid lying on a narrow bed propped up among snowy pillows.

Her face is an inspiration in itself, the ideal of brightness, patience and perfect rest.

To attempt to describe Mrs. Cooke's room so as to give any idea of its immaculate sweetness and neatness, seems an almost hopeless task. The walls from floor to ceiling are covered with engravings, portraits and texts. There are two windows looking westward draped with snowy curtains tied back with bright ribbons. At the window near the head of the bed a sort of little conservatory has been erected to hide the objectionable view of the saloon, and this is filled with growing plants and freshly cut flowers.

At one side of the woman is a highly polished stove where all the cooking is done, and where the tea kettle is always in readiness, for Mrs. Cooke is very hospitable, and many a tea party with some of New York's wealthy and fashionable women has been held in that little upper chamber.

Seated in a comfortable chair by Mrs. Cooke's bed I made my errand known, and she smiled as she answered, "Tell your good readers that I am still kept by God. I have been during all my life, and that all I ask is that He will use me for Himself every moment of my life."

Then, continuing, she said, "You wouldn't think, would you, to look at this house now, that when I came here it stood back from the road in a green field where cattle grazed? There was a great green tree, too, that shaded my window and gave it an air of seclusion and quiet. But that was forty-five years ago, and naturally many changes have taken place. When I came here, the owners promised that during my lifetime this house should never be torn down, but the place was almost in the country then, and now it is in the heart of the city."

For a year before coming to Second Avenue, Mrs. Cooke had been at The Woman's Hospital, where the physicians had pronounced her disease incurable, and so kind friends had brought her to that little room to pass the remaining days of her life. Eight of her doctors have died since then, but she still lives.

During all these forty-five years she has been confined to her bed. Though each day has been one of pain and suffering, she has not only endured her affliction patiently, but has ministered to the spiritual and temporal necessities of others; not only of those in her immediate district, but of a circle that has gradually increased till it embraces a large area between First and Fifth Avenues.

The missionary spirit was early born in Bella Cooke. When only a child in England she would gather poor men around her, and bringing them home to her mother would remark, "Ma, here are some hungry men." Once she noticed a little beggar girl shivering with the cold, and took off her own pretty green silk petticoat to give her.

She was the youngest of nine children, of whom she was the pet and plaything, and from a generous, impulsive girl she grew into an earnest woman, and later became a Christian wife and mother. The death of her husband in 1849 left her in America with three little ones depending on her for support.

It was at this trying time that she made a solemn vow to consecrate two hours daily to God's work. Her first labors were among the poor in Bellevue Hospital, and in First and Third Avenues to the river. She had nothing to give, and so she would beg food and clothes for the needy cases from the storekeepers, who never refused.

These two hours which she took from her daily work were made up during the evening, when the busy fingers would stitch all the harder; for she supported herself and little ones by sewing.

In 1855 her health failed, and at the urgent entreaties of friends she went to The Woman's Hospital. There she inaugurated morning and evening prayers. All those who were able would gather round her bed, and there she just began the work of exhorting and praying from her bed.

When after a year she was brought from the hospital to the four little rooms which she now occupies, her heart yearned toward those whom she had formerly visited, and one by one they came to her little room, and sitting at her bedside would pour out their troubles to her in the old way. And while practical advice was given, practical help was also generously bestowed.

She wrote to her friends who had learned to love her at the hospital, telling them of the necessities of her poor friends, and few could resist her appeals on their behalf. It was as if the voice of God spoke through her pen.

Her influence increased with her own spiritual growth, her earnestness and zeal communicated itself to all who fell under her influence, and from all over the land remittances began to come for her poor.

She numbers on her list one hundred and seventy-five families who are looked after personally.

Mrs. Cooke is accessible at all hours of the day to those

who need her help, and her little room has become a sort of refuge to her neighbors when they are in trouble. Her sympathy is of a most practical kind.

While I was there, a timid rap was heard at the lattice door, and in response to Mrs. Cooke's "Come!" a little Italian woman burst into the room in a perfect frenzy of despair. She was in a dark calico dress with a woolen shawl over her head, and the great tears were streaming down her cheeks.

"Well, well," said Mrs. Cooke cheerfully, "my good friend, what's the trouble now?"

"It's my husband again, Mrs. Cooke. I can't do nothing with him. He's just awful. He came home today while I was out, and scared the children, and went all through my bureau drawers, and took out the few pennies I'd hidden away to get milk for the baby. And he says he's coming tomorrow when I go out to work and he's going to sell all my furniture. Oh, dear Mrs. Cooke, you won't let him do it, will you? You'll stop him. Oh, please do! What shall I do if he sells my furniture? And I've got to go to work or the children won't have anything to eat." And the poor little woman wiped her eyes on the corner of her shawl.

"Now, don't you worry. Go right home and get your dinner, and tomorrow go to work as usual. Your husband shan't sell your furniture, and he shan't annoy you again," said Mrs. Cooke decidedly. "I'll attend to it." And as she shook the woman's hand before she left, she slipped something into it.

"Oh, thank you, Mrs. Cooke," said the woman, gratefully. "You're awful good, and you don't know what a load you have taken off my mind." And she was almost cheerful as she left the room.

Later I met her, and I questioned her, asking her if she was not afraid her husband might sell her furniture as he had said.

She looked at me in surprise as she answered, "Why, Mrs. Cooke won't let him."

"What can she do to prevent it," I continued.

"You don't know Mrs. Cooke, do you?" she asked in turn.

"Oh, yes, quite well," I answered.

"Well, it don't seem like it, because if you did, you'd know that when Mrs. Cooke says a thing won't be done, it won't; and when she says it will be done, it will. We don't know any more about it than that, but that's enough," and with these words she left me.

Mrs. Cooke gives excellent Thanksgiving and Christmas dinners to her poor friends, with clothes and money and candies and toys for the little ones.

She has a most original and characteristic method of distributing her Christmas dinners to her big family. She obtains lists from ministers and doctors of deserving people who would otherwise be unable to have any holiday cheer, and each receives an invitation to call for a personal interview. After a frank conversation, in which Mrs. Cooke endeavors to help her visitor by encouragement and advice, a memorandum is made of each one's special requirements.

Before the appointed day of distribution, cards are sent out inviting these persons separately to call, each at a specified hour. In this way there is no crowding, but a continuous procession of women through the narrow passageway leading to the house in which Mrs. Cooke lives.

For these occasions, a room is rented on the first floor of the house, and the turkeys and bundles are arranged in piles on long tables. Each one is carefully labeled, and a bit of helpful literature, a religious paper, or a pretty text is always included in the bundle. In the hall are barrels of potatoes and turnips, cans of tomatoes, and an immense trough of bread.

Each woman as she enters presents her ticket which

bears her name and requirements, and is given her portion. She then departs with an upward glance and wave of the hand at the bright face looking from the upper window.

The following extracts from Mrs. Cooke's journal give a practical exposition of the work done during one year from her busy corner:

"I have had 2,894 visitors, besides the visits of my poor. I received and gave away $2,024. Thanksgiving I gave out 1,085 pounds of turkey, 259 pounds of chicken, 32 3/4 pounds of geese, 31 1/2 pounds of duck 169 pounds of sugar 169 pounds of rice, 5 barrels of potatoes, 4 barrels of apples 169 loaves of bread, 30 pounds of tea." And she adds, "All the recipients come to me personally in order that I may know them well, and hold out to them the bread of life."

Mrs. Cooke distributes from thirty to forty tons of coal every winter. Certain women call regularly for their rent, while others receive a small weekly stipend. Erring children are returned to their homes, the sick are sent to the hospitals, and work is found for the unemployed.

This is all very remarkable when it is considered that the work is originated and planned and the money collected by a woman who has been unable to leave her bed for the past forty-five years. But Bella Cooke possesses rare executive powers, keen judgment and wonderful intuition.

She keeps her books with great accuracy, and her character and consecrated life exert a powerful influence on all who become acquainted with her.

Bella Cooke is now nearly eighty years old. Time has left few lines on the calm, beautiful face lying against the white pillows. Grace has glorified it with an inner radiance that shines out and sets it apart as belonging to one of God's saints.

This was Mrs. Cooke's motto, and hung on her bed for years:

"KEPT BY THE POWER OF GOD" (1 Peter1:5).

"That ye might walk worthy of the Lord unto all pleasing, being fruitful in every good work and increasing in knowledge of God" (Colossians 1:10).

Kept by the Lord Jehovah,
Kept for His use alone,
Kept, evermore remembering
That we are not our own.

Kept to reflect His image,
More like Him daily grow;
Kept to be all for Jesus
In this dark world below.

Kept for the Lord's good pleasure,
That we may give Him joy:
Kept that our highest glory
Be in His best employ.

Kept His "peculiar treasure,"
Ransomed by precious blood;
Kept to be found well pleasing
In everything to God.

Chapter 36

Translation of Loved Ones

In 1901 a great blow came to Mrs. Cooke in the sickness and death of her son-in-law, Dr. Joseph Pullman. Since January he had seemed to be failing and had at intervals been far from well. It was thought at first to be the effects of the shock of the death of his son in December, but it proved not to be that.

There had been since Dr. Pullman's young manhood a growing affection and interest between him and Mrs. Cooke. The relation that existed was that of a son to a dearly loved mother. He belonged to the old Rose Hill Church, so dear to Mrs. Cooke. In the earliest years of his Christian life he went to her weekly, for counsel and encouragement.

When he left the city in 1858 to go to study, they kept up a regular correspondence, and he always realized that he owed very much to her Christian sympathy and advice. In later years Mrs. Cooke felt she could lean on him, and in every perplexity receive his sympathy and help. The short accompanying note is indicative of the oneness of spirit that existed between them.

From Joseph Pullman
Stamford
May 18th 1901
Dear Grandma, [Grandma presumably being the family name for his mother-in-law]
This beautiful little poem touched my heart, and made me think of you and of life, and so I send it to you.

The radiant morn hath passed away,
And spent too soon its golden store;
The shadows of departing day
Creep on once more.

Our life is but a fading dawn,
Its glorious noon, how quickly past,
Lead us, O Christ, when all is gone –
Safe home at last.

Where saints are clothed in spotless white,
And evening shadows never fall,
Where Thou, Eternal Light of Light,
Art Lord of all.

With love from all and prayers for you,
Joseph

During the early summer Dr. Pullman continued to fail, and in August there was a marked change for the worse. He tried to fill his appointments as Presiding Elder, but it was with difficulty that he could endure the strain of preaching.

The local physicians began to feel that some serious cause must exist, and in September held several consultations. Deciding there was an internal cancer, advised that he go to the Brooklyn Methodist Hospital for examination by Drs. Fowler and Pilcher.

After the necessary plans had been made, his sons, one a physician in Brooklyn, took him down on the 11th of October. While in the hospital, not yet knowing that his illness must prove fatal, though realizing from the doctor's words that it was very serious, he wrote the following letters:

Methodist Hospital
October 16th 1901
Dear Grandma,
Here I am in this strange place, who has heretofore been so well. And the outcome of it is known only to our Heavenly Father. There is some internal growth but I don't know what it is, except that it is very serious.

Dr. Fowler is reluctant to operate till absolutely necessary, and wishes to wait for some time. They think I may go home, and I am very desirous to get home, and may leave here today or tomorrow.

This illness is a terrible disappointment to me. I want to live to preach Jesus Christ for some years yet, and I pray that our Heavenly Father may order a reprieve.

Wonderful if you should outlive me — so many years since we thought you were going home — wonderful has been your life and your suffering and your faith.

I am sorry I can't go to see you, but have orders to keep very quiet.

Great love to dear Grandma. Pray for me.
Affectionately,
Joseph

From Joseph Pullman
Methodist Episcopal Hospital
Brooklyn
October 18th 1901
Brethren Beloved,
Sad news has come to me, brethren. The doctors tell me that my work is done, that my case is beyond their skill. They advise me to return to my home in Stamford.

I am trying to be quiet and look to my gracious Redeemer. Your great love for me is a comfort, and now again let me cast myself on your prayers.

Give my tender love to my churches, and tell them that to them is committed everything that makes precious our human life.

Affectionately,

Joseph Pullman

On Saturday, October 19th, he was taken home by his wife and son, Dr. James Pullman, and he requested that on the way the carriage stop at Mrs. Cooke's, as he felt he must once more see and talk with her. He now knew this would be the last visit he would make her.

When they reached the house, his son took him in and left him, returning to his mother who remained in the carriage feeling the meeting and parting would be more than she could bear to witness. Mrs. Cooke knew he was coming and had directed the tenant on the first floor to lock the hall door and admit no one during Dr. Pullman's stay, as she felt the time would be too sacred to admit of any intrusion.

He remained with her about an hour. It was one of tenderest and most sacred communion. When his son returned and brought him out to the carriage, not a word was spoken, a quiet solemnity rested upon them, and the ride to the Grand Central Station was one of devout silence.

Several times afterward, in referring to this visit, Dr. Pullman said, "That memorable hour with dear Grandma was one of the most precious in my life." In connection with this visit we find a page of diary that Mrs. Cooke wrote:

October 20th 1901

Yesterday went through a very trying ordeal. Had a visit which to all appearances will be the last one from my dearly beloved son-in-law, who has been to me as a beloved and loving son, Rev. Joseph Pullman, on his way home to Stamford from the Hospital where he went for examination and where the doctors told him his work was done, that he would never preach again.

He told his wife and son he must call and see me. James brought him in and left us alone. We had a solemn time. Both felt it was the farewell till we meet above.

He sat beside me, few words were spoken; after a while he said, "Ma, pray with me." I could not. Tears choked my utterances. He slid down on his knees and offered a prayer never to be forgotten.

Soon his son came in for him. After kissing me goodbye, he turned to go, and as he stood by the door he waved his hand and said, "Goodbye, dear Ma, you will never know, till eternity reveals it to you what a help, what an inspiration you have been to me in my work all these years, and what a helpmeet dear Mary has been to me. Goodbye, God bless you."

In the yard he stopped and looked up to my window and waved farewell for the last time.

Saturday morning
January 4th 1902
The spirit was released, and Dr. Pullman joined the Church triumphant.

January 7th 1902
A beautiful service was held in the Stamford church, which was attended by about two hundred and fifty ministers. Bishop Andrews and a number of his closest friends paid rare tributes to his memory.

The next morning the family accompanied the precious remains to Greenwood, where he sleeps with four of his children till the Resurrection morn.

Though Mrs. Cooke was daily expecting to hear of Dr. Pullman's death, it came with a decided shock to her, and she really never seemed to rally from it.

From Ann Evans
Rahway, N. J.
August 1st 1902
Dear Sister Bella,
Do you know a sweeter word than, "Come unto Me and rest?" So I come to Jesus and lay my weary head upon His loving breast and fold my hands and rest.

We will meet beyond the River.

Your loving sister,

Ann Evans

The above letter is from the only surviving sister of Bella Cooke, who was in her eighty-ninth year at the time the letter was written.

The following year, January 8 1903, brought another great sorrow to her heart, when Ann Evans, her sister, was called home. Mrs. Cooke writes, "My beloved and last remaining sister went to her reward, a shock of corn fully ripe, a true servant of the meek and lowly Jesus, a faithful steward ever planning to help the Master's cause: a loving, tender sister."

Since the death of her husband in 1883, Mrs. Evans had made her home with Mrs. Cooke's youngest daughter, Mrs. William Hillier, and living in the city for years had made a weekly visit to her sister.

After Mrs. Evans' death, Mrs. Cooke could not throw off the feeling of loneliness as she realized that she was the last of her generation, and with her constantly increasing feebleness it had a marked effect upon her. Not that she was ever gloomy. No one ever entered her room to find her anything but cheery and bright. She was a marvel of sunshine

The word of welcome as one entered her room was wonderful in its characteristic cheerfulness. This probably was responsible for the question so often asked by strangers, "Mrs. Cooke, do you ever suffer?" Or the other remark, "Mrs. Cooke, you look so well," when in reality she was at that moment in great pain. She had learned to conceal her suffering.

About a month after Mrs. Evans' death, the very sudden taking away of Mrs. Cooke's oldest grandson, J. E. Paisley, was a blow that utterly prostrated her for several days. He had been with her only a day or two before, seemingly in perfect health. This was the fourth death in the immediate family since December 1901, yet Mrs. Cooke in her great feebleness was spared.

Chapter 37

A Severe Ordeal

On February 24th 1903, it seemed as though the end had come and that the poor body could no longer endure the terrible strain. After a night of pain and wakefulness, Ella, her maid, was asked to fill the hot water bag and place it at Mrs. Cooke's feet. This was done and the maid left the room.

Almost immediately the side of the bag burst and let a gallon of boiling water cover her feet. As they were always kept a little higher than her body to relieve the strain on her spine, the water rushed up, scalding her body to the waist.

The shock was so sudden and severe that she was unable to throw down the scant bedclothes or call Ella, and of course she could not move her poor feet and limbs, paralyzed for years, out of their scalding bath. Finally she was heard making a strange noise which brought, almost at the same time, the maid and Mrs. Bush, the tenant downstairs.

By this time Mrs. Cooke could speak, and after sending Ella for the doctor and Miss Shaw, a trained nurse, she gave directions to Mrs. Bush what to do. When Miss Shaw came, she found Mrs. Cooke's injuries were far worse than they had supposed. She sent out for the needed remedies and at once tried to relieve the terrible distress.

The doctor came as soon as possible and prescribed. He feared the shock would be more than his patient in her feeble condition could survive, and he watched her most closely from day to day.

So low was Mrs. Cooke that it was feared to attempt to take any of the wet bedding off for six weeks. Even after that length of time the mattress was still wet through.

A day and a night nurse had to care for her, with Miss Shaw always at hand to dress the burns. She had nursed Mrs. Cooke through many illnesses and knew well how to handle her.

For days it was feared she could not survive, and no one but the family was allowed to see her; yet she never complained or was the least impatient.

As soon as she seemed the slightest improved, the dear friends who had been so anxiously sending and calling daily to know how she was, were admitted, and the beautiful pleading prayers offered at her bedside by Mrs. Field, Mrs. McAlpin, Mrs. Pyle and others, to the dear Father to relieve her, and if possible spare her to them and her work, were most touching.

Mrs. Cooke said she had never suffered as much, even with the severe operations she had undergone, and they were many and severe, as she was suffering at this time. It took months for her to recover, and greatly reduced her vitality.

Within the last month of her life, she had an extreme case in which she was deeply interested, and though suffering intensely and unable to take nourishment, she felt she must secure help to liberate this poor family from the severe straits they were in.

When those with her would beg of her not to use up the little strength she had, planning for others, she would reply, "I must work while it is day. I can't care for my poor long."

Chapter 38

Words from Distant Friends

In Mrs. Cooke's folio have been found a number of letters which will add interest to these pages. They show the communion that existed between her and her friends, though widely scattered.

From C. D. Morris
Pyeng Yang
Korea
July 15th 1903
Dear Mrs. Cooke,
Mr. Moore has told me that he is writing to you, and I have asked the privilege of sending a few lines in his letter. I had the pleasure of calling on you twice: once when I was a student in Pennington Seminary, and once later when I was preaching in New Jersey.

I often think of the wonderful testimony that God enabled you to bear to His sustaining grace. Several times, when preaching to the Koreans, I have told them about you and used you as an illustration of how God can enable us to rejoice in Him, in the midst of great suffering. They were much interested in your story, and I want to tell you how your testimony has reached even to this distant land.

My own heart has often been strengthened as I have thought of you and the conversations we have had together.

With gratitude to God for the remarkable way He has

glorified Himself through you, and with my kindest regards, I am,

>Yours in Christian love,
>C. D. Morris

From Wm. G. Taylor
Central Methodist Mission
Sydney, Australia,
January 2nd 1904
My Dear Sister,
I am sending this letter to assure you of our love and continued good wishes. You are one of the Lord's honored ones. His dealings with you are marvelous, and we cease not to thank God for your witness-bearing life.

May the comforts of His grace be yours in all abundance, and may you yet be spared to us for years to come, as a much needed illustration of the much needed grace that is stored up for us all in Jesus.

How often I think of that sacred afternoon I spent in your room towards the end of 1894. Little did I expect then that you would be spared to us all so long. I am a better man today for that meeting, and often speak of you in my sermons. My dear wife also, though she has never seen you, loves you very tenderly and sends you her love.

The work of the Lord here continues to prosper. We have just concluded another very successful year. Conversions every week. Our great hall is crowded every Sunday and our income is nearly $40,000 each year. I am feeling the strain of the work more than formerly – am 60 years old on the 18th of this month.

God bless you, my beloved sister in the Lord. In your quiet little room, put up a prayer occasionally for yours affectionately in Him,

>Wm. G. Taylor

From S. H. Hadley
Superintendent
The Bowery Rescue Mission
New York City
October 30th 1904
Precious Mother,

I just want to let you know I'm thinking of you and that I love you. Dear, patient soul, lying there in your corner, where every speck on the wall and every pattern of the paper and every picture has been looked at thousands of times. Precious Mother Cooke, you truly have been so faithful, so prayerful, so tender and loving, and your patient life has been a benediction to tens of thousands all over the world, and especially to the one who pens these lines.

When the time comes for you to rise from your bed of pain and put on the robe of immortality, and enter the golden chariot with fiery steeds who will bear you away to Him Who has loved you and bought you with His own blood, thousands of ransomed souls who have been led to Jesus by you and have long since gone on before, will, I believe, be permitted to convey your glorified spirit to the heavenly home. Praise the Lord for such a hope!

Your loving son,
S. H. Hadley

From Mary Fowler
St. Ann's, Sefton Park
Liverpool
December 13th 1904
Dear, dear Mrs. Cooke,

The joy your letter gave, I cannot tell you. To see your writing and read your tender, loving words, so full of the coming glory – I thank God with all my heart that he had left you with us a little longer, to teach us how to endure hardness as good soldiers of the Lord Jesus Christ.

How wonderfully His grace has been made manifest in you! My very heart bounds as I think of the welcome home awaiting you! Near the throne is your place – may I be there!

Thank God the great purpose of my life is to please Him – to do His will here as it is done in Heaven. Pray for me, dear Mrs. Cooke, that I may bear fruit to His glory and fight loyally for my Lord. My Bible class – pray that I may be able to bring everyone for Christ. I have talked to them of you and told them how you prayed for them.

I have a large class of splendid young women, consisting of teachers and others in most responsible positions. I want every member of the class for Christ. They belong to different churches, even the Roman Catholic. I feel it a great responsibility, as well as a great joy.

I make you my little Christmas thank offering, rejoicing that you are still with us. May you have a very bright, happy time, making many others happy. Christmas brings up so many memories of the loved ones above. Pray for me, dear Mrs. Cooke, that in all things I may please God. Life will soon be past – I must work while it is called day. It is glorious to live for God, to know His Will and to do it.

With much love and earnest good wishes, for the happy Christmas for you and yours, believe me, dear Mrs. Cooke,

Lovingly yours,
Mary Fowler

Undated letter from H. R. Higgins
Melbourne
Australia
My Dear Friend,
I am so very pleased to receive your kind letter and the three photographs. All came safely this week. I felt I must give you

a kiss; you look so very happy and the sunshine of God's love shows clearly on your dear face. I am sure you are weary and so am I.

Suffering wears our poor bodies, but the peace our Lord gives is more than tongue can tell. No, dear one, my voice has not come back. "I am dumb, for Thou didst it," for some wise purpose, all in love. [Psalm 39:9]

With much love and sympathy; we shall soon meet in our heavenly Father's home.

Lovingly,

H. R. Higgins

From William H. Wills
138 East 40th St.
New York City
December 23rd 1904
Dear Sister Cooke,
I see by your bookmark, which I keep in my Bible, that this is your forty-ninth Christmas "Shut-in," and when I was reminded of it, the marvelous loving kindness and tender Providence of the Heavenly Father, as displayed in your individual experience, is truly wonderful, your life being a monument of His glory and praise.

We all, who know what God has done for and by you, should have the greater faith in His promises and power. I am looking forward to seeing you before many days are gone, and although I have not stood beside you for some time, yet you seem very near, as you are often in my thought.

The passing away of Brother De La Mater, no doubt brought many memories of the past before you, as it did to me, and made one more of the Rose Hill active workers preceding you to the heavenly country.

We are very happy in the West Church, but would be thankful to see more growth and spiritual power there, as elsewhere. My dear wife joins heartily with me in love and kindest good wishes for your Christmas season.

Goodbye – yours in Christian hope and fellowship, as ever and always,

William H. Wills

[Undated letter]

From John Wyburn

New York City

My Dear Sister Cooke,

Brother Hadley went to heaven this morning at 5:45. Funeral service from Mission at 10:30 Monday morning, and from the Old John Street M. E. Church at 1:00 o'clock.

Sincerely yours,

John Wyburn

January 1905

"Have faith in God." [Mark 11:22.]

"Faithful is He who has promised." [Hebrews 10:23.]

The past year has been one in which I have had much severe suffering. In March a severe attack of grippe and mumps; in June a long and hard attack of my old trouble laryngitis; in August very low with bowel trouble, and a relapse in September.

Doctor said the children must be sent for, as he felt I could not recover. Again the Master said, "Return to thine house and tell what great things the Lord hath done for thee." [Luke 8:39.]

I wonder why I am so often brought to the river's brink and then turned back. It must be the Master has a little more for me to do for Him.

During the year very many needy, suffering poor have come to me, and I have sometimes been sorely perplexed planning to do the most possible with the funds I had. As November was passing along, I was anxious about the

Thanksgiving dinner for my poor, and quite a number were sick and needed coal, and rents were due.

Daily I lifted my voice to my Father to send help for His needy children. He heard my cry and raised up a new helper in my friend, Miss Grace Dodge. Miss Dodge called and I talked to her about my work. She told me she had not intended coming to see me, but was impelled to do so. I felt my Father had sent her.

After she returned home she sent me a very liberal check, also one from her mother. Thus I was enabled with the funds sent by other friends to give a good substantial dinner to over one hundred families, and send coal and pay the rent where it was needed.

December came, and increased cold and stormy weather. Daily, mothers come, or send the children, begging for a little coal, or some bedclothes, or shoes for bare feet. My funds are almost gone, and again my dear friend comes to my help.

My long tried and true friend, General McAlpin, also sends me a fine donation. At once I send orders to the coal yard, and get Miss Shaw to attend to the rent of some very worthy cases.

I will just refer to one case. Mrs. Robinson, widow who was a nurse, had been shut in at home with one of her children sick with diphtheria. The child died. Just as she was able to go to work, another, and later a third child was taken with the same disease. She was in great need.

I paid twelve dollars rent and sent her some food and coal. Another month comes and she is not yet allowed to work. She came to see me on Monday. I told her I had not the money to pay her rent, but gave her a dollar to get some groceries, and said she could come on Wednesday and I would give her the rent.

I told my Great Banker, and left it with Him to help this

poor feeble widow and her children. Early on Tuesday morning a letter came from the *Christian Herald* with a check for seven dollars, sent by some unknown friend. In the evening a note from dear Mrs. Hunton, saying, "Dear Mrs. Cooke, Yesterday my husband picked up six dollars in the street. He inquired of those around, but found no owner, so I send it to you for your work."

I said aloud, "Praise the Lord." Here was the money for my poor widow who was to come in the morning: twelve dollars for the rent and the dollar for the groceries.

Many similar cases come to me, and are relieved in many instances in some unlooked-for way.

Why should I doubt my Father's care for His little ones when so often I have "felt the power of prayer, to strengthen faith and sweeten care."

As this New Year has opened with new and numberless mercies and blessings, grant, Father, that in me more and more Thine image may be manifest. Amen and amen.

From John Z. Moore
Pyeng Yang
Korea
July 11 1908
My Dear Mrs. Cooke,
Away off here in this corner of the world, I have been thinking of the very pleasant hour I spent with Miss Birch, of Hedding Church, at your home one day last February.

I remember you said that day, a friend from up the State wrote you, saying she thought you would be pleased to hear from one so far away, not knowing that you received letters from all over the world.

Now, I want to tell you an interesting little story. Last Sunday, I walked some five miles out in the country to one of our beautiful Methodist churches with one of the older missionaries. He preached to the natives and I listened. I understand but very little Korean, but two or three times I heard him use a word that sounded like "New York." I thought, of course, it was some Korean word and asked him about it on the way home, thinking I was sure of one more word that would stay, by the law of association.

He said, "Oh, that was the word 'New York.' I was telling them the story of the wonderful life of Mrs. Bella Cooke." So you see you have preached the gospel of our blessed Lord and Master in far-off Korea, though not out of your room for years, and yet you have been out of that room in a more real sense than most of us get our lives out into the world in the Master's service.

I do trust you keep able to see folks, and I am sure, whether here or "gone beyond," you are well, and all is well with you. I left your book in America, and it has been traveling among my friends ever since, leaving, I am sure, a trail of blessedness. I ask for your prayers for myself and for Korea, that His kingdom may come.

With very best wishes,
Very sincerely yours,
John Z. Moore

From H. B. Higgins
Melbourne
Australia
October 25th 1908
My Dear Fellow-Sufferer,
Just a few lines to let you see that you are remembered in this little corner; yes, and often prayer offered for you. If you are spared to see another Christmas and New Year, I pray that it may be the most blessed you have ever known, so full of peace and happiness that the world knows nothing about, and, if possible, with less suffering.

Will you please give Mrs. Chauncey Hamilton one of the enclosed bookmarks with my love and the season's greetings, and keep the other for yourself?

Pain and weariness prevent me from writing more. My voice has not come back yet, but in glory I will be able to sing (with a perfect voice) praises to my Lord and King. What a meeting with loved ones that happy time will be.

With loving sympathy from my attendant,

Yours affectionately,

H. B. Higgins

Bella Cooke at the age of 86

Chapter 39

Notes from the Press

A Pillow Saint

By Clara Marshall

When our Ladies' Aid Society meets at Mrs. Cooke's, I never miss attending it," said a benevolent lady to a friend a few days ago. Mrs. Bella Cooke is the sufferer, who hasn't been outside of her bedroom since 1857, but who, all the same, is one of the busiest members of the Rose Hill Methodist Church, the church to which Emma Abbott left $5,000 because she had received so much spiritual benefit there.

Well, if ever Emma Abbott found time to make a visit to Mrs. Cooke, she received as much spiritual benefit in that sickroom in a rear tenement, on Second Avenue, as she ever did in church. Yes, it was as far back as 1857 that Mrs. Cooke received what might be called a life sentence, but she is the most cheerful "lifer" that anybody ever saw, and she is the leading spirit in all the work of the church.

If it is a fair, she knows what is best to offer for sale at it, and that without having been inside of a store within an ordinary lifetime. If there's trouble of any kind in the church, she is the first to see the way out of it, and she is helpfulness itself where there is any worthy person in need.

She bears her affliction with fortitude, cheerfulness and patience. She does not love to be pitied. Think of how many times she must have heard her helplessness spoken of in the last forty-four years! She, herself, is ready to jest about her bedridden condition.

At a meeting of the Ladies' Aid Society when a fair was in contemplation, someone proposed putting Mrs. Bella Cooke on the Purchasing Committee, whereupon she replied, "I should be glad to serve, my dear, but I have neither hat nor shoes."

"Nor a dress, I suppose," added one of her listeners.

"Yes, I have a dress," she replied, smiling. "A nice white silk dress, and you will all see me in it at church one of these days, when I shall be taken there in my coffin."

I know that all present, except Mrs. Cooke herself, hoped that that white silk might be yellow with age before it would be needed.

The Saint of Second Avenue
By Kate Upson Clark
The Christian Herald 1908

The wonderful life of Mrs. Bella Cooke, who has for fifty-two years lain upon a bed of pain and weakness, and is yet full of love and cheer, is well known to *Christian Herald* readers. Although she was eighty-seven on the 13th of July last, her beautiful eyes are as bright and clear as ever, and her whole fine face shines with her unselfish and affectionate interest in others.

Yet the past year has been one of the hardest among the many distressing periods through which this devoted servant of Christ has been called to pass. It has been a time of constant pain and illness, and has left her so weak that she tells her friends, "I am not Bella Cooke any more. I am just a plain old woman who can do little but suffer on until the time of my release comes."

In spite of these words, she is still visited by hundreds of the poor, and by even more of the well-to-do who come to lay gifts in her hands to be distributed among the needy, whose wants no one knows like Bella Cooke. They love to come, not only in order that they may thus accomplish some good to the poor, but that they may be strengthened and refreshed in spirit by the tide of faith and joy which seems always at the flood in the heart of this noble and altruistic "shut-in."

Left a widow at twenty-seven, and bed-ridden at thirty-five, one would think that Bella Cooke might properly be exempted from charitable work for outsiders. But from the first, her great heart has yearned over the unfortunate. Even when, as a widow she was working for a mere pittance to put bread into the mouths of her children, she would manage to snatch an hour or two to visit those worse off than herself.

The storekeepers in her neighborhood soon came to know and to trust her. If she said that anything was needed in a certain quarter, they knew that it was so, and stood ready to help her.

A nurse dropped her when she was only two years old. This was the beginning of her physical disabilities. Later, largely as a result of this first fall, she had others. As a child and a young woman, she was always frail and feeble. The cares of motherhood rested heavily upon her, and before she was thirty, her life had been often despaired of; but her powerful will kept her upon her feet for five years longer.

Nearly every distinguished physician in New York has studied her case, but it has baffled the highest skill. She has been fortunate in having enjoyed, during all the years of her shut-in life, the services as her regular physician and devoted friend, of Dr. Miles W. Palmer. It is to his wise care that she is largely indebted for her continued life and power of usefulness. Even at his present advanced age of eighty-seven, he visits and prescribes for her daily.

Mrs. Cooke has ten grandchildren and eleven great grandchildren. She herself was one of nine brothers and sisters. Born in England and coming to this country during her early married life, she has kept throughout to the good old British tradition of large families, though she lost several of her own children during their babyhood.

Even the most hardened infidel must admit that a religion which can uphold its followers, as this saintly woman has been upheld through long and weary years, is a good working faith for the world. If everyone could but possess it, the millennium of perfect love and purest joy would be gloriously upon us.

Mrs. Cooke does not pray to live. She says that she is not tired of the work, "But, oh, the pain, the pain!"

Still, we cannot help hoping that she may be spared to the world a little longer. No one else can ever do the unique work which has so strangely and providentially been given into her feeble, yet powerful hands.

Chapter 40

Not Changed but Glorified

During the Easter season of 1908, Mrs. Cooke felt impressed she would not be with us another Easter season. She was daily becoming feebler and suffering more and more, yet always wearing a cheerful smile and trying not to waste her time, as she would say. If not busy with her hands, her head and heart were working out some problem of relief for some case of trouble and distress.

As the warm weather came, increasing weakness and pain came also. In June a severe and long attack of sciatica gave her sleepless nights and restless days; still the patience and endurance were ever manifest.

On July 12th, the day before her eighty-seventh birthday, her pastor, the Rev. F. J. Shackleton, administered the sacrament of the Lord's Supper in her home, some twenty members of the Helping Hand Circle of the King's Daughters and Sons being present and participating. At that time, the pastor presented her with a silver loving cup, a token of the love of the Circle for its aged President.

Mrs. Cooke gave a bright testimony to her friends of her faith in the keeping and directing power of the Heavenly Father. During the service other friends from Brooklyn joined them, and though the communion of saints was precious, it proved too much of a tax upon her, and increased her suffering to a great degree.

The next day a few of her grandchildren were to lunch with her, in honor of her eighty- seventh birthday. On coming, they found her so very ill that they were reluctant to remain, but she insisted that they enjoy the luncheon she had planned, and which one of her granddaughters had prepared.

They were all impressed with her serious condition, and from that time she failed steadily till October, when all realized that she could not be with us very long. From the fact that Mrs. Cooke had suffered repeated attacks of illness, from each of which it had seemed that she could not recover, her friends could not realize it was possible for the time to come when she would not recover.

This was even the case with her children and grandchildren, as is seen by an extract from a letter her grandson, John S. Pullman, sent to his mother,

From John Pullman
Dear Mother,
It hardly seems possible that Grandma is really leaving us. She has always rallied before, and my earliest memories are so linked with associations of her lying there, serene, sweet, cheerful, wise in her corner, that it scarcely seems to be possible that she can go and leave it empty.

She was in that corner when I first saw her. When I first got to know her, and then when I first began to love her, and later when I began to realize how truly great a woman she was, she was still there in her little corner. Always through the years, as I thought of her, I could picture her right there, and so it hardly seems that it must not always be as it always has been.

A ring at the outer door, a walk through the dark hall; the little yard, with the stable, and in early years the hydrant. Then into the lower hall and up those narrow stairs. A peculiar odor of cleanliness, so different from the smells of the street, the dark hall or the yard, made one feel he was at the same old place. And then the latticed door, the knock, the cheery "Come in," and there she was, sweetly smiling out her fond welcome.

Other people move about from place to place, and when they die it does not seem so strange, but Grandma has become so identified with one dear spot that it is harder for the mind to think of that spot as vacant. I think that the fact of her permanency there has helped in fastening her in the minds and hearts of thousands, who can in their mind's eye picture her and remember her words of love, advice and comfort.

She has thus been able to aid others more than if she had had the same characteristics and same afflictions, but had been moved about from place to place. She will leave you there and all her grandchildren and great grandchildren a rich heritage. I hope she will slip away soon, very soon, peacefully and without pain, and I hope she will soon be enjoying that life for which she has so often longed and which was so real to her.

Lots of love,

John

There are many things one cannot understand, and to those who know of the intense suffering Mrs. Cooke endured during the last six months of her life, from what proved to be a malignant growth, it was an unanswerable mystery why one who had been so long in the furnace of affliction should require that it be heated even seven times hotter.

Many times during those last months she said to her daughters, "You don't know what agony I am in." And when nearer the end, the only time in her years of suffering she was ever heard to murmur, she said, as they stood around her trying to relieve her, "It seems more than my share of suffering, but it is all right."

The news of Mrs. Cooke's critical condition spread rapidly, bringing many of her loved and loving friends to find if it could indeed be true that her days were numbered, and one of her daughters was kept busy answering the multitude of notes asking about her.

It was very touching to see the deep, tender affection manifested by many of the wealthy friends who had been visiting Mrs. Cooke for years, as they came to her room and were shocked at the change in her appearance, and only a word from her, and later only the cheerful smile that always greeted everyone as long as she was conscious.

When the time came that it was best that none but those ministering to her should see her, still many of these friends continued to come daily to inquire how the dear one was, and add, "If she should be conscious, give her my love."

Not long before Mrs. Cooke failed to recognize those about, she looked up at her three daughters, and said, "Thank God for my three dear, faithful girls. Don't look for any last words. I have been trying to live my last words for years."

A night or so after this, she said to her daughters, "What am I waiting for?"

Mrs. Pullman replied, "Waiting for the boatman, mother."

Mrs. Cooke then exclaimed, "And I shall see my Pilot face to face, when I have crossed the bar." Then looking up, she said, "If I am worthy, yes – praise the Lord!" These were her last words of consciousness.

Those present can never forget the sacredness of the place one day, as dear Mrs. Pyle came in, and realizing Mrs. Cooke was soon to pass over the river, knelt by the bedside in silent prayer, clasping the feverish hands.

Up to the last week Mr. Charles Stickney brought, as was his custom, the choicest grapes, though he realized the days were past when Mrs. Cooke could enjoy the fruit or reply to his pleasantries. He and his beloved wife were among those who came every day, ever asking "Is there anything we can do for dear Mrs. Cooke?"

The last two weeks of anxious watchings seemed lengthened into months to those who with sad hearts were asking that the spirit of their mother might be free, and the poor weary body might be at rest.

At last, on Sabbath afternoon, November 15th, the release came, and being "perfect through suffering," she entered into rest. The telephone was kept busy, and friends were notified that Mrs. Cooke had joined the Church triumphant.

There was a service at the Twenty-Seventh Street Church at 4p.m., November 18th, which was conducted by former pastors. Addresses were made by Rev. M. Y. Bovard and B. F. Kidder, and letters read by Rev. F. J. Shackleton, the pastor of the church, from the Presiding Elder, Dr. J. E. Adams, and Rev. E. L. Thorpe, who could not be present.

In the evening at 8 o'clock another service was held, in order that those employed in the afternoon, and the hosts of Mrs. Cooke's pensioners, might have an opportunity to look once more at her dear face. Dr. Edwin Whittier Caswell, who had been a very frequent visitor in her little room, delivered the chief address at this service.

At the close of the service, after the throng had looked, many of them through tears, at Mrs. Cooke, their best earthly friend, they pressed around Miss Sarah Shaw, the Church Missionary, and begged for just one flower for a last link that should keep them in touch with one from whom they would never more receive the needed help.

Those who bore Mrs. Cooke into the church were her own loved ones: a son-in-law, four grandsons and a great-grandson. They counted it an honor to perform this last service for her.

The next morning, the family, Dr. Shackleton and Miss

Shaw accompanied the precious remains to Greenwood where they were laid with her dear husband and child to await the time when "The dead in Christ shall rise first." [1 Thessalonians 1:16.]

Dr. Shackleton read the burial service, and the newly-made grave was covered with the most beautiful of earth's flowers.

When leaving for Greenwood, a quantity of flowers were left to be carried by Miss Shaw in the afternoon to many of Mrs. Cooke's sick poor. This, the family knew would be her wish if she could speak.

Many will ask what became of that sacred little upper room where so many were led into the better life, so many enabled to lay down the spiritual burden and leave rejoicing in a Saviour's love; so many, weary of life's struggles, inspired with new purposes to try again; where the naked were clothed and the hungry fed.

In September 1856, Mrs. Cooke was brought to this house, which stood in the midst of flowers and fine plots of grass, till 1860 when the front house was built. For some years she merely rented the floor she occupied.

Later, when the property changed owners, she felt it would be wise to have the whole house under her control, and after consulting some friends decided to rent the house, subletting the lower and part of the upper floor. The latter was generally occupied by a widow.

In this way she was able to choose her tenants, and have those who were quiet and desirable people who would in a degree be interested in her and her work.

After Mrs. Cooke's daughters were all married it became necessary to select, as one of the tenants, someone who would be responsible to care for her when her maid was out, or in times of emergency, as she was often taken very ill suddenly. For this service they were paid monthly.

Many were the improvements made in the house to add to her comfort by her old and devoted friend, Mr. John Stephenson. Mrs. Cooke's friends, whether from home or abroad, were always sure of finding her in the corner by the window, always sure of the quiet smile of welcome as they opened the latticed door after hearing her gentle "Come in," in response to their knock.

Now, when she has been called to her heavenly mansion, and there is no one to occupy the rooms and carry on her work, though the associations are sacred and dear and many would be glad to have the place to come to as a Mecca, yet it has not been found feasible to keep them, for the neighborhood is so poor and the immediate surrounding such that no one belonging to her could live there.

Many expressed the wish that the property might be bought and turned into a mission named for her, The Bella Cooke Mission. This would require a large amount of money and a capable manager to establish and carry on the work, two requisites difficult to find, so the idea could not be entertained.

Hundreds as they pass that house will say, "Here lived Mrs. Cooke, who always helped us when we were in trouble."

It does not seem fitting to close this short account of Mrs. Cooke's last days without adding a word about the wonderful devotion of her friends. Since Volume 2 of *Rifted Clouds* was written, a number of those who delighted to give her pleasure by making her their almoner to the poor have died. Many others remain and continued to aid her to the last.

Among these are a number whose names are in the first volume of her book, and who have been for over thirty-five years devoted friends both to Mrs. Cooke and her work: Mrs. Field, Mrs. Charles Stickney, Miss Callender, Mrs. F.

W. Vanderbilt, Mrs. J. Crosby Brown, Miss C. A. Bliss, and hosts of others.

In the city and scattered all over the world are many more who, though they have not known her so long, have been equally devoted and have helped her personally as well as in her work. Since Mrs. Cooke's death, Miss Shaw has done what she could to carry on her work, though lacking funds.

Since this volume has been in the hands of the printer a friend who called weekly for Mrs. Cooke's message to the Class Meeting told me that two weeks before she entered into rest, though suffering intensely, her testimony was,

> "I know in whom I have believed,
> And am persuaded that He is able
> To keep that which I've committed
> Unto Him against that day."
> [2 Timothy 1:12.]

[The following letter to Mary Pullman is from Bella Cooke's grandson, John.]

Bridgeport, Conn.
November 15th 1908
Dear Mother,
I was out walking with Missie, and when I got home Dora was here and they told me Grandma was gone. For days I had been expecting it and hoping for it, but when it did come, it came with a distinct shock. One is never ready to have death come to a dear one, without its being a shock. It is the consciousness that they are absolutely gone that hurts so.

We may have been hoping for it, so as to spare the loved one further pain, yet when it does come there is always that awful wrench, and so I know how sad your heart is tonight, and how you feel more alone than you did before.

She was a wonderful mother to you and to your sisters, and so to lose her comes harder than if she had been an ordinary mother, and to lose a mother is next to losing a wife or a husband.

She had lived a marvelously full life. She had done a great work, she wanted to go, and now she is enjoying that other life for which she so deeply longed. Her suffering is ended, her loneliness is all gone – she is at rest. Oh, what a relief. Had she been made of less stern stuff, she would have ended it all long ago.

Her faith, her endurance, her patience, her bravery, were wonderful, and what a benediction she has been to many, what a truly marvelous disposition.

I have never known anyone that equaled her or came near it. You have our love and our heartfelt sympathy, mother dear. We join you in your sorrow and share with you in the great loss.

Love from us all,
John S. Pullman

<><><>

The full Introductions to the three parts of *Rifted Clouds*, and the addresses preached at Bella Cooke's funeral and memorial services, follow.

About White Tree Publishing

There are more than 70 Christian books currently available from White Tree Publishing in non-fiction and fiction for adults and for younger readers. All books are available in eBook formats, and some in paperback. The full list of published and forthcoming titles is on our website:
www.whitetreepublishing.com
Please visit there for our full catalogue.

White Tree Publishing publishes mainstream evangelical Christian books for people of all ages. We aim to make our eBooks available free for all eBook devices, but some distributors will only list our books free at their discretion, and may make a small charge for some titles – but they are still great value!

We rely on our readers to tell their families, friends and churches about our books. Social media is a great way of doing this. Take a look at our range of fiction and non-fiction books and pass the word on. You can even contact your Christian TV or radio station to let them know about these books. Also, please write a positive review if you are able.

Full Introduction to Part 1

By John Stephenson
47 E. 27th St.
New York
1884

Records of the dealings of God with His people form a large part of the Sacred Volume, from which His children have during the ages derived instruction and comfort. But in these later times the idea is extensively entertained that the divine administration is not as of old, but as "He sendeth His rain on the just and on the unjust" [Matthew 5:45] we need not seek to obtain protection from ills or relief from trouble.

The subject of this narrative had no common experience. Indeed, a marvelous life of physical disability and suffering mingled with peace, joy, and usefulness, seemingly combining the extremes of human possibilities.

Physicians and friends (among whom it has been my happiness to be numbered for thirty-five years) have repeatedly looked with wonder at return of vitality to the apparently lifeless frame, and witnessed subsequent years of beneficent accomplishments by frail physical organism, not to be accounted for by any known laws of natural causes.

The Controller of the ravens who fed Elijah, [1 Kings 17:2-6], sent His children to take care of this helpless one, not for "forty days" only, and a faithful descendant of St. Luke has not ceased his professional services, though having to wait the settlement of account until the day of final reckoning.

He who "chose the weak things of this world that He might put to shame the things that are strong," [1 Corinthians 1:27], has used this feebleness for His glory, happifying homes and pointing restless ones to the inviting arms in which are peace and everlasting joy.

By Henry Dickinson.

Brooklyn, N. Y.

In my early life in Sheffield, England, I well knew Bella Cooke. She was a neat, attractive child, and evidenced the careful training of her godly parents, Methodists of the old time, who endeavored to lead their children in early life to Christ.

Bella Cooke's narrative may tell how in early womanhood in the providence of God she was led to give her hand and heart to one in every way worthy; how she removed from Sheffield to Derbyshire, one of England's most lovely counties, rich in minerals, in which I believe her husband had some interest, and how, moved by visions of the New World, they bade adieu to their native land and settled in the United States.

But "man proposes and God disposes." Their bright hopes were not realized. The divine thoughts were not their thoughts. In His own way God works out His own plans.

What a course of discipline followed the steps of this young wife and mother! Her own account will tell of the sickness and death on the voyage, the interment of the loved one in the stormy sea, the sorrowful landing, the illness and death of her earthly dependence.

In the midst of these trials her health failed, and the weakness so much more manifested in later life began to appear. Then every hope of self-help was reluctantly surrendered. "Every door seemed closed but one, but that was mercy's door."

I well remember the last time she visited my family, probably in 1854. From that time to the present, though her afflictions have been extreme and continuous, she has experienced the upholding of the divine power, while the faith which honored God has been marvelously answered by the divine provision.

The Christian reader who follows this providential story to its close will find new proofs that the God and Father of our Lord Jesus Christ is a living and unchangeable God.

By Mrs. S. A. Lankford Palmer
316 E. 15th St.
New York.

My introduction to Mrs. Bella Cooke was at a social religious gathering of ladies in March, 1848. By her tears and expression of sadness my sympathies were moved, and on making inquiry, I learned that financial embarrassment was pressing heavily upon her. Her husband could find no employment, and her little children were in want. By the aid of friends, and the blessing of the Heavenly Father, a happy change came to them. Mr. Cooke secured steady employment, and the family found a home in a pleasant cottage on the banks of the Hudson.

But still this doubting disciple was not happy. She cherished her griefs, and was not able to cast her burden on her Lord. But in good time there was a wondrous change.

The reader will be pleased to learn the story. Only a few days after they were settled in their new home, this dear sorrow-stricken one called on me, and to my great surprise said, "We cannot remain here." In answer to my inquiry, she said that she, "Could not endure the dashing of the waves upon the sandy beach."

On Mrs. Cooke's passage to America, the mortal remains of the idol of her heart, her angel babe, as she called her, was buried in the deep, and every wave that dashed upon the shore seemed to open afresh the wound. I assured her that she would soon become accustomed to the waves and enjoy them as we did. But no, she replied that she could not. It seemed as if "every wave would go over" her – go they must.

I felt a strong impression that there was some concealed reason for the haste to leave, and asked if there was not some need unsupplied to make them more comfortable, but with convulsive weeping she replied, "We have everything we need, but we cannot pay for them, and we cannot live upon strangers. It's enough to live upon one's own people."

In my effort to comfort the weeping one, I said, "You are not living upon strangers. Your husband is at work and receives wages." With sobs she replied, "He gets his wages, but does not earn them." Sympathy seemed unavailing; something must be done. It was cruel to try severity, but the sufferer must surrender or she would die.

She spoke often about her nervous body, her little children and feeble husband. I asked her if she left us, where would she go? She did not know, but she could not stay here. I remarked, "The Lord has placed you here. If you take yourself out of His hands you may find more trouble."

She was reminded that the Lord had said, "Cast thy burden on the Lord and He shall sustain thee." [Psalm 55:22.] Her reply was, "How can I? How can I cast this nervous body and little children on the Lord? I must care for them!"

She was again reminded that He who commanded her to do so, would give her the power. Still she wept, and wept, and could only repeat, "How can I?"

Her friend, feeling it was a desperate case, dared to say, "Mrs. Cooke, do you know that you are sinning against God? You are sinning against your husband, you are sinning against your children. You are bearing a burden which the Lord has commanded you to cast on Him. It will crush you,

you will die, and it will be suicide. Your husband will soon be without a mother for his children, unless you cast this burden on the Lord. It must be possible, or it would not be commanded. The poet says,

> "Is it possible that I
> Can live and sin no more?
> Lord, if on Thee I dare rely,
> The faith shall bring the power."

We knelt to ask divine aid, and the dear one, who had not yet been heard to acknowledge the sin of not casting her burden on the Lord, commenced her prayer (to the great joy of her friend) by saying, "Lord, is it possible that I can live and sin no more? Lord, help me to cast myself, my children, my all upon Thee. Help me, Lord, to live and sin no more."

Deliverance came very soon. The precious one reached the sunlight of faith and exclaimed, "I am Thine; all the Lord's." After giving thanks and rising from prayer, the first expression of the quieted spirit was, "All the Lord's. I have no poor nervous body, I have no husband, I have no children. All the Lord's. Let Him do with us just what He pleases."

For thirty-six years since that day of gracious release have I had my eye on this witness to the faithfulness of the living God. Her trust in her Heavenly Father has been beautiful. We have often heard her say that, "Not one thing hath failed of all the good things the Lord spake – all are come to pass – not one thing hath failed."

Tests of faith have been many, but after these thirty-six years this child of God writes, "My Father gave me this promise when, in my twenty-eighth year I was left a widow, that He would be a Husband unto me – and has He not kept His promise? For in all these years He has never suffered me to ask a dollar for myself, and I have never been one dollar in debt."

The life of Bella Cooke is truly a life of faith, and believing that her testimony, as it is found in her journal and letters, will strengthen the heart of many fearful ones in Zion, we ask for her offering a prayerful acceptance.

The volume is published at the request of many friends. A few letters written by old friends were solicited and inserted by the Editor [Rev. Joseph Pullman, Mrs. Cooke's son-in-law] in the belief that they will add to the interest and usefulness of the book.

Its records were penned by their author amid much suffering as she lay upon her couch. The kind reader may fail to find high literary merits in these pages, but he will not fail to find a touching tale of singular providences, of patient endurance and overcoming faith.

In gratitude to the adorable Lord, they were written as a sacrifice of praise, and on the wings of prayer they are sent forth, in the hope that they will prove a comfort to the children of sorrow, an inspiration to the workers for the King, and a blessing to many hearts.

Full Introduction to Part 2

A good name is rather to be chosen than great riches, and loving favor rather than silver and gold (Proverbs 22:1).

By her Pastor, W. W. Clark, D.D.

Man handles the diamond roughly, that he may shape it into "a thing of beauty," and clothe it with brightness; so God often subjects His children to painful and protracted discipline that He may fashion them after His will, and make them shine in His likeness. Such, it seems to me, has been the method pursued by the Divine Providence with my dear and cherished friend, Mrs. Bella Cooke.

The Master has, indeed, chosen her "in the furnace of affliction." Like her great Exemplar and Lord she is to be made perfect through suffering. The gem is now in the moral laboratory. The Divine Lapidary is cutting and polishing it; but soon it will ornament the region and reflect the light and glory of immortality.

I first became acquainted with Sister Cooke in the spring of 1875 when I became her pastor, and from that time to the present I have enjoyed the high honor of an uninterrupted friendship. I cannot undertake in the limited space assigned me to give anything like a complete analysis of her wonderful character, but must content myself with a few points in outline. Let me call the reader's attention to the following characteristics, viz.: *Her resignation, usefulness, thankfulness, and cheerfulness.*

1. *Her Resignation*

Sister Cooke joined "the people called Methodists," over fifty years ago, and during all those years she has retained a sincere and hearty attachment to the church of her choice, and "meddled not with those who are given to change."

It pleased the Lord, however, early to withdraw her from personal activities in the church, and to place her permanently in circumstances which demanded the cultivation and exercise of the passive graces of the Christian character. For over thirty years her physical condition has been that of a confirmed invalid. It is not in language to describe the sufferings through which she has passed during this lengthened period.

That "beloved physician," Dr. Miles W. Palmer, has been constant and unwearied in his attendance upon her for over thirty-four years, ever esteeming it a privilege to minister daily to the necessities of this suffering saint. His reward will certainly follow.

To say that under all her afflictions Sister Cooke has been resigned and patient, would be to present but a small part of the truth. Depressing as her manifold infirmities have been, and severely trying as she has felt it to be debarred from the activities of the church and the enjoyment of its privileges, she not only has not "charged God foolishly," or indulged in a spirit of fretfulness and repining, but, on the contrary, she has ever exhibited, even in times of the utmost physical prostration, a serene and holy resignation such as words cannot worthily picture. Again and again she has been brought down to the gates of death by acute attacks of her complicated disease, and her family and friends have waited in tearful silence for the coming of the chariot and horsemen; but they came not. On one of these occasions the writer stood by her bedside and asked for her last testimony before going hence. After a moment's pause she repeated the following stanza:

> "Pain's furnace heat within me quivers,
> God's breath upon the flames doth blow,
> And all my heart in anguish shivers

And trembles at the fiery glow;
But yet I whisper, 'As God will!'
And in His hottest fire lie still."

Was not that Christ-like! Was it not imitating the spirit of Him who in Gethsemane said, "Not as I will, but as Thou wilt!"

2. *Her Usefulness*

She is never unemployed. Many churches and benevolent institutions have profited by the skillful work of her fingers. Her hours and days of pain are spent in earnest work for the Master. She is ever ready to instruct the ignorant, to comfort the sorrowing, and to relieve the needy. I have frequently sent earnest seekers of salvation to her room to be taught the way more perfectly. Her Heavenly Father has endowed her, not only with a rich personal experience in divine things, but with strong common sense and a marvelous insight of character, thus qualifying her to lead others from darkness into light.

Her trials and sorrows have prepared her, as nothing else could, to enter into the feelings of all who are suffering and sad, and to truly sympathize with them. And then the money placed at her disposal from month to month by those who have chosen to make her, in part, their almoner, has enabled her to supply the necessities of life to a little colony of needy ones.

Every Christmas and Thanksgiving Day witnesses busy scenes in her little room. I have seen turkeys, chickens and vegetables piled up in one corner sufficient to provide dinners for *more than one hundred families of the poor!* How they will miss her when her Father calls her home!

3. *Her Thankfulness*

Dr. McDuff says, "Thankfulness has been spoken of as the lovely shadow cast by our sorrows. And it is an undoubted truth that it is found most frequently side by side with sorrow. Sorrow is the best builder of these shrines and Ebenezers of thankfulness which crowd the believer's pilgrim way.

Were I asked to go in search of thankful hearts, I would go, not to circles of unbroken prosperity – not to those dandled on the lap of luxury – not to the man of style and equipage, of state and fashion and fame; but I would go to some child of sickness, for years chained down to a couch of distress, shut out from the light and sunshine of a busy world, the dim midnight lamp burning in the silent chamber; a solitary bird with broken wing, from whom, as we see it pining in its lonely cage, we might expect nothing but the wailing note of sadness. There is everything, one would suppose, to lead to repining, yet there is ofttimes nothing but sweet resignation – "nothing but recounted mercies; the bright spots are alone seen and the dreary are forgotten."

How these words have been verified in Mrs. Cooke's experience, those who are intimate with her are able to judge. She was early left a widow, with a little family and a shattered constitution, and compelled to struggle alone with her early sorrow and with poverty. Still she has been contented and cheerful, and "the goodness of God" has been her song in the house of her pilgrimage.

Many a storm has swept athwart her sky, but yet the sunshine of heaven rests on her heart. Her stores are scanty, but yet she has not wanted. She has been fed from the Divine table and clothed from the Divine wardrobe. In all her afflictions her grateful heart has responded to the sentiment of the most *sorrowing,* yet the most *thankful*

One: "I thank Thee, O Father, Lord of Heaven and earth; even so, Father, for so it seemeth good in Thy sight." [Luke 10:21.] Such a heart is like the aromatic plant which sends forth its richest odors when broken and crushed.

> "Its fragrance from the wounded part,
> Breathes sweetness out of woe."

Thus it is, dear reader, that the grandest attributes of our nature are only brought out in affliction; the highest elements of our being, like the stars, are seen only in the night. When the sun of prosperity goes down and the night of adversity comes on, then the brightest orbs of virtue come out and light up the moral firmament. The sweetest songs of the nightingale are warbled only in the darkness; and so the clearest notes of thankfulness and joy are heard only in the midnight of affliction. It is "God, our Maker, who giveth songs in the night." [Job 35:10.]

4. *Her Cheerfulness*
One would naturally suppose that after so many years of constant pain and suffering there would be a tinge of sadness and gloom in her conversation and deportment. How many suffering saints seem to regard it as a necessary part of their religion to be melancholy and sad. They carry a face as long as Lent and as gloomy as Ash Wednesday. But nothing of this kind mars the spirit of this imprisoned child of God. She is ever cheerful, and when free from paroxysms of pair, can enjoy sanctified wit and humor with a zest truly refreshing. And why not?

> "Why should the children of a King
> Go mourning all their days?"

Blessed be God, there is such a thing as *"joy in tribulation"* and *"pleasure in infirmities."*

Sister Cooke's cheerful disposition has ever made her a great attraction to childhood, and none are more welcome to her little room than the children of her friends. To them she is always *"at home."* I remember when I first became her pastor she was very anxious to see "the Parsonage boys," as she called my little sons; but they hesitated to accept the invitation, for they thought that a lady who had been so many years confined to her bed must be very gloomy and sad. But after their first visit, the difficulty was to keep them away. It was always a great treat to them to get permission to see "dear Auntie Cooke."

To her little room I frequently turned my footsteps on "Blue Monday," that her bright spirit and cheerful converse might "minister to a mind" jaded and exhausted. That little room is a stranger to "Blue Monday." Like the sundial near Venice which bears on its face the care- dispelling inscription, *"I count only the hours that shine,"* so this cheerful heart takes note only of the bright hours of life, and buries in oblivion the cloudy ones. Sister Cooke's cheerful disposition, viewed in the light of her surroundings, has often brought to my mind Madame Guyon's little hymn, written while she was a prisoner in the dungeons of France:

"A little bird I am,
Shut in from fields of air,
And in my cage I sit and sing
To Him who placed me there;
Well pleased a prisoner to be,
Because, my God, it pleaseth Thee.

"Naught have I else to do;
I sing the whole day long;

And He whom most I love to please
Doth listen to my song:
He caught and bound my wandering wing,
But still He bends to hear me sing."

Dear reader, let us learn from Sister Cooke's experience the wisdom of trusting God at all times and under all circumstances. "Let those who suffer according to His will commit the keeping of their souls to Him in well doing, as to a faithful Creator." "Afflictions from His sovereign hand," if received in the right spirit, "are blessings in disguise." Trust Him, my brother! Trust Him, my sister! "What I do thou knowest not now; *but thou shalt know hereafter.*"

"Trust in the Lord in days of sorrow,
And meekly tread the thorny way;
It may be thou shalt see tomorrow
The love that chastens thee today."

By Murray Shipley, of Cincinnati, O.
Minister in the Society of Friends.

One seldom finds, even among sincere Christians, that symmetry of life, that even balance of character, which the promise of Scripture holds out to our expectation, and which makes the life of our Lord the ideal life. Where we find great amiability there is apt to be a want of steadfast manliness. Where great force of character exists, we are apt to be disappointed in the lack of the ornaments of a meek and quiet spirit. Where great faith has enabled a soul to step beyond the ordinary reliance of most Christians, we are so often disappointed to find the fullness of a complete faith marred by the divergences of fanaticism and superstition taking the place of reliance on truth.

George Muller, of Bristol, England, is known throughout the world for his life of faith in connection with the orphanage under his care, where about two thousand orphans have been provided for during many years, and the millions of dollars that have been expended have all been sent by willing hearts in answer to prayer.

It was my privilege to have George Muller as my guest for some days. His testimony was that, though his direct duty was felt to be to care for the orphans, his particular calling was to make manifest to the world that a living God takes cognizance of the affairs of men now, and answers the believing prayers of those that put their trust in Him. And while the doubting heart might carp at such a reliance, none could fail to admire in George Muller the cool judgment, the clear wisdom and discretion, the steadfast adherence to his apprehended line of duty, the extreme gentleness of his nature, and the positive decision of character of this man of God, whose faith for a lifetime has been beyond the narrow boundary of most Christian lives, circumscribed and governed only by, "Thus saith the Lord."

Living thus a life of faith, he daily drew from the Scriptures fresh realizations of the breadth of God's power, and witnessed His promises changed into personal realizations, and saw every day fresh manifestations of His abiding presence.

About the year 1850 I visited for the first time my friend Bella Cooke, and from that time she has ever been to me a witness of the power of the Holy Spirit to make manifest the divine life in the quiet retirement of a confirmed invalid, in the midst of nervous debility, dependent alone upon the Lord for the needful things of life. One of my first queries, for I shrink from bodily suffering, was, "Do you suffer much?"

"I am never five minutes in forty-eight hours without

pain."

The answer impressed me, as it cannot impress those who have not looked upon the great restful face of one who has been for over thirty-five years a sufferer. Not living in the same city, my visits have often been a year or more apart, but whether at times of comparative ease, or suffering from the changing vicissitudes of life, in that chamber there has seemed to reign the kingdom of peace.

With a distinct faith in and claim on God's power to provide, moment by moment, for the need of the body as well as of the soul, and evidently never exchanging profession for experience, there has been unwavering testimony to His faithfulness to supply *all* our needs.

I leave it to others to narrate the instances of these evidences. To me, the calm unperturbed mind, the restful waiting the Lord's will, the riper fruit of the spirit in long-suffering, gentleness and meekness, were convincing proof that love, joy and peace, so manifestly present, were held in due relation to His perfect work. Thus in the retired life of one without means, without publicity, the power of the divine life has been manifested.

I asked my friend at one time a question which I would seldom ask of any, "Does the Lord keep thee from sin?"

The answer was given, but it was the humble reverence of tone, of voice and manner, it was the entire absence of self, it was the inward witness to your own mind that one of mature judgment, of well balanced mind and of deep spirituality was answering, that her prudent, guarded, quiet answer, "I may reverently say, that He keeps me moment by moment," carried conviction to my own mind.

The circumference of her religious life, so much broader than that of most religious professors, the application of God's promises to the daily realities of life so very direct, that which in others has produced ranterism, and, worse than every other thing, lowering the standard of truth to accommodate it to the defective experience of actual life, has in the life of my dear friend only brought forth the matureness of that singleness of life, that uniformity of trust, that due relation of dedication of body, mind and spirit to the Lord, which evidences itself in the use of each phase of our nature, moment by moment, under the renewing power of the Holy Spirit; the complete roundness of a Christian life, of which Christ is the center.

What has impressed me has been the uniformity of her life, uniform as the ocean, always full, and like the ocean, with its tides and waves responsive to God's winds, but whose waves are still at His command.

By Rev. S. A. Seaman
One of her Pastors

The true minister of the gospel loves his work, yet he often meets with experiences that are painful. If he has genuine human sympathies, and without them he cannot be a proper representative of the Master, he will find them deeply moved by the scenes of the sickroom and dying bed.

But no painful impressions were produced by visits to Sister Cooke. During the three years that I was her pastor I do not remember a call that was not a pleasure to me. When absent, if my thoughts turned to her, her helpless, suffering condition frequently excited painful feelings, but on entering her beautiful room these feelings always failed to appear. She was always cheerful, and her interest in events around her seemed to be little, if any, less than it would have been in health. The welfare of her children, the health and prosperity of her friends, the state of the church, social and political interests – everything, in fact, that a healthy person would think of, occupied her attention.

There was none of the selfish egotism sometimes seen in

invalids. I could hardly realize I was in a sickroom. There was the cheerful tone, the pleasant smile and not seldom the merry laugh. Often when several days had passed without my calling, have I excused myself on the plea that pleasure must give way to duty, and that I did not come to see her as much for her sake as for my own pleasure and profit.

I shall ever value the friendship to which my ministry in her church led me.

By her Class Leader, Mr. Holman
My first acquaintance with Mrs. Bella Cooke dates back to May 17th, 1847. The vividness of my first impressions on being introduced to her remains as distinct as it was at first.

In May, 1857, under the charge of Rev. Thomas G. Osborn, pastor of the Rose Hill M. E. Church, I was appointed leader of the class of which Sister Cooke was a member, and continued in that capacity for fourteen years. It was my duty, as her leader, to visit her regularly, and on these occasions I was always greatly blessed, and at times quite on the verge of heaven.

The record of but few has been characterized by more unassuming and retiring modesty, and has presented so eminent an example of what the grace of God can do for poor humanity.

Full Introduction to Part 3

By Rev. Edwin W. Caswell

I count it one of the greatest blessings of my ministerial life that I ever became acquainted with Bella Cooke, and that I have enjoyed the privilege of assisting in compiling and arranging for publication this memorial volume. [Part 3.]

Her two books, entitled *Rifted Clouds* [Parts 1 and 2], have passed through many editions and will no doubt become more widely known in future years as the ablest devotional work since *The Pilgrim's Progress*, or *The Imitation of Christ* by Thomas à Kempis. These volumes are an evidence of Mrs. Cooke's superior mental ability, as well as of the great depth of her spiritual experience. The present work is the continuation and completion of the series.

The chapter giving her continued diary during the last years of her eventful life will be of great interest to those who have followed her in her other books up to this period, and will inspire the thousands who read this last volume to secure *Rifted Clouds* previously printed.

Mrs. Joseph Pullman's [Mary's] graphic account of her mother's last days will be highly prized by Bella Cooke's world-wide friends. No one else could have written it so truthfully and so vividly.

It is a delightful after-glow of her life, to think that the saintly sufferer had every earthly want supplied that her three loving daughters could bring in affectionate care and attention, and all that the wealth of New York City could give in sympathy, in personal visitation and kindly offering.

From the multitude of sympathetic letters, written by the friends in many countries, we have selected a number as samples of the esteem in which Mrs. Cooke was held by many who never even saw the face of the patient, peaceful invalid.

It has also been thought best to preserve in book form selections from various publications, showing the universal appreciation and admiration which the press of many countries manifested for this most distinguished martyr to pain, of a century.

Bella Cooke truly lived a double life: the one, visible in the valley of sorrow; in the other, she dwelt high upon the Delectable Mountains, a transfigured life, full of glory, whose heavenly beams she often transmitted to those who saw her, and, through her books, to a multitude of readers. Her departure will not end her earthly glory. It will only draw wider attention to her matchless character and unexampled heroism in her life-long agony.

Bella Cooke is now enjoying a blissful compensation for all her sufferings: in the purity and holiness of her own character; in the delightful consciousness of having led so many lost ones to Jesus, so many saved ones into the fuller Christian life; in thinking that, while she endured the long fight with affliction, she relieved the sorrows of the poor and needy around her, and also became a blessing to the rich, who found in her a channel for their benevolence, and who, beholding the reflection of the Divine halo that shone upon her face, followed her, as she followed Christ. But this is not all – think of the compensations, of the vast number of intimate friendships she has made, while enduring her great ordeal.

The rich and great have bowed at her lowly lintel, carrying away with them the aroma of her devotion to Jesus, an inspiration that will never leave them. Even the children loved her. It is said that one day when the boys were playing about her yard, one of them was heard to say, "Boys, don't make a noise – the Good Samaritan lives here, and she is sick."

All know that the poor and the lowly were her friends, and hung about her home as they did about the Man of Sorrows, and today hold her in everlasting remembrance, because she was so like her Lord.

Let me give you a few words from the lips of Bella Cooke, which will be like a window through which you can see into her heart home. "All this has caused many sleepless nights and weary days; but the work is very sweet, and I am very happy. I earnestly ask to be given the right words to speak to each one who comes to see me, rich or poor; to bring them into a closer union with the precious Saviour, Who is ever ready to bless all who come unto Him."

Rev. Dr. Carey said when dying, "When I am gone, do not say much about Dr. Carey, but speak much of Dr. Carey's Saviour." So I am sure Bella Cooke would say to us, if she could make us hear, "Tell my life story, but tell more about Bella Cooke's Saviour, for His presence made me perfect through suffering. His blood washed my robes and made them white. His love and power has enthroned me with Himself in His glory."

When the beloved sufferer left her earthly friends, she no doubt heard Jesus say, "Peace, be still," to the troubled waves of life's ocean. She dwells now in the land of the Morning Calm, where no wave of trial rolls across the sea of glass, where all things have become new, beautiful and divinely good.

The question will no doubt arise in the minds of many who read these words, why this volume has not been edited by the same skillful and sympathetic hand that compiled the first two volumes of *Rifted Clouds*. Alas, one of the hardest blows that came to Mrs. Cooke in these later years was the loss of that strong arm on which she had leaned as on a beloved son.

Struck down while still in the vigor of middle life, the

death of Rev. Joseph Pullman was one of those mysterious providences to understand which we must await God's own interpretation. No apology is offered for the space given in these pages to Dr. Pullman's illness and death, for it will be read with great interest by the many who have felt his personal touch in the editorship of the first two volumes of *Rifted Clouds*.

I can think of no words with which to close this introduction, more beautifully expressed, than the poem written in honor of Bella Cooke by Mrs. Helen R. Hamersley Stickney, who was one of Mrs. Cooke's devoted friends.

To Mrs. Bella Cooke
By Helen R. Hamersley Stickney
[Note: this is one long, single verse in the original.]

Down through the lattice
Each sunny day
The golden rays
Shine cheerily;
Over the lattice
Each somber day
The storm-clouds
Lower drearily.
Within the lattice
A sweet face lies,
And you never would dream,
As you look in her eyes,
That day and night
She had suffering lain
For many long years
On a couch of pain.
Like a bird from afar,
Her heart ever sings,

And her words are of heaven
And heavenly things.
And daily she lists
For the Master's "Come,"
For earth is but fleeting,
And Heaven her home.
In her radiant face
There's a restful calm;
'Tis the "peace of God"
That no fear or alarm
Can swerve from the path
Of patience and rest;
With always the trust
That "God knoweth best."
And many in want
Or in despair,
She has led to the light
Through heartfelt prayer.
Full many a soul,
When their faith grew dim,
She has tenderly, lovingly,
Led to Him;
And many a one
Through this saint of God,
In that "upper room"
Has found the Lord.
I count 'mong my mercies,
Again and again,
The inspiring words
From that bed of pain.
She holds ever upward
A beacon light,
And brighter it will grow
Till faith becomes sight

So she waits for the Bridegroom,
Her lamp burning clear,
While she lists for the cry,
"Behold, He is here!"
When her task is done,
And her work laid down,
What glories will shine
From her starry crown!
The reward will be hers
The reward that is meet,
When her life-work is laid
At her Saviour's feet.
And the joyful "Well done"
To her will be given
In her mansion prepared
'Mong the chosen in Heaven.

The Heavenly Meeting

Can it be possible no words shall welcome
Our coming feet?
How will it look, that face that we have cherished
When next we meet?
Will it be changed, so glorified and saintly,
That we shall know it not?
Will there be nothing that will say, "I love thee,
And I have not forgot"?
Oh faithless heart, the same loved face transfigured.
Shall meet thee there,
Less sad, less wistful, in immortal beauty
Divinely fair.
The mortal veil washed pure with many weepings,
Is rent away.

And the great soul that sat within its prison
Hath found the day
In the clear morning of that other country
In Paradise,
With the same face that we have loved and cherished
She shall arise!
Let us be patient, we who mourn, with weeping,
Some vanished face,
The Lord has taken, but to add more beauty
And a diviner grace
And we shall find once more, beyond earth's sorrow,
Beyond these skies,
In the fair city of the "sure foundations,"
Those heavenly eyes,
With the same welcome shining through their sweetness,
That met us here;
Eyes, from whose beauty God has banished weeping
And wiped away the tear.

Anon

MEMORIAL ADDRESSES

Address delivered by Rev. Melville Y. Bovard

Ascend, beloved, to the life;
Our days of death are o'er;
Mortality has done its worst;
The fetters of the tomb are burst.
The last has now become the first,
Forever, evermore.

Ascend, beloved, to the feast;
Make haste, thy day has come;
Thrice blest are they the Lamb doth call
To share the heavenly festival
In the new Salem's palace-hall,
Our everlasting home.

Horatius Bonar

The life of Mrs. Bella Cooke is so exceptional and so interesting, that it is in one way a pleasure to speak of her and her work in the presence of her friends, even though we are sitting in the shadow of death. I count it one of the gracious privileges of my life in the ministry to have been her pastor for a few brief years. Her interest in the prosperity of her church and the success of her pastor are well known facts among her friends.

No one will ever be able to express his full gratitude for such inspiration and wise counsel as were received from time to time in that quiet little room by the pastors of Mrs. Cooke. At this time, when our sympathies are awakened and we look at her life in its splendid concrete, we must acknowledge that one of the great elements of her power for good was her deep sympathy for those who were weary with the burdens and misfortunes of life; for this fine and almost superhuman sentiment as it appeared in her life's workings, was never without that substantial help which by the strange providences of God she was able to give.

I speak mainly to those who are familiar with the great work she has done for the poor and needy in the Kingdom of God. The multitudes were helped by her; the lonely, straying soul was set right; the penitent groping in darkness was pointed to the true light which shines from across the sea of infinite mystery. With this sympathy so timely and well appointed, was a wisdom, practical, and which seemed never to fail her in the emergencies common to her life of suffering. I am not speaking merely of a well poised judgment, a sagacity like that of the statesman, but of a wisdom which has in it the true heartbeat of the child of God.

Thus we do not wonder at her wonderful sway over the hearts and lives of men and women. Mrs. Cooke never boasted of these gifts, but must have felt conscious of them in the presence of so many perplexing problems. With what was certainly, from the mere human point of view, a sad handicap, nevertheless, from the shut-in room of love and light, she exercised such supreme patience, by the grace of God, as to make the weak soul who came into her presence strong, and the poor one rich towards God.

Hawthorne in his *Mosses of an Old Manse* writes of a fishing excursion which he made with Ellery Charming up the River Assabeth, and as the river and wood were hushing one another to sleep, amid the showers of broken sunlight, "up-gushed their talk like the babble of a fountain." But he says their chief profit in those wild days lay in the freedom which they won from all custom and conventionalism.

Even when they had gone from these delightful

surroundings, the leaves that overhung the river were whispering to them, "Be free! Be free!" Mrs. Cooke could not claim such freedom, but her fellowship with souls who were free, and especially her fellowship with Jesus made her superior to every difficulty and free in her mastery of patience. So she lives today as a fine example of almost perfect endurance. Her burden of soul was that of an effort for the emancipation of those who were enslaved by one form or another of sin.

She was the center of a great fraternity of friendship. One said to me, "You have lived in New York City, then you must know my friend Mrs. Bella Cooke?" On entering her room one day in answer to that gentle word of welcome, "Come in," I was introduced to a company of her friends of wealth and influence with these simple words, "These are my friends" and "This is my pastor." There was no distinction, no classes with her heart-record; all were children of one Heavenly Father.

So it came to pass that more frequently than otherwise, the very poor were among her most devoted friends, for they needed her most. One not familiar with her wonderful life might not suppose her to have been a close student of the great literature of the world. It was true that she studied most and held closest to her heart the pure religious type of learning, but incidentally she was well acquainted with the great leaders of thought in many departments of learning. One, the great Teacher, was ever first and nearest to her heart, in this business of seeking the truth, but every devout scholar was given his place as a torch-bearer of the light of truth.

In the very nature of the situation, it was evident that Mrs. Cooke must be a teacher; for she was surrounded by those seeking light and help. It was seemingly easy for her to impart the message which she had received, making those who came to that humble shrine of love, wise unto salvation before they left.

The very gifted and successful in life often called upon her for inspiration and consultation. Well do I recall that afternoon when the genial and scholarly Bishop Andrews was introduced to her. There was no want of appreciation on the part of Mrs. Cooke for her distinguished visitor. Their conversation was dignified and well balanced. The beloved Bishop was conscious of the presence of a great soul with a rich and almost divine experience. It was a rare scene when the man of God bowed in her presence and offered a brief, touching prayer, and there came from the patient sufferer the gentle, prevailing "Amen."

In closing, I must call attention to her personal evangelism. Mrs. Cooke knew where to put the emphasis – it was ever to be on the message of her Lord and Saviour. She belonged to that school of religious workers who go to the very verge of earnestness, but hold themselves well in hand. While she was the chosen agency under God to minister to the physical necessities of thousands of needy persons, her opportunity to put the living truth into their hearts was seldom overlooked. She "must be about her Father's business." [See Luke 2:49.]

In this connection, we must believe that somehow her personal touch, in kindly word and deed, made sure the word and work of God in their souls. This is not easily explained, but like the magic life of Henry Drummond, her presence was the key to unlock the door to the inner life of the penitent soul seeking pardon.

Yet there was a power in her prayers which made her life an effective evangel. Her friends felt stronger for the battle of life when they knew that she was remembering them in prayer at stated hours. Her prayers were prevailing, fervent, effectual. That sweet story of President Cleveland, and his faith in his mother's prayers, is most applicable here. On the day of his election to the position as Governor of New York State, he wrote to his brother telling him what he would be doing that hour "if mother were alive." He would have been writing a letter to her.

Then speaking of her death, he tells his brother how much he misses her prayers; that he would feel "safer if mother were alive, for he had such faith in her prayers." My dear friends, some of us would feel safer if Mrs. Bella Cooke were alive; we had learned to believe so definitely in her prayers for us.

Mrs. Cooke was a great believer in prayer. On one occasion when calling at her quiet little chamber of devotion and life, I mentioned the fact that I had recently read that sweet little poem, *Song of the Mystic*, by Father Ryan. She requested me to recite it for her, which I did with a deeper sense of its beauty and devotion than ever before or since. I shall quote it here as appropriate in illustrating her love for that hour of divinest communion:

"I walked down the valley of silence,
Down the dim voiceless valley alone,
And heard not the fall of footsteps
Around me, save God's and my own;
And the hush of my heart was as holy
As hovers where angels have flown.

"Do you ask what I found in the valley?
Tis my trysting-place with the Divine;
And I fell at the feet of the holy,
And about me a voice said, 'Be mine!'
And there rose from the depths of my spirit,
An echo, 'My heart shall be Thine.'

517

"Do you ask how I live in the valley?
I weep and I dream, and I pray;
But my tears are as sweet as the dewdrops
That fall on the roses in May;
And my prayer like perfume from censer,
Ascendeth to God night and day.

"Do you ask me the place of the valley?
Ye hearts that are narrowed by care –
It lieth afar, between two mountains,
And God and his angels are there;
And one is the dark mountain of sorrow,
And one is the bright mountain of prayer."

Address delivered by Rev. B. F. Kidder, Ph.D.

If I were to attempt anything like an analysis of the marvelous power for good which this beautiful life has exerted for more than half a century, I should fail to even approximately satisfy the inner feelings of those who really knew her. There are lives that no more need analysis than the sunlight needs it. The sunbeam is its own best interpreter. It simply needs a place to shine. And wherever it comes, there is light and warmth and power. There new life appears, and old forms of life become more luxuriant.

In Bella Cooke the light of a beautiful, pure, divinely-sustained soul shone through a broken, scarred body, and transfigured it, until every line of suffering became a line of beauty and of glory. Through more than half a century of affliction, that light shone forth with ever increasing brightness; and thousands and tens of thousands directly, and hundreds of thousands indirectly, felt its blessed warmth and power in their lives. Many found the way into the kingdom of God's love and fellowship and service because of its shining.

Bella Cooke's life might be likened to a brilliant jewel. It does not need analysis, or definition. Its imprisoned glories simply await the lapidary's touch and a proper setting. Then it is its own best witness. Archbishop Leighton said: "God has many sharp-cutting instruments and rough files for the polishing of his jewels; and those whom He especially loves and intends to make most resplendent He has oftenest His tools upon."

The Divine Lapidary makes no mistakes. Many wondered why one so pure and good should be permitted by the Heavenly Father to suffer so much; but such thoughts are always born of ignorance and human limitation. God knows, and that should be sufficient for us. It was sufficient for Bella Cooke.

The last time I saw her in life, only a few months ago, I said to her, "Sister Cooke, I want to ask you a question that may seem almost improper, even impertinent."

And with a beautiful smile upon her face, and with that sparkle in her eye which was so often there, she replied: "What is it?"

I said: "Have you ever felt like questioning God's wisdom or love in his dealings with you, or wished that he had led you by some other way?"

I shall never forget the expression that came into her face, or the deep, soulful meaning that she put into her words as she answered, "I do not know that I ever have. And I do know now that I am perfectly satisfied with the way my Father has led me."

As the Master kept at his work, by day and by night, in that little upper room on Second Avenue, how those glories of the inner life, the spiritual life, shone forth! Her soul was filled with the glory of the Infinite. Her afflictions, sanctified of God, worked for her "a far more exceeding and eternal weight of glory," [2 Corinthians 4:17], while she looked, "not at the things that are seen, but at the things that are unseen." [2 Corinthians 4:18.]

The finishing earthly touch has now been put upon the priceless brilliant, and it occupies its place in the crown of the King.

These simple figures of speech suggest only a part of what cannot be expressed in words. The Master's test is, after all, the best one to apply to this, as to every other life: "By their fruits ye shall know them." [Matthew 7:16.]

I shall ever count it one of the greatest privileges of my life that I was permitted for a period of five years to be Bella Cooke's pastor. Practically every week during that time, and frequently several times a week, I was a visitor at her bedside. And since that pastorate closed in 1894, whenever I have been in the city I have seldom failed to visit her.

As one who was permitted by the Divine Husbandman to be associated with Him in the care of this choice branch of the Living Vine, I am going to say a few words concerning the fruit of her spiritual life as I saw it grow and ripen.

The first fruit of the Spirit is "love." "He that loveth is born of God" [1John 4:7], and "love is the fulfilling of the law." [Romans 13:10.] The love that Bella Cooke bore toward the Heavenly Father and toward her Saviour was real, and vital and supreme. It was not simply one among many impulses of the heart, or one among many influences that touched her life and helped to make her what she was.

It was her very life. Without it, the beauty and glory of her peerless personality would have been only as the fading flower, and her power would have been only that of the branch when severed from the living vine. None would be so quick to declare this as Sister Cooke herself, if she could speak to us today. That love cast out all fear, and sanctified everything that came into her life. It gave her visions of the Infinite, and power which only God can supply. It was the deep secret of what she was, and of what she accomplished.

Bella Cooke's love for her fellow beings was not less real than her love for God. It never failed. While few, if any, suffered more in the flesh than herself, yet she largely forgot her own afflictions in her solicitude for others. It seemed as though the sorrows of all humanity through her heart made their thoroughfare. Many who came to see her were in dire affliction. She had for each a word of sympathy and good cheer, and through the generosity of wealthy friends she relieved as far as possible the temporal distress of those who seemed at all worthy.

And even when she found that she had been shamefully deceived and imposed upon, as was sometimes the case, there was never a tinge of bitterness manifest in her spirit. Paul says: "Love beareth all things, believeth all things, hopeth all things, endureth all things. Love never faileth." [1 Corinthians 13:7.] And I have never seen another who quite so fully manifested this precious grace as did Bella Cooke.

The strongest and richest manifestation of her love for her fellow beings was seen in her tender and intense desire that they should be saved. And many, through the influence of her prayers and loving words and beautiful life, became followers of Christ.

The second blessed fruit of the Spirit is "joy." One would hardly expect to find this grace very largely developed in one whose life was so hemmed in by disappointment, affliction and pain. Sister Cooke once said to me, in answer to a question, "There is hardly a moment of my life that I am not in acute pain." Yet I never once looked into that wonderful face when if was not radiant with holy joy. I remember, years ago, to have come across a rare and beautiful flower, in full bloom, away up in the Simplon Pass in the Alps, not far from the eternal snow. I wondered at finding it there.

But the little flower, from its sheltered nook, had been looking full into the face of the sun, and its heart could not but sing for joy. So, if you would know the secret of Bella Cooke's abiding and blessed joy in the midst of such adverse outer conditions, you will find it nowhere but in the fact that she was constantly looking, by faith, into her Saviour's face.

The third blessed fruit of the Spirit is "peace." I cannot speak at length of this grace, as it was manifest in the life of Sister Cooke. But it has sometimes seemed to be that Mrs. Stowe must have written her beautiful little poem, *The Calm of the Soul*, in that upper room on Second Avenue, or with Bella Cooke before her mind.

> When winds are raging o'er the upper ocean,
> And billows wild contend with angry roar,
> 'Tis said, far down beneath the wild commotion, That peaceful
> stillness reigneth evermore.
>
> Far, far beneath, the noise of tempests dieth,
> And silver waves chime ever peacefully;
> And no rude storm, how fierce soe'er it flieth, Disturbs the
> Sabbath of that deeper sea.
>
> So to the heart that knows Thy love, O Purest,
> There is a temple, sacred evermore;
> And all the Babel of life's angry voices
> Dies in hushed stillness at its peaceful door.
>
> Far, far away, the roar of passion dieth,
> And loving thoughts rise calm and peacefully;
> And no rude storm, how fierce soe'er it flieth,
> Disturbs the soul that dwells, O Lord, in Thee.

The time would fail me to tell of those other blessed fruits of the Spirit: "long sufferings, gentleness, goodness, faith, meekness, self-control," all of which were found in rich abundance in this one marvelously beautiful life.

Some are quick to say, regarding such qualities of mind and heart as Bella Cooke manifested, "It is largely a matter of temperament." But no greater mistake than this was ever made. Paul reveals the true secret of spiritual power when he says, "By the grace of God I am what I am." [1 Corinthians 15:10.]

Read Sister Cooke's personal testimony, as she gives it in *Rifted Clouds*. On the voyage to this country, when baby Agnes died and was buried at sea, the mother's heart was plunged into inconsolable grief. She did not lose faith in God, but the deep wound was not healed. She says: "Oh, how my heart rebelled, and would not be submissive."

Not until the wonderful victory of faith that came to her when she was in prayer with Mrs. Lankford did "the peace of God that passeth all understanding" [Philippians 4:7] fill her heart and mind. She says, in speaking of this experience, "The Lord stretched out His arm and I was saved. Yes, saved with a full salvation. It seemed to me I was stripped and clothed, unclothed and clothed upon, filled with the love of God. ... I was a new creature in Christ Jesus. Oh, the sweet, calm, settled peace. It was beyond expression. ... There was no outburst of feeling, but a calm, serene resting in the arms of my Beloved; a persuasion that I had given myself with all my powers over into His care, to do with me just as He pleased, only to make and keep me fully His."

If Sister Cooke could speak to us today, this would be her message, "Yield yourselves fully to Christ, and the fullness of the blessed life shall be yours."

Bella Cooke has gone from us, but her influence remains, and will remain, an abiding benediction upon all who ever knew her, and upon all who shall ever hear of the way she was "kept by the power of God," and of the beautiful, triumphant life that she lived in the midst of life's sorest trials.

What men call death was to her only the entrance into larger life. She has gone forth "to join the lost of love again, in endless bands and in eternal peace," to mingle with that "great multitude that no man could number" who are constantly before the throne of God and of the lamb. [Revelation 7:9.]

She has taken her rightful place among those glorified spirits "who came out of great tribulation and washed their robes and made them white in the blood of the lamb." [Revelation 7:14.] Above all, she has seen the face of her King, for she has awaked with His likeness.

In life her favorite hymn was this:

> "Jesus, Thy blood and righteousness
> My beauty are, my glorious dress;
> Midst flaming worlds, in these arrayed,
> With joy shall I lift up my head."

Now faith has turned to sight, and prayer to praise.

Sermon by Rev. Edwin Whittier Caswell
Delivered at the Evening Service

Text, Revelation 7:14. "And he said to me, these are they which came out of great tribulation, having washed their robes and made them white in the blood of the Lamb."

Mrs. Bella Cooke, the sublime sufferer, the mother of the poor of the East Side, the guardian angel of New York City, the most saintly woman of a century, is no longer with us. On Sunday afternoon, November 15th, 1908, the beautiful spirit of one of the most afflicted women since the world began escaped from her body of pain and ascended, "Where heaven's morning breaks and earth's vain shadows flee."

Multitudes who have inquired after Mrs. Cooke's health during the sixty years of her illness have passed away, while the patient sufferer lived on. Today we can reply to such inquiries, "Mrs. Bella Cooke is entirely well." Among her last words was the exclamation, "It is well with my soul."

A few days before the exaltation came, she said to her daughter, Mrs. Joseph Pullman [Mary], after enduring the most excruciating agony in one of the spasms of her disease, "My dear, what am I waiting for?"

Mrs. Pullman replied, "Mother, you are waiting for the Boatman to come."

A calm peace settled upon the sufferer's face, as she triumphantly exclaimed, "Yes, I shall see my Boatman face to face when I have crossed the bar."

Her weary spirit is at rest forever; she has awakened in His likeness and is satisfied. The stormy voyage is past, as Faber sings:

"The land beyond the sea,
Sweet is thine endless rest,
But sweeter far thy Saviour's breast,
Upon thy shores eternally pressed;
For Jesus reigns over thee,
Calm land beyond the sea."

Mrs. Cooke realizes now that sixty years of pain are but a moment compared with immortality. Her long illness appears now as "light afflictions" in the scale over against "the eternal weight of glory." Mrs. Cooke was the whitest saint we ever knew. Tribulation lifted her soul into the secret abiding place under the shadow of the Almighty.

To be in her room, to look into her face, was like "days of heaven upon earth." Her face was illumined with unearthly beauty. She wore the smile of rapture, the gleam of life eternal. None who saw her can ever forget the expression of peace, patience, contentment and joy that looked from her countenance. After leaving her presence, one would reflect that Mrs. Cooke had riches without money, sweet fellowship without mingling with society, influence without strength, contentment without health, rest of spirit in a body of unspeakable unrest.

The only way to account for happiness amid such conditions is that the Divine Christ, her Creator and Redeemer, gave her the power of His life, supplying all her spiritual needs according to the riches of His glory.

Mrs. Cooke held sweet communion with her Saviour every day of all those years of deprivation and pain. At last, when the journey was ended, she heard the voice of Christ whisper to her the enrapturing words, "This day shalt thou be with Me in Paradise." [Luke 23:43.] Today, like Enoch of old, she "is not," for Jesus, the Lover of her soul, has received her to serve Him in the higher sphere, up among the "no mores," where there is no more sorrow, no more pain, no more tears, no more temptation, no more night, no more death, no more crying, where all things are new and beautiful.

> "Beautiful heaven where all is light,
> Beautiful angels clothed in white,
> Beautiful strains that never tire,
> Beautiful harps through all the choir,
> There shall I join the chorus sweet,
> Worshipping at the Saviour's feet"

God built us for his best mansions in his best world; the homeland of immortals. We feel that we are as indestructible as our Father. The quenchless spirit within us flames with love and hope eternal. When our earthly house is dissolved, we are forever with the Lord. One moment we sing the song of loss and bereavement; the next we join the Hallelujah chorus around the Throne. Jesus knows when to put on the last touch to make the soul beautiful and complete in Him. Mrs. Cooke waited patiently till her Lord said, "It is finished."

Mrs. Bella Cooke was born in Hull, England, July 13, 1821, and was in her eighty-eighth year when she passed away. In her early life, she gave her spare hours to the work of laboring among the poor in her neighborhood and among the sick in the Bellevue Hospital. Even at this time she was a partial invalid.

Mrs. A. G. Phelps and her daughter, Mrs. Stokes, aided her financially, and in giving clothing and supplies for the needy at this time. Later, when she entered upon her long illness, the William E. Dodge family took great interest in caring for Mrs. Cooke and in making her the dispenser of their gifts, as also did Mrs. Haxtun, Mrs. Jaffray, Miss Callendar, Mrs. C. De Peyster Field, Mrs. Fred. Vanderbilt, Mrs. John Crosby Brown, Mrs. Helen E. Hamersley Stickney, Miss Catherine Bliss and many others.

This vast work of benevolence which the wealthy allowed Mrs. Cooke to perform, delightfully occupied her lonely hours, lessened her thought of pain, and gave exercise and opportunity to her generous nature.

Think of a woman never taken from her bed for fifty-four years, carefully investigating each individual case of poverty who received aid from her hands, and never allowing one to go from her bedside without a word of warning or encouragement, prompted by love for Christ and

His children.

Delegations from various church associations, such as from Sunday Schools, Epworth Leagues, Woman's Home and Foreign Missionary Societies, Thanksgiving and Christmas Committees, all were entertained by her, and invited to give brief services in her presence, receiving words of cheer and counsel, gifts of goods and money that gave a new inspiration to their work in the Christian life.

Truly, sanctified suffering lifted Bella Cooke up to the wonder and admiration of all her worldwide friends, and extolled the power of her Lord in His ability to elevate the soul infinitely above its trouble.

Mrs. Cooke's husband died at the beginning of her illness, in the year 1849. Since 1855 she has occupied rooms at 492 Second Avenue. A large whiskey saloon stood in front of her apartments. It was necessary to ring the bell of the side entrance to the saloon and to pass through a long hallway beside the saloon to gain an entrance to her home. If she could have been moved, her friends would have given her more pleasant surroundings and accommodations.

She occupied much of her time answering correspondence from all over the world, and in writing two books, entitled *Rifted Clouds*, which have passed through several editions and have made her known and loved among a multitude of people, even in foreign lands. The capacious volumes are her autobiography, giving an account of God's providential dealings in her life of trial, and especially describing the multitude of visits which averaged about two thousand calls a year, that were made by her friends, as well as those seeking aid from her beneficence.

All the physicians who attended her occasionally, such as J. Marion Sims and Fordyce Barker, have passed away, except the one who has been her daily attendant for fifty-nine years, namely, Dr. M. W. Palmer, the last of the celebrated Palmer family, who founded the Tuesday Holiness Meeting. This beloved physician, who is the same age as Mrs. Cooke was, survives her, waiting for the same chariot which bore her to take him through the gates of that city whose inhabitants never say they are sick. Probably the annals of a century or of the world record no other instance of such prolonged suffering and such faithful attendance of medical care from an individual physician.

Among those who prayed with Mrs. Cooke at her bedside for healing was the sainted Dr. Cullis, of Boston. Mrs. Cooke believed in healing by faith in Jesus, but in her case she enjoyed the will of God in the answer given to Paul, "My grace is sufficient for thee." [2 Corinthians 12:9.] She believed from that moment that the mission of her life was in the sickroom, rather than in health.

Among the many lovely traits of Bella Cooke's character, the one that shone brightest was her deep solicitude for the welfare of others. She forgot her own needs in her absorbing devotion to her church, her loved ones, to the poor and lost ones, and to her God.

She seemed surrounded by an atmosphere of spiritual gentleness, tenderness and benevolence, wafted from Paradise and breathed forth from her meek and quiet spirit, giving spiritual strength to all attracted to her side. Words are insufficient to picture the gentle manner, the affable bearing, the chaste nature and the enduring, unmurmuring submission to the Divine will under all the trying emergencies of her almost lifelong illness.

Her soul is a gem of rare beauty for the Master's crown, a brilliant, undimmed, even to mortals, while earth and time endures. The secret of her beautiful life, in its triumph over pain and disease, was the consciousness that the everlasting arms of the Divine Christ were underneath her. She saw by faith her Friend and Elder Brother, Jesus of Bethany, sitting on the throne of the universe. She heard His voice, telling her not to be troubled with her tribulation.

All things were working together for her good. One day she would be crowned a queen by His side. He who had died for her would control all the forces of His world for her welfare. He who had gone to prepare a place for her was coming to bring her home, that where He was, there she should be also.

Jesus walked on the storm tossed sea of her life and often said, "Peace, be still." Then there "was a great calm." [Mark 4:39.] This is the secret of her tranquility and triumph.

Sometimes in the last long years of waiting she felt with Paul, "in a strait betwixt two, having a desire to depart and be with Christ" – a kind of sacred discontent, a holy homesickness. But sweet submission was mingled with these desires. [Philippians 1:23.]

Bella Cooke lived and died doing good, as Livingstone suffered and died for Africa, and as Jesus lived and died for all mankind. Her spirit, with theirs, and with all the mighty throng in the procession of the holy of all the ages is marching on, giving inspiration to earth's millions for all future time.

May the multitude of her admirers follow her as she followed Christ. She was useful and joyful in the midst of painfulness, wakefulness and burdens innumerable. How many there are who are useless and miserable in the lap of luxury, amidst honors and powers and personal comforts unlimited.

Mrs. Cooke lived in the centre of Greater New York for sixty years, without the privilege of beholding the grandeur and glory of its material progress. Today she gazes down upon us from the Upper Galleries in God's capital city of all worlds, surrounded by the millions of the redeemed. Now she is a traveler in all climes, a visitor to all cities, a ministering spirit, a guardian angel, re-enforced with the unsearchable riches of Christ.

She is still the dispenser of gifts. Once we went to her; now she comes to us. Is she not with us still? But our dull eyes of sense cannot behold the matchless beauty of immortals. We rejoice that her sphere of usefulness is infinitely enlarged and eternally extended, for her imprisoned spirit, like a bird of Paradise, has broken through the bars of the flesh and, forever free, roams all spaces of God's infinite dominions.

Queen Victoria, who became a friendly correspondent of Mrs. Cooke through reading her autobiography, once said to the Dean of Canterbury, who had preached on the second coming of Christ, "I wish He would come while I am living."

"Why?" said the dean.

The Queen replied, "Then I would have the exalted privilege of casting the crown of England at His feet."

Mrs. Cooke has joined Victoria, where all are crowned kings and queens unto Him, and where all have helped to crown Him Lord of all, amid the anthems of the Invisible Choir, and the acclaim of the general assembly of the redeemed.

A sacred shrine is in our hearts today, containing the inscription, "We loved her." Her words to us in this hour of our grief are,

> "Say not goodnight,
> But In some fairer clime,
> Bid me good-morning."

Till then, we say, "All hail, and farewell, Bella Cooke!"

"Beautiful spirit, free from all stain,
Ours the heartache, the sorrow, the pain;
Thine is the glory and infinite gain –
Thy slumber is sweet.
Peace on the brow and the eyelids so calm;
Peace in the heart 'neath the white folded palm;
Peace dropping down, like a wonderful balm,
From the head to the feet.

"Beautiful toiler, thy work is all done –
Beautiful soul into glory gone –
Beautiful life, with its crown all won,
God giveth thee rest.
Rest from all sorrow and watching and fears;
Rest from all possible sighing and tears;
Rest through God's endless, wonderful years,
At home with the blest."

Mary T. Lathrop

To weary hearts, to mourning homes,
God's meekest angel gently comes;
No power has he to banish pain,
Or give us back our lost again,
And yet, in tenderest love, our dear
And Heavenly Father sends him here.

There's quiet in that angel's glance,
There's rest in his still countenance;
He mocks no grief with idle cheer,
Nor wounds with words the mourner's ear;
But ills and woes he may not cure,
He kindly learns us to endure.

Angel of Patience! sent to calm
Our feverish brow with cooling balm;
To lay the storms of hope and fear,
And reconcile life's smile and tear;
And throbs of wounded pride to still,
And make our own our Father's will.

Oh! thou, who mournest on the way,
With longings for the close of day,
He walks with thee, that angel kind,
And gently whispers, "Be resigned!
Bear up, bear on, the end shall tell
The dear Lord ordereth all things well!"

Whittier

THE END